The Brain Makers

The Brain Makers

Harvey Newquist

PUBLISHING

A Division of Prentice Hall Computer Publishing
201 West 103rd Street, Indianapolis, Indiana 46290

Trademarks

To my mother,

who taught me the value of many things, especially words,

and

To my father,

whose influence is far greater than he will ever know.

Contents

Acknowledgments

A great many people helped me with my understanding and appreciation of AI over the past decade, either by sharing their thoughts and insights or by giving me an outlet for my own opinions. In many ways, this book is a compilation of their influences. They are Jerry Barber, John Barnabas, Judy Bolger, Hubert Dreyfus, Thomas Farb, Neal Goldsmith, Richard Greenblatt, Tom Halfacre, Ann Hamlin, George Harrar, Robert Harvey, Joanne Kelleher, Kay Keppler, Justin Kestelyn, Alex Lilley, Christopher Locke, Tom Madden, Neil McGlone, Steve Mott, Nancy Parker, Debra Rachleff, Randy Raynor, Daniel Salas, Rosann Schwartz, Tony Scofield, Caroline Seward, Julie Shaw, David Shlager, Keith Styrcula, Marty Tacktill, Gene Wang, Tom Werge, and Dennis Yablonsky.

In addition to these people, I want to note the singular importance of the original staff of DM Data, the company that granted me an entrance into the world of artificial intelligence: Howard Dicken, Loretta Mahoney, Marge DeRiso.

Certain individuals made themselves available at crucial times during the writing of *The Brain Makers*. Most notably, the following people provided services and stories above and beyond the call of duty: Russell Noftsker, Randy Parker, Arthur Schwartz, Alex Jacobson, Bill Hoffman, John Clippinger, Stan Curtis, and Ken Tarpey. In addition, Philip Chapnick served as redactor extraordinaire for this book, and his insightful comments and intimacy with the subject matter have proven to be a most worthy sounding board. This book is better because of it.

Many people interviewed for *The Brain Makers* asked that their names not be used, and I have respected their wishes. Their contribution, however, was important to many of the stories that I have included, and I want to acknowledge that here.

I am indebted to the following people and institutions for making the agony of research—and its attendant time spent away from home—that much more bearable: The MIT LCS and AI Library, the MIT Barker Library, Neil and Maureen Ferris, Tucker and Linda Greco, Randy and Nancy Parker (for providing me with an East Coast office), the Boston Public Library, The Arizona State University Engineering Library, and The Maricopa County Library. Thanks also go to my editors—Rosemarie Graham, Carolyn Linn, and Stacy Hiquet, as well as to the ongoing efforts of Matt Wagner.

Over the last ten years, I have talked to countless reporters and editors of magazines and newspapers that span the gamut from *The Wall Street Journal* to the *Phoenix Business Journal*, *Newsweek* to *Information Week*, and *PC World* to *Computerworld*. I am thankful to them for taking me seriously, even if I didn't act that way, as their reporting put my concerns and opinions into perspective.

Inspirations and diversions were provided during the writing of *The Brain Makers* by Catherine Wheel (Chrome), Curve (Cuckoo), Jimmy Page (complete), Pearl Jam (vs), The Sisters of Mercy (A Slight Case of Overbombing), Joe Satriani (Time Machine), Machines of Loving Grace (concentration), and the staff at Cherry Lane. Further credit goes to my brothers and sisters and their families, as well as to my immediate circle of relatives.

Most of all, I am indebted to Trini and Madeline, who survived this book and its idioscyncrasies. Now that it is finished, you can both have me back.

Introduction

Artificial intelligence may be the most important technology ever developed by modern man.

Having said that, and having made it the first official line of this book, I now have to qualify it. Ostensibly, *The Brain Makers* is the story of man's need to create—in almost godlike fashion—an image of himself in the confines of a machine. Over the years, the attempt to make machines that can do what humans do has come to be known as artificial intelligence. Called AI, this technology has been fixed in the popular psyche since before the days of Frankenstein and science fiction robots. As you'll see in the following pages, man has made such machines for years, starting with figures of clay and tin and evolving now to boxes of sand and silicon. The fact that persists throughout history is that man has always done this, as if it were part of his nature. Never quite sure of his own origins (God, the primordial soup, evolution), man has continually sought to recreate himself in a form that is under his control. In modern times, this endeavor has taken on the face of the machine, and our most modern machine is the computer. Hence, artificial intelligence.

Even though the technology of AI advances at mind-numbing speed, and man gets closer to achieving his goal of building a thinking machine with each passing day, there have nonetheless been tremendous failures along the way. These failures are not so much the failures of the technology, for AI technology itself has moved along quite swiftly. Today there are machines that can make medical diagnoses better than emergency room attendants, make better and more profitable trades than Wall Street brokers, and position tanks and warships into the best killing zones during battle.

The failures of artificial intelligence have been at the hands of men and women running AI companies and AI labs, men and women who have tried to develop this technology and make it part of the world's business culture. Their egos, frailties, and foibles—something not yet found in machines—have been part and parcel of the attempt to put intelligent computers into the world around us. In a large number of cases, these people were their own worst enemies, as well as the worst enemies of the technology. On the other hand, a small group of people did manage to make AI work, and they succeeded in putting thinking machines into daily use in corporate cultures where one might not expect them: the credit card division of American Express, the aircraft maintenance group at American Airlines, the trading floor of the Chicago Board of Trade, the bullet trains of Tokyo, and the subways of Paris.

These people, good and bad, are the brain makers. As brain makers, they have attempted to recreate human intelligence in machines. Many of them are researchers; others are business people who saw the various potential benefits of AI. All of them were intimately involved in making artificial intelligence a reality.

I am not a brain maker in any way, shape, or form. Rather, I have observed the brain makers, worked with them, analyzed them, applauded them, and even antagonized them over the last decade. My job—in nearly a thousand separate newsletter, newspaper, journal, and magazine articles—has been to make some sense of their pursuit of artificial intelligence. Over the last decade, I have worked with the brain makers, their benefactors, and their clients in order to translate what they were saying and doing into a form that could be understood in both a traditional business and popular sense. I have attempted to do that same thing in this book as well. If I have failed, it is my fault. In another age—sometime in the distant future, perhaps—I could probably shrug my shoulders and say, "Blame it on the machines." Unfortunately, by that time, a lot of people will.

This book is about humans, but it is also about machines that do what we humans do. Making thinking machines is neither right nor wrong, no more than the search for the origin of the universe or the study of dinosaurs is right or wrong. It just is. However, many people don't see it this way. They think that it is wrong to give machines the same reasoning capabilities as humans. Reasoning, they say, is what separates us from the animals. The fact that artificial intelligence is part of "advanced technology" only makes it worse, because these same people tend to think that mankind should hold itself in check when it comes to new technologies. There are dangers out there, they claim; things which should not be toyed with and are better left alone. This makes the pursuit of technology—which is also a pursuit of knowledge—sound like some overactive hormonal condition that should be reined in and tamed with cold showers.

I believe that technology, once developed, is unstoppable. It can be regulated, but ultimately technology is like the contents of Pandora's Box—you cannot shove it all back into the little space from whence it emerged. The discovery of new technology is a form of knowledge, and thus, like knowledge, it cannot be unlearned. This may come as a shock to people who feel that everything and anything can be legislated, including the use of knowledge. But the discovery of knowledge moves forward, never backward. It is only in the approach to knowledge that man occasionally retreats and recants, usually in some religious or political fervor.

Once established, knowlege is something that cannot be undone. In a sense, all new technologies are like the discovery of fire. You can't undiscover fire because you find that it is threatening. The same is true of any knowledge, not just technical knowledge. Knowledge can be modifed, altered, even lied about and debased, but it is nonetheless something that exists. How man uses his technology and his knowledge is up to him, but it is ludicrous to think that not using it is the same thing as not having it.

This book does not label any particular pursuit of AI as good or bad, better or worse. I do not claim to be an empiricist or a rationalist or a humanist or any of those terms that belong in first-year college philosophy books. It is just such labelling that got a lot of the early AI researchers into trouble and kept them from really doing serious work. The arguments in those days seemed to take their cues from old Three Stooges sketches: "Well, I think knowledge can only be codified through empirical means." "Oh yeah? Well, you pinhead, I know that cognitive reasoning can be developed through nondirect absorption of concepts." "Why, you idiot! I oughta knock your block off." Fistfights, if they had ever been a part of the computer research culture, most assuredly would have ensued. Instead of fights, pompous diatribes appeared in scientific journals, complete with name-calling. Broken noses were avoided, but careers were ruined and reputations were besmirched. It all had the same end result, though, in the long run: the opponent got bloodied.

Finally, and above all, this story is a chronicle. The events that take place in this book are the cornerstones of a computer evolution and revolution that will inevitably create machines that appear to think. These machines may ultimately be smarter than many of us, and someday they may even do our jobs for us—whether we want them to or not. But the thing to remember as you travel these pages is that man has been trying to create thinking machines for centuries and will continue to do so until one of two things happens. Either man will stop creating smart machines because he feels he has created true artificial intelligence, or he will stop because the machines tell him to.

Chapter 1

The Zenith of Artificial Intelligence

It Was the Best of Times, If You Were a Machine

The crowd stood in the last light of sunset on a cliff one hundred feet above the Pacific Ocean, drinking margaritas and watching the waves smash the sand. From that high above Malibu Beach, the sound of the surf was barely audible, but the party-goers took little interest in the sights or sounds of the natural world. They had something more important on their minds.

They were gathered to pay homage to a machine. A machine constructed of plastic and silicon.

A machine that could think.

As usual for a Hollywood-style bash, many of the guests had arrived by limousine, chauffeured to the party compliments of the evening's host, a small computer company called Symbolics, Inc. headquartered three thousand miles away in Cambridge, Massachusetts. The guests included selected members of the federal government, especially the Department of Defense, as well as the strategic planning groups of major corporations from around the world.

The date was August 20, 1985. Symbolics, then a five-year-old company that employed just over four hundred people, had been able to accomplish in those four years what billion-dollar computer behemoths like IBM, Hewlett Packard, and Digital Equipment could not: It had brought an intelligent machine to market. This thinking computer was created through a technology called artificial intelligence. Known as AI, artificial intelligence was a relatively secret computer technology that computer researchers had been working on for the better part of twenty years. The motivation behind AI was to give computers the capability to behave like humans—to make them think and act logically, to enable them to understand the spoken word, to give them the capability to communicate in conversational language, and to provide them with practical expertise in everything from stock trading to brain surgery.

Although virtually unknown to the general public, Symbolics was the pre-eminent player in AI and one of the most important suppliers to the federal government, working closely with agencies such as the Pentagon, NASA, and the Internal Revenue Service. Companies like American Express, General Motors, and Boeing were all waiting in line behind the feds to get at Symbolics' machines.

In keeping with its astounding success, the company had spared no expense in setting up its Malibu celebration. The party was an extravaganza of a scale not often hosted by companies of Symbolics' size. Most start-ups in the computer business, from Apple to Intel, were known for their beer blasts and pizza parties. Symbolics had chosen instead to rent a cliff-side Malibu mansion and had stocked it with catered Mexican food and fountains that bubbled over with margaritas.

Symbolics was fundamentally different from other computer companies of any size. It was the recognized leader in a technology that promised to change the world, and Symbolics executives were planning a complete overthrow of the existing computer establishment. A Symbolics vice president had once remarked that it was "only a matter of a few years before every computer in the United States, and then the world, would become obsolete in the face of Symbolics' technology." Who would want to use plain old personal computers and monstrous corporate mainframes for word processing and calculating when they could have a computer that could decide—on its own—how to best run an entire business?

This was a fairly brash prediction from a small company, but there just happened to be a lot of well-placed people and important government organizations that were willing to bet on the same vision of the future.

Symbolics' president interrupted the party festivities momentarily to discuss his company's corporate successes and product plans. Russell Noftsker, the boyish-looking forty-three-year-old founder and president of Symbolics, also announced record sales levels for the current quarter. Noftsker was one of a growing clique of computer scientists who had found new careers in the early 1980s as technology entrepreneurs. At one time, Noftsker had worked on the development of the SR-71 spy plane, and then had overseen the world's largest artificial intelligence laboratory, which was at the Massachusetts Institute of Technology. Yet at forty-three, with years of sophisticated high-tech expertise behind him, he still managed to look like a computer kid made good, sparkling blue eyes peering out from behind wireframe glasses, ready to discuss the most intimate technical aspects of any of his—or his competitors'—products.

The crowd listened as he discussed the newest version of Symbolics' computer, known as a LISP machine. The machine was named after a high-level programming language called LISP, which was short for LISt Processing. The computer he described sounded like the ultimate thinking machine—something as advanced as HAL, the fictional computer from the movie *2001: A Space Odyssey*. HAL, the make-believe icon that the artificial intelligence industry pursued in real life, could understand spoken language, see and recognize its surroundings, speak with its own voice, and most importantly, think and reason using both universal concepts and its own experience. Thus, it behaved in the same way a human being would. The fact that HAL had ultimately been too smart for its own good, had run amok and then outwitted and destroyed its human creators, was considered an improbable part of the *2001* story.

The people at the party had long been frustrated in their desire to possess a system with HAL's mythical level of computerized intelligence. Part of the problem was the price tag for intelligent systems: $1 million minimum for the cost of the computer hardware, software, and trained personnel needed to build a computerized brain. Symbolics' own high prices were responsible for much of the expense; its computers typically cost $100,000 or more for each person using the machine. Software and consulting services often added at least $200,000 to the cost.

But Symbolics was ready to offer an alternative to high-cost machines. In a move to put more AI out into the commercial market, the company was planning to give the partiers a chance to buy intelligent software and hardware components for less than $100,000. To every member of the crowd, it was a bargain.

Users of the newest Symbolics computer would be able to quickly develop intelligent systems that could mimic the behavior of research chemists, financial advisors, neuroscientists, and lawyers. These systems relied heavily on the use of complex logic, reasoning capabilities, and built-in rules of knowledge that would bring any traditional computer—from a PC to a mainframe—to its knees. Creating relationships between objects and executing rules of logic, traits normally considered human, just weren't part of what ordinary computing systems did. But Symbolics' machines could easily perform these operations. Other computers had always been designed essentially for making mathematical calculations and producing text, and could do little else. Trying to get an IBM mainframe to run programs the way that the Symbolics LISP machine did was like trying to get a Mack truck to drive like a Lamborghini.

For the party-going technical elite, the possibility of owning a Symbolics machine, any kind of Symbolics machine, was the stuff of which hackers' wet dreams were made. And tonight, Symbolics was celebrating an affordable intelligent machine: a computer that would bring AI to the masses.

The audience understood and appreciated the significance of this conceptual breakthrough. All of them were working on their own intelligent systems, many under the strictest codes of government and corporate secrecy. They represented the most powerful organizations in America, from Fortune 500 companies to the FBI, and all their organizations wanted the Symbolics computer for the same basic reason: They could create applications that would be smarter and more efficient than their human personnel. Using machines to do the work of people would save countless hours in training and millions of dollars in salaries, not to mention sick leave and vacations. You didn't have to pay a thinking machine, it never got tired, quit, had pangs of conscience, or suffered a nervous breakdown. It was the perfect replacement for a human being.

Many of the party-goers stood to make their own financial and career fortunes by using the new Symbolics hardware. First, there were researchers and academicians who were pursuing the theoretical aspects of the smart machine. Second, there were executives of software companies with brainlike names such as IntelliCorp, Teknowledge, and Inference who had begun developing software for it. Then there were journalists who saw AI as the biggest ongoing story of the decade. And finally, there were venture capitalists, investors who had put millions upon millions of dollars into the companies working in this field. These financiers had already decided that artificial intelligence was the most influential, and potentially most profitable, technology ever devised. It was bigger than the personal computer revolution and bigger than biotechnology. AI represented everything that any technology could ever aspire to.

As if to validate that point, Symbolics had had its first piece of hardware featured on the cover of *Business Week* the previous summer with a headline that screamed "ARTIFICIAL INTELLIGENCE: IT'S HERE!" Suddenly, scores of other companies like Symbolics were getting huge AI development contracts from entities like DuPont, American Airlines, MIT, Harvard University, NASA, the U.S. Air Force, Texaco, Ford, and General Motors. Any major corporation that knew anything about technology was rapidly pouring large sums of money into smart technology. The business of artificial intelligence seemed like a no-lose situation.

The AI business in the mid-1980s already owed much of its success to an unlikely source: the secretive technocrats within the Pentagon. The Department of Defense had actually funded the development of AI hardware at MIT throughout the 1970s, hoping to create computer copilots for fighter aircraft and tanks that could maneuver over obstacles and attack an enemy without any human intervention. Russell Noftsker, who was director of MIT's AI Lab in the early 1970s, saw the potential of bringing the fruits of this research to the commercial market. In 1980, he recruited the best programmers from MIT and founded his new company right across the street from the university in Cambridge, Massachusetts, within sight of the lab's front door.

Noftsker's plan to commercialize the technology distressed a small group of AI scientists and academicians who had worked in MIT's private enclave for years. Many of these individuals felt that the development of AI technology should be closely guarded by those who had worked on it and who, therefore, best understood its potential. This, of course, meant that these same academicians and scientists felt that they alone were entitled to the privilege of guardianship. Turning AI over to the commercial sector would both cheapen their efforts and endanger further research for the sake of making money and creating product lines.

Outraged and fearful, one disgruntled MIT researcher threatened to strap dynamite to himself and blow the new Symbolics building and most of Cambridge off the face of the earth. He never followed through with this plan, but Noftsker and Symbolics succeeded in theirs, beyond their wildest dreams.

The company had an extremely successful public offering in 1984, and the summer of 1985 was on its way to more than $100 million in sales. Now, it was being courted by the biggest names in the computer industry. Companies like IBM, Apple, Digital Equipment, and Hewlett Packard—all wanted to get a piece of Symbolics' technology. These companies knew that machines that behaved like humans were the next generation, the natural evolution, of the computer business, and they saw that Symbolics was sitting in the cat-bird seat.

Not even Japan, Inc.—the conglomeration of Japanese electronics firms that was quickly eating its way into the world's computer markets—could compete with Symbolics. Although the Japanese government had set up a research project in 1981 that was attempting to develop a fully functioning form of artificial intelligence by 1990, it wasn't even close to achieving what Symbolics and its U.S. compatriots had already done. The AI industry was one technological area in which the United States still had undisputed dominance; the Japanese were so far behind that they weren't even considered competition.

The general consensus at the Malibu party was that artificial intelligence would be in widespread use throughout the world by 1990. Sold and marketed properly, there wasn't a single business sector in the United States or anyplace else where AI couldn't make a phenomenal difference to its users. Intelligent computers would be programmed to make more money than any trading floor full of MBAs. Hospital emergency rooms would use AI to make life-saving decisions more quickly and accurately than any attending surgeon. The technology would begin to take humans out of the loop in military combat, making the decades-old science fiction notion of wars waged by robots a reality. Smart software would soon scan more data and analyze more facts in an hour than a single person could hope to in a year, and in the process, business and government would change: oil would be drilled more efficiently, telecommunications networks would be designed without errors, the IRS would catch more tax cheats, airlines would optimize their flight schedules, the SEC would be able to detect the slightest level of corporate fraud, the automakers would make safer cars, and the FBI would quickly be able to catch the nation's serial killers.

All of these AI projects, from efficient oil drilling to the improved criminal investigation, were either under way or on the drawing board at the time of that summer party of 1985. The technology was already in place. Framed by the Malibu sunset, the promise of AI seemed limited only by the abilities of the people entrusted to make it work; almost nothing could stop the progress of man finally creating a machine in his own image. AI—the pinnacle of human technology—was about to make the dream a reality.

That was all true on the evening of August 20, 1985. But in less than thrity-six months, Symbolics and the artificial intelligence business would become the pariah of the computer industry.

Yet the pursuit of a thinking machine, an intelligent creation made in man's image, had just barely begun.

❧

Suffering from undelivered promises, unrealistic user expectations, and over-whelming media hype, the vendors of smart machines experienced a market backlash unprecedented in the computer industry. To a large degree, the AI vendors were victims of their own success. Customers who had experienced huge successes with intelligent computers were unwilling to publicly discuss a technology they wanted to keep as a competitive secret. Companies that were unable to get smart applications up and running, on the other hand, were only too happy to criticize the technology. The vendors were caught in a situation where nothing positive was being said about artificial intelligence, and sales into new markets stalled. As revenues began to flatten, many of the AI vendors sought out private funding to provide working capital. But in the harsh economic climate of the late 1980s, they found the investment well had gone completely dry. Companies that had raised millions of dollars in start-up financing on the promise of smart machines were now shunned as bad risks by the investment community. By 1993, half of the major develop-ers of AI were shut down.

On January 28, 1993, Symbolics, Inc. filed for protection under Chapter 11 of the U.S. federal bankruptcy code. It had gone from sales in the hun-dreds of millions of dollars to revenues that barely cracked the $10 million mark. From its standing as the preeminent developer of computer technol-ogy in the United States, it had become a corporate weakling that no longer even sold computers, but sold consulting services. The company's intelligent machines were—and are—regarded as perhaps the most advanced in the world, but in a customer-driven marketplace, having the best technology was only one of many prerequisites necessary to maintaining long-term success. Symbolics and other AI companies failed not because of their technology, but as a direct result of the egos, idiosyncrasies, and even the recklessness of the people who ran them. These people were selling products that they be-lieved would fundamentally change the way that business was run, and their unyielding commitment to seeing that happen—on their terms—was their downfall. Having created the ultimate computer, they ignored the basics of how to run their businesses. They failed to acknowledge the needs of cus-tomers, and often regarded their corporate and government clients as unen-lightened and technically naive.

Ultimately, the AI researchers who were suddenly taken from the relative obscurity of the labs to entrepreneurial roles on Wall Street simply had no clue how to manage the growth of start-up companies. Many of these people, including the man who first envisioned the commercial potential of AI—Symbolics' Russell Noftsker—would end up being unceremoniously and acrimoniously thrown out of the companies they had founded by impatient investors and long-time partners. At the same time, users learned enough about artificial intelligence that in many cases they were able to eliminate the need for vendors altogether. Large industrial corporations like Boeing, DuPont, and General Electric eventually created internal AI groups that were many times larger and better staffed than those companies that had previously been selling them intelligent systems. Instead of buying intelligent machines, they developed their own.

Today, the success of smart technology continues despite the stunning collapse of the companies that achieved notoriety during the 1980s. And the technology still promises to change computing in ways that only science fiction writers could have dreamed of. The IRS has its tax monitoring system in place, and the FBI can now create psychological profiles of suspects. The U.S. military used smart computers to assist in the rapid deployment of men and equipment during the Persian Gulf War; American Express claims to save millions of dollars a year in credit card processing by using a system—developed with Symbolics—that authorizes member purchases; Mrs. Fields Cookies has been so successful in creating software that manages its retail stores that it sells the package to other retailers such as Burger King; and a controversial system called APACHE (Acute Physiology, Age, and Chronic Health Evaluation) is now in use at a number of hospitals, making medical recommendations on the care of critically ill patients.

The following chapters look at those individuals and organizations that created the first thinking machines and explore what remains of their legacy. They also examine the next generation of intelligent systems already under development—devices modeled on the biological structure of the brain. These computers will be able to translate the spoken word into foreign languages, guide automobiles safely from one place to another, identify faces in a crowd, and adapt to their surroundings by learning from experience. This new generation will extend beyond the province of large corporations and government research centers. It will address the individual user, putting machine intelligence in the hands of consumers for the first time. Smart appliances, such as VCRs that continually scan cable channels and record programs based on knowledge of users' interests and preferences, or washing machines that know how dirty a load of clothes is, are already in the testing stage.

Computer tutors that can monitor a student's progress and structure lessons accordingly are being developed at universities such as UCLA and Stanford.

Dow Jones is building an information system that understands concepts and ideas, which will be used to create customized newspapers for each of its subscribers.

Apple Computer has promised to deliver a personal computer that is controlled by the human voice—and not by a keyboard—within the next several years.

Motorola has outlined plans for an intelligent microchip that will provide kinesthetic instructions to damaged or paralyzed limbs and organs. The chip will not be part of a computer: it will be embedded in the human nervous system.

This is the future of artificial intelligence. How the computer industry will get there—and the growing pains that it has already been through—is the story of *The Brain Makers*.

The Computer Industry Seeks to Create AI

Stupid Machines, Relatively Smart People

We want all of our machines to have artificial intelligence.

In a day and age when most of us do not change our own oil, cannot program our VCRs, and can only turn on the TV with the remote control, we expect our appliances, devices, and machines to do these things for themselves. Or, at the very least, we expect them to be able to tell us how to do them.

We no longer know how to do the mundane things because there are too many important things to worry about. Who has the time to read through a twenty-page manual just to get the VCR to record reruns of "Gilligan's Island"? Not me, and probably not you. So what would it take to make machines simple enough to use that we wouldn't have to fumble around with manuals and buttons and complicated instructions?

Artificial intelligence.

Since the beginning of time, man has wanted his machines to take on a disproportionate amount of his work. He has always accomplished this by making machines act as extensions of his own limbs and organs. Plows and tractors are extensions of the hands, shoulders, and back. Blenders and washing machines are extensions of the hands and arms. Cars are traveling machines—extensions of the feet and legs. Telescopes are extensions of the eyes. Telephones are extensions of the vocal cords and ears. There are mechanized extensions to every part of the body, some of which are probably better left unmentioned at this point.

The one organ that we have not truly extended beyond our physical selves is the brain. The calculator does some of the functions of the brain, as do personal computers. But neither of them really thinks; we tell them what to do and they do it. These machines do not take the initiative to do our mental work for us, yet that is what we expect from them.

It is because of this expectation—that computers are to ultimately be the logical extension of our minds—that the field of artificial intelligence has become so visible and talked about in the last decade. Once we get computers to do our thinking, the reasoning goes, then we can get VCRs to program themselves, microwaves to set their own times, TVs to find the right cable stations, and cars to take care of themselves. Self-supporting machines. All we have to do is turn them on and never bother with them again. End of story, right?

Wrong. Beginning of story.

The creation of artificial intelligence is more involved than making a wish list of technical capabilities, and it is not as simple as examining today's state-of-the-art technology. The attempt to create thinking machines is actually several hundred years old. Only recently has it become a story that most of us can relate to, filled with gigantic egos, spoiled brats, military spending, corporate intrigue, get-rich-quick schemes, and ruined lives. Of course, it is also a story of one of the greatest technological undertakings since the shaping of the wheel.

Surprisingly, it is not a story of computers, although they play a major and recurring role in all modern AI endeavors. The story of artificial intelligence is about people and how people want their machines to behave. More specifically, it is about what people have done and will do to make their machines think.

The people who have built thinking machines are predominantly from universities and large corporations. It would be nice to think that in a noble pursuit such as the creation of a machine with its own intelligence that personal politics, egos, and pettiness would be removed from the equation at the outset.

It would be nice, but it would be completely unrealistic.

Artificial intelligence wove a web of research organizations and academic institutions in the 1970s that were more than happy to jump on the bandwagon because the U.S. government—and your tax dollars—were footing the bill. During the Vietnam War, when researchers were accusing the military of unspeakable horrors on a daily basis, the Department of Defense was paying for their AI research. When these researchers left academia for the legitimacy of the commercial world, guess who their first customer was? The Department of Defense. The contradictions didn't end there, and many of the first companies in AI often seemed touched with lunacy. Only in the artificial intelligence business could a company like Teknowledge, flush with millions of investment dollars from General Motors, try to sell a revolutionary new business technology to major accounts by demonstrating a program that selects the best wine for dinner parties. When IBM announced publicly that it was going to legitimize the artificial intelligence market by coming out with its own AI products, it neglected to tell its salespeople. Hewlett Packard saw a big chance to make money in AI by capitalizing on its engineering expertise, only to have that chance disintegrate during an embarrassing shouting match involving a small group of mid-level engineers.

Of course, there are some remarkable stories that show just how much really can be accomplished with this unique technology, some of which were mentioned in the previous chapter. We'll get to them all in time.

The point is that in the story of man and machines, man is the story. There are plenty of outsized egos to match the normalcy of the people who worked tirelessly to make AI a reality. People who had been unable to keep a job in any other area of the computer business often found a safe haven in AI. Others, with no pretensions of greatness, made remarkable breakthroughs that pushed the technology further than it was ever expected to go.

You do not have to know anything about machines to understand what has taken and is taking place in the business of creating artificial intelligence. If you've never used a computer, you won't be at a loss in the pages that follow. Nor do you need to know anything about the age-old quandaries concerning what is thinking and what is not thinking. Indeed, much of what has already been written about artificial intelligence is rife with philosophy, some of it interesting, much of it mundane and repetitive, and all of it a little too clever for its own good. While many of philosophy's great debates do lead naturally to a discussion of man and his thought processes, they don't necessarily make required reading for a story about artificial intelligence. There are plenty of places to learn about philosophy and computers and all their intricate little details and idiosyncrasies. This, however, isn't one of them. All you have to do here is sit back and read.

Or wait until a machine can do it for you.

~

A few thoughts on what makes artificial intelligence different from regular computing are in order here just to make sure that your eyes don't glaze over during any of the more prosaic passages in the following chapters. This will only take a minute, so bear with me.

Today's handheld calculators, which are roughly the size of a credit card, are capable of performing all the basic math functions: addition, subtraction, multiplication, and division. Most of them also handle more complex functions like square roots and percentages. We take these little devices for granted because they are so cheap and nearly omnipresent. You get them free with minimum purchases at electronics stores or as bonuses for opening charge accounts. They are so trivial in today's society—from a consumer point of view—that it is cheaper to throw them away when their batteries run dry than to get new batteries.

In 1950, though, it took nearly 6,000 cubic feet of electronic equipment to do what a plastic calculator does today.

Descriptions of the first digital computers, which appeared in the 1940s, usually include mention of the fact that these machines contained thousands of vacuum tubes, had lots of blinking lights, and even "filled a room." Such descriptions hardly touch the immense scale of those first machines. Built one at a time, they had mind-numbing names like IBM's Mark I and the University of Pennsylvania's ENIAC, the Electronic Numerical Integrator And Calculator. Yes, these machines were as big as a room, but they would have hardly fit in anybody's family room or master bedroom. Instead, they were actually the size of small houses, running up to fifty feet long. Room-sized, perhaps, but only if you're living in Buckingham Palace or the Louvre.

In the early days of computing, the machinery essentially did one thing, which was calculate numbers. Similarly, the toaster in its early incarnation just toasted bread to one shade of brown. Today, computers can do a number of things, and although we may not understand the details of how they operate, this does not limit our interaction with them. Modern toasters have an almost limitless number of settings, including things like "top brown only" and "light." Do you know how the toaster gets its coils to know the difference? Does it matter? Of course not. The same is true of computers.

The important thing to know about computers is that they are digital and very good with numbers, but not so hot with symbols and concepts. Digital simply means that they use a system of electrical 1s and 0s instead of moving parts, which is what analog devices use. Two examples of digital devices and their analog counterparts are compact disks versus vinyl records and digital watches versus watches with sweep second hands. The 1s and 0s represent bursts of electricity through transistors, or in the early days of computers, through vacuum tubes. These 1s and 0s, which are the core of binary mathematics, are generated so quickly (as "on" and "off" pulses) that they can be grouped together to represent numbers and words. The number 79, for example, is represented by the binary code 01001111. With enough proper planning, or computer coding, these binary bursts form words, numbers, pictures, and even sound and video.

Computers are designed from the outset to accept binary information. A programmer must then convert that binary information into a workable format so that the binary code can be used for specific tasks. Overwhelmingly, these tasks are mathematical in nature, and are used for calculations. When a programmer instructs the computer to do something, it only follows the instructions given to it; there is no deviation. Simply, a computer is commanded to "Do this. When this is done, only do this and this after it." Thus, the operation of computers is well-thought-out and predetermined. This accounts for the extremely finicky nature of most programmers and their obsession with detail. Any deviation from the programmer's intent is considered a bug that must be eliminated. Bugs drive programmers—and users—crazy.

A calculator only adds four and four when you tell it to, and the answer is always eight. The computer is unable to speculate about possible variations in the adding of four and four because it has been programmed to always and only give a reply of eight. This is one of the annoying things that many first-time users encounter with computers—they only do what they're supposed to. They don't make allowances for the user's lack of familiarity, or they aren't flexible enough to understand when something is "close enough." This inflexibility is a good thing, though, because it allows huge calculations to be performed without strange deviations that might result in wrong answers.

People do not think or behave in the same way that computers do. We take into consideration any number of variables when making a decision or trying to solve a problem that is not related to mathematical equations.

Driving a car, for example, requires that we process a huge number of data points and concepts in order to get from the driveway to the office. We have to accelerate, slow down, stop, start up again. These are variables that have no specific order; we apply them as they are needed due to external conditions—or inputs—such as traffic lights, weather, the proximity of the cars nearest to us, or the jerk who cut in front of us at 80 miles an hour.

To make things even more difficult, these variables have different values at any given time: speed can be 10 miles an hour or 60 miles an hour, stopping can be done quickly or gradually. A standard computer program that encountered a variable with no specific value would not be able to proceed to its next step because it needs a defined value in order to carry out each of its instructions. Since these variables in driving cannot necessarily be predetermined, they would make for a lousy computer program.

Artificial intelligence overcomes these traditional limitations through a form of programming known as *symbolic processing*. Instead of creating programs that rely on strict adherence to instructions from one operation to another, symbolic processing uses the concept of symbols to make the computer more flexible, and hopefully more "intelligent." Symbols are variables that can have a number of attributes as well as relationships with each other. "Car" can be programmed as a symbol with attributes such as "moves forward," "moves in reverse," or "stands still." Depending on the situation, the proper attribute would be assigned to "car" by the computer. If we were trying to direct the computer to navigate through traffic, the attribute it would use would be "moves forward" and certainly not "moves in reverse." Traffic itself can be a symbol (symbols also represent concepts and don't need to be persons, places, or things). Thus, when car and traffic are brought together in a computer program, the machine can determine that this involves "moves forward" without the programmer's actually having to specify that this must be done. As long as the attributes of the symbol, and its relationships with other symbols, have been established by the programmer, the computer can do much of the processing work on its own from that point forward. This imbues it with the capability to handle situations that standard computer programs cannot. And since it theoretically resembles the way in which humans go about the process of making decisions and solving problems, this is considered intelligence.

Of course, intelligence is a subjective term. There are arguments about true intelligence versus apparent intelligence, mental intelligence versus conditioned responses and instinct, and a load of other philosophical blustering that never seems to get resolved. Many computer scientists believe that if a computer can process symbols, it can be taught to think. Others believe that symbols are not important; rather, it is the connections that occur between different areas of the brain and nervous system that enable us to think. Both factions have their supporters, and both sides consider their beliefs to be worth defending at all costs.

The result of this near-religious fervor in the AI business has created the computer industry equivalent of a Holy War, complete with preachers and evangelists, fundamentalists and extremists. Still, the questions linger: Can a machine think? And if so, does that mean it has a mind? Would pulling the plug on a creature with a mind be the equivalent of killing it? Would the machine know it was being killed?

Maybe this is closer to a Holy War than any of us would care to admit. But moral considerations aside, we are talking essentially about giving machines those abilities that are normally thought of as belonging to humans. This includes the ability to understand the spoken word (as well as the ability to speak), the ability to communicate in a common language, the ability to reason and to understand concepts, and the ability to recognize patterns and make sense of them. It was the use of symbolic programming that first provided computers with the potential to mimic these characteristics. And, up until the last decade, symbolic programming was done almost exclusively in research and academic labs.

The unleashing of the concept of symbolic processing into the commercial marketplace, as well as the first electronic age arguments over what constitutes thought, created the crack that allowed artificial intelligence to sneak out of the labs and into the light of day. From there, it begat its own technological subcategories—including expert systems, neural networks, and voice recognition—and provided the impetus for the creation of hundreds of companies throughout the 1980s and 1990s.

The lust for thinking machines, however, did not begin in modern times. Instead, one needs to look back to the beginning of recorded history to realize that man has been working up to artificial intelligence for almost as long as he has been able to understand the concept.

Chapter

3

The Dawn of Thinking Machines

Brazen Heads, Brass Balls

Artificial intelligence is about power, pure and simple. Power of man to re-create human intelligence in machines. Power over other men through the manipulation of these machines. Power to thumb one's nose at the rest of the world and make them stand back in awe of one's accomplishments.

Therefore, it is exceedingly strange that the spiritual mentor of the artificial intelligence industry is not a revered scientist, a wizened sage, or the first person that managed to make a machine think.

It is, instead, a nineteen-year-old girl.

In particular, it is a nineteen-year-old girl who has been dead for more than one hundred years.

While most of the story of AI centers on events that have occurred since 1980, there is an illustrious history of attempts to create thinking machines that dates back nearly to the beginning of recorded history. It is necessary to describe some of these earliest endeavors in order to understand the modern attempts to create thinking machines.

And, as will be evident momentarily, these pursuits were characterized quite succinctly by a young woman named Mary Shelley, the author of the novel *Frankenstein*.

Ever since the day man discovered that he could shape mud and stone into statues, he has been trying to make those statues look and act like himself. After all, statues are primarily representations of individual beings. The difference between statues and people, however, is that statues don't do anything; they just stand there. Statues have always lacked a number of things that would make them truly human like, the most obvious being life. To remedy this situation, people throughout the centuries have tried to make statues and human icons more than just slabs of clay, marble, or metal. They have tried to make them real—or at least realistic—and thereby make them more interesting.

The priests of early civilizations such as Babylon and Israel found that—after a few centuries of getting people to worship statues of golden cows and winged humans—their minions began to catch on to the fact that there wasn't much substance to these idols. Their followers wanted more from their false images. They wanted them to do something, to be intelligent, to be wise, to give them direction. Thus, out of the need to keep the masses at bay came the first efforts at making inanimate objects do what humans could do.

❧

Not surprisingly, the first references man to making smart copies of himself—without God's help—come from classical mythologies and early religious traditions. Roman, Greek, and Egyptian cultures are filled with boatloads of stories about gifted humans creating robot like slaves that grew beyond their makers' original intentions.

Perhaps the best known of them was Hephaestus, a master Greek craftsman renowned for his skill in shaping and forming metals. Known in Roman mythology as Vulcan and in Egyptian lore as Ptah, Hephaestus was born lame, even though his mother was Hera, the goddess of women and marriage. Shunned at an early age by his mother and other gods because of this handicap, Hephaestus became a whiz at creating things out of metal. In a foreshadowing of the "I'll show you!" attitude of the computer generation's oftentimes quirky geniuses, Hephaestus created a golden throne for his mother that bound her in a seated position forever. He also made the infamous armor that protected Achilles.

His greatest feat was creating Talos. In legend, Talos was the embodiment of the greatest accomplishments of the Bronze Age. He was a bronze being crafted by Hephaestus to act as a servant for the god Zeus. If he had been created two thousand years later, Talos would have been considered a robot. As it was, Talos was employed as a weapon to keep surveillance on the island of Crete. His job was to act as a tireless servant, making sure that no one either entered or left the confines of the island without the permission of King Minos. Talos could walk around the entire perimeter of Crete three times in one day because he never got tired, bored, or hurt—which is a big selling point in modern day AI. Possessing incredible strength, this metal man was supposed to be able to throw boulders and rocks huge distances, thereby discouraging anyone from either invading or exiting the island by boat.

But boulders were not enough to stop all invaders, and Talos was oftentimes required to use his own powers of intelligence in order to thwart these interlopers. Making fine use of his metallic machinery, Talos would walk into a raging fire until he and his bronze skin became white hot. At that point, he would hunt down his potential enemies and then embrace them— warmly. Think of it as hugging a smart furnace, with the outcome that his foes were burned to death.

In the bizarre pantheon of classical gods, many of whom were sleeping with their own moms or who actually fathered themselves, Talos was intimately related to another great craftsman named Daedalus. Depending on which tradition you follow, Daedalus was either Talos' uncle or his real creator. In the latter scenario, Talos was forged by Daedalus when Hephaestus wasn't around, even though Hephaestus went on to claim all the glory. Regardless, there came a time when Daedalus and his son, Icarus, were imprisoned on Crete at the invitation of King Minos. In order to escape the ever watchful eye of Talos, Daedalus molded wings of wax for Icarus to use in his escape from Crete. As we know today, the wings of wax were no match for the hot summer sun, and Icarus plunged into the sea like a badly maintained Third World fighter jet. Talos, though, went on to live a full and rich life as a mechanical slave until a woman named Medea cut off his big toe and killed him. Given such a lame ending to one of mankind's first thinking machines, it is obvious that the Greeks were a little weak on the concept of personal security.

Interestingly, this same scenario—killing the hero with a simple act— would be repeated many years later in the "Just pull the plug!" school of thought for controlling intelligent computers.

Robotlike creatures showed up in various other classical myths and writings, notably *The Iliad*, everybody's favorite high school reading assignment. Even Plato and Aristotle both perpetuated the myth of Daedalus creating mechanical men in his workshop. Of course, the Greek myths were fictitious stories. They required nothing in the way of a physical manifestation to prove to the population at large that they were true. Just as it was obvious to everyone on the street that Apollo dragged the sun across the sky from morning until evening, it was obvious that metal-based creatures forged by men existed somewhere, if only in the superstitious minds of believers.

Around the first century A.D., the classical gods began to die off as people stopped believing in them. In their place, both Christian and Jewish traditions became the increasingly dominant forms of religion. In order to win converts away from the Greek and Roman adherents, the new religions appropriated some of the classical fascination with man-made humans. With the increased sophistication—if such a term can even be applied here—of people in the first century, however, the new churches had to substantiate their claims that sentient manufactured beings actually did exist.

A number of luminaries in the early Catholic church had "brazen heads" created for their own use that were rumored to act as advisors. Brazen in this context had less to do with the sheer audacity of the heads' supposed powers than it did with the fact that brazen means "made of bronze." These heads, which sat in exalted places such as their own altars or to the side of their owners' thrones, occasionally had moving parts like mouths or eyes to correspond with real human features. They were consulted on matters of great theological importance, which most often had to do with protecting or furthering their owner's station in life, as opposed to religious quandaries. Remember, early church leaders weren't necessarily known for their piety or commitment to saving the masses, what with charging people entrance fees to heaven and all. Talking heads were just part of the charm of getting a new religion up and running.

Interestingly, religious leaders used their access to talking heads and thinking machines to establish themselves as the most powerful men of the realm. In what would foreshadow the AI research mentality of the 1970s and 1980s, control of the talking heads meant domination and superiority over the less well-informed members of the society. Access to the machines was both a privilege and a divine right—albeit one foisted on unwary subjects by the creators themselves. This mindset would barely change at all by the time MIT and Stanford started working on AI more than ten centuries later.

The first of the religious talking heads belonged to Pope Sylvester II, who headed up the church in the year 1000. Prior to becoming pope, Sylvester was known as Gerbert, a well-schooled intellectual and part-time sorcerer. One of the best educated men of his time, Gerbert was extremely knowledgeable in many fields, including astronomy, literature, mathematics, and music. He was also a consummate politician who carefully plotted his rise through the ranks of both French politics and the Roman church. His unusual command of diverse sciences and arts, coupled with his apparently easy rise to the papacy, caused many to believe that he had made a pact with the devil to advance his own interests and career. In return for his soul, it was said, Gerbert was given the instructions to create a brazen head that would advise him as well as deliver prophecies to him.

The most important thing that the head told Gerbert, after he had become Pope Sylvester II, was that he would not die until he had said Mass in Jerusalem. Thus, in order to live forever, Gerbert chose not to include Jerusalem in any of his travel plans. Yet, while saying Mass in a church in Europe in 1003, Gerbert began to feel weak and saw himself surrounded by demons and evil spirits of the satanic type. Feeling as if he was about to die, but confused about the head's promise, Gerbert was told that the church he was in had been dedicated to the Holy Cross of Jerusalem. It was, in effect, a little piece of Jerusalem set up outside of the Holy Land. Gerbert made his last confession upon learning this obscure but wholly relevant fact, and died a few minutes later.

Interestingly, it is widely believed that Gerbert may have been the man who introduced the abacus—the ancient forerunner of the electronic computer—to the Europeans. Supposedly, in his ongoing quest for knowledge, Gerbert actually learned to operate the device from Arabs who had been trading goods in Spain. He then used the machine to perform complex calculations that were beyond the scope of arithmetic traditionally used by Europeans. Gerbert's world thus became one of the first places in history where computing devices and humanlike "thinking" devices came together. Although he didn't put the two devices together into one machine, Gerbert was intimately involved nearly one thousand years ago with the concepts that would later flourish into artificial intelligence.

The next Catholic dignitary to dabble in the mechanical arts was Albertus Magnus, a Bavarian bishop born in 1204 A.D. Albertus spent nearly thirty years of his life building a head that could think for itself. The head was able to answer questions that were put to it and was capable of solving mathematical problems. Eventually, according to legend, Albertus was able to affix a body to the head, creating a mobile machine not unlike an ancient C3PO. When this marvel was demonstrated for the benefit of St. Thomas Aquinas, the leading Catholic thinker of the time, Aquinas went berserk. Aquinas attacked the machine with a fury, ripping it limb from limb and destroying each of its metal parts in the process. By the time St. Thomas was done, the thinking machine was not much more than scrap metal. His explanation for destroying three decades of Albertus' work was that this creation was the work of a sorcerer, and thus not fit to exist. From that point forward, Albertus and Aquinas had little to say to each other.

One of Albertus' comtemporaries, Roger Bacon, was another Christian leading light who employed a brazen head. Bacon had an obsession with war-related activities—a strange pastime for a clergyman—and undertook to surround all of England with a great wall made of brass. Realizing that this was a somewhat gargantuan task, Bacon decided that he needed some intellectual support in undertaking the building of the wall. With the help of the devil (or perhaps a sorcerer; accounts are a bit sketchy), Bacon built a brazen head to assist him in the design of the wall, as well as to give him moral support in his endeavor. Like all good brazen heads and early smart machines, this particular head took a long time to complete—namely, seven years' worth of labor. As it turned out, though, any modern day visitor to England—including the country's various World War II enemies—can attest to the fact that the talking head was of little help in assisting Bacon with his ambitious scheme to protect the island.

Four centuries later, in 1625, the term "automaton" first appeared in English writing. The word served to describe and categorize all of those brazen heads and humanlike machines that had been created by men over the centuries. It implied both mechanical and mental capabilities, although it was often used to describe simple devices that moved only when wound up or activated by pendulums.

Only a dozen years after automaton made its way into the vernacular, renowned thinker and mathematician René Descartes came up with the single phrase that would ultimately lay the conceptual groundwork for whether artificial intelligence could be more than just machines with logic circuitry. His *cogito, ergo sum*—"I think, therefore I am"—has been the rallying cry that many in the human race use to distinguish themselves from animals, vegetables, and minerals; indeed, it is often used to distinguish some humans from others. Descartes was obsessed with putting forth a philosophical determination that would verify existence, and he did this by positing thinking as a proof of existence. Part of his beliefs, though, included the notion that men and machines were both complex automata that had similarities in their nature, even though this did not extend to their spiritual and intellectual nature. Both had bodies, but both did not have minds.

Like all the other noted philosophers of his time, especially those with major religious affiliations, Descartes (a devout Catholic) was reputed to have fashioned his own version of the brazen head and primitive robot. In this case, though, the machine was a traveling companion, and said companion was a "she" that Descartes referred to as "my girl Francine." This being the mid-1600s, a lot of people didn't quite take to the idea of a respectable man carrying on with a mechanical girl. On one trip that Descartes and Francine took aboard a ship, the combination proved to be too much of a travesty for the vessel's captain. In a veritable replay of St. Thomas Aquinas' earlier rage against a machine, the captain tossed Francine overboard. While mariners have always had a superstitious fear of women on their ships, the captain justified this particular action by claiming that Francine had been created by the devil. One can only surmise that Aquinas would have been proud.

~

At this point in history, our story detours out of the Christian mainstream and works its way over to Jewish tradition. Since Old Testament times, Hebrew mythology had embraced the idea of the golem, a manlike creature made out of clay through magical means. Psalm 139:16 specifically mentions the golem as being an unformed human being still waiting to take its final shape. It is in various legends, however, that the nature of the golem is related to a man-made entity. The basic story is this: Mud or clay was sculpted into the form of a man. When the word "aemaeth"—the Hebrew term for truth or God's truth—was etched into the clay figure's forehead, it came to life to do its creator's bidding. Not considered an intelligent being, the golem was ordered to do manual labor around its master's house, things like cleaning up or fetching water. Essentially, the golem served as free labor, but there were a number of catches. For one thing, the golem was not to leave the home of its owner. Also, it could take orders, but could not always speak. The primary drawback to having a golem around the house, however, was that it got bigger every day. A lot bigger. Its strength also increased on a daily basis, to the point that it became a potential threat to those living in the house. Before the golem could get out of hand, its owner had to grab the golem and wipe off the first two letters of the word written on its forehead. This turned "aemaeth" into "maeth," which is the term for death. As soon as this occurred, the golem reverted to a muddy corpse.

The golem myth grew rapidly in Eastern Europe, where the creature evolved into a sort of Jewish bogeyman. Stories of golems running amuck replaced the earlier stories of the helpful assistant, and the legend took on malevolent implications. One of the first tales of the danger involved in making one's own golem involved a man who had let his creature grow to monumental proportions. When the man realized that he could not reach the golem's head in order to perform the all-important letter scrubbing function, he began to fear for the safety of his family. In what he believed to be a stroke of genius, the man ordered his gargantuan slave to bend down in order to converse with him. Seizing the opportunity of dealing with the golem face-to-face, the man quickly erased the letters from its forehead. Instantly the monster turned to clay, its life having been sucked away. Unfortunately, in its now inanimate state, the golem toppled forward and crushed its creator to death under the sheer weight of its clay bulk.

Far and away the best known golem was the work of Judah Loew ben Bezaleel, the High Rabbi of the city of Prague. Known by the horrendous pun name High Rabbi Loew, the rabbi created his own golem around 1600, which roughly coincides with the time period that René Descartes' mechanical girlfriend Francine was learning about the lack of buoyancy in metal. Rabbi Loew created the golem every Monday morning after the Sabbath was over and commanded it to do all his housework and temple cleanup during the week—notably, fetching pails of water for his use from a local well. Adhering to the Jewish law that commanded all things to rest during the Sabbath, the rabbi would turn his golem back into clay every Friday evening before the Sabbath Eve liturgy took place. The Jews in the Prague ghetto were well aware of the golem's existence, and many believed that it even protected them by uncovering nefarious plots concocted by anti-Semites. The Jews were frequently accused of participating in ritual murders and their enemies plotted to execute them, given the right opportunity, in a seemingly endless series of persecutions, known as pogroms. The rabbi's golem—who was thought to be generally stupid yet possessing a certain canny intelligence—was able to warn various members of the community about these impending plots and therefore saved many of their lives. He may have been a monster, but the Jews in Prague had a certain respect for him.

Being only human, though, Rabbi Loew was bound to eventually slip up at some point in his weekly rituals. One Friday evening in particular, the rabbi hurried to the synagogue and forgot to do the required forehead-scrubbing. As he started to lead the congregation in prayer, the sound of mayhem and destruction in the city reached the ears of the worshippers. The golem had wandered out of Rabbi Loew's house and was smashing through houses and tearing up the streets. The rabbi interrupted the religious service and ran out to confront the golem. He managed to attack the now-maniacal golem and scrape at the word on his head, rendering him lifeless. For some unknown reason, the rabbi had the dusty remains of his creature entombed in Prague's Altner Shul synagogue, where they supposedly remain to this day.

The Eastern European Jews certainly had an influence on their non-Jewish counterparts in countries like Germany, Austria, and Russia—and vice versa. This, after all, was the land of vampires and werewolves, creatures that were aberrations of God's law. But the golem story, especially as portrayed in the exploits of Rabbi Loew's creature, found its way into one of the most popular tales in German literature as the basis for Johann Goethe's *The*

Sorcerer's Apprentice, written in the late seventeenth century. In a bizarre clash of cultures, this same story serves as the primary animation segment in the Disney film *Fantasia*. Known for appropriating truly gruesome European folk tales and turning them into nonthreatening children's entertainment, Walt Disney had Mickey Mouse give life to a broom—a fairly harmless household tool that lacks the inherent menace of a golem—in order to do his housework. The broom fetched water until it flooded the house belonging to Mickey's boss (the sorcerer), at which time the master reappeared to invoke the command that returned the broom to its original inanimate state.

Substitute the golem of Rabbi Loew fame for the broom of Mickey Mouse fame and you begin to get an idea of how pervasive the golem legend truly is. More than any other single cultural artifact, the golem is the precursor of modern man's fear and fascination with thinking machines that have the power to conquer and even dominate their masters.

༺

As civilization boldly pushed into the eighteenth and nineteenth centuries, the oral tales of talking heads and metallic men and women started to abate, due perhaps in equal measures to a slight increase in literacy, a propagation of authenticated written histories, a lessening of various religions' stranglehold on the mind-set of the populace, and better communication between individuals in geographically separate regions. The fictional automata gave way to real machines, which were put on display or traveled the land in expositions and carnivals. These machines mimicked animal and human activities, but were not mistaken for living beings. The most pervasive of these automatons were the glockenspiels that became fixtures of bell and clock towers in cities throughout Europe. Life-sized artificial men and women marched out of their clock closets every hour on the hour to pirouette and play instruments, and generally cavort about in a mechanical frenzy for a few minutes before returning to their enclosures. It was clever and captivating—at the time—but it didn't approach real life.

There were a few attempts at continuing to create lifelike machines, most notable being some undertakings by a French artisan named Jacques de Vaucanson. He built a realistic mechanical flute player that could play a dozen different tunes on a real flute, but he is best known for a duck that he constructed in 1738. Vaucanson's mechanical duck contained more than four thousand parts and was actually able to walk, flap its wings, and peck at grain. The impressive thing about the metal duck's ability to peck at grain was how thoroughly Vaucanson imitated the eating process. The duck could grab the grain with its bill, swallow it, perform some rudimentary digestion via a simple chemical process, and then excrete the result. This was accomplished through a complex set of gears, tubing, and various other unknown mechanisms that Vaucanson refused to reveal during the course of his lifetime. The duck was presented in numerous shows throughout Europe, with the proceeds going to fund Vaucanson's own research into artificial life.

From Vaucanson's time forward, mechanical beings were gradually relegated to the role of toys. An impressive large-scale piece was constructed by Pierre Jacquet-Droz in 1774 that involved a boy, sitting at a table, who could hold a pen and write selected poems on a piece of paper (it currently resides in a Swiss museum). But Droz's family was more interested in creating amusing playthings and moving figurines than in creating wondrous examples of mechanical life. Surprisingly, even as craftsmen achieved a better understanding of gears and hydraulic systems and had better tools at their disposal, the interest in creating truly marvelous pieces waned. In fact, the whole art of creating automatons actually regressed, with the result being that the machines were primitive, crude, and not very complicated at all. Wind-up organ grinders and their monkeys became a common mechanical theme that maintained its popularity well into the twentieth century, as did automated fortune-tellers of the kind featured in the movie *Big*. Yet, the improvements in technology did not stop the decline in the creation of automatons, which disappeared almost entirely by the end of the 1800s.

This decline dovetailed with the onset of the Industrial Revolution. Suddenly, people found that their jobs and their workplaces were being invaded by large mechanical beasts that could do the work of many men in half the time. Maybe the idea of little machines that looked like people was too closely associated with the terror of being replaced by a machine like the Jacquard loom, a device that had already supplanted thousands of textile workers across Europe by the middle of the 1800s. Maybe the time and effort required to make automatons wasn't worth it in an era of growing hostility toward machines. Maybe man creating machines that had the potential to replace humans just wasn't amusing anymore, and it was all hitting a little too close to home. Maybe people just didn't like the idea of artificial people showing up in a time of technology overload.

Or maybe a lot of them had finally gotten around to reading *Frankenstein*.

❧

As the Industrial Revolution was crashing down upon the heads of humans who never expected to compete with machines, the young wife of poet Percy

Bysshe Shelley published the only book for which she would be truly remembered. Not only did this novel tap into the growing nineteenth-century fear of technology running amuck, but it upped the ante of just how far that technology might go. Mary Shelley's book intimated that man might just be able to build the creatures that would eventually make the human species obsolete.

And she basically wrote it out of boredom.

Mary Wollstonecraft Shelley was born Mary Godwin in 1797, the daughter of a famous politician father and a famous activist mother. Both of her parents had devoted a great deal of their lives to writing about political issues that often focused on the need to improve the human condition. Even though her mother died only eleven days after she was born, by most accounts Mary Godwin had a pleasant upbringing, one that was inflamed during her adolescence with the passion of the Romantic literary movement.

At the tender age of sixteen, Mary became emotionally and physically involved with Percy Shelley, one of the leading figures—along with William Wordsworth, Samuel Taylor Coleridge, and Lord Byron—of the Romantic movement. The fact that Shelley was still married to his wife Harriet did not keep him from traipsing around Europe with Mary to spend candlelit evenings with the leading thinkers and artists of the day. When Harriet Shelley decided—two years after Percy left—that her husband was not coming back, she committed suicide, a dismal yet convenient act that allowed Percy and Mary to get married in 1816.

That same year, Percy and Mary took an extended summer vacation in Switzerland to spend time with Shelley's fellow Romanticist, George Gordon Byron (better known as Lord Byron). The unusual grimness of the summer weather, coupled with discussions of the evolutionary inklings of Erasmus Darwin (Charles Darwin's grandfather) and the nonstop Romantic need to express themselves, led Lord Byron to suggest a particular literary diversion for the group. Byron proposed that each of them—he, Percy, Mary, and a friend named Dr. Polidori—should undertake to write their own ghost stories. As the Romantic poets were not exactly known for embracing horror or suspense in their writing, the assembled group saw this as a challenge, and they rose to it enthusiastically. Besides, they didn't have much else to do until the weather lightened up.

Contrary to popular belief, the four did not retire that night to their bedrooms and show up for breakfast the next morning with completed novels. Each of them agonized for days over the development of their stories, but in the end only Mary's story proved of any interest to the group. It was entitled *Frankenstein, The Modern Prometheus.* Much of its inspiration was drawn from the ongoing discussion about Erasmus Darwin and his thoughts on creating life in inanimate entities.

Two years later, in 1818, *Frankenstein* was published. The book told of the experiments and eventual downfall of one Dr. Victor Frankenstein, a man who had no business messing around with a technology that he could not control. A pieced-together monster had been created by Dr. Frankenstein as a demonstration of his own human intellectual prowess—a sort of slap in God's face, so to speak. Unlike the monster in the version of *Frankenstein* popularized in the 1931 Universal Studios film, the novel's monster was a fine physical specimen with flowing black hair and beautiful features (he did have rather hideous eyes and lips, though) who was ultimately able to communicate intelligently with his creator. (Incidentally, the novel's monster never had a name; the book's title refers to the doctor who made him.) Yet like his Boris Karloff incarnation, the monster in the book was misunderstood by all those he encountered and was driven to violence by the abuse and victimization that he experienced. The monster ruined Dr. Frankenstein's life by killing the doctor's young brother and wife, and Frankenstein took it upon himself to destroy his living creation. The end came not at the hands of angry Bavarian villagers carrying torches, but on a ship in the Arctic where the monster killed both his creator and himself. In all, Frankenstein was a scary book that also had a strong sense of morality, and it became popular very quickly.

Without delving into the juvenile socio-psychological analysis that so frequently accompanies most discussions of Frankenstein and his monster, suffice it to say that something about the book tapped into the collective consciousness of the Industrial Revolution. Its publication followed the 1816 demise of the Luddite movement by only two years. The Luddites were a band of aggressive toughs who fought viciously against the industrialization of business—not unlike today's Teamsters. Their leader was the legendary Ned Ludd, who may or may not have been a real person. Accounts vary as to his actual existence because nothing is known of his life or how he died— not unlike Jimmy Hoffa. The Luddites took it upon themselves to destroy factories throughout Britain that used modern machinery—such as looms— which they perceived as being threats to their jobs. Never mind that the machinery was usually employed to do difficult and dangerous work that had kept the lifespan of the average worker to under forty years. The Luddites didn't like machines doing men's work, and they couldn't have cared less about the supposed benefits. These men were the first true technophobes, and they gave physical expression to a certain type of fear that is prevalent to this day. There are even modern day Luddites who are fighting hard against the commercialization of artificial intelligence, but today these men and women are not wage slaves and blue collar workers. They are part of the white collar work force: doctors and lawyers. Their Luddite reasoning and technophobia will be explored later on.

So we have more than Mary Shelley just telling a wonderfully good tale about man creating life and intelligence where there was none before, just like God and the dirt that he turned into Adam. The fact that the monster was actually a better being than its creator—it was more reasonable and less driven by its own selfishness—didn't help matters any. Man replacing himself with his own creation just didn't sit well with the man on the street in the mid-nineteenth century. Perhaps for that reason, the book has always managed to be relevant. It mines a vein of fear that man has always had about himself and his origins—an act of God? a fluke of evolution? Most thought that it was better to let sleeping dogs lie and not pursue the matter of man's power too strenuously. Leave the God-playing to God, and keep technology in its place, wherever that might be. Toying about with insects or lab animals, one presumes.

The strength of the Frankenstein legend is verifiable simply by noting its ongoing popularity. The most recent film version of the novel starred Robert De Niro, who is among the most popular actors of this generation, as the tragic monster. An enormous number of movies and novelistic rip-offs have capitalized on Mary Shelley's ideas, and the reason is simple. People relate to them at a visceral level. It hits them where they live, especially as technology takes more control over their daily lives.

The message of *Frankenstein*, as well as stories about the golem and other automatons, was that mankind should leave the creation of life to God and keep to his own affairs. But the message was too late to prevent the march of technology towards thinking machines, because the first digital computer was already in the planning stages. There was no turning back.

∼

Charles Babbage was a man who, by all accounts, could be accurately described as both a genius and a boor. Spoiled rotten by wealthy parents, Babbage was given everything he demanded in his childhood. To make matters worse, he also happened to be brilliant. The image of a spoiled Poindexter holding his breath until he got the proper scientific equipment for his playtime is not out of place here.

Babbage was born in 1792, and early on showed an uncanny ability for dealing with mathematics. He quickly bested his professors at Cambridge University in his understanding of math and took it upon himself to look for more stimulating avenues of study. Using his parents' vast reserve of funds, he traveled the world to meet and spend time with those he considered his intellectual equal. This included notables of the time such as Charles Dickens; Alfred, Lord Tennyson; and Charles Darwin. Freed from having to actually work for a living, Babbage became a toast—and host—of the intellectual elite, all the while trying to find something that would keep his attention. He ultimately found it in the world of mechanical calculators.

Calculators had been around in one shape or another, most notably in the form of the abacus. Blaise Pascal, though, had created a little mechanical device that could perform addition and subtraction in the mid-1600s, while Gottfried Leibnitz had improved on the same device to include a multiplication capability a few years later. But young master Babbage had plans that were bigger than the rudimentary applications of plus, minus, times, and divide. He believed that whole sets of mathematical procedures, specifically logarithmic tables, could be handled by a machine.

The thing that Babbage hit upon was to use the mathematical concepts of one of his contemporary thinkers, George Boole. Boole had developed a form of algebra—called Boolean algebra—which could use the binary system of 1s and 0s as a means to represent rules of logic. A "1" would equal "yes" while a "0" would equal "no." Charles Babbage saw that this form of math could be utilized in a machine that would flip switches to indicate 1 or 0, yes or no. This scheme, as devised by Babbage, would serve as the basis for creating the first computing machines, and is still the principle on which all computers are built today.

Given the fact that the wide scale use of electricity was still about a century away, Babbage had to construct his calculating machine out of a complex system of gears, wheels, cylinders, rods, and switches, each of which was extremely intricate in and of itself. To imagine its scope, the construction of the machine was similar to trying to construct Big Ben out of watch innards. In order to subsidize his work—his parents' largesse only went so far—Babbage managed to obtain money from the British government as part of a contract to build his first calculating machine for the British Post Office in 1823. Calling his device the "Difference Engine," Babbage undertook to make the machine a reality. Unfortunately for both Babbage and the British Post Office, he was way ahead of his time in what could be realistically manufactured given the tools of the day. The state-of-the-art skills of even the country's best craftsman could not produce mechanisms to meet the tolerances that the Difference Engine required. It simply wasn't feasible.

Additionally, a lack of manners that would have been termed "petulance" in his youth proved to make Babbage a complete curmudgeon in his maturity—or lack thereof. He alienated many of the people that he had hired to help him build the computer and his turnover rate was dismal, making today's fast-food chains look like career opportunities in comparison. When it looked like the Difference Engine might collapse under its own complex weight, Babbage began looking to develop another machine, which he called the Analytical Engine. This machine would use more conventional components and have the added feature of being able to perform any logical computation. Yet, there was no mad rush to join him in this venture—his personal reputation being of less than stellar quality. One woman stood by him in all his work, though, because she believed that Charles Babbage could make a sophisticated calculating machine a reality. Her perseverance brought her lifelong fame, and also brings another nineteenth-century teenage girl into the AI family portrait.

The young lady in question was Ada Lovelace. She was the only legitimate daughter of the aforementioned George Gordon, Lord Byron—the same man who put Mary Shelley up to writing *Frankenstein*. Lord Byron, who was actually the first person in literary circles to be described as "mad, bad, and dangerous to know," certainly had no compunctions about the propriety of his sex life. In fact, if one takes into account the number of children sired by Percy Bysshe Shelley and Lord Byron in their various nefarious and incestuous affairs, it's not inconceivable to suppose that Ada and Mary Wollstonecraft Shelley were related in some way. It made for a small world.

Ada was taken with the notion that Babbage's machine could be used for more than math. She imagined that, if properly directed, the Analytical Engine could be "taught" to mimic certain human behaviors such as playing chess. Working closely with Babbage and the few associates who could tolerate him, Ada began to develop ways to "program" the device, using a methodology based on the punch-type cards that had already become prevalent in programming Jacquard looms. This same type of punch card would survive well into the 1980s in the form of the ubiquitous IBM card.

For her work with Babbage, and her dedication to making his machines do something, Ada earned the title of being "the first programmer." For nearly a century she could also have been called the world's "only female programmer," due to the complete male control of the computer business through most of the twentieth century. Her greatest posthumous honor came when the Department of Defense undertook to have all of its software written in a common programming language. The language that resulted was named Ada. Hmmmm. The same government agency that undertook to create artificial intelligence in the manner of Mary Shelley names its primary programming language after Ada Lovelace. Interesting that two British women from the same social circle in the same period in history get immortalized through the efforts of the biggest military agency in the history of the world. Seems a little strange in retrospect.

Ada died from cancer at the age of thirty-six. Her death left Babbage with no one who shared the same commitment to the Analytical Engine that he had. The crankiness factor of Babbage's character as he got older served to doom his projects as much as the limitations of the technology: the Difference Engine was never finished, and the Analytical Engine was never built. The last reports of Babbage's activities had him ripping apart delicate machinery with his bare hands to try and improve on some craftsman's long hours of hard work. He regularly feuded with his neighbors, and children who lived on his street often taunted him. It was as if he became the living embodiment of Scrooge, the character created by his friend Charles Dickens.

Babbage did not complete either machine, although he spent every last bit of his family's fortune trying to build working models of each. For all his cantankerousness, he did manage to develop concepts that would result in the creation of the first digital computer, and that legacy has certainly outweighed the lack of humanity that he demonstrated in his lifetime.

❧

Thus ends the history of man's tinkering with thinking machines before modern times. After the death of Ada Lovelace and Charles Babbage, work commenced almost exclusively on developing workable calculating machines with little thought to their ability to behave like humans. It became a much more mechanically oriented pursuit, possibly as a reflection of the interest in machinery as a tool with limited functionality. It may also have lost some of its motivation and inspiration with the passing of the Romantics.

Mass production gradually became an accepted part of society, and people really couldn't complain when they saw that cars, clothes, toys and other goods were more readily available than ever before. The idea that these machines inside big factories were serving the public good replaced the initial horror of machines becoming masters of society. It was left to various forms of fiction and film to keep alive the idea of artificial intelligence until World War II. At that time a brilliant and socially inept young mathematician named Alan Turing, who had been instrumental in Germany's defeat by the Allies, wrote a paper claiming that machines could ultimately think like humans.

4

Nazi Codes, Computers, and a Poisoned Apple

The man who defined the beginning of the modern age of artificial intelligence was Alan Turing. Far from being a quiet little man toiling away unknown in the confines of a research lab, Turing was an incredibly complex individual both as a person and as a scientist. He has been credited with helping the Allies defeat the Nazis during the height of World War II. His work on thinking computers inspired the date 2001 for the movie of the same name. He was chemically castrated by the British government for sexual deviance. He killed himself by eating a poisoned apple at the age of forty-one. This was not your normal computer scientist.

In the decade prior to Turing's birth in 1912 and continuing through the early 1900s, computing dedicated itself to building bigger and better calculators. National Cash Register (later just NCR), Computing-Tabulating-Recording Company (later to become IBM), and Remington Rand (later Sperry Rand, then Sperry, and then Unisys) were all busy with all kinds of machines that built on the ideas put forth by Pascal and Leibnitz. Babbage's work, while revolutionary, was still considered suspect by those who felt it just couldn't be manufactured. That would have to wait until the power of electricity could be brought to bear on such complex equipment.

These machines were most often used for accounting functions in accounting departments, instilling a certain amount of fear in accountants about the future of their jobs. (Amazing how machines do that to people every time the machines invade a particular work force.) Yet one of the most complicated—and some might say insidious—uses for the mechanical calculating machines was developed by the military.

Cryptography—the scientific word for creating secret codes—has always been a part of warfare. Messages that must be passed from one location to another during wartime are always in danger of being intercepted by enemy troops, with possibly disastrous results. Say command post A needs to send a message about its next attack to command post B. Should this message fall into enemy hands, the secrecy of the planned attack would be negated, and the attack could be completely undermined by the enemy. Long ago, warring parties determined that they needed to transfer and transmit these messages in a language or code that would be understood only by those who knew the code. For centuries this involved simple alphabet substitution like those used on secret decoder rings found in cereal boxes. The letter Z might actually be represented by the letter A, the letter Y by the letter B, X by C, and so on.

As cryptography became a branch of science unto itself, the military trained cryptanalysts—decoders—to meet the challenge. They devised elaborate schemes to prevent the enemy from deciphering messages. One of the most popular in this century came to be the note pad, which also served as the basis for numerous spy novels and movies. A pad would be issued to the appropriate personnel with tear-off sheets that would have a different code for each day. With a pad, the sender and receiver of a message had to make sure that they were using the same page on the same day to utilize encoded messages. This was all well and good until a pad was captured or stolen by the enemy, eliminating any future use of that pad. New pads would have to be made up and then issued to qualified personnel all over again.

A German machine called the Enigma was manufactured for coding use in 1923 and became readily available for use after World War I. It was used primarily by financial institutions for sending proprietary data to and from various branches and affiliates. The Enigma device involved the use of three cylinders that were rotated to new positions and also placed in a different one of three spaces each day. For instance, cylinder one might be in place one on Monday, but in place three on Tuesday. On Monday, this same cylinder might have had its letter A set to letter Z, and on Tuesday its letter A might have been set to G. Though this sounds complicated, it really amounts to nothing more than putting the cylinders in a new spot each day.

The operation of Enigma involved entering a number or letter into the first cylinder as an electrical current. Depending on the settings of the remaining cylinders, the letter would be given a new designation as the current passed through each of them, resulting in a completely new letter designation. The letter Z could become the letter H due to the setting of the cylinders, yet this would make no apparent sense or have any logic to any person who attempted to figure out why the letter Z came back as H. The only way to decode a message that had been created using Enigma was to have another matching Enigma machine with the cylinders at the exact same setting. No amount of human guesswork could conceivably break an Enigma-generated code.

As the Nazis geared up for World War II in the 1930s, they added an electronic plugboard to the front-end of the Enigma rotor system to make it more complex than the commercially available system. The plugboard (which resembled a small, old-time telephone switchboard) had the effect of adding an extra level of encoding to the entire machine. Thus, even if a German enemy had miraculously stumbled on the ability to match its own Enigma rotors and settings to a Nazi machine, it still would not be able to break the German Enigma code with the additional encryption created by the plugboard. Needless to say, this somewhat hampered the British efforts to decode Enigma-generated messages sent by the Nazis. By the time Britain and Germany were locked in full-scale war, the German cryptographers were so far ahead of their enemies that it appeared as if their Enigma system could not be cracked.

With unfailing determination, though, Britain decided that it had to try to break the German codes in order to stem the tide of a war that was increasingly going in Germany's favor. In the summer of 1939, the British government began Project Ultra. A group of leading scientists and mathematicians were gathered together in a small village north of London called Bletchley Park to work on breaking Enigma. Into this military enclave was thrown Alan Mathison Turing.

He was born on June 23, 1912 in Paddington, England. Turing's father was a career British diplomat, taking his wife to live in the far-off regions of the British Empire while Alan and his brother were left to attend various boarding schools in England. Alan was a precocious boy who had a consuming interest in science and nature, but otherwise he was an unremarkable child. So unremarkable, in fact, that after a few years in primary school, many of his teachers felt that he wasn't cut out for higher education or the upper ranks of English academia. Alan's grades were mediocre, and he tended to disregard his personal appearance, especially his clothes. He also lacked an interest in organized sports and military-style drills, which were both mainstays of the British educational system of the 1920s. In all, Alan Turing simply did not fit in with those class-defined British pursuits that were—and still are—considered essential to personal discipline and proper upbringing.

He had few friends throughout his school years, further advancing the opinion of those around him that he just didn't fit in. Turing finally found refuge in astronomy and mathematics, for which he showed a keen aptitude. It had taken him awhile, but Turing had found his calling in the complexities of mathematics. He passed the exam to get into King's College, Cambridge, and eventually succeeded in getting a fellowship there. It was evident early on in his college career that Turing didn't know how to play the politics that went along with being a scholar, nor did he care about the way that the "system" worked, with its oftentimes unspoken rules of conduct, compromise, and deference to those in power. Such ignorance, or neglect, of day-to-day social behavior would follow Turing out into the real world and cause him no small number of problems.

He was considered a bit of an oddball while at King's College, but managed to gain the grudging respect of students and teachers alike with his unusual explorations into areas of mathematical theory. In 1936, while still only twenty-three, Turing published a paper called "Computable Numbers" (actually, the full title was the barely comprehensible "On Computable Numbers with an Application to the Entscheidungs Problem") that dealt with some highly disputed mathematical problems of the time.

The actual problems are not relevant to this story, but they had kept the math community tied up in knots as to whether certain things were provable or could be proved to be unprovable. Ultimately, Turing came up with an unsolvable problem, which had to do with trying to solve equations that involved infinite amounts of numbers. He said that any math problem involving infinity would never be solved because it was infinite. Looking back on this now, it might be taken for granted that this was the case, but it was not so clear in 1936 as it is today because most mathematicians—with the exception of a small fringe—assumed that the ability to solve problems involving infinity was possible. At any rate, Turing was lionized and became a math guru at the age of twenty-three for the insights put forth in Computable Numbers. The respect given to this paper served to make him a little bit more acceptable in polite society, and, as a result, he also learned some of the graces that he had disdained throughout his life.

Part of his work in Computable Numbers included descriptions of how conceptually difficult math problems could be solved mechanically, using a kind of super-typewriter calculator. Turing also proposed that this single machine could be designed to do the work of all the different machines currently in use. This "universal machine" would be almost as complex as a human in the number of tasks that it could perform. And finally, he argued, any logical process that could be done by a human could theoretically be done by such a machine. Therefore, it was not unthinkable that a device—a symbolic machine—that could think and behave like humans could be constructed.

From this seemingly secondary component of Computable Numbers came Turing's greatest triumph, the idea that a machine could perform the same logical activities—thinking—that human minds could. The Universal Machine, which came to be known as the Turing Machine, gave science a basis for pursuing mechanical thought.

The outbreak of World War II prevented Turing from doing more immediate investigation into the universal machine. His mathematical notoriety made him a perfect candidate for the cryptanalyst hideaway in Bletchley Park in 1939. The fact that Bletchley had as one of its most important directives the breaking of the Enigma-based code must have appealed to Turing. Here was a machine that did not think, but whose output was impenetrable to human scrutiny. He undertook the dissection of the machine and its code-making mind with unmitigated zeal.

Turing came up with a scheme for decoding Enigma via a machine that would recognize certain encoded letters by their frequency, probability, and other factors. He applied his ideas to an existing decoding instrument known as a Bombe, so named for the ticking noise that it made as it clicked through letter possibilities. But Turing's Bombe was different in that he programmed it to embody his own methodologies for mathematically breaking Enigma codes. In late 1940, with the critical assistance of others at Bletchley Park, Turing's decoding device succeeded in decrypting messages about the movement of the German Navy, especially its U-boat submarines. Even as the

British Navy began to intercept these boats on a regular basis with coordinates obtained from transmitted Enigma messages, the Germans could not believe that it was actually Enigma messages that were being decoded. They decided that since there was no possibility of Enigma being broken, the coordinates had to have been discovered by well-placed spies for the English. Thus the Germans, secure in their belief of Enigma's impermeability, continued to use the device while Turing's group continued to break its codes.

Even as his group was doing what had previously been thought impossible—and receiving secret praise from Winston Churchill—Turing and the British Government began to work with research teams in the United States to further develop new encryption and decryption technologies. Turing was sent across the Atlantic—made somewhat safer since Enigma had been broken—to spend time at RCA and Bell Laboratories, the leading electronic technology U.S. think tanks of the 1940s. While his visits were ostensibly intended to share and gain new knowledge about cryptographic techniques, Turing found some kindred spirits in the U.S. science community in 1943 who wanted to do more with computing machines than just send and decode secret messages.

The most important person Turing met during this time was Claude Shannon. Shannon had been at MIT prior to working for Bell Labs and had worked extensively on the possibility of making electronic versions of calculating machines based on Boolean algebra. It was critical to Shannon that these machines would also have some sort of memory. Through his work, Shannon was laying the groundwork for the first electronic computers. He and Turing had many philosophical discussions about what such a machine could do—the term computers was not yet applied to these mechanical beasts—and they both believed that such a device could imitate the human brain. The time spent with Shannon allowed Turing to give free rein to ideas that he had proposed in Computable Numbers, and he was encouraged enough to pursue them on his own.

As the operations at Bletchley Park took on a life of their own, Turing gradually removed himself from day-to-day tasks. He neither liked nor agreed with the increasingly political nature of the operation, for it was now an integral part of the armed services and various British intelligence services. The war was also beginning to favor the Allies, and the mood at Bletchley was one of accepting that an Allied victory was a done deal. So in 1944, Turing began talking openly about the possible creation of a thinking machine. He and his ideas were taken more seriously after the war ended, when it became understood, though not explicitly, that his group of code breakers had turned the tide of the war. Turing was increasingly sought out by other respected mathematicians when he returned to King's College in 1947 to resume the teaching duties he had forsaken for God and country when he left for Bletchley.

There was a considerable downside to his newfound notoriety. Throughout his early years at college, Turing had come to terms with the fact that he was homosexual, something that didn't need to be hidden within the sheltered walls of Cambridge. Indeed, as described by his biographer Andrew Hodges, Turing's sexuality was not out of the norm at King's College, where he was just an "ordinary English homosexual atheist mathematician." Homosexuality was considered to be such a primary diversion of the British elite during wartime, especially amongst its intellectuals, spies, and politicians, that the Germans actually derided the British for trying to win the war using the brainpower of homosexuals. Turing's own inability to see that the outside world didn't share the casual college and Bletchley attitude towards sexuality would prove to be his ultimate downfall. He was occasionally seen in less than proper bars and sometimes with less than proper companions, which sent tongues wagging about the extracurricular doings of the young professor.

Nonetheless, Turing became active in conferences and seminars that explored the potential of the computing power that had been developed during the war. In 1951, Turing wrote a paper called "Computing Machinery and Intelligence," which was published by *Mind*, a philosophical journal. His intention was to show that if a computer's actions could not be differentiated from those of a human, then the computer could be said to be thinking.

He did this by proposing a test—or more accurately, a game—to define intelligence. The game involved three people: a man, a woman, and an interrogator, who could be of either sex. The man and the woman were hidden from the interrogator's sight, and the goal was for the interrogator to determine which of the two hidden people was actually the woman. The interrogator would ask the two people a variety of questions to determine which was the woman, yet it was the hidden man's duty to try to trick the interrogator into believing he was the woman. The replies were written so that voices would not give away the identity of the two. The interrogator continued asking questions until he believed that he had determined the specific identity of the man and the woman. Whether the identities were actually deduced, said Turing, was of no consequence. Gender could not be determined simply through the use of written words that might or might not be truthful.

On the other hand, he asked, what if a machine were used to act out the part of the man or woman? If it could mimic the answers of one of the hidden participants well enough for the interrogator to be unable to determine whether it was human or machine, wasn't this an adequate test of its ability to think? Since the machine is hidden during the "Imitation Game," as Turing called it, then it would be judged purely on the merits of its thought processes and not on its appearance or "its inability to shine in beauty competitions." Similarly, the machine would be judged on the strength of its ability to mimic human characteristics because a human would be too slow to compete against a machine, especially if the two were asked to perform mathematical calculations.

It is important to understand just how Turing perceived the brain. To him, the organ's chemical and biological makeup had nothing to do with the process of thinking. Turing stipulated that the physical structure just served to support the "mechanism" for thinking, and served as the container that gave this "mind" a place to reside and live. This view, then, stated that the brain—being a repository for processes called thought—could be duplicated by a machine, since the organic components were of no practical import. And since Turing believed that the brain's behavior was actually based on a logical foundation that could be broken down into rules, there was no reason to believe that these same rules—and thus the essence of the brain—couldn't reside somewhere else. In Turing's mind, that somewhere else would be inside a machine.

To quote from Turing's paper:

> *I believe that in about fifty years' time it will be possible to programme computers to make them play the imitation game so well that an average interrogator will not have more than a 70 percent chance of making the right identification after five minutes of questioning. I believe that at the end of the century the use of words and general educated opinion will have altered so much that one will be able to speak of machines thinking without expecting to be contradicted.*

Given that this paper was written at the end of 1950, a belief in machine intelligence fifty years hence would have put Turing's date around the end of the year 2000, or right on the eve of 2001. Could this date be leading somewhere? Most assuredly, but not until another chapter of this book.

In his paper, Turing also addressed many of the arguments that were posited against the question "Can machines think?"—including theological, moral, mathematical, and even biological arguments. Considering that this was contained in a twenty-page article written in late 1950, his arguments still hold up quite well, and manage to have presumed the whole spectrum of objection to artificial intelligence that would be revived in the 1980s and 1990s. His game, in particular, eventually came to be the cornerstone of testing a machine for intelligence. The imitation game took on the name Turing Test, and its man and woman were permanently replaced by a computer terminal and a human. If the interrogator was unable to tell which of the two hidden subjects was man and which was machine, then the machine would have passed the Turing Test and thus be considered intelligent. Turing had no problem defending this: How can we prove intelligence in other people unless it resembles our own? And if the machine's intelligence resembles our own, doesn't that make it as obviously intelligent as another person?

Turing's philosophical and academic approach to computing moved him out of the government and corporate mainstream that he had been part of during the war, especially when he was working with American partners like Bell Labs. As such, the computer "revolution" started passing him by. Amazingly, it appeared as if he really didn't mind. Turing had already started turning his attention to biology, specifically embryology. He was fascinated with the fact that cells "knew" how to grow and link themselves into organisms greater than their individual selves. He began to apply mathematical principles to the process of cell division and the chemical reactions that accompanied this division. While Turing was bringing new and revolutionary insights into areas of biology that had not been previously explored, his personal life took one wrong turn too many.

On January 23, 1952, Turing reported to the police that his house had been robbed. Several days later, he went back to the police and changed the initial story that he had given them. It was readily apparent that Turing was lying on his second trip to the station, and the police decided to investigate further. When they came to his house to question him, he admitted—in a moment of rather elaborate candor—that the burglary had involved a young man named Arnold Murray that he was "seeing" at the time. He and Murray had since made up, prompting Turing's second trip, which was intended to divert suspicion from him. But once again, Turing's obvious lack of understanding as to the ways of the world put him into trouble. The crime was no longer one of burglary, or lying to the police. It was quite suddenly a crime of "gross indecency" in that Turing had engaged in homosexual relations with young Mr. Murray. Typical of Turing, he was bewildered that such a charge would be brought against him because he considered the relationship an honorable one. Of course, the British legal system didn't see it that way.

Turing was charged and convicted of the crime of gross indecency in March 1952. He pled guilty to the charges, although he firmly believed that he was guilty of nothing. He was given a choice of punishments: to spend time in jail or to undergo "chemical castration." This latter punishment involved an injection of female hormones that would serve to eradicate the sex drive from the male offender. Turing considered this organo-therapy preferable to being locked up, and he consented to take estrogen for a year. Presumably, its effects would wear off once the treatment was stopped.

Turing continued working—most of his associates already knew of his homosexuality—and appeared to put his conviction behind him. He was self-deprecating when discussing his legal problems. For a while, Turing saw a psychiatrist in an attempt to understand himself better, but there was no underlying sense of shame or dread. After his year of treatments was over, Turing even went on vacations hoping to find male companionship. He devoted more time to understanding the organic sciences, leaving the field of computers to a new generation. Life seemed to be quite normal for Alan Turing.

It was this normalcy that made his suicide on June 7, 1954 such a shock. His cleaning woman found him dead in his bed, a half-eaten apple on his night stand. A jar of potassium cyanide was found in the house, and cyanide was determined to be the cause of death. It was apparent to all concerned that Turing had dipped the apple in the cyanide and then eaten it. Unlike his complex life of mathematical equations and military codes and government politics and dissertations on thinking machines, Turing's death was taken directly from the romance of children's fables and the simplicity of their imagery. The poisoned apple was as pure and innocent as everything else was not.

Turing's mother never believed that he had committed suicide, claiming that it must have been accidental. He left no note, so his motivations were not clear to anyone, including his closest friends. What he did leave were well-thought out, brilliant ideas that gave shape and substance to centuries of speculation about the possibility of endowing machines with intelligence. In Turing's view, and in the view of those he inspired, thinking machines were not only a technological possibility, they were an eventuality.

Only two years after his death, a proper name was given to the ideas that Turing had so passionately developed. The name was "artificial intelligence."

Chapter

5

The Dartmouth Conference of 1956 and the Influence of MIT

Almost Heaven

The Massachusetts Institute of Technology is located in Cambridge, Massachusetts, a couple of stone's throws down the Charles River from Harvard University. The two schools are so close, in fact, that they share bookstores and merchandise outlets. Yet, since its founding in 1861, MIT has been the preeminent engineering and computing institution in the United States, a fact which oftentimes puts it worlds away from many of the economically driven business types that enroll down the road. MIT attracts only the best of the brightest in applied sciences and mathematics, and its students—who are increasingly not from the United

States—are perhaps the most sought-after graduates for high-paying technical positions in companies around the world.

From the outside, MIT is a think tank that is developing many of the most important technological breakthroughs of this age, ranging from high definition television to virtual reality. From the inside, however, it resembles a backwoods West Virginia town, complete with incestuous relationships and an exaggerated fear of outsiders.

The incest is not of the sexual sort, but of the professional sort. MIT students, graduates, and professors interact with each other throughout their lifetimes in a way that few other universities and their alumni could even imagine. It is no surprise that many of the first AI companies established their headquarters on the streets that physically bounded the MIT campus. While this provided a geographic link to the university and its constant stream of innovations, it also gave rise to the notion, said only half in jest, that MIT graduates would die if they worked too far away from the campus. Fish out of water, and all that.

Yet the current state of AI in the world owes its orgins to these lads who dwell in the shadow of their brethen down the road. And it is all those Harvard lawyers, doctors, and MBA grads that MIT will one day hope to replace with thinking machines.

❧

The first person to truly represent this MIT-or-die mentality is also the person that picks up the thread of AI history from about the time that Alan Turing was moving towards more biological pursuits: Norbert Weiner, professor of engineering at MIT from 1919 to 1960—more than 40 years. A child prodigy who had received his Ph.D. from Harvard at the age of 18, Weiner championed the belief that the transfer of information was the most important way to model scientific phenomena. This ran smack into the face of the conventional wisdom of the 1940s, which said that energy was the driving force in the universe—a belief that went back to Isaac Newton. According to Weiner, in his 1948 book, *Cybernetics*, the most important thing that happens in living cells is not the transfer of heat and energy to create chemical reactions and larger life forms, but the use of information that allows the cells to instigate and manage these processes. It is information that makes reproduction possible, in the form of passing on genetic code. Such information management is true not only in cells, but in large organisms, in molecular activity, and in the machines that man was just then creating; namely, computers.

Weiner's pride in his prodigy status did little to endear him to those who had to spend any quality time with him. He was similar in lack of personality and charm to his forebears Babbage and Turing—a trait that we will see appears to be almost genetic in the makeup of people involved in AI research. In Norbert's case, this character defect was oftentimes blamed on the fact that his father, a Harvard linguist, kept telling the boy that he was no different—linguistically speaking—than a machine.

While Weiner is idolized within the computer research community, especially among those affiliated with MIT, his fame stops right there. This is unusual in that Norbert successfully predicted the replacement of analog devices with digital devices, a fact of life that today accounts for digital watches, personal computers, portable telephones, and CD players. Yet, he is best remembered for defining cybernetics, the science of control through information. The term cybernetics was even briefly considered as the catch-all term for what was eventually called artificial intelligence, but it was too broad in its theory to apply only to thinking machines.

Although his is not a household name, the concepts that Norbert Weiner developed are accepted as a matter of course today. This is due in no small measure to the amount of groundbreaking work that his students and fellow academicians performed at MIT in the 1950s and 1960s, work that carried his influence well beyond the hallowed halls of that institution. Weiner is the MIT icon from whom most of the other humans in this tale descend.

Claude Shannon, who had encouraged Alan Turing to pursue his work on intelligent machines, was a graduate student at MIT in 1937 during Weiner's tenure there. At the time, he worked on a mechanical computer-like device that was used to help determine trajectories for artillery shells during World War II. In 1941, Shannon went to Bell Labs, where he oversaw work on a number of projects, including communication systems. Despite meeting Turing during this time, it is conceivable that he may not have known the actual reason why Turing was visiting Bell Labs, since Shannon had little to do with the cryptography group.

His interest in thinking machines resulted in a February 1950 *Scientific American* article that addressed the problem of a machine playing chess. Shannon felt that a machine could not and should not try to calculate all of the possible moves it confronted on a chess board because there are on the order of 10^{120} potential moves to be considered. Calculation of every move limited the computer and its potential by defining it as a massive calculator and nothing more. Instead, Shannon argued, the machine should be programmed to work not only with numbers but also with symbols and concepts, enabling it to take advantage of the same analytical processes that humans use.

By using the game of chess as a yardstick to help measure intelligence, Shannon planted a seed in the heads of all future MIT researchers interested in thinking machines. Chess became something of a raison d'etre for many of those researchers, something that they pursued as if it were the proverbial light at the end of the tunnel. If those same researchers had spent a little more time watching Roadrunner and Coyote cartoons, they would have realized that the light was actually a train coming from the opposite direction. But they wouldn't learn that until 1967, when they were challenged on the chess problem by one of their own MIT brethren.

There is ample reason to use chess as an indicator of intelligence. Clearly, it requires a great deal of strategy in the form of conceptual thinking. Sheer number-crunching, trying to process all of the possible moves and their related outcomes, is not possible unless the game is to last for decades. Plus, an individual's technique in playing chess can be measured as part of the infamous rating system that determines everything from grand master status to lowly incompetent. Chess is rigidly organized in this aspect, yet it provides players with the flexibility to test their own logic strategies in pursuit of a win.

The idea of a machine playing chess did not originate with the MIT researchers, although they have made it an art form. As far back as 1835, Edgar Allan Poe wrote an essay called "Maelzel's Chess Player," which exposed the fraudulent creation of one Baron Wolfgang von Kempelen. (The essay is also a good introduction to automatons of that time, including Vaucanson's mechanical duck.) A machine called the Automaton Chess Player—a mechanical man who played chess against unwitting challengers—was created in 1769 by Kempelen, a Hungarian nobleman who had also created a famous mechanical model of the human vocal cords. This automaton, dressed flamboyantly as a Turk, was attached to a large box that concealed his machinery. Atop the box was a chess board. The arm of the automaton would move—in robotic fashion—to pick up chess pieces and move them according to the rules of chess. Invariably, the Automaton Chess Player beat its opponents.

The machine was exhibited throughout Europe by one Mister Maelzel, a kind of carnival barker who traveled about solely to show off Kempelen's device. Challengers were allowed to examine the interior of the automaton's box, which proved to contain gears and pistons and all sorts of confusing machinery. However, the box was opened only briefly, and its contents shown while it was being wheeled about a stage, thereby keeping the audience from getting a complete look at it for any length of time, or from any continuous angle. To enhance the mechanical appearance and disposition of the artificial Turk, when it would occasionally miss a piece that it was intending to pick up (if the piece were slightly off-center, for instance), it would still continue moving as if the piece were actually in its grip. A neat trick, but it didn't fool Poe.

Poe's article exposed Maelzel and Kempelen as frauds when he wrote that the box actually contained a man who was an incredibly good chess player. The machinery that appeared to hide him was an elaborate magic trick, an illusion along the lines of the stage boxes used today that allow a woman to be sawed in half. Poe managed to thoroughly shatter the notion of the chess machine's having any mechanical intelligence by explaining point by point how the machine operated. Maelzel died the year of the essay's publication, which probably appealed to Poe's sense of the macabre, and the chess player was retired to the home of a private collector.

But Claude Shannon managed to tap into the same kind of fascination with mechanical chess playing that had been prevalent in Maelzel's day more than 100 years before. At MIT, plenty of students were willing to explore the possibilities outlined in Shannon's *Scientific American* paper, even though he had already left for Bell Labs. His departure, however, didn't end his relationship with the university, and it was only a matter of time before he fostered more work on thinking machines at MIT.

During the summer of 1953, Shannon employed two Princeton University graduates, John McCarthy and Marvin Minsky, to work with him at Bell Labs. These two men would soon become the physical manifestations of MIT, even though neither one had any connection with the university at the time. Both McCarthy and Minsky were in the process of getting their Ph.D.s from Princeton, although McCarthy had done his undergraduate work at CalTech and Minsky had done his at Harvard. The two had a strong interest in thinking machines, which was fostered by Shannon during their summer together. Minsky, in particular, had already explored the possibility of creating an electronic representation of a brain cell—an artificial neuron—during his Harvard days.

Upon receiving their doctorates, Minsky returned to Harvard as a junior fellow and McCarthy opted for the more idyllic Dartmouth College campus, located about two hours north of Cambridge in Hanover, New Hampshire. Minsky was spending his time in the realms of mathematics and neurology, while McCarthy became an assistant professor of mathematics. The two men kept in frequent touch, with their interest in thinking machines providing a strong intellectual link. They felt that there was a great deal to be done in exploring the "mental" capabilities of computers, but lamented the fact that no one was doing anything about it.

In 1956, two years after the death of Alan Turing, McCarthy and Minsky approached their old summer job mentor, Claude Shannon, with the idea of bringing together a group of people who were interested in pursuing machine intelligence. The conference would focus solely on the potential of thinking machines and would include those most active in the field. Shannon liked the idea and agreed to participate when the two men were ready.

At the same time, McCarthy approached Nathaniel Rochester of IBM to solicit his participation. The previous summer, McCarthy had worked at IBM—another summer job that panned out better for McCarthy than any fast-food experience might have—and had come into contact with Rochester. As the designer of IBM's first mass-produced computer, Rochester had practical experience in making computers work in the real world, still a rare accomplishment at that point in time. However, Rochester was also interested in making these computers act similar to the human brain, and had developed a program that acted like the brain in the way that it handled various problems. His approach to this mechanized brain structure—called neural networks—was different than Minsky's construction of an artificial neuron, yet Rochester was willing to explore new possibilities that might be presented at a gathering such as the one McCarthy was suggesting. Rochester signed on as an organizer.

Not only did Shannon and Rochester agree to participate in McCarthy and Minsky's proposed gathering, they provided the name recognition that allowed the conference to actually take place. Armed with the "endorsements" of Claude Shannon and Nathaniel Rochester, McCarthy and Minsky went to the Rockefeller Foundation to solicit a grant for pursuing work on thinking machines through their conference. The Rockefellers, through various foundations and investment companies, were constantly on the lookout for new and possibly exploitable technologies. The Rockefeller Foundation found the conference idea worthwhile and gave McCarthy and Minsky $7500 to run a two-month long symposium. It was the first of many Rockefeller family investments in AI; unfortunately, most of the others would prove to be disastrous.

With their $7,500 in hand, McCarthy and Minsky went about setting up the conference. It was going to be held at Dartmouth, McCarthy's home turf, and already had a confirmed list of four, each of whom would receive organizer credit: McCarthy, Minsky, Shannon, and Rochester. In all practicality, this was barely enough participants to have a decent poker game, let alone a conference on the future of computing. The organizers had promised the Rockefellers that they would have at least ten people in attendance and went about finding their remaining six.

By the time the conference began in the summer of 1956, McCarthy and Minsky had their full number of conference attendees—barely. The additional members of the group were drawn from both industry and academia. Oliver Selfridge was working at Lincoln Labs, a military research facility overseen by MIT, in an effort to teach machines to recognize patterns such as the shapes of letters in the alphabet. Selfridge had another credential: he had been an assistant of Norbert Weiner's and had helped Weiner put together the first version of *Cybernetics*. Ray Solomonoff was a friend of Marvin Minsky's at MIT who believed that machine intelligence was possible through the use of symbols and not just brute-force calculation. Arthur Samuel was an IBM researcher who had worked with Shannon at Bell Labs. While Shannon had followed the chess playing route, Samuel had gone off to work on building an intelligent checker playing machine. He succeeded, but his success brought heaps of woe to IBM, as we shall see. Alex Bernstein, a co-worker of Samuel's, attended the conference because he, too, was exploring ways to make machines play intellectually challenging games like chess. Trenchard More, a graduate student at Princeton, came to the conference as sort of a philosophical observer. He was writing a thesis on mathematical logic and wanted to observe how this might be applied to computing machines.

This handful of participants was culled largely from people who were friends or working acquaintances of the four conference organizers. It was a fraternity, albeit a loose-knit one, of people from Princeton, MIT, Bell Labs, and IBM. Not surprisingly, the organizers liked this cliquish arrangement, but they were obliged to ask two "outsiders" to come to the party. In hindsight, this invitation seems to have been offered rather grudgingly, but to omit these two men, Herb Simon and Allen Newell, would have meant having an incomplete, misleading, and seriously imbalanced conference. For in the summer of 1956, Newell and Simon were the only ones to show up who had actually created a thinking program for a computer.

Herbert Simon, a professor at Carnegie-Mellon University in Pittsburgh, specialized in industrial administration—the study of people working in groups. His main area of interest lay in the motivation of organizations or bureaucracies to achieve goals. Simon, who would later win a 1978 Nobel Prize in economics for his work, viewed corporations as entities that were comprised of smaller organizations. Each organizational unit had its own sets of goals, but it was the responsibility of the corporation to direct these smaller-scale goals into a unified goal that would benefit the entire corporation. Simon was consulting for the RAND Corporation (RAND stood for Research AND Development) when he met Allen Newell in the early 1950s.

Newell was a trained mathematician who had found the theoretical life of academia too stultifying; this was quite the opposite of McCarthy and Minsky's opinions on career pursuits. Newell opted for a job with the RAND Corporation rather than pursue graduate work in math at Princeton, and he immediately went to work on various projects for the Defense Department. He developed modeling programs on RAND's company computer, programs that ranged from creating air defense centers to simulating personnel organizations and their structure. When Newell and Simon met, they found an immediate kinship in their fascination with organizations and the various behaviors exhibited by organizations. The fact that Newell was doing his work on a computer—a revolutionary idea at the time—lent additional excitement to their mutual interest.

Aware to some degree of the potential "logic" capabilities being discussed in the emerging computer industry, the pair wondered if the machine could solve problems of logic that occurred in humans at a level beyond the traditional "if this, then that" kind of logic. Specifically, they wondered if machines could be used to mimic human behavior in goal-driven situations, where a human has to decide what to do next in order to reach a goal. This involved more than simple logic functions such as "If A equals B and B equals C, then A equals C." It required an understanding of "heuristics," or the rules-of-thumb that people use to get through daily life and to succeed in attaining goals. For instance, a daily heuristic might be "It's below freezing outside; I'd better dress warmly." While not spoken out loud, this is a logic statement that most people make unconsciously in a cold winter situation. In a work environment, a heuristic might be more along the lines of "I'd better not take all of the credit for this project or my boss will get really bent out of shape." Again, this is a logic function that manifests itself in a situation that has no apparent "logical" guidelines.

Due to their interest in the way that people behave in organizations, Newell and Simon decided to test whether or not a computer might act like a human in similar situations. They opted to create a program that was based on certain principles of logic, and they chose Bertrand Russell and Alfred North Whitehead's *Principia Mathematica*, a system based on propositional calculus. The decision was not exactly one that they agonized over: Simon claimed that they chose the text for no other reason than that it happened to be on his bookshelf. But the *Principia* had a number of theorems that Newell and Simon wanted to put to the test on a computer.

Unfortunately, computers were not the machines that they are today, and programming was not exactly something that someone did in a few hours of their spare time. Keyboards were not part and parcel of the machines then, and the method of input—punch cards—was long and tedious. To make sure that the program could run on a computer, Newell and Simon wrote the entire thing out on index cards, and then acted out the role of the computer using friends and family. The index cards served as possible paths of thought for the computer, acting as branches of a decision tree. If the computer was faced with several different decision possibilities, it would pursue each one to find out which might yield the proper solution.

Using the office metaphor mentioned earlier, a worker might encounter a situation in which he had single-handedly finished a project. The first truth is that the worker has finished the project. The decision that must be made now is what to do with it. The worker can decide either to take credit for the entire project or to share the credit with his coworkers, and perhaps his boss. But each of these decisions has further ramifications that create more branches. If he decides to take all the credit, he may win points with senior management. This could lead to a raise or a promotion. It could also lead to dissension among his coworkers and unhappiness on the part of his boss, who might feel that the worker was hogging the glory and not being a team player. On the other hand, the choice to share the credit would make life in the office easier, but not necessarily elevate the worker's status in terms of career or salary.

These are examples of how a single truth might have numerous possible decision paths, and how the branches form a decision tree. Actually, a decision root system is probably a more accurate description: from a single truth the decisions branch downward, like roots, and each of the various roots has its own endpoint; together, the endpoints represent all of the different conclusions that might be reached. For Newell and Simon, the only way to test their program without using a computer was to use the index cards to represent all of the different branching points in the *Principia*'s theorems. To keep track of this, they used a number of people during Christmas vacation of 1955—their friends and families—to turn up certain cards whenever a particular decision needed to be made. It was primitive, but it kept track of all the variations that could be encountered. And as far as they could tell from their index cards, the program worked.

Simon informed one of his Carnegie-Mellon classes after the Christmas break that he and Newell had created a thinking machine. By the time that Newell and Simon arrived at the conference, the word had already spread about their program, even though it still didn't actually reside on a computer. The two called it the Logic Theorist, and it was the only computer-based system to mimic human thinking that existed in 1956. For the Dartmouth conference organizers to overlook this accomplishment would have been shortsighted on their part, and Newell and Simon got their invitation.

Hanover, New Hampshire, is not exactly the easiest place in the United States to get to, and it was certainly less so in 1956, which put a crimp into some attendees' travel plans. During the course of the two weeks, the participants mentioned above showed up for some but not all sessions, depending on their own schedules. As it turned out, there was no single occasion when all of the participants were in the same room at the same time. Because of this, the conference served primarily to introduce all of the participants to each other and their respective work and research. It did not produce any groundbreaking ideas or courses of action in guiding the future of thinking machines. In retrospect, it might be best to think of it as a get-acquainted mixer.

One shared ideology that was fairly evident at the conference was the attendees' belief that thinking machines should be created using symbols as opposed to connectionist theories. Proponents of connectionism—also known as neural networking—believed that the best way to mimic the activities of the brain was to attempt to re-create its structure through large interconnections of neurons. The Dartmouth AI group tended to pooh-pooh this idea, feeling that just because a machine was constructed like a brain didn't mean it worked like a brain. Symbolic processing made much more sense, at least from a practical point of view. Newell and Simon had employed this technique in creating the Logic Theorist, and it seemed to work better than trying to create an artificial neuron—something both Minsky and Nathaniel Rochester had toyed with. Minsky, however, would never be fully comfortable with either concept and flip-flopped between the two, which would put him at odds with his fellow AI researchers in the future.

While John McCarthy expressed some disappointment at the outcome, the conference did accomplish one thing for which it would live on in infamy. A formal term for the work that all of these men were pursuing was agreed upon: artificial intelligence. A number of ambiguous and cryptic words and phrases had been bandied about to describe the endeavors that could create thinking machines, such as cybernetics, complex information processing, machine intelligence, and automata studies. None of these seemed to capture the feeling of what they wanted to do with computers; yet no one liked anybody else's suggestions much better than their own. McCarthy came up with artificial intelligence, although to this day he isn't sure if he first heard it somewhere else or came up with it at the conference. However, he was certainly the one most in favor of the term, even though some of the others regarded it as being a bit too overblown or fantastical. Artificial intelligence, as a phrase, "keeps our eye on the goal," according to McCarthy, who felt that it was the only term to encompass all of the different ideas that were brought to Dartmouth that summer. With some grumbling from the conference participants, artificial intelligence became the official term for a new field of computer science.

The conference broke up and the members went their separate ways, but at least they were all now on a first name basis with each other. Though they would communicate with each other over the next two decades, most of these men would never spend any time working together on AI again. They all had their own ideas and their own careers, and except for McCarthy and Minsky, most of them would dabble in AI more as a hobby than as an actual area of dedicated study. (There was little progress, or fallout, in the aftermath of the Dartmouth gathering. The idea of a national network or even a regional concentration of AI researchers fell through the cracks. Though they managed to form an AI "community" of sorts by the end of 1957, the following year, the primary souvenir that each had taken away from Dartmouth was a name for his research work.)

Marvin Minsky and John McCarthy, however, would soon be battling it out for the title of "Father of Artificial Intelligence."

꩜

The year after the Dartmouth AI conference, John McCarthy accepted a teaching position at MIT. He immediately began working to create a programming language that might somehow improve a computer's capability to process logic in a human manner. Existing languages treated the computer as nothing more than a mechanical calculator and primarily sought to take advantage of its capability to perform arithmetical equations. McCarthy wanted something that understood symbols, which humans use in the form of printed words and pictures.

Another preoccupation of John McCarthy's at the time was the tiny amount of operating time that individual users could get on MIT's computer. Long sign-up lists and programs that had to be run in the middle of the night were part and parcel of getting access to the computer. McCarthy felt that there was a way to use the computer continuously so that it could handle multiple jobs at once. While things were slow with one job, the computer could do certain chores for another job. The computer would be using all of its assets at any given time, instead of having some remain idle while it worked on just one program at a time. McCarthy called this system of multiple access to the computer "time-sharing." In effect, it gave a number of people the chance to use the computer as if they were the only ones on the machine.

McCarthy's new post at MIT brought him geographically closer to Minsky, who by that time had bailed out on his fellowship at Harvard to spend quality research time at Tufts University, a mere twenty miles from MIT. Unfortunately for Minsky, Tufts closed the department he was working in during the course of 1957, and Minsky was soon out of work. Looking for more challenges, and a steady job, he joined fellow Dartmouth AI participant Oliver Selfridge at MIT's Lincoln Laboratories in Lexington, Massachusetts. Selfridge was developing a program of his own that he called Pandemonium, which he hoped would be able to learn from its own experience.

Minsky spent a year at Lincoln, where he and Selfridge worked on a few projects that were peripherally related to AI, especially in the area of pattern recognition. After his year was up, though, Minsky headed to MIT proper back in Cambridge, where he was less restricted than in the confines of Lincoln's military-oriented environment. (Lincoln Labs was allegedly the site of government-sponsored plutonium testing on humans during this period.) He signed up for the mathematics department, but soon switched over to electrical engineering, which was where McCarthy was working. Not coincidentally, the nascent work on computers was also done in the electrical engineering department, since most college administrators had no idea where else to put it. It involved electrical components and electronics, so why not stick it into the electrical engineering department? This was an early example of bureaucratic confusion over computers and their study that would unite computers and electrical engineering in some universities until well into the 1980s.

McCarthy and Minsky had already established themselves as the AI community's dynamic duo—Newell and Simon were busy with other things—and having the two mathematicians together in 1958 was the start of highly visible AI activities at MIT. To top it off, Claude Shannon returned to MIT that same year as Donner Professor of Science (Donner is an endowed science chair at MIT). The 1956 AI fraternity was once again intact and the schoolboys were going to capitalize on being together once again, because for all intents and purposes, MIT had most of the AI brainpower in academia by the end of the decade.

The first order of business for McCarthy and Minsky was to establish a true center of AI at MIT. It was not enough that MIT as an institution was laying claim to being the center of the AI universe; McCarthy and Minsky needed something within the MIT organization that they could call their own.

In 1959 they established the Artificial Intelligence Laboratory, which was called the AI Lab. It occupied the seventh, eighth, and ninth floors of the Tech Square building on the Cambridge campus, just as it does today. There, McCarthy and Minsky began holding forth on the philosophies of thinking machines—what it would take to create them, how they should be built, what issues they should be programmed to handle. It did not attract a lot of attention at first, but gradually managed to gain a small but avid following.

McCarthy and Minsky became their own two-man cult of personality. Their names were combined into a single utterance at MIT, used in the same way that Gable and Lombard, Martin and Lewis, and other famous pairs were used in the entertainment business. They were co-founders of the AI Lab, and they shared equally in its formation and growing pains. They were partners.

Well, at least that was true in the beginning.

꘠

Meanwhile, Alan Newell and Herbert Simon had gone back to Carnegie-Mellon University to complete the Logic Theorist. They were using RAND Corporation's IBM computer to build their thinking machine, but by the time it was up and running, the Logic Theorist didn't really mimic humans very well. Instead, it mimicked rules of logic very well. Newell and Simon embarked then on a follow-up, or evolutionary, program to better emulate human behavior. They called this the General Problem Solver, or GPS. The concept behind the GPS was that it would be programmed to achieve a certain goal, and then must find the means to reach that goal. As opposed to starting from a truth and working towards an eventual solution, this involved a certain amount of mental backtracking or backwards thinking, going from the final solution to the present state. Thus, most of the process resembles working one's way backwards through a maze.

In the same way, let's say that you wanted to be president of the company you work for. Right now, however, you are a mail room clerk. Your final goal is obvious: the presidential suite. How do you figure out how to get there from the mail room? You could start forward and say you want to go to a higher paying job—say on the loading dock—but that doesn't necessarily lead forward to the president's desk. Instead, you work backward from the job of president. There are vice presidents, then senior managers, then middle managers, then the rank-and-file, followed by entry-level office personnel, clerical staff, and you—just above the janitorial staff. By working backwards through the organization, you have seen that the loading dock is not in a direct line of succession from you to the president. This makes your task easier, and it took less time than trying to figure out where every single job ahead of you led. GPS worked the same way.

Newell and Simon worked on the GPS on and off throughout most of the 1960s. Their fame in AI was already carved in stone due to their development of the Logic Theorist, but the GPS helped to cement their reputation as pioneers of new ways to program machines. Increasingly, Simon's presence at Carnegie-Mellon began to attract new recruits into the AI fold, in much the same way that McCarthy and Minsky were AI beacons at MIT. Among Simon's students during this time was a young man named Edward Feigenbaum who was studying concepts about human memory and its use in solving problems. Twenty years later, Feigenbaum would almost single-handedly pit the United States against Japan in an attempt to get greater funding for AI, and he would make a lot of money doing it.

Carnegie-Mellon would also become a hotbed for other intelligent technologies over the next two decades, primarily in robots and in the development of machines that could understand human speech. But most of that would not happen until the mid-1970s. In 1960, the AI mantle was draped squarely over the shoulders of the MIT contingent.

Newell and Simon made their mark and then got Carnegie-Mellon on the right track towards creating a stimulating environment for developing AI. Then, however, they both bowed out of the AI community. Herb Simon returned to his work studying organizational behavior, which would result in his being awarded the Nobel Prize for economics in 1978. He had little to do with AI after the General Problem Solver, and besides, then as now, AI was not an area that merited Nobel prize consideration.

Allen Newell would eventually become the first president of the American Association for Artificial Intelligence in 1979, but it was an honorary title more than anything. His work in AI had been only moderate since the early 1960s. He died at the age of sixty-five in July 1992.

❧

Back in Cambridge, Massachusetts, the McCarthy and Minsky show was already betraying signs of stress. As personalities, the two men could not have been more different. John McCarthy had enough hair on his face and head to qualify as an extra in a werewolf movie, and he was somewhat spacey in his relationships with his students and peers. He also wanted to work on specific problems related to AI and to create computer programs that would demonstrate advances in the technology. Marvin Minsky, on the other hand, was prematurely bald, had a biting if not somewhat condescending manner— Norbert Weiner comes to mind—and wanted to deal with the "big picture" of AI. He was more concerned with the philosophical questions of what really constituted intelligence in humans, and his attention to the details of creating thinking machines was noticeably lacking.

MIT was also beginning to court government dollars to fund its new research into computer science, and this turned out to be a devil's deal. The money came in, but so did the politics and restrictions that were mandatory baggage with government grants. McCarthy's time-sharing system got caught in the maelstrom, and various factions within MIT started demanding more computer time for their pet projects. McCarthy, for one, didn't like it. He had always been on the fringe of mainstream society, and his personal beliefs leaned further to the left than most of his fellow mathematicians. As far as he was concerned, MIT was getting too constricted, and perhaps in a way that McCarthy couldn't handle, it was also getting a little too chummy with the military.

In 1962, McCarthy was offered the opportunity to go to Stanford University to set up a new artificial intelligence lab at the school. Stanford had begun to establish itself as the leading intellectual bastion of the West Coast, and it was eager to begin its own work in AI. McCarthy would be getting more power at Stanford—he alone would run the new lab—along with more money and a chance to move back to California. He had attended CalTech as an undergrad student in the 1940s, and had enjoyed California and its somewhat more liberal surroundings. Apparently, McCarthy didn't need much prompting. In the fall of that year, he left MIT and Minsky behind, forever.

A footnote to the event was that McCarthy was one of the first people to ever break the stranglehold that MIT held over its spawn. And to prove that MIT wasn't the only place that had the brainpower to develop AI, McCarthy put together an AI community that equaled MIT's over the ensuing years. When the whole field of artificial intelligence started turning out commercial products in the 1980s, there was very obviously a West Coast AI and an East Coast AI—one inspired by McCarthy and the other by Minsky. The two communities have little respect for each other, even to this day, and find no end of joy in belittling each other's efforts.

The most evident fact of this separation between the two coasts is that both McCarthy and Minsky are called "The Father of Artificial Intelligence." Father, as in one father—singular. The AI community justifies this by figuring that Minsky is the father of the East Coast AI faction, and McCarthy is the father of the West Coast AI faction. The fact that popular opinion says there is really only one AI community in the United States doesn't matter; neither does the fact that the rest of the world considers Alan Turing to be the "Father of Artificial Intelligence." The MIT group and the Stanford group each have their own father, and if the other side wants to make some spurious claim to the contrary, that's OK by them. They each know the real truth, facts be damned.

This insularity on the part of MIT and Stanford will go a long way to explaining some of the bizarre attempts to commercialize AI in the 1980s. But from a purely academic view, MIT would act as if Stanford never existed from that point forward. Stanford's AI lab couldn't ignore its roots in MIT, but it didn't feel the need to acknowledge them publicly. They would each go their own ways and try to ignore any of the accomplishments of the other. There was business at hand, and each group needed to attend to it.

For Marvin Minsky, that business was getting the military to fund the research for the boys in his AI Lab.

6

The Nation's First AI Lab and the Defense Connection

Marvin Minsky and Military Money

Marvin Minsky is a strange person to be the father figure for artificial intelligence, be it the West Coast or East Coast or anywhere in between. He admits to little interest in programming computers, and it is doubtful whether he has written an entire AI program by himself in the last twenty years.

He is, by all accounts, a genius. He has had insights into the concept of mind that no one before him considered. His work has influenced the course of modern artificial intelligence research. He has overseen the studies and work of some of the most important computer scientists of our time. But genius is a subjective term. Many people think that Jerry Lewis is a genius, so go figure.

Minsky is a complex and well-respected man. He was good friends with Isaac Asimov, the twentieth century's most important science fiction writer. He was the technical consultant to the film *2001: A Space Odyssey* and was mentioned by name in the book version of the movie's script. He was the first American ever awarded the Japan Laureate prize for technology by the Japanese government. He has been featured in countless books and magazine articles as one of the great thinkers of the past three decades.

His foundation is in mathematics, yet he plays the role of philosopher king, trying to get a rise out of both his followers and his detractors. In years gone by, he would have fit nicely into the role of the mastermind that incites the crowd to riot, and then casually steps over the carnage after the dust has settled.

What Minsky does is coax, tease, ridicule, prod, and belittle people into doing things that he thinks about, yet has little time to do on his own. He is in the business of getting reactions, oftentimes for the pure satisfaction of doing so. Reactions are an integral part of Minsky's modus operandi.

He claims no one paid any attention to a robot arm that he built as a boy until he put the sleeve from a flannel shirt on it. That, he claims, got quite a reaction. He got a bigger rise out of the AI community when he once referred to the brain as nothing more than a "meat machine."

Minsky looks the part of the mad scientist. Not the wild, nearly insane-looking one with the frightening shock of gray hair—that would be McCarthy—but the diabolical one with the shifty eyes, thick black glasses, and gleaming bald pate. His eyes shift constantly as he talks to you, almost as if he's looking for a way out, or possibly for someone more important to converse with. His voice is at once grating yet preternaturally soft and whining. He continually scratches his bald head, making him the epitome of all the deep thinkers of the world who allegedly spend all of their time thinking about thinking. Minsky would make a great cartoon character.

Born in 1927, Minsky went to Harvard after graduating from the Bronx High School of Science, initially to study physics. He had a keen interest in optics, but his attention wandered—a foreshadowing of the way he would live his professional life—and he sought out different academic pastimes while at Harvard. He spent a great deal of his time in the biology lab, where he learned to manipulate the pincers of a crayfish by attaching electrodes to the creature's nervous system. He also took music courses and began a lifelong fascination with what makes some music pleasing to one culture while completely irritating to another (native American music, for instance). One of Minsky's biggest passions in his undergraduate days was psychology, and he was lucky enough to have one of the world's most famous psychologists performing experiments down the hall from him.

B.F. Skinner is best remembered as the guy who kept his kid in a box to monitor the kid's psychological growth. Giving his name to "the Skinner box," B.F. is often the object of derision in introduction to psychology classes. But in the 1950s, he was pushing the limits of psychological research. His methods for observation set strict standards of research that are still applied today, and his theories on conditioning people is the basis of many forms of behavior modification therapy (such as weight loss, quitting cigarette smoking, etc.). Most of Skinner's work at Harvard was considered breakthrough and revolutionary, if not radical and extremist, by the psychological community. Marvin Minsky, as an undergraduate looking to find his calling, was in awe. He got to know Skinner fairly well, although Skinner was another splendid example of an MIT curmudgeon. The psychologist had an extreme distaste for those who put any importance on the mind, believing that all human behavior was a matter of complex responses to stimuli. The same belief formed the basis of his theories on conditioning, which have their roots in Pavlov and his salivating dogs.

Skinner's affect on Minsky cannot be understated. Minsky has spent most of his adult life trying to define what a mind is, and whether or not it exists. In many ways, the field of artificial intelligence gave him free rein to play with those ideas of mind versus behavior without having to submit to any critical scrutiny from the psychological community.

Unfortunately for his studies, Minsky's interest in so many diverse fields severely impacted his undergraduate grades. In order to salvage his undergraduate career, he decided to write a thesis. It didn't really matter on what; it just had to be stunning. Since the physics department had no provisions for thesis work, Minsky switched majors to mathematics, where he wrote a thesis discussing the mathematical variables of heat on the Earth's surface. It wasn't very pretty or even very useful, but it was stunning, and the thesis saved his grade point average. His advisor was so impressed that he persuaded Marvin to become a full-time mathematician.

From Harvard, Minsky went on to Princeton and to Bell Labs and to Lincoln Labs and to Tufts and then back to Cambridge and MIT. The rest, as they say, is history. He has been at MIT ever since. Like Norbert Weiner before him, Minsky is firmly enshrined in the university's popular and mythical culture. He even held Claude Shannon's old position of Donner Professor of Science.

❧

Shortly after John McCarthy left MIT for warmer and less politically correct climates, the AI Lab—under Minsky—became beholden to the Department of Defense.

The U.S. Department of Defense had been severely humiliated in 1957 by the Russian success of Sputnik, the first successfully launched space satellite. To have a bunch of Communists pushing the envelope of technology research with Stalin-era equipment was a very nasty slap in the face, and many in the Pentagon took it personally (they always have and probably always will). To avoid further embarrassment at home and abroad, the DOD decided to put a great deal of its research money into funding development of new technologies. It created ARPA, the Advanced Research Projects Agency, in 1958. The goal of ARPA was to invest in strategic areas of technology, especially computers, to make sure that America stayed at the forefront of technology research. Money would go to research institutions and universities with the intent of creating new technologies, though what was to be done with them once they were created was anybody's guess.

A number of particular universities wanted the DOD's money: MIT, Cornell, Princeton, Stanford, Carnegie-Mellon, Yale, and just about every other school that could boast of a respectable science lab. But MIT had an inside track and its own secret weapon: the director of ARPA—the man charged with disbursing funds—was J.C. Licklider, a former Harvard professor who just happened to have taught Marvin Minsky during the latter's undergraduate days. Not only that, but Licklider was apparently fond of Minsky and believed that Minsky was destined for greatness. Licklider's policy was to invest in people and their ideas and not necessarily in any specific existing research. In no time at all, the relatively new AI Lab was near the top of the DOD's list of grant recipients. Things couldn't have worked out better for MIT if ARPA had been run by Santa Claus.

The first big ARPA project that affected the AI group at MIT was a 1963 grant worth more than $2 million. The money was to be used for two specific computer-related projects that fell under one heading: Project MAC. The acronym MAC stood for two things. The first was Machine-Aided Cognition, which was a novel way of saying "artificial intelligence." The second thing it stood for was Multiple Access Computer, another term for the time-sharing project that John McCarthy had begun during his tenure at MIT. The idea behind Project MAC was to throw money at both endeavors and see what cropped up. The AI Lab alone was entitled to nearly a million dollars worth of the funding, which was an estimated 10,000 percent increase in its annual budget. The rest of the money, however, would still be floating about the various computer groups at MIT, many of which had some association or link to Minsky and his lab. Marvin had a virtual stranglehold on the entire grant.

But Licklider's largesse didn't end there. The university was promised approximately three million bucks per year after the first year for as long as Project MAC was in operation. It was this money that allowed MIT to take the lead in computer science in the early 1960s and to create the first environment in the world conducive to that unusual breed of humans known as hackers.

In current parlance, "hacker" has a somewhat derogatory connotation. It tends to refer to teenagers who use their computers to unleash all manner of mayhem on other people's computers. Modern-day hackers steal, destroy, pilfer, rob, corrupt, and delete the computer files of big corporations and unsuspecting users—or so the conventional wisdom goes. When the term was coined, however, hacker was a prestigious word, used only in reference to the very best computer programmers.

In appearance and personality, there was not a lot of difference between hackers and what the rest of the world delicately called "nerds." Indeed, *Random House Unabridged Dictionary* charts the initial use of the term "nerd" to this time. Hackers, though, were the elite nerds, the crème de la crème. It wasn't enough to sport pocket protectors and horn-rimmed glasses, and to spend all your free time playing chess or reading science fiction. For the hackers at MIT, especially those in the AI Lab, commitment to the computer was all-encompassing. Looking the part wasn't enough; you had to eat, drink, and sleep it. This is not a cliché. Eating meant only Chinese food or take-out pizza, drinking meant anything as long as it was caffeinated, and sleeping meant on the floor of the AI Lab.

A "hacker ethic" developed very quickly at MIT for a number of reasons. The most important reason was that there were very few people in the whole world who were given the opportunity to work on computers whenever they wanted, twenty-four hours a day, seven days a week. And, computers were literally still being invented. They were not mass produced in the way that PCs are today; they were sold in lots of one and two at a time. The total annual shipment of product for the computer industry in the early 1960s was measured in tens and hundreds. PC industry shipments are currently measured in millions.

The hackers represented the first generation of humans who got to cut their teeth on computers. The men in companies like Westinghouse or General Motors that had to learn to deal with those "new-fangled computer things" were taken from places like accounting and electrical engineering and tossed into the arena. There, they were expected to make computers work, whether they had any training or not. It was a lot like learning to fly an airplane once it's already in the air, and the pilot has just died.

Hackers had no such pressure. They were school kids or grad students or professors who didn't really have to report to the outside world. They lived in the comfortable insularity of academia and could do whatever they wanted because they wouldn't be fired and had no bosses. ARPA didn't know enough about what the hackers were doing to be any sort of nuisance, so they were left on their own. And the hackers' main computer, a new machine called the PDP-1, had been donated free to MIT by its developer, Digital Equipment Corporation. It was like living in a big playpen.

Another driving force in the hacker environment was the fact that these individuals were getting to do work on computers that was radically different from what anyone else was doing. Certainly they were pushing the boundaries of traditional computing just by toying around with the machine on a continual basis, which was giving them the opportunity to make advancements that no corporation or more structured research organization could achieve. AI research was a different matter entirely. Being allowed to make the computer do things that it wasn't designed for—especially not in the product plans of companies like IBM and Sperry Rand—was an added bonus for the hackers. It gave them an elite status that went beyond the nerd community; it was something that could be held up as a pursuit that would put almost anyone, including the average Joe, in awe. AI justified the hackers' existence.

And what an existence it was. Although McCarthy's time-sharing mechanism was in place, it still did not take care of all the needs of everyone in the AI Lab. Cots were brought in and desks pushed together to provide sleeping areas for hackers who wanted to be ready for the first free moment on the computer. It was too much trouble to have someone call a dorm room and then have to trudge across campus to the lab. It was better to be right there when opportunity knocked. Plus, no one wanted to miss anything in case someone else ran a really neat program or came up with a cool new idea.

Such strange hours lent themselves to a number of personality quirks that became pervasive throughout the computer science groups at MIT. Since many hackers weren't on traditional schedules, they missed meals in the cafeteria and even in local restaurants. The only establishments other than convenience stores that were open late into the night were Cambridge's Chinese food restaurants and pizza places. As such, both forms of sustenance became the de facto food of choice for hackers.

Spending all one's waking hours at the computer site also didn't allow for much time to attend to basic bodily needs, such as bathing or changing clothes.

Many hackers became notorious for the amount of time—measured in weeks, not days—that they went without showering or washing their clothes. Neither of these activities was important to the hackers, who viewed them as a waste of valuable time that could be spent at the computer. Even after the hackers got real jobs, the situation didn't change much. The president of Symbolics, as late as 1991, had to issue an edict to the company's hackers about attention to bodily hygiene in the workplace: Clean your clothes or clean out your desks. In essence, it boiled down to four words: Wash or don't work. Many hackers were actually torn over how to handle this demand. Salary . . . or soap? Hmmm. Tough choices.

Another thing missing from the hackers' daily lives was an interest in the opposite sex. There was no outward dislike of women, no "He-Man Woman Hater's Club." Women just didn't fit into the environment or the mind-set. These guys were fairly nerdy to begin with, so they didn't possess all the social graces that might endear them to any particular woman. Besides, what could be better than creating a truly great program that really tested the limits of MIT's computers? Certainly not sex.

When a hacker did break out of his shell and start dating, he oftentimes became the object of derision. He was believed to have forsaken his commitment and loyalty to his first love—computing—for a female, and was thus no longer ranked among the leagues of the hacker elite. This stigma broke up many casual relationships and marriages over the years.

It was this group of roughly two dozen people that Marvin Minsky oversaw as Project MAC got under way in 1963. All were highly motivated individuals with a disdain for conventions, outsiders, and interference in their pursuits. Minsky realized this and allowed them to take over the AI Lab in the way that he saw best suited them. The cots, the empty pizza boxes, the smell—all were okay as long as the hackers spent quality time exploring the potential of the computer. Minsky didn't interfere, and in fact was known for his hands-off style. Oftentimes the hackers didn't see him unless he had an idea that he wanted them to work on.

Within MIT, Project MAC was known as "Man Against Computers," a reference to the need to make the machines do exactly what they were ordered to. As stated at the outset of this book, much of artificial intelligence is about power, and the hackers wanted to exert their own brand of power over the hulking behemoths from IBM and Digital Equipment that took up floor space in Tech Square.

At first, little of the research in Project MAC had any military orientation. The programmers were primarily trying to find out what the infantile computers were capable of. One of the primary undertakings of the project

within the AI group was the continuation of work on a computer programming language that John McCarthy had invented in 1958. When the first
commercial computers were manufactured in the 1950s, a programming language called FORTRAN was used to write the instructions and programs
for them. AI researchers like McCarthy and Newell and Simon found this
language too number- and calculation-oriented to handle symbols and symbolic representation. Newell and Simon wrote their own language, called the
Information Programming Language, to address this problem, and wrote the
General Problem Solver with it.

McCarthy wanted something that better represented the way that people
think, something along the lines of lists, concepts, and experiential values.
He came up with a language called List Processing, which was given the
unfortunate acronym of LISP. The programming language could group symbols together in lists or particular relationships by means of parentheses, which
are also used to group sections of mathematical equations together, as in ((4
x 4) + 3). A long LISP program involved innumerable parentheses, prompting the adherents of more traditional languages to claim that LISP stood for
"Lots of Inane Stupid Parentheses." McCarthy was unfazed, and his LISP
language became the primary tool for developing AI on the MIT campus. It
also had the distinction of being the second formal computer language ever
invented (after FORTRAN), coming into existence well before more widely
known languages like BASIC, COBOL, and C.

After McCarthy left MIT and just as the ARPA money was coming in,
the AI Lab spent considerable time reworking the LISP language to take
advantage of the almost daily progress that was being made in the design of
computer hardware. A version called MacLISP was created by a young
student named Richard Greenblatt, who showed remarkable aptitude for writing programs that the majority of hackers at MIT considered nearly impossible to write. So committed was Greenblatt to the AI Lab that he would go
for weeks without leaving its offices. The consequence of such devotion was
that Greenblatt never went to classes, either. He eventually flunked out of
MIT, a fact that did not keep him from coming in to work at the lab every
day. Greenblatt was considered the archetypal hacker in his day, being both
a stellar chess player and nonbather, and was held in high esteem by the other
hackers—even the ones that were passing their courses.

Richard Greenblatt would eventually create the machine that moved artificial intelligence from the lab and into the commercial marketplace after
nearly twenty years of research isolation. The only drawback to that accomplishment was that Greenblatt didn't want to have anything to do with it
because it meant leaving the MIT playpen.

❧

Practical work on artificial intelligence in the lab tended to be largely theoretical, much like the hackers' sex lives. Minsky's main concern was determining what actually constituted thinking. Was it the ability to take random pieces of information and tie them together into something new? Was it the ability to use experience and apply it as necessary to problems? It wasn't just the ability to solve logical equations, because most of everyday life did not involve problems and situations that could be broken down to logic statements. Besides, humans didn't think in the largely mathematical terms of formal logic. Thought seemed to be based rather on a slew of factors: past experiences, pattern recognition, and information gleaned from nonpersonal sources such as books or movies. The question that began to haunt AI researchers was, "If we don't know how humans think, how can we get a machine to think like a human?" At first this seemed like a minor problem, one that most researchers believed would be overcome within a matter of years. It is a tell-tale example of their egos that this same question is still the major obstacle to artificial intelligence as we approach the year 2000.

One of the peripheral benefits of this study of thinking was the creation of programs and concrete models that allowed psychologists to test their hypotheses on computers. Trying to define thought so that it could be programmed into a computer also showed psychologists that the more they found out about thinking, the less they really knew about it. AI gradually became something of a sounding board for psychology—a fact that was not lost on Minsky in the years to follow.

A few programs were created in the early 1960s at MIT, but none that came close to accomplishing the goal of creating a true thinking machine. These programs could do specific jobs in a manner that resembled human thought, but were completely incapable of doing other jobs. Clearly, there was more to the scope of intelligence than just being able to solve a few problems of logic. The men in the AI Lab knew they would find it eventually, either through some brilliant piece of programming from a guy like Greenblatt or from some off-the-cuff remark made by Minsky. Besides, they had plenty of time to work on the problem, and ARPA was more than happy to keep funding their efforts year after year.

While many of their paychecks were coming directly out of the DOD grants, the AI researchers tacitly ignored any political implications about the source of the money. The DOD wanted to win the Cold War, and it wanted to get some useful technology from places like MIT. This technology would go—for better or worse—to making more efficient killing machines and for improving administration of war-time efforts. Even though this was not ex-plicitly written out in the grants, it was an obvious expectation on the part of the military. Anybody who denied that this was the case was either fooling themselves or lying.

The AI Lab people were the sort that tended to fool themselves. During the Vietnam War, many of their fellow students and peers—people like John McCarthy—were extremely vocal about their opposition to America's involve-ment in Vietnam. No one on a college campus in the mid-1960s could es-cape it, even the removed-from-reality denizens of the AI Lab. Yet, various MIT researchers—including Greenblatt—have been quoted as saying that although their money came from the military, they weren't really doing any military work. People like Minsky sidestepped the issue, noting that DOD money was designed for research, and research alone. If the technology ulti-mately found its way onto the battlefield, that was the DOD's doing, and not something related to the day-to-day work being conducted in Tech Square.

The AI community was faced with a philosophical argument similar to the one concerning the essence of the mind, and no one seemed to have all the answers. So they put on their blinders and continued working, pretend-ing to be blissfully unaware of who was holding the purse strings. The money kept flowing in.

✑

While Project MAC plodded along unimpeded, the DOD itself was getting more concerned with the way the Vietnam War was going—which was badly. Manpower and traditional weaponry were not routing the Communists out of Southeast Asia as expected, and other means needed to be employed. Piqued by—but not completely satisfied with—the theoretical work in AI coming out of MIT, the Defense Department started looking around to see what else was going on in the field of thinking machines. It even changed the name of ARPA to DARPA, which stood for *Defense* Advanced Research Projects Agency, so that no one would mistake the fact that it was looking for sub-stantial gains in technology that would help the military. It found that both Stanford and Carnegie-Mellon University were doing some interesting things with robots, and both were working on specific applications of artificial in-telligence; not just theoretical applications. These universities began lobby-ing more actively for research dollars, and they both started getting them. Every dollar that went to Stanford or CMU, however, was a dollar that didn't go to MIT.

Minsky, in particular, was well aware of the ramifications of this monetary equation. He didn't like government funding—the major source of his research dollars—going to someone else when he felt that he and the AI Lab deserved it. This is not at all unusual; territoriality exists in every organization. But Marvin knew that the golden goose had only so many eggs, and he wanted them plunked down in Cambridge. Like a mother hen, he would do his best to ensure that MIT got them.

One episode strikes right to the heart of government funding and helps to define the importance of the Department of Defense to AI research. It also provides some insight into Minsky's mind-set at the time.

As mentioned earlier, Marvin built an artificial neuron during his days at Harvard in the early 1950s. The concept behind artificial neurons lies in the physical structure of the nervous system and the brain. The brain alone is composed of approximately one trillion neurons that are linked together by axons and dendrites. If you think back to junior high school biology, you will remember that axons are the long tails that emanate from neurons, while dendrites provide a weblike connection at the end of axons that allows many neurons to be connected together. There may be as many as a thousand cells linked to a single dendritic connection. Thus, the firing of an individual neuron can affect many other neurons, because they are not simply linked one after another, but in all different directions.

Neurons transmit information to each other along different pathways, depending on the situation. In the early 1940s, two MIT researchers (surprise!) named Warren McCulloch and Walter Pitts theorized that this same mode of information transmission—via a network of neurons—could probably be reproduced using electronic components. They didn't specify computers as being the components in question, as those devices were not in regular use in 1943.

Minsky took this idea to heart, in hopes that it might be a way to create a mechanical model of the brain. Using hundreds of vacuum tubes, Minsky assembled a simple neural network in 1951. He designed it as a maze in which a signal worked its way from beginning to end. Using an automatic pilot from an airplane as a controller, the signal navigated the maze by determining which "neurons" provided the strongest link to the end point of the maze. Eventually, the signal could run the maze quickly because it had established all of the strong points on each of its successive runs. The auto pilot increased the strength of the connections based on the performance of the signal. In this way, the system appeared to "learn" the maze.

Minsky's creation was possibly the first neural network, quite an achievement in light of current interest in the technology. Yet Minsky felt that neural networks were limited in that once they had learned to accomplish a goal, they couldn't apply that knowledge or information to other goals. Essentially, they acted as Skinner would have expected them to: responding over and over to stimuli, a repeated behavior without a mind. Despite what Skinner thought, Minsky felt that he was on to something, but that it probably required a larger network consisting of perhaps millions of neurons. So obsessed was he with the notion of neurons that could learn that he structured his Princeton dissertation around it. Still, the answer eluded him in practice, and he sought other mechanical ways of re-creating the mind.

Had Minsky pursued neural nets at the time, they might have become the most important form of AI in the 1960s. There were, however, other researchers who also felt that neural nets might be the way to create rudimentary thinking machines. Minsky was irked by the fact that some of them claimed to be making headway in neural nets while he was struggling with the basics of the problem. Chief among these researchers was a man named Frank Rosenblatt, who had gone to high school with Minsky in the Bronx.

Rosenblatt was a Cornell psychologist who had invented a neural network device he called the Perceptron. He used sensors to provide input to the machine and lights to indicate the neural connections that were being made by the machine during its operation. The Perceptron actually had a methodology for showing why it made its decisions, which were based on "weighted" information. These "weights" would help the network to determine a solution path without having to run through the entire system, by indicating that a certain connection was "more" or "less" favorable to the goal it was searching for. Rosenblatt, who was something of a self-promoter, claimed that this was a much more feasible approach to creating thinking machines than the use of symbols, which was something that Minsky had begun investigating more intently in the early 1960s.

Such claims irritated Minsky, and many MIT researchers, to no end. Rosenblatt and Minsky often engaged in public arguments during technical conferences that showed just how little love was lost between the two men. And even though Rosenblatt wasn't able to physically demonstrate everything that he claimed the Perceptron could do, there were a number of other researchers who were able to make the machine perform as promised. Rosenblatt began making a lot of headlines for himself in the computer community of the 1960s, and the Department of Defense was seriously thinking about funding Rosenblatt's work on the Perceptron.

In any given year, the DOD can realistically finance only a finite number of projects, although it may not seem that way from looking at its annual budget. It needs to invest in projects that can give it some value for its dollar, and return a payoff at some point in the not-too-far-distant future. As more and more schools of thought regarding AI came into conflict with the original ideas of Minsky, McCarthy, Newell and Simon, et al, DARPA was obliged to investigate each of them seriously. Rosenblatt's neural network was embraced by a whole new group of AI researchers in the mid-1960s, people who had little or no connection to the original Dartmouth group or the MIT AI Lab. They believed that intelligence could be created in machines that mechanically reproduced the process of the brain at the cellular level. As such, they were outsiders—at least as far as the MIT group was concerned—but they still managed to make a good enough case to be considered an alternative to the work going on at MIT or Carnegie-Mellon. (Stanford was actually promoting the research on its campus.)

Minsky began working on a book in 1965 to show that neural networks simply could not work as promised, and that symbolic processing was the only way to make a thinking machine. Assisting him in this endeavor was Seymour Papert, a psychologist and mathematician who had joined MIT immediately after John McCarthy left. (Papert and Minsky eventually shared the directorship of the AI Lab in 1968.) Both had an intense loathing of the connectionists, as the neural net researchers were called. The book that they wrote was called *Perceptrons*, and its stated intent was to debunk the whole idea of neural networks. Even the title, which was the name for Frank Rosenblatt's machine and not the field of study itself, suggested that there was a personal underlying grievance involved in the book.

Minsky and Papert convincingly argued that neural nets could not—at their most basic level—learn new things from past experience. They had to perform every activity over again in order to solve a problem, or "complete the maze" as it were. Even though a single-level neural net might improve its problem-solving ability over time, it needed to test the problem anew at each pass, thus acting like a rat that had to start over again each time in order to complete the entire maze. Like the rat, learning one maze or set of problems did not help the neural net in a completely new environment. Conversely, symbolic processing made relationships during its problem solving that could be used in the future. Using our earlier example, the lessons learned in driving a car on a city street ("moves forward," "moves in reverse," and "stands still") could also be applied to driving a motorcycle on a dirt road. This form of processing would not require that the entire process of driving be relearned, since the system already understands certain symbolically-based information about driving.

The concern about this inability of neural networks to learn was true, but only at the most basic level of operation. Rosenblatt and his peers, however, had successfully argued that a complex system of multilayered neural nets working together could learn from experience by devoting certain parts of the system to specific problem areas, thus eliminating the need to run an entire problem through the system each time. Minsky and Papert side-stepped this issue by stating, "We have not found any other really interesting class of multi-layered machine." This was not an altogether up-front statement since multi-layered systems were what most connectionists considered to be the real benefit of neural networking.

Minsky and Papert circulated portions of their paper throughout the research community for about three years, making sure everybody of any circumstance knew where they stood on the issue. In 1969, *Perceptrons* was published with great fanfare by MIT Press. Any person or organization getting their information on neural networks from this book found out that the technology was not worth pursuing. Unfortunately, one organization that relied on the book was DARPA. Taking a cue from its favored son, DARPA discarded its plans to fund Rosenblatt's research. After all, if Marvin Minsky said it didn't work, who were they to argue?

Within minutes, neural networks were anathema in the AI community. All major sources of funding disappeared in the months following the publication of the book. Rosenblatt's projects were shelved, and he couldn't even get his papers published in technical journals. No one would listen to him no matter how loudly he screamed. He and his beloved neural networks were passé. Minsky had guaranteed that, for the time being, his own work would not be underfunded because of the efforts of Frank Rosenblatt, and the money pipeline flowed as if nothing had happened.

With a huge cry of anger and outrage, the neural net community claimed that Minsky had used his influence to sabotage work on neural networks for his own economic gain. They pointed out his book's glaring omissions as well as his personal differences with Rosenblatt. DARPA was unmoved. The book was closed on neural net funding.

The tirade could have continued, but Frank Rosenblatt died the following year in a boating accident. He was, by many accounts, a thoroughly defeated man who felt he had been cheated and abused. Even if he had not died, Rosenblatt probably wouldn't have had the inclination to continue championing the cause of neural networks. Much of the spark of the connectionist movement died with him, a stake driven through its heart by Minsky's book. The technology was literally forgotten about through the 1970s and most of the 1980s, lost like some Egyptian mystery in the dust of passing years.

Nearly twenty years later, fueled by an underground movement, neural networks came back in a big way. A very big way. In the late 1980s, the Japanese government found that neural networks were superior to symbolic systems as a method of instilling intelligence in certain devices. It touted the ability of the technology to such an extent that many U.S. researchers wondered where neural nets had been hiding. They wondered why they hadn't heard of such an innovative computing method when it had supposedly originated in the United States. All of a sudden, neural network companies began sprouting up like weeds, and neural nets were at the top of the list of DARPA's most important research projects. So what had happened?

Like some dark and shameful secret, *Perceptrons* was nailed as the culprit. The controversy over Minsky and Papert's work started all over again, this time with the two MIT researchers as the obvious bad guys. Papert wrote an essay in 1988 that defended the book and its findings, but he also admitted that its tone was dictated to a certain extent by the very funding considerations which Minsky had denied. "Did Minsky and I try to kill connectionism?" he asks in his paper. "Yes, there was some hostility in the energy behind the research reported in *Perceptrons* . . . By 1969, AI was not operating in an ivory-tower vacuum. Money was at stake." Papert goes on to state that "part of our drive came from the fact that funding and research energy were being dissipated on what still appear to me to be misleading attempts to use connectionist methods in practical applications."

Both Minsky and Papert feel today that much of their original work was taken out of context at the time of publication, and that their intention was to promote further research into possible avenues of use for neural networks. In retrospect, such sentiments do not accurately reflect the feeling of the times, when getting DARPA money was as necessary for places like MIT as a fix was for a junkie. It was research lifeblood, and without it, the institution might wither away or even die.

As the 1960s evolved into the 1970s and the Vietnam War petered out, DARPA's interest in AI waned. It would come back with a vengeance in the 1980s, and with more money than ever. Only this time, MIT would not just be competing with other universities and research organizations for AI dollars. It would be competing with the hackers who had deserted the AI Lab to form their own companies.

❧

There is one last point that makes for a telling footnote of the days of Project MAC and early AI government funding. J.C. Licklider, the ex-Harvard professor who funneled millions of dollars into the AI Lab in the 1960s as director of ARPA, went back to teaching after his administrative stint was up. Licklider did not, however, return to Harvard. He went to MIT.

7

The Research Groundswell

Stanford and Carnegie Get into the Game

The Stanford University campus in Palo Alto, California is as idyllic as the campus at MIT is industrial. Surrounded by rolling hills that are a lush green in the rare years when there isn't a drought, the campus lies on the peninsula just south of San Francisco, only a few miles from the Pacific Ocean—much the same way that MIT in Cambridge is just across the river from Boston and a few miles from the Atlantic.

It is actually Berkeley, California, some fifty miles to the north of Stanford, that shares a cultural bond with Cambridge, Massachusetts. Both are quintessential college towns that promote a good deal of freethinking and liberal behavior. In many ways, Cambridge and Berkeley set the tone for alternative trends on their respective coasts.

But it is Palo Alto that is the West Coast academic equivalent of the town of Cambridge, and this is due exclusively to the presence of Stanford. The California

Institute of Technology in Pasadena has a better reputation for turning out the kind of engineers who go straight to places like NASA, but Stanford has a more well-rounded curriculum. With a respected business school and one of the best computer science departments in the country, Stanford embodies the essence of both Harvard and MIT in one location.

Having pointed out all these similarities, however, it is now necessary to mention that the two schools couldn't be more different if they were located in separate dimensions—which, some might argue, they are.

In many ways, they are caricatures of their own locations. Stanford, its architecture reflecting a Spanish influence, is relaxed and open, with lots of outdoor areas for in-line skating and sunbathing. MIT has utilitarian concrete towers and classically inspired buildings connected by long hallways, with an occasional patch of lawn set aside in deference to nature. Every square foot of MIT is dedicated to cramming as much learning into available space as possible. Stanford has acre upon acre of trees and grass.

These differences are outwardly determined by the weather and environment of the cities of Cambridge and Palo Alto, but they carry over into the attitude of the people who live, study, and work in each place. People at MIT are more intense, yet also more willing to engage in philosophical arguments about the nature of their work. This resembles the Boston work ethic that compels many to work long into the night, yet spend whole weekends arguing about the virtues of this year's version of the Red Sox. Those at Stanford are much more laid back, yet driven to do something practical with their work. This attitude can be found throughout Northern California, where people will ride their bikes to work seven days a week while wearing spandex shorts— as long as they have their cellular phone with them. MIT as an institution is prone to act as a closed castle, rarely inviting scrutiny of its work. Stanford is more than happy to open its doors to the outside world, which has occasionally turned up embarrassing revelations—like grants for research that went to decorate the president's office. In their off hours, MIT computer students can be found perfecting their skill at video games; those as Stanford might be more inclined to work on solar-powered bicycles.

These are sweeping generalities, but as in any generality, there is some basic truth inherent in them.

John McCarthy came to Stanford in late 1962 to get away from the increasingly heated and political atmosphere of MIT and the East Coast. Stanford was a blank slate when he arrived, and he was given carte blanche to structure the infantile computer sciences department to his liking. McCarthy's personality would become the model for West Coast computing that exists to this day.

McCarthy, born in 1929, grew up in a liberal California family. He went to college in Pasadena at prestigious CalTech, but was eventually kicked out of school because he would not attend gym classes. This left him eligible for military service, and he was drafted during the waning months of World War II—even though he and his family strongly objected to the war. Fortunately, peace broke out before John had to do anything too militaristic, and he went back to CalTech to resume his studies. He graduated from CalTech in 1948 and went on to graduate school at Princeton to study mathematics. There he would make the acquaintance of Marvin Minsky.

It is strange that in their physical appearances, he and Minsky seem to have swapped roles. Minsky is the diminutive balding nerd with the plaid shirt and t-shirt that one would expect to shuffle along hallways muttering to himself while making every attempt possible to avoid physical and social contact with other members of the human race. McCarthy, somewhat stiff and imposing in his gait, has a mass of hair that covers most of his face and head, allowing his eyes to peer out in imitation of Lon Chaney, Jr. He looks like he could bite your head off and then continue nonchalantly on his way to teach a class.

Yet McCarthy is the quiet, somewhat reclusive one, while many believe Minsky has taken aggressiveness and antagonism to the level of art form amongst academicians. McCarthy is known simply as "Uncle John" by most of his peers and students, an affectionate appellation he was tagged with even in his earliest MIT days. The term "uncle" says something about McCarthy's persona when you think of the colloquial way that people use the word to refer to unusual friends or relatives—like Uncle Fester or Uncle Ernie. Stories about McCarthy and his eccentricities are part of Stanford legend and lore and have been for decades. He speaks only when he has something to say, and will occasionally walk away from questions that are asked of him—with no warning—only to return to the inquisitor several days later with an answer. The DOD used to get severely bent out of shape when McCarthy failed to write up progress reports on his government-funded projects; he always claimed he had something better to do.

For all his overt aloofness, McCarthy has always wanted to do something tangible with artificial intelligence. He was not content to reside among the Boston techno-Brahmins who were most interested in addressing the philosophical concerns and foundations of technology than putting it to work. Stanford, unlike MIT, gave him the opportunity to make intelligent systems that could be viewed, touched, and felt by the outside world. McCarthy and his acolytes wanted to show the world how artificial intelligence could be used practically, while MIT kept its AI work secretive and exclusive.

Not that McCarthy ignored the philosophical underpinnings of AI. Like Minsky, he felt that there were a number of issues that needed to be addressed in order to create a thinking machine. Yet he felt that it was less a question of psychology than one of logic, and that incremental developments in applying logic machines could help to further the progress of AI research. McCarthy felt that most thinking problems really were issues of logic, while Minsky felt that logic was only a tiny part of the answer. Minsky's view also leaned toward the premise that AI wasn't ready until it had successfully answered all the tough questions, and the use of logic was only the first answer to many questions.

Unfortunately, beliefs like Minsky's tend to prevent much practical work from happening in the research stages. In context, this would have been similar to telling Henry Ford to hold off on producing any cars in the early 1900s until he had perfected the mechanisms for power windows and airbags. Ford, and others, knew better than this, realizing that any primitive form of the product was better than no product at all. This same argument was soon championed by the West Coast AI contingent, which knew that the technology could be put to use while it was still being developed.

John McCarthy's second AI lab was informally called SAIL, the Stanford Artificial Intelligence Laboratory. Founded in 1963, it was created to support the Stanford AI Project, which was designed by McCarthy specifically to build an intelligent machine by the mid-1970s. The project, like AI research at MIT, would be based on McCarthy's LISP language, and would take advantage of his experience in computer time-sharing.

McCarthy put the word about SAIL out to various members of the fledgling AI community, inviting them to join him in the pastoral and relatively non-political environment of Northern California. Although Uncle John was well-liked at MIT, few people took him up on his offer. There was a belief at MIT that one—and only one—place could truly cultivate the atmosphere necessary for intense AI research, and it happened to be in Cambridge, Massachusetts. Stanford might be offering more money and better weather, but it wasn't "tough" enough for the hackers who were camping out on the tile floors of the MIT AI Lab. It would require a huge leap of faith for someone from MIT to follow McCarthy and, in effect, break the chains of loyalty as he had. In the mid-1960s, no one was prepared to be that foolish, or perhaps that brave.

Instead, the California sunshine and McCarthy's reputation had a magnetic effect on a completely different area of the country: Pittsburgh, Pennsylvania.

❧

Alan Newell and Herbert Simon had gone back to work for The RAND Corporation and Carnegie-Mellon University after the Dartmouth Conference with the feeling that they were really quite a bit further along in their research than their younger colleagues from the Northeast. Simon continued his work as a consultant to RAND, and he and Newell pursued various AI projects together when time permitted. As noted earlier, they developed the General Problem Solver, but that program would prove to be their last great contribution to AI research. Instead, they were destined to become the "grand old men" of AI (although many at CMU consider them to be the true "Fathers of Artificial Intelligence") and foster a new generation of apprentices and students who would carry on the fruits of their work in the manufacturing haven of Pittsburgh.

Simon taught a number of classes at CMU and indoctrinated many of his students into the ways of AI, albeit on a relatively theoretical level. CMU in the very early 1960s did not yet have the computer clout or brainpower that MIT had. Rather, it was oriented more towards manufacturing automation and industrial concerns than were the research purists at MIT. If corporate America wanted to build a new factory using the latest technologies, it went to Carnegie-Mellon. The attitude there was one of "Give us a problem and we'll find the answer" coupled with an emphasis on solving existing business problems. CMU was a school where "Can do, Chief!" and rolled-up shirt sleeves were the expected responses to any challenge.

Amongst Simon's students, one who showed particular interest in AI was Edward Feigenbaum. He had been at CMU in 1956 when Newell and Simon developed the Logic Theorist and had assisted Simon in his later work on the General Program Solver and the Information Processing Language. Young master Feigenbaum's area of study was cognitive psychology, and he agreed with Simon that machines could be used to mimic certain cognitive functions. Under Simon's tutelage, Feigenbaum began spending lots of quality time on CMU's computer. In particular, Feigenbaum was interested in developing a computer program that could mimic the decision-making processes of business people. The idea fit in well with CMU's industrial bias, and Feigenbaum proceeded to work on a program that might be able to demonstrate some of the underlying psychological principles of decision-making. The result was a program called EPAM (Elementary Perceiver And Memorizer), which ultimately had much more to do with psychology than business. EPAM was a simple program that showed that certain "thinking processes" involving memorization could be simulated on a computer.

Looking to make a mark in the psychology field, Feigenbaum went out into the world with EPAM, only to find yawning indifference. He spent time in London as a Fulbright scholar (where he became friends with Seymour Papert, whose future alliance with Marvin Minsky was still some years away), and at the University of California at Berkeley as a teacher. Neither place fully accepted his ideas on AI or put much stock in EPAM, but Berkeley did give him free rein to create the first AI textbook, a compendium of papers published in 1963 entitled *Computers and Thought.*

Not pleased with the reception he was getting in trying to peddle the ideas underlying EPAM in the psychological field, Feigenbaum switched gears and jumped into computer science. Almost immediately, John McCarthy asked Feigenbaum to come down from Berkeley to Stanford in 1965 to help run the computer science department, an invitation based in part on Ed's activity in artificial intelligence. After only two years at Stanford, McCarthy was feeling the pinch of administering a computer organization and being involved in such distasteful things as politics and applying for funding—the very same things that he had hoped to leave behind at MIT. He wanted and needed more time to work on AI, and to spend less time as an administrator. Thus, within a matter of months, the task of running the entire Stanford computer center fell by default into Feigenbaum's hands, and McCarthy moved into a lab off-campus. This arrangement gave Feigenbaum more autonomy and McCarthy more privacy and suited both men perfectly.

He didn't know it then, but John McCarthy had put Edward Feigenbaum into the driver's seat of the AI business. From his position of power and influence at Stanford, Ed would eventually start two of the largest AI companies in the world and unleash the biggest Japanese scare in the American military since Pearl Harbor.

❧

Though only a few years younger than Marvin Minsky, Edward Feigenbaum is considered part of a separate generation of artificial intelligence researchers. The first generation consisted primarily of the 1956 Dartmouth Conference attendees. The second generation included people who were disciples of Newell and Simon, Minsky, and McCarthy—the men who made up the first generation. The second generation individuals differed from the first in two ways: They were using computers from the outset of their research, which was a luxury that the first generation did not have (since computers weren't always readily available), and they saw the commercial potential of the work they were doing, which totally escaped the research-funding mentality of the first generation.

While McCarthy was ceding control of the Stanford lab to up-and-comer Ed Feigenbaum, Minsky was overseeing a bunch of MIT students and even fellow professors who themselves were eager to make their mark in the AI community. The leader among the student contingent at MIT was Richard Greenblatt. Even though he was no longer technically a student after being booted for failing his courses, Greenblatt was still held in high esteem by his fellow hackers, and his scholastic status was of little importance to them. After flunking out, Greenblatt was hired as an employee to work in the MIT lab, using money from Project MAC. Most of his time was devoted to tweaking the LISP programming language so that it would run on MIT's computers, thereby facilitating more AI work on the part of other programmers. When not immersed in LISP code, Greenblatt was beholden to another MIT technical quest: the intelligent chess-playing machine. From roughly 1964 to 1966, it would be his own personal crusade to build the machine that could beat a human chess player.

While such pursuits did little in the way of advancing the practicality of AI, especially as it applied to the Department of Defense, Greenblatt was not the only one at MIT guilty of what could be considered frivolous endeavors. No one in the lab was creating practical applications that would necessarily find their way into general or commercial use; but then again, they weren't necessarily supposed to. They were chasing the big questions and trying to find out what machines could do at certain levels of "alleged" thinking. Practical considerations were to be handled at a later date, presumably by DARPA.

An innocent bystander at MIT who contributed a great deal to making the machines act like real humans during this time was Joseph Weizenbaum. A faculty member who had been a computer programmer at General Electric , Weizenbaum had a keen interest in both psychology and language, especially the way that language could be modified and interpreted to form both questions and answers based on context. In his spare time—Weizenbaum was not a part of Project MAC—he created small programs that could answer simple questions that were phrased in English and not written in computer code. A question such as "What is your name?" would trigger a response from the computer based on the words "your" and "name." The computer was programmed to recognize that the word "your" in a question referred to the computer itself. "Name" would trigger the appropriate term for the computer (almost all lab-based computers are given names by their users). The machine could then answer something like "My name is Hal."

Weizenbaum took this basic question-and-answer procedure quite a bit further, gradually applying his interest in psychology to the program. With the help of Stanford psychiatrist Kenneth Colby, Weizenbaum created a question-and-answer program called ELIZA that mimicked a psychotherapist talking to a patient. A user, acting as the patient, would type a statement such as "I'm depressed" into the computer. ELIZA would lock on to the syntax of the sentence, noting that "I" referred to the user and that "depressed" was a verb. It could then rephrase the syntax to ask a question of its own: "Why are you depressed?"

The use of terms such as "no" or "not" by the user would trigger computer statements such as "You are being a bit negative" or "Are you saying 'no' just to be negative?" These replies sounded exactly like the ambiguous and faintly bemused comments one would expect to get from a psychiatrist. ELIZA also engaged in mind games that got it through difficult passages or questions from the user, using key phrases like "Why do you ask?" or "Is that why you came to me?" or "Please go on." These innocuous comments got it out of situations it was not programmed to respond to.

Weizenbaum didn't design ELIZA to be a quasi-professional shrink; he used it as a demonstration program. In fact, after a few minutes with ELIZA, most users could trick the machine into making ridiculous statements or into repeating itself. Nonetheless, the program gave the distinct impression to the uninitiated of the mid-1960s that there was something more than plastic and steel behind the blinking lights of the computer. To all outward appearances, ELIZA was asking questions and making comments as if it truly understood the conversation it was having with the user.

In truth, ELIZA's only intelligence was in being able to manipulate words to give the illusion of thought. It understood nothing of the actual words or their meaning, but it did understand basic rules of grammar and sentence structure. This language orientation of ELIZA gave Weizenbaum the inspiration for the program's name; it was in honor of the character Eliza Doolittle in the novel *Pygmalion* and the musical *My Fair Lady*, the peasant woman who learns the idiosyncrasies of language to raise her status in life.

ELIZA was a step forward for computers in the 1960s in that it showed how they might be programmed to recognize the grammar, context, and relationships of normal conversation. This normal conversation, called natural language in the computer community, was much more desirable than communicating with machines via strange lines of code or bizarre technical jargon. Unfortunately, computers are designed to respond to these unusual instructions and not to normal conversation; it is how they are built. Yet, the pursuit of communicating with computers via natural language will figure prominently later in our story.

Interestingly, Joseph Weizenbaum and Kenneth Colby had a falling out over ELIZA. Weizenbaum was—and still is—skeptical of what AI can do, and he downplayed the ability of ELIZA to be anything more than a game or a demonstration of basic language capabilities in machines. Colby, however, felt that the software could be used for actual therapy, allowing individuals access to the benefits of psychotherapy in the privacy of their own home. Colby went on to promote ELIZA as a bona fide machine therapist, although he changed the system's name to DOCTOR.

Today, ELIZA is available as an inexpensive game that runs on any personal computer. Despite the fact that it is nearly thirty years old, it still provides those who have never encountered AI with a glimmer of the possibilities to be found in the technology. There are even those that continue to argue, as Colby did, that some people are more comfortable talking to a computer because it won't judge them as another person might. They might be inclined to be more forthright and honest about what they are thinking when dealing with an inanimate object. Therefore, the argument goes, these people are better off using a machine-based program like ELIZA than spending $100 an hour for a therapist. Freud would probably have a lot to say about that.

Weizenbaum's concerns about language did strike a responsive chord among others at MIT. It was clear that a thinking machine had to be able to act logically and also understand nuances of communication. Since conversational—or natural—language is the most common form of communication in humans, an intelligent computer would also have to be able to use this same type of language to communicate with people.

One of Minsky's students, a doctoral candidate named Daniel Bobrow, tackled natural language and logic together in a program he called STUDENT in 1964. The goal of STUDENT was to interpret mathematical word problems and solve them. Bobrow took word problems specifically from algebra and broke them down into their component parts for his program, using tried and true staples such as "Jean's mother's aunt is twice as old as Jean's mother. In two years, Jean's mom will be three times as old as Jean. The sum of their ages is 92. How old is Jean today?" This is the kind of word problem that separates the mathematically impaired from the true math fans in high school, and Bobrow found that his STUDENT behaved at about the high school level.

The important goal for Bobrow's program was that it had to be able to understand relationships within the problem. It was programmed to understand that Jean, Jean's mother, and her mother's aunt all had ages, all of which were different. Each age would also have to have a numerical value. The words "twice as" and "three times" represented mathematical equations. In this way, STUDENT could take the basics of a word problem and break it down into a workable algebraic problem. Though limited in scope because it could only solve certain types of word problems, STUDENT was one of the first programs to combine two components necessary for mimicking humans: reasoning and language.

Yet STUDENT was still experimental in that it only laid preliminary groundwork for some unknown application to be developed down the road. At MIT this was part of the plan. At Stanford, it was not.

～

Stanford attracted a wide variety of researchers and scientists in the 1960s, readily establishing it as a haven where an individual studying, say, the acoustic principles of electronic music could converse with a biologist on one of the many benches dotting the campus. Cross-fertilization of ideas was encouraged and fostered.

Joshua Lederberg, a Stanford researcher who had scored a Nobel Prize for genetics, became interested in Edward Feigenbaum's notions of imitating human decision-making on a computer. One of the tools of Lederberg's trade was the mass spectrometer, a device used to analyze organic compounds and determine their molecular structure. Essentially, the instrument determines the basic chemical makeup of a compound by identifying its various atomic charges, but it cannot specify how the molecules are linked together or what the actual structure is. In this way, it is equivalent to having all the parts of a car laid out on a floor, but not being told how they fit together or what kind of car they will finally form. A chemist must take the component data from a mass spectrometer, knowing that it does indeed form a complete compound, and then determine how this data fits together. It results in a trial and error process of oftentimes excruciating complexity, and ultimately all the pieces do fit together, but only in one way. For instance (using our car metaphor again), the researcher might decide to build a Ferrari from all the car parts based on all the data he has, but may find that after the Ferrari is complete, a few extra screws and body panels are still lying on the floor. It may take multiple attempts, but eventually he will realize that the parts fit together perfectly to form a Lamborghini.

Lederberg, who had little working knowledge of computers, suspected that

Feigenbaum's ideas could be used to help chemists by having computers make decisions about mass spectrometer data. He approached Feigenbaum in 1965 with a proposal for developing a system that would make the same type of decisions that chemists did when they were presented with the analysis from a mass spectrometer. Feigenbaum eagerly agreed to work with Lederberg, and they set out to develop their program.

They named the system DENDRAL, a name derived from the Greek word for tree. The term related to the decision tree and its branches, which must be searched in order to find an answer to a problem. All of the different possibilities represented the branches of the tree, and the answer to a specific problem lay at the end of only one branch. But as our car builder found out, many different branches had to be explored in order to come to the proper conclusion, which meant a lot of time backtracking after reaching various dead ends. It was this "search through the tree" that DENDRAL was going to speed up and hopefully automate, doing the work of a chemist in far less time with the same accuracy.

Feigenbaum and Lederberg began their work by encoding certain facts into the computer about mass spectrometer data. Relationships between these facts were also programmed into DENDRAL in the form of rules or truisms, such as, "If a compound contains a carbonyl group and possesses at least one hydrogen atom covalently bonded to the carbon atom, then it is an aldehyde." These rules ran the gamut from simple and obvious chemical knowledge to extremely complicated rules regarding the valences and atoms and the mass-to-charge ratio of ions. Many of these rules could have been taken directly from chemical texts and reports and encoded directly into DENDRAL, which then might have acted as an interactive encyclopedia of chemical knowledge. That, however, was not what Feigenbaum was attempting to do. He wanted to recreate the thinking process of chemical experts, who do not have to look up every law of chemistry in a textbook each time they analyze mass spectrometer data. It was more important to capture the essence of the human decision-making process in DENDRAL than to have it search exhaustively through each rule it encountered. This was not what experts did, and it was not what DENDRAL would do.

Feigenbaum then hit on the rarely explored notion that human experts often rely on facts and rules that aren't part of the textbook approach to solving problems. They rely on certain rules that they have created for themselves based on their own experience. This ability to use experience appropriately is what made these people experts in the first place. If not for their expertise, they would have to look up all their information in reference works just like amateurs or inexperienced personnel. This expertise is unique to them as individuals and could best be described as "gut feelings" or "rules of thumb" that they employ in their daily work, often without giving it much thought. The technical term for these feelings or unstated rules is "heuristics." Feigenbaum realized that heuristics plays a huge part in the decision-making process of chemical experts, and their own particular heuristics helps them do their jobs better than non-experts. For instance, experts often have to make educated guesses when they encounter vague or conflicting data. Their decisions, or choices, are then based on intuition and heuristics, since the data they have does not lead them to any particular conclusion.

In observing chemists who made decisions that were not based on textbook-style facts and procedures, Ed Feigenbaum asked them how they arrived at such decisions. Frequently, the answer was something ambiguous along the lines of "That's just the way I do it," or "I don't know, it just seems like the right way to go." Clearly, their heuristic knowledge was operating at a level below the surface of their more obvious thoughts, but the heuristics were integral to the complex web of activities that were involved in human thinking.

Feigenbaum began encoding this heuristic information by interviewing the experts during the decision-making process. His "Why did you do that?" questions soon bore fruit when he tapped into replies that demonstrated the chemists' rules of thumb. Back to putting our car pieces together, the expert knows that the steering wheel doesn't get connected to the fender, even though there is no specific rule or law stating that this is true (perhaps because it is "obvious"). He knows, from experience, that fenders and steering wheels aren't linked, so he doesn't take fenders or their related parts into consideration when assembling the steering mechanism. In a scientific mode, such knowledge can be phrased plainly: "I know that I can skip this particular line of inquiry because the mass spectrometer showed me the presence of X, and this inquiry is designed primarily to establish the presence of Y, which I am not interested in at this time."

Heuristics, however, are not universal truths. They apply specifically to a given task or job. A baker knows that icing goes on a cake after it is baked, a painter knows that you don't attempt to use sandpaper on wet paint, a plumber knows that water flows downhill. All of these are heuristics which apply to particular professions, but they have absolutely no bearing on the other jobs described. Thus, heuristics are not a set of laws or maxims that can be applied to all decision-making processes. Heuristics have to be tailored to specific tasks.

Feigenbaum called DENDRAL an "expert system" because its purpose was to emulate a human expert in a particular field. It contained much of the expertise that a human had and could accurately mimic that expert's method of problem solving. DENDRAL and future expert systems would be based not just on facts, but on facts coupled with heuristics, which formed the basis of an expert's practical knowledge. This use of knowledge in developing a computer program led many people to refer to Feigenbaum's expert system as a "knowledge-based system." The two terms are used interchangeably today.

What finally emerged from the work on DENDRAL, which lasted nearly a decade, was a system that knew how to analyze mass spectrometer data— and nothing else. It could not play chess, and it could not solve algebra word problems. It was, in effect, an idiot savant. It knew how to do one thing extremely well, but could do absolutely nothing else. There was no problem with this; DENDRAL wasn't designed to do anything else.

The rest of the AI community saw things differently, however. One of the concepts that drove Newell and Simon's development of the General Problem Solver, and even some of MIT's research, was that a true AI program should be able to solve any problems put to it simply by the way it was structured. The methodology was the important consideration in thinking, not the area of expertise. AI researchers thus believed in form over content: once form was validated, content could be easily plugged in. It was like constructing the framework of a house. As long as the exterior was stable and structurally viable, then specific rooms of any type could added to the interior at a later date.

DENDRAL, though, demonstrated that content was at least as important as form, if not more important. It didn't really matter how the machine arrived at its answers, as long as it had all the appropriate data with which to make a decision. Furthermore, that data couldn't easily be structured in a logical way because it depended in every situation on specific heuristics.

This revelation threw a monkey wrench into the conventional wisdom of the 1960s' AI community. If DENDRAL was indeed a smart system, but could only do one thing well, did it actually possess intelligence? Didn't intelligence involve more than being an idiot savant? For that matter, did idiot savants of the human variety possess intelligence? It all boiled down to one thing: what exactly was intelligence?

The question of what constituted intelligence—which by some miracle of faith or ego had never really been put to the test before—suddenly caused AI researchers to rethink exactly what it was they were pursuing. Debate about the nature of intelligence and thinking soon began in a friendly way during seminars and informal get-togethers, with all interested parties believing that they could come to some kind of agreement over time. The issue of what intelligence really was seemed to be nothing more than a little intramural squabble between AI factions that would be cleared up in no time at all. It was still all in the family, where it belonged.

By the mid-1960s, however, AI was no longer being developed in a vacuum, and like some strange lab experiment, it started to attract the curious stares of other researchers. Some were computer scientists who couldn't quite believe that the AI community was really trying to get big IBM computers to think like humans. Others were psychologists who were still trying to figure out the human mind for themselves. Still others ranged from biologists to theologians who didn't quite know what to make of this attempt to give machines human characteristics. Plus, these were not just any human characteristics; they were the ones that helped define and separate man from the rest of the universe.

More than a few people thought that the AI researchers were charlatans similar to the wizards and magicians of old, with their brazen heads and metal maidens. In the normally restrained politeness of academia, words like "fraud" and "liar" began to rear their heads in intellectual conversation. The whole concept of artificial intelligence gradually came under attack from various corners of the research world, and many AI researchers found themselves with their backs up against the wall, defending their work and their careers in the face of a modern-day Spanish Inquisition. And, perhaps not unexpectedly, the most harmful attack came from two brothers who had defected to the University of California at Berkeley from—where else?—the Massachusetts Institute of Technology.

8

Can Machines Think? Better Yet, Should They?

The Philosophy of AI

Can machines think? This is the one question that motivates the world's artificial intelligence community. The answer is yes. Or no. Or maybe. It depends on who you talk to.

A still bigger question than that of the possibility of thinking machines has baffled and intrigued mankind since Day One. That question is "What is thinking?" This question is oftentimes accompanied by the equally puzzling "How does man think?" After all, if we are to believe that a machine can think, don't we first have to know what thinking actually is?

All of these questions have their roots in philosophy, man's favorite intellectual pastime for the last fifteen hundred years. Philosophy deals with three major issues: man, his mind, and God. It attempts to explain the relationships between these three in a way that makes them understandable and easier to live with. These relationships can be narrowed down to first, man's relationship with other men as part of mankind; second, man's relationship with his own mind; amd third, man's relationship with God. All other philosophical and social discussions derive from these three relationships, including issues such as free will, morality, personal identity, the existence of good and evil, heaven and hell, and all the other heady concerns that people struggle with then they aren't worried about other things, such as making a living for paying the rent.

ॐ

This chapter could have been either the longest one in the book you are now reading, or one of the shortest. Because there are thousands, maybe even hundreds of thousands, of books that have thoroughly investigated the fundamentals of philosophy, I have opted to make this among the shorter chapters. All the great arguments on thinking can be found in other books, and rehashing them here would neither break new ground nor serve any purpose except to add mind-numbing pages of text to this particular chapter. To give you the background for our big question, though, I'll give you a sampling of the various schools of thought, so to speak, on thinking. It will be a brief detour from our story, I assure you.

Philosophy by its very nature is not an exact science, and it is open to interpretation by all who choose to indulge in it. To complicate things further, philosophies come in two types: personal and social. Our own personal philosophies affect how we perceive the world around us and how we act in that world. Social philosophies, on the other hand, are the basis for governments, laws, and group behavior and interaction. No single philosophy of either type is constant, and they all change from country to country and person to person.

One relatively constant aspect of philosophy is that people tend to believe that their personal philosophies are right, and opposing philosophies are wrong. This is not always true, but a lot of people are willing to die for the belief that their philosophies are the right ones. When it comes to philosophies of the mind, though, people are less inclined to give up their lives defending ideas that have very little tangible representation and cannot be proven to exist. These people are, however, quite happy to argue about it for years at a time, the louder the better.

No one really knows what the mind is, mostly because we can't take it out and dissect it or break it down into small working parts without killing it. This tends to defeat the purpose of an investigation. We do, as a species, generally believe that the mind is where the action of thinking takes place, and that physically the mind resides somewhere inside the brain.

That's all we know. That's it.

Some people get paid to study the mind and the process of thinking. Getting paid, however, is about the only qualification they possess that separates them from the common man in terms of knowing exactly what goes on in the three pounds of gray matter that sits inside your skull. These people have thought more about thinking than most of the rest of us, just as priests think more about God than the rest of us, but they don't really know factually more than we do about thinking. No one knows it all, which should give some people pause to stop and think. There are so many theories about thinking that almost everybody qualifies in their own way as an expert on the mind. Most of us just don't put it on our resumes.

From a purely physical perspective, the study of the brain as a biological entity has resulted in impressive findings over the last several decades about which parts of that organ are responsible for certain activities related to thinking. This is especially evident in pictures taken via a technology called positron emission tomography (PET), which shows glucose activity in the brain during specific mental processes such as remembering or solving a puzzle. Still, we don't know how images and words are transformed into thoughts or memories. We don't know where those memories are stored, why they are stored, or most importantly, how they are recalled at the time they are summoned. And what part of the brain is doing the summoning, anyway? (The hippocampus is the current favorite in popular scientific literature.) As you can see, we're dealing with a lot of ambiguity and uncertainty here.

Yet the processes involved in thinking have been studied by the most respected minds (pun somewhat intended) in history. Their names read like an alphabet soup of great philosophers past and almost present: Aquinas, Aristotle, Descartes, Hegel, Heidegger, Hobbes, Hume, Kant, Kierkegaard, Leibniz, Locke, Mill, Nietzche, Pascal, Plato, Pythagoras, Rousseau, Russell, Sartre, Schopenhauer, Socrates, Spinoza, Voltaire, Whitehead, and Wittgenstein. All of these men had opinions on what thinking and intelligence is, and very few of them agreed completely with any of the others. Their individual and unique thoughts on the philosophies of man and his mind have distinguished them from the run-of-the-mill thinkers and from each other and have entitled each to his own cult of personality in various college curriculums and academic pursuits.

Regardless of the philosophies of these particular men, there are some basically accepted ideas about what thinking is, and how it relates to intelligence and knowledge. In essence, thinking is an activity that we associate specifically with intelligence. The stripped-down dictionary definition of thinking is the "ability to reason, remember experiences, and make rational decisions." Intelligence, on the other hand, is "the capacity for learning, reasoning, understanding, and similar forms of mental activity" as well as "an aptitude for grasping truths, relationships, facts, and meanings." Finally, knowledge can be described as "acquaintance with facts, truths, or principles, as derived from study or investigation." We can group these together in a hierarchy: intelligence is dependent upon thinking, and thinking in turn is dependent upon knowledge. In purely mechanical terms, intelligence is the car, thinking is the engine, and knowledge is the gas.

Yet nowhere in our definitions do we see that these are traits limited to the minds of humans. For instance, animals must make decisions based on their own forms of knowledge. A dog chasing a cat must determine whether to cross the street and catch the cat right now, or wait until an oncoming car has gone past. Not very intellectual, but it is still a process that requires knowledge (an oncoming car is dangerous) and thinking (the cat will still be on the other side of the street, even though the car has obscured the view of it). Most people also agree that certain mammals have relatively high intelligence, especially gorillas and dolphins. So we can accept that intelligence and its attendant components, thinking and knowledge, are not limited to humans. If humans and animals have intelligence, what is keeping it from being possessed by machines?

The problem is that thinking in animals still occurs in the brain, an organ about which we know very little. It is an organ, and it is alive, but our understanding of this living thing relative to thinking is still feeble. Brains, alive or dead, are substantially different than manufactured components made out of silicon or steel. Intelligence, by popular consent, resides in living tissue and not in inorganic factory products. We have observed intelligence in living things since the dawn of time, and we have an innate understanding of this intelligence, probably because we can relate to it. But never has a nonliving thing—a rock or a window, for instance—demonstrated intelligence, nor do we expect it to. After all, nonliving things don't have brains.

The only way we can appreciate the possibility of machine intelligence is to realize that life-based intelligence may not be the only kind. Why does intelligence have to be limited to entities with brains? As Alan Turing argued, if a machine "brain" can do all the things that a human brain can, wouldn't that constitute a similar form of intelligence? Without worrying about consciousness and immortal souls—another whole set of books we won't be condensing here—a computer that reasons and uses knowledge like a person is displaying something akin to our dictionary definition of intelligence. Given this fact, maybe we need to reevaluate what intelligence is.

There is much more to all of this than a simplistic picture of organic and inorganic intelligence. People supplement their intelligence with a host of other facilities unrelated to out-and-out thinking as it applies to the logic functions of a brain. Emotions, pain, pleasure, and experience all serve as components—although they are based on sensory experience—that contribute to comprehensive human intelligence. These are things that again are considered to be the personal property of higher mammals, especially humans. Most importantly, this is the area where most people believe that machine intelligence diverges substantially from human intelligence because an inanimate object cannot produce these typically organic activities. Whereas many thinking processes can be schematically mapped out and observed via various forms of logic, such as predicate calculus, we have no methodology for mapping out emotions. No mapping mechanism; hence, no way to get them into a computer.

Or so goes the primary argument against complete machine intelligence. Those who view thinking machines as an inevitability have a different view, as you can imagine. This faction argues that emotions, as well as response to pleasure and pain, are the end result of complex chemical processes. These processes are governed by laws of physics and will ultimately be mapped out so that they can be simulated at will. Researchers of this camp point to the use of mood-altering drugs and medication to establish certain emotional levels in individuals, especially those with mental and physical imbalances and disorders. It is only a matter of time, they argue, before emotions can be completely controlled and created through chemistry. If this is the case, such chemical processes can then be moved outside of the human body and applied to machines. This could be in the form of actual chemical applications, or as programmed information about the reactions caused by the chemicals. This information could then be encoded in a computer to simulate specific processes such as elation or depression. The end result? Computerized love, lust, pity, passion, anger, and angst. Everything necessary to complete the foundation for intelligence, right? Yes. No. Maybe.

Both sides have reasonable and unreasonable arguments. History favors those that do not believe a machine can ever think, while technology has quickly become the willing and able tool of those who are determined to create artificial intelligence. Even in the AI business, researchers from both sides have been known to switch sides after a few years of intensive labor and introspection.

So while people like Minsky and McCarthy firmly believe that someday there will be artificial intelligence—even if they disagree on the methods of achieving it—other people just as firmly believe it will never happen. Machines will never think, no matter what. In this latter category are the two renegades from MIT who took their heresy to Berkeley: the Brothers Dreyfus, Hu and Stu. We resume our story to find them in the early stages of their fervent quest to expose AI researchers as a bunch of frauds.

Heretics

AI as Smoke and Mirrors

For the better part of AI's first ten years, no one challenged the idea that machines could be made to think; it was deemed inevitable. Most people were so in awe of the massive computers that were being used to help run companies and to make government work more efficiently that they didn't have reason to question computing's potential. It was taken for granted in the brave new world of the technology-based 1960s that marvels ranging from flying cars to artificial intelligence were just a few years away.

In the same climate that produced manned space missions, live TV broadcasts, and other accomplishments far beyond what was thought possible a decade before, the earliest AI researchers jumped on the optimism bandwagon with little or no thought to the possible consequences. The phrase "ten years" became the catch-all that was applied throughout the industry, as in, "We can accomplish just about everything that can ever be accomplished in the next ten years." While not willing to go quite so far as to make this particular claim (in a rare example of self-restraint), the AI community still did not hesitate to use the magic ten years as fuel for the fire of its goals. Newell and Simon predicted that systems based on artificial intelligence would be world chess champions within ten years of 1957, and that such machines would also be investigating mathematics and creating art and music on a level equal to or greater than their human counterparts. Stanford's AI project planned on developing a thinking machine with government funding by the early 1970s, and Marvin Minsky claimed that most of the problems associated with creating artificial intelligence would be solved in a relatively short time. He even asserted, wrongly, that when it came to neural networks, he had already solved all of the difficult basic problems associated with the technology, leaving little else to be investigated. Such was the hubris of the AI pioneers well into the 1960s.

This absurdly naive but prevailing belief that computers could accomplish almost anything helped to keep those who might criticize artificial intelligence at bay. A few dissenting opinions were heard, usually via academic papers or speeches that received little attention. In general, the dissenters were ignored, since they ran against the prevailing wisdom regarding AI. Like the doomsayers who were scoffed at just prior to the stock market crash of 1987, no one wanted to listen to party poopers.

Hubert Dreyfus didn't mind being a party pooper. In fact, he seemed to be the kind of guy who would spoil the fun just for the sake of doing it. He might even manage to draw attention to himself in the process. The convenient thing was that he was on the faculty at MIT, which meant that he was already guaranteed an invitation to the fun.

Dreyfus is a difficult man to understand, in the same way that it is difficult to understand the motivations of people like Rush Limbaugh or Morton Downey, Jr. (remember him?). These are people who make their reputations based on their uncanny ability to irritate and agitate, to get under people's skins and gnaw at their sensitive spots like unchained pit bulls. They have a basic understanding of the issues, perhaps even a correct understanding, but they use this more to their own benefit than to further any cause. For instance, does anyone really believe that Rush Limbaugh is best known for his heartfelt personal convictions rather than for being a bombastic loudmouth? Highly doubtful. In the always tumultuous world of political commentary, a Limbaugh rises above the rest by dint of being both the most abrasive and the one making the most noise.

While such antics are usually reserved for those in the media, politics, and various religious factions, artificial intelligence in the gee-whiz 1960s was ripe for someone to make rude noises of a contrary kind. Hubert Dreyfus was the man for the job. What makes this so unusual is that in person Dreyfus is soft-spoken, even congenial.

Hubert and his brother Stuart Dreyfus were both working at MIT when Project MAC came to rest its benevolent pocketbook down at the doorstep of Marvin Minsky's fledgling AI lab in the early 1960s. Minsky himself was just going into full promotional mode, and Newell and Simon were staking their reputations on their aggressive assertions about the probable future of AI. While many AI researchers were claiming that the goals and timetables of achieving true computer intelligence—within the next ten years—were right on track, the Dreyfus brothers weren't buying it. Not for a minute.

Hubert Dreyfus was a young MIT professor of philosophy in 1961. As you might guess, philosophy—and even humanities study in general—is not among MIT's better-known scholastic offerings. Most of MIT's students would probably prefer intensive weekend courses in quantum physics to being forced to sit through even rudimentary philosophy lectures. Humanities as a body of study is a wayward child at MIT, and is spoken of with a smirk and a knowing smile.

Thus, from the outset of his career, Dreyfus was not exactly part and parcel of all those engineering and mathematical pursuits for which MIT is so highly respected. However, when the school started dabbling in the concepts of creating a machine that could think, Dreyfus found a cause that was near and dear to his heart. After all, he was teaching philosophy, and what is philosophy if not the study of thinking? The technical geeks were treading on his territory now. And, as a humanities anomaly in a school dedicated to the "pure" sciences, Dreyfus also found the issue of thinking machines a pedestal from which to berate the barbarians and their computers.

Not that he had always frowned on his scientist peers. Dreyfus had actually studied physics as an undergrad at Harvard before deciding to switch to philosophy. This was a bigger leap than the jump that Minsky made from physics to mathematics at Harvard, but Dreyfus managed to make the transition smoothly. From Harvard to MIT was a short career jaunt down the street in Cambridge, and it was there that he began teaching his beloved philosophy to a bunch of kids that worshipped at the altar of new science. It wasn't the rambunctious kids that Dreyfus found the most difficult to handle, though; it was his academic peers.

Neither Hubert nor Stuart Dreyfus, who was a little less verbal in his disagreement with the MIT artificial intelligence group, could believe that serious researchers were wasting their time and efforts pursuing a goal that could never be accomplished. As far as the Dreyfuses were concerned, there could be no emulation of human intelligence without all of the attendant biological human components, especially a body. People learned and thought in the context of their world and their specific environments. Learning, then, required having a body with which to experience the world. The body and the senses all contributed to intelligence. Therefore, intelligence required a complete being.

The Brothers Dreyfus anticipated arguments against intelligence and its relationship to the body, and prepared for them. If perchance intelligence was only limited to the mind, and didn't need the body, then our whole idea of intelligence in humans was wrong anyway, argued the Dreyfuses. If this was indeed the case, intelligence needed to be redefined; and, if it needed to be redefined, then the current research into AI was based on the flawed existing definition and was itself misguided. A perfect catch-22 was in effect, they reasoned. Thus, pursuing machine intelligence was a no-win situation as laid out by the Dreyfus brothers.

Like spies inside of enemy lines, the Dreyfuses began to attack the status quo at MIT. The first provocation was in 1961, when the two attended various lectures held on the MIT campus to promote awareness of AI. These lectures featured homegrown pioneers like Minsky, as well as respected outsiders such as Herbert Simon. Hubert Dreyfus found Simon's discussions on the ability to create models of memory in computers especially ludicrous and decided to make a public statement about his opposition to Simon's work.

Hubert Dreyfus wrote a rebuttal to Simon's speeches. Somehow, he and Stuart managed to get the rebuttal inserted into the printed transcripts of the lectures. When the copies of the speeches were published at the end of the lecture series, there was the Dreyfus rebuttal included right along with them. This happened even though neither of the Dreyfuses had made a presentation during the actual sessions.

Having accomplished an end-run around standard protocol—one is supposed to speak at a symposium or conference before one's ideas are published in the proceedings—Hubert Dreyfus greatly irritated those who had actually made presentations. Not only were the Dreyfuses disagreeing with the speakers, but they had gotten their views aired without working through the proper channels. It was a direct affront to the lab work that the AI community was trying to promote, and most researchers took an immediate dislike to the brothers, with Hubert attracting the lion's share of the disdain.

But knowing that people were angered by his views only served to motivate Dreyfus further. He had found the Achilles' heel of AI—its sensitivity to criticism—and he was determined to hack away at it.

His next opportunity came about due to the graciousness of Newell and Simon's benefactor, the RAND Corporation. RAND, as a large corporate research center, was in the habit of hiring various professors and academic researchers as consultants to assist in the publication of its topical reports on technologies. This kept RAND and its customers up-to-date on new research, and it provided the academics with an extra paycheck and some potential notoriety. Stuart Dreyfus had landed one of these plum consulting roles with RAND and suggested to his employers that his brother might be able to help the company in its investigation of artificial intelligence. Having received positive feedback from sponsoring Newell and Simon's Logic Theorist and General Problem Solver, RAND decided in 1964 to give Hubert Dreyfus a shot at developing some new AI perspectives.

It was Hubert's big chance. During his stint with RAND, he wrote a paper called "Alchemy and Artificial Intelligence," a general criticism of the work going on in the research community. In essence, Dreyfus compared AI to the centuries-old attempt to create gold through sorcery and medieval chemistry. The term "alchemy," since it implied a certain amount of primitive magic and charlatanism, was enough to send the intended targets into foaming fits of rage. This, of course, was the reaction that Dreyfus desired.

Popular history diverges at this point, and like all history, memories of the events tend to favor the teller of the tales. The report was published as a research memo by RAND in 1965, a relatively low-level offering compared to some of the company's more high-profile reports. Dreyfus counters by saying that the paper was the biggest-selling diatribe published by RAND up until that point in time. Various individuals associated with RAND, however, claim that they were embarrassed by the tone of Dreyfus' work, and were unaware of Dreyfus' preexisting antipathy towards the AI community. In addition, AI researchers such as Simon tried to dissuade RAND from publishing the work, feeling that it was not only somewhat slanderous but also poorly thought out.

Hubert Dreyfus had taken the same tack that was to prove so popular with Marvin Minsky and Seymour Papert a few years later in their assault on the concept of neural networks. Like those two, Dreyfus attacked some of the most primitive aspects of artificial intelligence technology without addressing the possibilities of more advanced systems. This was like laughing off the Model T as a form of transportation because it was only slightly faster than a horse. It missed the potential of such a vehicle to be improved upon over time, especially when it was used for specific applications such as racing. Dreyfus' approach was: "Why bother with AI since it currently can't accurately mimic human intelligence?"

Dreyfus' primary disagreement with AI researchers—whom he disparagingly referred to as the "artificial intelligentsia"—had to do with trying to separate mind from body. He agreed in principle that the brain and its various neural components were the center of thought and intelligence, and that computers might even be able to mimic some of the processes that occurred in the brain. However, he argued, intelligence is not limited to the chemical and electrical functions of the brain. Intelligence includes an awareness of the outside world—through the body and senses—which is not dependent upon the brain's physical structure. This is a "phenomenological" connection with the world that transcends the more mundane neurological and physical link to our environment.

Once he came back to earth from the rather mystical realm of phenomenology, Dreyfus actually hit on a more tangible concept that made his claims worth paying attention to. This concept is that of fringe consciousness, whereby humans deal with situations based not only on the obvious set of facts presented to them (navigating through traffic, for instance), but on a whole range of peripheral and unconscious information that is processed by the mind. Much of this peripheral data is immediately filtered by the mind (which is different than the brain, remember) according to its relevance and importance to the situation at hand. Driving through a heavily congested downtown street at lunch time may create a signal to the mind to beware of a higher density of pedestrian traffic, while the time of day or type of weather may have an effect on how good visibility is and how much caution needs to be exercised in this downtown traffic. The driver doesn't overtly think of these things—he or she is not aware of specific pedestrians or individual cars, but of all of them—and thus his or her awareness in this situation is operating at a fringe level of consciousness.

A more universal example, and one actually put forth by Dreyfus, has to do with our ability to hear sounds. People hear sounds, regardless of their source, as cohesive and understandable representations of audio frequencies. A single song is made up of hundreds and thousands of different combinations of frequencies, each generated at different levels of intensity and pitch. We do not interpret these frequencies as frequencies, per se, although that is what they are. We interpret them as a unified whole—namely, a song. It is our intelligence that turns these frequencies into recognizable sounds, even though we never give it a second thought.

Note that this idea of fringe consciousness is different than Edward Feigenbaum's notion of heuristics, and the two should not be confused. Heuristics are the mental functions that assist in making decisions based on facts and unspoken rules of thumb. Heuristics ultimately are rooted in experience or knowledge of relevant data, while fringe consciousness is based on a vague awareness of the events and obstacles in a specific situation. The individual then uses this level of consciousness to deal with specific situations.

The reliance on phenomenology in "Artificial Intelligence and Alchemy" prompted many of the AI academics to heap layer upon layer of derision upon Dreyfus' less-than-humble head. Phenomenology had been a core theory of certain philosophies in the mid-1900s, but had been widely panned and discarded as of the 1960s. Dreyfus' belief in phenomenology was held up as an example of his amateurishness and his being out of touch with advances made in the research of both technology and human behavior. The elite among the artificial intelligentsia all but laughed him out of town over phenomenology.

They also tried to shrug off his musings about fringe consciousness by claiming that he was making a mountain out of a molehill. Fringe consciousness, they retorted, was another aspect of intelligence that would eventually fall victim to improved methods of computer representation, whether mathematical or symbolic. Programming methods would be found to deal with inputting fringe consciousness into computers. It was only a matter of time.

Time, in this case, was on Dreyfus' side. As research progressed through the 1960s and into the 1970s, the codifying of fringe consciousness—as well as perception—proved to be an almost intractable problem. There was simply no easy way to program a computer to deal with things that were barely understood, let alone barely perceived, in any given situation. Too many random occurrences happened simultaneously (as in the traffic example), and no one was quite certain as to how and when these events affected decisions or conscious activities. If it was difficult to track this process in humans, it was even harder trying to program it into a computer. Dreyfus, then, had actually hit upon a crucial point that AI researchers were naively ignoring.

It was unfortunate that this point was lost in the bombast of Dreyfus' writings and speeches. The vitriol that he spewed in trying to make his case against AI was more intense than his message, and the persona of Hubert Dreyfus actually offset the credibility of his viable suppositions. The louder he screamed, the less people paid attention to him.

Yet, he was really just getting started.

His fellow academicians began to make life rather difficult for Dreyfus after the 1965 publication of "Artificial Intelligence and Alchemy." In the manner of school kids around the world, he was given the silent treatment by other members of the MIT faculty. The sole exception appears to have been Joseph Weizenbaum, the creator of the ELIZA psychologist program. Weizenbaum himself had difficulty buying into the entire AI elitist research mentality; he was particularly at odds with Marvin Minsky over some of the projects that MIT students and teachers were spending their time on. Almost by default, Weizenbaum was lumped into the same category as Dreyfus by the AI believers, even though Weizenbaum himself didn't particularly care for Dreyfus' methods or his ideas.

Weizenbaum disliked the childish squabbling that had become so dominant within the still young artificial intelligence community more than he disliked Dreyfus' ideas, however. It reeked too much of narrow-mindedness and showed a distinct lack of professionalism. (Weizenbaum himself would become persona non grata within the AI industry upon the publication in 1976 of his book *Computer Power and Human Reason*, which questioned the viability of AI's using then-current research methods.) Despite Weizenbaum's concerns about this behavior, many members of the AI community were just getting comfortable with the notion of institutionalized backbiting. Dreyfus was more than happy to egg them on.

The first cut, and perhaps the deepest to the pride of people like Minsky and Newell and Simon, was a mention of Dreyfus' "Alchemy and Artificial Intelligence" in *The New Yorker* magazine of June 11, 1966. Qualifying as perhaps the first mainstream media commentary on artificial intelligence research, *The New Yorker*'s "Talk of the Town" column made reference to a specific Dreyfus contention that computers could not be programmed to play chess well enough to beat any self-respecting human. In fact, Dreyfus pointed out, Newell and Simon's very own chess-playing expert had been beaten quite handily by a ten-year-old boy. *The New Yorker*—which was then at the peak of its intellectual popularity—made light of the computer's chess loss and threw its tongue-in-cheek support behind Dreyfus.

While it was all proper and professional to slander fellow academicians' reputations in technical journals, laying the issue before the public in one of the most highly respected magazines of the day was more than most AI researchers could bear. It was like airing dirty laundry in public, and the laundry happened to belong to AI pioneers like Newell and Simon. The gauntlet had been thrown down.

Seymour Papert picked up the gauntlet and threw it back in Dreyfus' face.

Papert devised a scheme that had the potential to really do some damage to Hubert's ego and perhaps get him to shut his mouth for good. He wanted to pit a computer's intelligence against Dreyfus' intelligence. Specifically, he wanted a computer to beat Dreyfus at a game of chess.

As mentioned earlier, MIT hacking icon Richard Greenblatt spent a great deal of his free time using MIT's computers to work on an intelligent chess player. Although he was no longer a student, the AI Lab had managed to give him a job under the auspices of Project MAC, and he spent as much time in the lab—if not more—than most students and professors. Greenblatt was both a superb programmer and an exceptional chess player, and his work towards combining the two resulted in a chess program called MacHack. It was a substantial improvement over the other chess programs that had come before it, including Newell and Simon's. Seymour Papert recognized Greenblatt's achievement and decided it was good enough to give Dreyfus a run for his money in a man-against-machine competition.

Papert enticed Dreyfus to come to the AI Lab in mid-1967 to play chess against MacHack. Dreyfus, ego in full gear, could not resist the invitation, and showed up ready to put the AI group into its place once and for all. All of the appropriate interested parties were invited to watch the game, including Herbert Simon. Also in attendance was a young MIT administrator named Russell Noftsker, who had recently been hired by the school to help oversee the activities in the lab. Some bets were made, some odds given, and the game began: Hubert Dreyfus, phenomenologist, against a Digital Equipment PDP-6 computer running Greenblatt's MacHack software program.

Dreyfus lost.

Many in the room expected MacHack to put up a good fight and make Dreyfus look inept, but they were by no means certain that the program would beat Hubert. When the computer actually checkmated Dreyfus, some in the AI Lab were just as stunned as Dreyfus was. In the space of one match, machine intelligence had triumphed over a human mind, MIT's obsession with creating chess playing software had been vindicated, and Richard Greenblatt had entered the MIT pantheon of deities. The only thing missing was the trumpeting of angels from on high.

The victors wasted no time making the results of the match known to the world. The outcome of the game was submitted to and published in the bulletin of the Association for Computing Machinery under the banner "A 10-Year-Old Can Beat the Machine, But the Machine Can Beat Dreyfus." For the AI community, it was a headline that ranked right up there in the historical annals along with "Dewey Defeats Truman."

But Hubert did not tuck his tail between his legs and go away. Instead, he backpedaled over his previous claims with a number of fairly lame excuses designed to explain away his defeat. First off, Dreyfus stated that he never said a computer could never beat a human, just that it couldn't beat a human at the time of the publication of "Alchemy and Artificial Intelligence" in 1965. Besides that, he whined, he was nothing more than a "rank amateur" when it came to playing chess anyway, so the success of MacHack was really not that big a deal since it had beaten a relatively unskilled opponent. It was a mismatch, according to Hubert. Needless to say, his words fell on deaf ears.

The victory over Hubert was not enough to completely sate the wounded pride of the denizens of AI, however. A few months later, in January 1968, Papert wrote a paper called "The Artificial Intelligence of Hubert L. Dreyfus: A Budget of Fallacies." While many of his comrades felt that the best way to handle Dreyfus and his headline grabbing was simply to ignore him and avoid lending credence to his views, Papert seemed to take the Dreyfus assaults personally. As the title indicates, Papert's response was a retort against Hubert the man. Terms like "cowardice" and "questionable honesty" were used in the paper, which shows the level of sniping that MIT academicians were willing to resort to in order to protect their interests. Papert deemed that the activities of people like Dreyfus—and most especially Dreyfus himself— would derail attempts to push computer research to new levels of innovation. These people, Papert claimed, created an atmosphere whereby all computer work was suspect, which could lead to a lack of appreciation for the successes that were being achieved. This was tantamount to standing in the way of progress.

It is interesting to note that although Papert never officially finished the "Hubert paper," MIT decided to publish it anyway as an academic memorandum under the auspices of Project MAC. Score one for the school's favored son.

One fact that Dreyfus finally did accept was that he was unwelcome at MIT. He may have realized this because no one on the faculty would talk to him. He took a job teaching philosophy at the University of California at Berkeley, where he was joined several years later by his brother, Stuart. Apparently, the stigma of having the Dreyfus surname was enough to send both brothers as far away from MIT as geography and career opportunities would permit.

Hubert Dreyfus went on to consolidate his anti-AI writings, including "Alchemy and Artificial Intelligence," into a book entitled *What Computers Can't Do*, published in 1972. It has since been revised and updated, but Dreyfus has found no reason to tone down his scathing criticisms of the AI community. The brothers also wrote a book together in 1985 called *Mind Over Machine*, which continued the decades-long Dreyfus crusade against AI. For all practical purposes, though, the Dreyfuses have faded into relative obscurity in the 1990s. Their names are still bandied about in news stories that address the shortcomings of AI, and they are more than happy to be associated with any "I told you so" perspectives on specific failures of the technology over the last few years.

Throughout all of his work, the biggest detriment to Hubert Dreyfus' thoughts, ideas, and criticisms is that he has never offered his readers or listeners a satisfactory alternative to the research methods used in artificial intelligence. Instead of tearing down ideals in order to build better ones, he just leaves those ideals laying on the ground, seemingly pleased by the mere fact of having beaten up on them. Even though this has proven to be a one-trick pony, Dreyfus has ridden it year after year, right up to the present day.

Still, it is important to note that Hubert Dreyfus made some reasonable observations about the limitations of AI nearly three decades ago. There are problems associated with perception that continue to plague today's AI developers, and Dreyfus had the foresight to see that these problems would be harder to address than was commonly believed in the 1960s and 1970s. If he hadn't left such a bad taste in people's mouths, he still might be given a small amount of credit where credit is due.

It is highly doubtful, though, that any AI researcher currently alive would be willing to publicly say, "You know, Hubert made an exceptionally good argument back then. Maybe we should reexamine his ideas on the subject." Most of these researchers would prefer to have their spleens removed with a fork than concede any merit to an argument put forth by Hubert Dreyfus.

Chapter **10**

The Common Man Finally Encounters Artificial Intelligence— at the Movies

By the end of 1969, much of the world was finally introduced to artificial intelligence. This happened not through the efforts of the researchers and universities that were developing AI, but through the fictional realm of television shows and Hollywood movies.

It is perhaps telling that for all the work going on in various labs, as well as all the money being spent on AI by the government, it was the entertainment business that brought the concept of artificial intelligence to the general public. While most people were completely unaware of AI in the 1960s—indeed, many of them had yet to encounter a computer—they did get an inkling of the technologies being pursued by individuals at MIT, Stanford, and Carnegie-Mellon through movies and TV. The most startling to AI, and still among the most famous, was via HAL, the computer menace in Stanley Kubrick's *2001: A Space Odyssey.*

For those of you who may have missed the movie or possibly forgotten its story line, the following is a quick review: A U.S. space mission unearths an obelisk on the moon. When the first rays of lunar sunlight strike the obelisk, it sends a shrieking radio signal towards Jupiter. Determined to find the significance of this event, the U.S. sends a crew on a voyage to Jupiter. The crew consists of two active men, three others in deep sleep, and a sixth member, the HAL 9000 computer, who functions as the omnipotent central information manager and "nervous system" of the spacecraft. All that the crew knows about the mission is that it is an exploratory flight to Jupiter; they know nothing about the obelisk and its mysterious signal. When HAL malfunctions during the flight, the two active crew members threaten to disconnect him. Disturbed at the prospect, HAL kills the three sleeping crew members and sends one of the two remaining men off into the emptiness of space. Since HAL is clearly out of control, the mission commander disconnects the computer, at which time he finds out the real intent of the journey. The purpose of the mission is not to explore Jupiter, but to confront the makers of the obelisk on Japetus, one of Saturn's moons, where the signal from the moon was sent. The U.S. space agency believed that such a confrontation would be hostile, so this information was not revealed to the crew members for fear of it being leaked to people on Earth, who would no doubt be frightened at the thought of such a prospect. HAL had killed off the crew members when they threatened to disconnect him in order to protect the integrity of the mission, which he alone knew, and to prevent the humans from interfering with the true purpose of the trip.

The movie was enormously successful, as was Arthur C. Clarke's novelization of the screenplay (the entire concept arose from a short story by Clarke). The star of both movie and book was HAL, who appeared to be more human than the humans he was stuck with in space. Especially as he is described in the book, HAL is a machine that has neuroses and even emotional conflicts, traits which are markedly absent from the people involved in the space odyssey.

HAL was an artificial intelligence unlike any that had ever been depicted in movies: he was not a robot, he was a stationary computer system. He could see, talk, hear, understand concepts, and make decisions, plus he had access to the sum total of mankind's knowledge. His malevolence came from the fallibility of his programmers in not anticipating that he might have to choose between the lives of his compatriots and the sanctity of the mission he was given. This created dilemmas in his "thinking" that resulted in his perceived disregard for his human crew mates.

Clarke describes the birth of HAL in detail during the course of the book. He mentions both Alan Turing and Marvin Minsky by name during these passages, linking HAL's intelligence directly to their work. Thus, it is no coincidence that Minsky was hired as a consultant to the film, ostensibly to make sure that the movie depiction of HAL conformed to modern computer ideals and did not fall prey to the bulky robot concepts of previous generations.

Those that didn't really understand the state of the art in computing—which is to say, most of the viewing public—were concerned because HAL had turned on its human masters. Here was this machine that was able to do all these human things, and it had ultimately been smarter and more conniving than the people who had programmed it. Though there was no outcry over the possibilities of creating a real-life HAL, the concern did give rise to numerous editorials, cocktail party discussions, and at least one interesting rumor that persists to this day. Clarke states in his novel that HAL stands for Heuristically programmed ALgorithmic computer, although a more interesting story circulated through the research community about the origin of the name. The story says that Clarke (and researchers in AI labs) believed that IBM was on its way to worldwide domination of the computer industry, and that in time it would create an environment where intelligent machines like HAL would control businesses in the same way that HAL had actually controlled the Jupiter mission in *2001*. This was evidenced by the fact that if you take the letters H, A, and L, and then raise each of them to the next position in the alphabet (H to I, A to B, L to M), you get the letters IBM. Thus HAL equaled IBM, and *2001* took on new life as a sort of morality play about the computer business. It's a cool story, but one that Clarke has denied over and over again.

HAL was endowed with types of artificial intelligence that were not very popular in the labs of the three major universities doing AI research. These forms of AI included the ability to talk and to understand speech, to see and recognize objects, and to communicate via conversational English or "natural language" (the technology that Joseph Weizenbaum sought to address with ELIZA). HAL did possess reasoning faculties of the sort being pursued by Minsky, McCarthy, Feigenbaum, et al during the sixties, but this was only a portion of his "humanness." Voice recognition (also known as speech understanding), machine vision, natural language, and the ability to speak were all technologies that fell under the AI umbrella because they were believed to result directly from human intelligence. Yet these technologies were mostly overlooked by the big labs and by the media, which were more interested in the logic functions of the mind.

This lack of enthusiasm existed for a number of reasons. Many AI research-ers felt that abilities like speech understanding were easily achieved once the proper resources (namely time and money) were dedicated to them; thus, they were not "hard" problems to spend time on. Others felt that once the basic functions of the mind were programmed into machines that areas of speech and communication would naturally fall into place with relative ease. Still others just didn't see the glamour in spending their valuable time and research dollars on things as primitive and mundane as speech. It was very much a difference between the cerebral aspects of artificial intelligence and the more physical—even visceral—side of human behavior. These AI pur-suits were relegated to "second tier" status by the AI pioneers, who were in-tent on solving "first tier" problems.

The U.S. government, on the other hand, found these technologies to be fascinating. It began handing out money to smaller and less well-known or-ganizations to develop computers that could see and understand spoken words. These organizations, such as the University of Michigan and the Uni-versity of Texas, did not have the high profile that MIT or Stanford had, and their work did not attract headlines outside of technical journals for the academic community. They most certainly didn't get coverage in publica-tions like *The New Yorker*.

By and large, these smaller labs did not publicize their work the way that MIT would. They weren't large enough to attract a lot of attention, and their work was primarily at the investigative stages. However, an additional con-cern made these researchers on the second tier of AI more than a little reluc-tant to discuss their work-in-progress. This concern was based on a report called ALPAC, published in 1966 by the U.S. Air Force and the National Science Foundation. ALPAC had destroyed an entire segment of AI re-search—called machine translation, which gave computers the ability to trans-late text from one language into another—in less than three months, leaving dozens of projects without funding. ALPAC was so devastating to U.S. re-search efforts in machine translation that the only lab still willing to work on the technology was located in the remote setting of Provo, Utah. The lab was owned by the Mormon Church.

❧

In addition to the amazing computer abilities portrayed on the silver screen in *2001*, Americans were getting another, more continuous, dose of high-tech wizardry on their TV screens. Beginning in 1966, the same year that ALPAC was published, "Star Trek" brought the possibilities of AI into U.S. living rooms every weeknight for three years. Captain Kirk and his crew utilized voice recognition to activate all manner of devices and communicated with these devices using natural language.

One of the more popular devices used by the denizens of the Enterprise was an appliance that could translate words spoken by alien beings into a language understandable to Kirk and company—that language being English. The device was especially effective for helping Kirk to understand that some scantily clad alien female wanted his body, since for some reason he seemed unable to interpret the obvious body language displayed by these otherworldly nymphets. The language translator was a handy device indeed, as "Star Trek" demonstrated time and time again.

Although such a device was portrayed as a futuristic invention of science fiction, the computer community had been intrigued by the potential of a mechanized language translator since the 1950s. Human translation of one language to another was a slow and laborious process, and the world simply did not have enough humans to efficiently deal with the translating needs of businesses and governments. Documents ranging from formal correspondence to product instructions had to be translated in an ever-increasing flow of paper around the world.

The major problem with all forms of translation is that they cannot be done on a word-to-word basis. That is, you cannot take a sentence in English and swap out the individual words to their French equivalents and still have the translated sentence make any sense. Different languages have different sentence syntaxes, different placement of adverbs and adjectives, and different idioms that are peculiar to each language. For example, the exceedingly simple English phrase "I love you" translates word for word into French as "I you love" because French employs a different placement of subjects and objects than that which is used in English.

Without going into excruciating detail, suffice it to say that language translation is a difficult prospect at best. At worst, it can be nearly impossible. Translation between Romance languages—such as English, French, Italian, Spanish—is relatively straightforward because they share a common origin (Latin), while translating English into something like Vietnamese or Farsi is a monumental task because there are no common underlying language traits. It was exactly this obstacle that the U.S. government faced as it escalated its presence in Vietnam during the late 1950s and early 1960s. Messages, codes, and even magazines had to be translated so that the U.S. Army could better plan its strategies for dealing with the Vietnamese. Complete unfamiliarity with the language and the culture, as well as the inability to read local newspapers or captured messages, proved to be a severe impediment to U.S. military efforts in Vietnam. Additionally, the Pentagon was having problems translating its own English documents for its South Vietnamese allies who needed to read American directives as well as manuals for operating equipment.

Military officials in Washington got the brilliant idea of trying to bring the power of computers to bear on the problem. This statement is not meant sarcastically; computer power had helped to turn the tide of World War II for the British once the Enigma code had been broken. Using computers for translation seemed like an obvious strategy, but computers lacked one thing required to perform accurate and even adequate translations: intelligence. As noted above, word-for-word translations are not sufficient for converting whole sentences, and certainly not for converting lengthy documents. It takes knowledge of two languages and their various idiosyncrasies to make a proper translation. This knowledge includes rules of grammar as well as familiarity with slang, jargon, and even content. A computer would have to be familiar with these variables in order to perform usable translations of any piece of text, no matter how trivial. Even translating a dinner menu could prove to be a Herculean endeavor for a computer.

At first, computer researchers didn't realize that translation would be any more difficult than simply finding the proper computer programming techniques. As early as 1956, the same year that the term artificial intelligence was coined, researchers at Georgetown University submitted a proposal to the Central Intelligence Agency for machine translation using computers. This resulted in the creation of the GAT (General Analysis Technique) System, a simple translation device that did little more than word-for-word translation. However, GAT was used by various government agencies—including the Atomic Energy Commission, which was monitoring both U.S. and Italian nuclear sites—until the mid-1960s. Additionally, a word-for-word Russian-to-English system translation was developed by IBM in the late 1950s to work on its Mark II computer system.

These two efforts were pedestrian to say the least, but so was the understanding of what computers could and could not do. Remember, this was the era that believed technology would have us all in flying cars and George Jetson-style houses by the 1980s. The best example of how extremely naive the government was in expecting computers to rectify its translation woes is told in an apocryphal story from 1960. Concerned over Russia's growing preoccupation with accelerating the Cold War, the U.S. government ran some test programs to translate Russian to English and English to Russian. These tests involved simple phrases and idioms found in routine conversation and even literature. Among the chosen idioms was the popular English phrase "The spirit is willing, but the flesh is weak." After running this through a translation program, the computer produced a Russian version that bore no resemblance to the original: "The vodka is strong, but the meat is spoiled." This was hardly what one would call a successful translation. In fact, it was a lousy translation.

At about this time, most people realized that the computer needed more than slick programming to do a passable job at translation. The notion that some of the mechanisms of artificial intelligence might be used to improve translation caught the fancy of the government, and various small projects were funded to create intelligent translation systems. Institutions such as Georgetown and the University of Texas at Austin began to develop these systems, optimistically named "automatic translation processors." At the top of the government's wish list was translation involving Russian, Vietnamese, and English.

The intelligence that was added to translation systems involved programming rules about grammatical structure into the applications, such as "If the French words 'vous' and 'tu' are encountered, then the English equivalent for both words is 'you'" or "The French phrase 'Est-ce que' at the beginning of a sentence always signifies a question." Even though it was impossible to program every possible derivation of every possible sentence into a computer, these rules provided a basic methodology for structuring the conversion of routine sentences.

Automatic translation work was conducted outside the main centers of AI research, but there was little communication about technological advancements between the main AI labs and these "second tier" labs. For all intents and purposes, the developers of translation systems worked in a cultural vacuum and were not privy to the advancements being made at places like MIT and Stanford. And even though Georgetown University had close ties with the government, it was not known at the time for its advanced technology expertise in working with computers. In spite of the variety of approaches being used to study AI at the various labs, progress towards a computer translator that could work with the skill of a human was barely measurable.

The U.S. government was digging itself deeper into the Vietnam War, and to say that it was impatient for a good working translation system is to barely hint at its level of anxiety. By 1965, no working systems had proven to be substantially better translators than the word-for-word systems developed in the late 1950s. Merging AI and translation had not produced the desired results, and the government was not happy about it.

A joint commission of the National Science Foundation and the U.S. Air Force—both major funders of the machine translation projects—was formed to evaluate the existing computer translation work as well as potential benefits from continued work. The committee, called ALPAC (the Automated Language Processing Advisory Committee), was expected to offer some ideas on ways to improve research methodologies as well as to investigate new areas of technology that might help overcome the obstacles which were hindering translation development. Instead, ALPAC authored a scathing report in 1966 that blasted all of the efforts at machine translation as being a waste of time and money. It declared that automatic translation was an unsolvable computer problem that was not worth pursuing. Furthermore, it recommended that all funding for translation projects be immediately discontinued and put into hiring more human translators.

The small machine translation community was ill-prepared for such an indictment of its work, and promptly went into shock. Funding for projects dried up within weeks of the ALPAC report, and several research labs shut down soon thereafter. With no benefactors to support their work, researchers were forced to abandon projects regardless of their status or the amount of funding they had already received. So, by the time Captain Kirk was demonstrating his translator of the future on prime time TV, the government had already killed off its own plans for the exact same device.

ALPAC's ability to slam the door on computer research as it related to artificial intelligence projects struck fear into the hearts of second-tier AI researchers everywhere. Machine translation was intimately tied to the pursuit of natural language research, since both depended upon the ability of a computer to "learn" and "understand" the essence of languages. Plus, if a computer couldn't comprehend language, whether in communicating with humans or in translating text, then how could it be expected to understand the meaning of spoken words or even conversational commands typed in on a keyboard? In this light, ALPAC's ramifications went far beyond the domain of computer translation. Many researchers took good hard looks at where they were in their various AI projects and found that they didn't want to be caught with their pants down should another government report slash the life out of their professional babies. There were other, more stable, projects to get involved in that wouldn't be so susceptible to the funding knife. These researchers quietly slunk off to find those projects before it was too late.

Note that in discussing these second-tier AI projects that familiar AI names don't surface at all: Minsky, McCarthy, Newell and Simon, MIT, Stanford. Amazingly, all of these people and their respective organizations had stayed away from natural language and machine translation to a certain degree, and thus were unscathed by the ALPAC report. It was as if an arsonist had burned down the garage, leaving the inhabitants of the house blissfully unaware of the nearby destruction. When all was said and done, as far as the AI pioneers were concerned, the garage was just a minor structure anyway. After ALPAC, the rest of the AI community went about its work as if nothing more than a minor incident had occurred.

Yet ALPAC was a major incident. It certainly put the brakes on a number of AI-related programs throughout the United States. It dissuaded many universities from getting into the "hot" new field of AI in the 1960s by pulling funding from existing projects. Since program funding is the life blood of academic research, universities could ill afford to set up AI departments with the lingering fear of having the funding rug pulled out from under them. Nonetheless, the established AI labs managed to carry on in the face of ALPAC, and it is worth noting that no snide rebuttals or papers were written by these labs to contest ALPAC, since rebuttals were usually prompted by much more trivial events. The AI organizations that were left standing knew much better than to bite the hand that fed them.

~

Though the government discontinued funding for academic research into machine translation in 1966, this did not quite signal the end of the road for all forms of computer translation in the United States. A small company called Logos was founded in 1969 to translate technical manuals from English to Vietnamese, and its primary client was—surprise—the U.S. government. Logos is still in business today, although its focus is on European and Arabic language translation.

Far removed from the realms of military conflict, researchers at Brigham Young University had their own ideas about how to use machine translation. Run by the Church of Jesus Christ of the Latter Day Saints, the school is located in the Mormon enclave of Provo, Utah. It is the center of higher education for Mormons, where the teachings of founder Joseph Smith are studied by young adults who are expected to go and spread the Mormon word. These young men and women are sent to foreign countries for two-year "missions" to recruit new members for the church.

The primary text in the Mormon religion is the *Book of Mormon*, a document not unlike the Bible in its telling of tales related to the prophets and founders of the Mormon religion. It is carried by the young missionaries on their international journeys and handed out to all interested (and even uninterested) parties.

Being one of the world's younger established religions—it was founded in 1830—the Mormons have not yet had a worldwide theological impact on the order of, say, Catholicism. Whereas the Bible has been translated into virtually every language and dialect known to mankind, the *Book of Mormon* has not been around long enough to garner such widespread acceptance and translation. It is an obvious impediment to missionaries in foreign lands when their religious texts can't be read by the locals.

Realizing this from the outset, the Mormons have made huge efforts to translate the *Book of Mormon* into foreign languages. However, there are literally thousands of languages and dialects in the world, and the *Book of Mormon* is nearly 800 pages long—and that's the paperback edition. To make this a less formidable task, the Mormon Church sought to use computers to perform translations of the sacred text. In the early 1970s it set up the Translation Science Institute at Brigham Young University to develop an automatic translation system specifically designed for tackling the *Book of Mormon*.

Over the course of a decade, the Mormons put a lot of cash into the institute and developed some very practical translation technologies. But, like the U.S. military before it, the Mormon Church found that machine translation did not possess quite enough intelligence to tackle all the idiosyncrasies of its documents. The descriptive and occasionally archaic nature of the prose in the *Book of Mormon* made it an especially difficult nut for computers to crack.

Unlike the U.S. military, the Mormons realized there was value in what they'd done and decided to make the best of the investment it had already made in machine translation. Instead of killing its research project off, the church opted to turn it into a commercial enterprise that could tackle less demanding translation tasks. By 1980, the entire Translation Science Institute had been spun off into two companies, Weidner Communication Corporation and Automated Language Processing Systems (ALPS). Both companies were at the forefront of intelligent machine translation in the United States during the 1980s, succeeding where the government had failed. Weidner was eventually taken over by its Japanese investors, while ALPS has become a publicly traded company providing translation services to clients in most international markets.

Today, machine translation is one of the biggest areas of AI research in the world. Every major Japanese corporation has some sort of machine translation project or product it uses to help translate documents—especially product manuals and brochures—into the native languages of the countries

where it sells its products. The Japanese routinely list fully automatic machine translation as one of their primary computer-based goals for the next
decade. They realize there is an obvious benefit to having your written materials understood by your customers.

Europe has literally hundreds of machine translation projects under way,
most of them funded by national governments. It is the goal of the unified
European Community to make translation of documents between the nine
primary working European languages as efficient as possible, and it is expecting
to rely on machine translation for this efficiency. European governments and
corporations spend millions of dollars annually on this research, and the
Europeans hope to beat the Japanese to market with a fault-free machine
translation system by the end of this decade.

By way of contrast, the United States has a grand total of three companies
that sell machine translation products, and only five or six notable university
projects. As far as the university projects are concerned, it must be pointed
out that much of their research is co-sponsored by either Japanese or European investors. Apparently the stigma of ALPAC still lingers over U.S. machine translation research efforts, despite the fact that machine translation
has the potential to improve corporate competitiveness in the global market.

One would think that after nearly thirty years the sting of ALPAC would
have worn off. It hasn't. And, although I haven't checked, it's a pretty sure
bet that Captain Kirk probably got his translator from Fuji or Siemens.

Chapter

11

Facing Up to New Definitions of AI

As more and more people became aware of artificial intelligence, the definition of what constituted AI underwent considerable reworking. There has never been a completely satisfactory definition of AI, and this was especially true after the first full decade of AI research had been completed in 1970.

When John McCarthy came up with the term in 1956, it was meant to describe computers that could think like humans. With this definition in hand, the members of the Dartmouth Conference were determined to create computer programs that could act logically and solve problems. Aiding them in their quest was a conventional wisdom that stated that the things humans do could be broken down into mathematical equations and rules of behavior. This belief was based on the ability to represent human activities through formal logic systems such as propositional calculus and predicate calculus.

Many mathematicians argue (then and now) that there are ways to use mathematics to formalize human behavior. They believe that the proper systems of logic can account for all inevitabilities, or will be able to eventually since mathematicians are always coming up with new derivations of existing logical forms. For those of us who left our math careers in our school lockers upon graduation, it may come as something of a surprise to find that math is a dynamic area of study and that it is constantly evolving. There are those individuals still deeply involved with math who see no reason why math can't ultimately be used to explain almost anything. These are also the same people who hope to find mathematical order in chaos (like the growth of a tree or the movement of a storm), so I leave it to the reader to put as much or as little faith in this as he or she chooses.

Mathematicians hold no exclusive rights to thinking that human thought and behavior can be broken down into a rigid structure of rules and equations. As far back as the thirteenth century, a Christian mystic named Ramon Lull developed a mechanism for describing all of man's behavior and the events of nature. Based on a written work that he called the *Ars Magna*, the device was composed of a series of interconnecting wheels that could be aligned to give answers to questions of philosophy and physics. This mechanism appears to have been similar in concept to a metaphysical slide rule, or perhaps those cardboard disks by which amateur astronomers can plot the movement of the constellations. In any case, Lull believed that his invention was just what the world needed to answer all of its questions. As an artificial device, it was the earliest man-made creation that purported to explain the universe in terms of a formalized structure. The fact that Lull claimed his invention was given to him while he was having a vision of Jesus Christ seemed to be a big plus to those who put faith in Lull's creation.

Back in the twentieth century, the first AI researchers felt that rules of logic could describe any situation or problem. Take something as simple as learning to play the guitar. A set of basic rules for guitar playing could be set up in the following manner:

1. Matthew wants to learn to play the guitar.
   (This is a statement of fact.)

2. Matthew must have a guitar in order to play the guitar.
   (Another statement of fact.)

3. If Matthew does not have a guitar, Matthew cannot learn the guitar.
   (Again, this is a fact.)

4. If Matthew wants to learn how to play the guitar, but does not have one, then Matthew must obtain a guitar.
   (While this is factual, it also contains a condition which specifies an action that Matthew must take in order to learn the guitar.)

At this point, the condition must be resolved. Either Matthew has a guitar or he doesn't. If he does have a guitar, then he can move on to the next stage of learning to play the guitar. If he does not have one, then he must get one. Not having a guitar involves a new set of facts, such as:

1. Guitars are available at music stores.
   (Statement of fact.)

2. Guitars cost a lot of money.
   (Another statement of fact.)

3. Matthew must go to a music store to get a guitar.
   (This is true, but it is not a complete condition of obtaining a guitar. The statement needs to incorporate the additional condition of money mentioned just above.)

   The entire statement, then, in order to be completely true, should be as follows:

4. Matthew must go to a music store to get a guitar, and Matthew must have money to get the guitar.

   This line of inquiry then branches out into definitions of cost and transfer of ownership. Various conditions must be met in order to establish that Matthew now has a guitar, if he had not previously owned one. If Matthew did own a guitar, the conditions concerning getting a guitar would be unimportant because they are only relevant to not owning a guitar.

These are all rules and conditions that need to be resolved before Matthew can even get to the level of actually taking lessons on the guitar. They are simple and straightforward, and in the 1950s and early 1960s, it was believed that all activities could be broken down into a similar structure of rules and conditions. Most activities would be considerably more complex and lengthy than our guitar example, perhaps involving hundreds of rules before a resolution could be reached.

Whatever their complexity, these structures were still basic enough that they could be programmed into a computer, and the computer could decide, for instance, how to help Matthew learn the guitar. When the computer got to the point where it needed to know if Matthew had a guitar, and if the answer was "yes," then it could skip the line of inquiry regarding how to obtain a guitar. Although this was a programming function, the computer would appear to be intelligent because it would "know" that you don't need to go out and buy a guitar if you already have one.

Because the potential of the computer was untapped in the 1950s, it was expected that computers would be able to handle problems like this with relative ease. The dilemma was that computers as pieces of machinery were not up to the demand that AI researchers were already making on them. You couldn't make a Model T Ford drive 120 miles per hour in 1930; you had to wait until the Ford Cobra was introduced 30 years later. The AI pioneers were faced with the same problem, although they didn't know it at the time.

People like Minsky and Newell and Simon made their grandiose predictions about the future of thinking machines based on expectations that computers would be almost infinitely powerful within a matter of years. In hindsight, of course, this is ridiculous. At the time, though, computers were revolutionizing every aspect of society and science as part of the greatest technological upheaval of all time. In the context of the 1950s, all things seemed possible with the computer. It was an optimism that was destined for disappointment.

❧

While AI labs worked on breaking mental activities down into rules of logic and pushed the computer to its technical limits, researchers encountered the first problems with their own definition of artificial intelligence. The use of language, for instance, did not fit comfortably into a definition of intelligence that was based solely on the ability to think logically and to solve problems. By any measure, though, the use of language is an obvious example of intelligence; other examples are the ability to differentiate between two similar yet different objects (a softball and a grapefruit, for instance) and the ability to manipulate and arrange objects (such as making a play house from building blocks).

These were things that certain animals could do, but computers could not do. It was readily apparent that the ability to learn by communicating and speaking and manipulating objects affected intelligence. In fact, the ability to do these things efficiently was a mark of higher intelligence, and was even used to test human intelligence quotients (IQs). Could a computer be said to be truly intelligent if it could not do these essential things? At the end of the 1960s, more and more researchers answered with a resounding "no."

The early AI groups at Stanford, MIT, and Carnegie-Mellon began to split into factions in the early seventies as the problems of AI began to multiply. From the naive definition of AI as a computerized problem solver to the concerns about how to interpret the nuances of language, AI had suddenly become a field with a lot more questions than answers. The provocation of people like the Dreyfus brothers only increased the awareness that AI researchers were dealing with something a lot bigger than they had ever imagined. The issue was no longer just about the steps someone like Matthew needed to take to learn how to play the guitar; it was now about how Matthew actually got from his house to the music store, how he knew to ask for the right kind of guitar, how he learned which notes were which, and how he applied his fingers to the fretboard. The computer needed to know these types of things to become truly intelligent. In AI, a snowball had become an avalanche, and it threatened to bury everyone who thought they were on the verge of getting machines to think like humans.

The first tangible evidence that AI wasn't going to be a reality as soon as had been predicted was demonstrated in the performance of the actual computers themselves. The computers were too slow to solve problems with lots of rules, taking hours to make the correct decisions while they sorted through all the possible outcomes before arriving at precisely the right solution. Computers didn't have a lot of memory, either, which severely limited the amount of information that they could deal with. In 1970, the average minicomputer had about the same memory capacity as today's electronic organizers, or slightly more than a pocket calculator. Thus, the AI community was working on problems that computers were not physically capable of handling. A six-year-old child could solve simple logic problems faster than many computers.

The awareness of the disparate problems facing AI, in both hardware and software, created a new diversity in the study of machine intelligence. Areas of specialization developed almost overnight. One of the first groups to splinter away from the "problem solver" mainstream of AI was determined to leap-frog the computer's hardware limitations on its own. This group began making plans to create computers specifically designed to work on problems involving rules of logic, with the ability to manipulate and use objects. Ideally, John McCarthy's LISP language would be used as the basis for this whole new type of computer, which would transcend the boring kinds of traditional arithmetic-based applications like accounting and scientific calculating that most computers were used for. These machines based on LISP would be truly revolutionary, because they would be artificial intelligence computers from the ground up. Richard Greenblatt, slayer of Hubert Dreyfus' chess dreams, decided that he would be the man to invent them. Unwittingly, though, he would also pull AI from the insular protection of MIT, and he would be one of its first casualties. We will come to his story in time.

Other researchers moved into the area of natural language. Originally a sort of bastard child in the AI community, natural language caught the fancy of a number of people who realized the inherent complexity in understanding language. These astute people were mostly the students of the first wave of AI researchers, and they were able to see some sense of reality underneath the unabashed optimism of their mentors. Part of the overwhelming attraction they found in natural language was that it was such a basic skill found in all humans, yet it was almost impossible to duplicate on computers.

From the day they were invented, computers have been controlled by specialized languages that have little to do with normal human language. These specialized languages, with names like BASIC, FORTRAN, COBOL, and LISP, are virtually indecipherable by the average person. They tell a computer what to do and when, and they don't do it using common language forms. Instead, they rely on commands made up of lines of code that guide the computer through every single step of a process. Computers don't—and can't—do anything that is not programmed as a defined step in these lines of code.

Even those who have casually used personal computers are familiar with the bizarre and complicated schemes that make up computer languages. In the very popular DOS operating system, which was the cornerstone of the first generation of IBM-style PCs, every task—no matter how simple—required the use of strange commands based on "unnatural" language. For instance, if a PC user wanted to copy all the files from a floppy disk onto a computer's hard drive, the only way to get the computer to do this was to type

```
COPY A: *.* C:
```

This command had to be typed in exactly, not approximately or "pretty close." Any missing dots, colons, or spaces would result in a "bad command" message on the computer. DOS users had to learn dozens of these neat little hieroglyphs in order to do simple tasks such as delete or move files, or even search for particular lists of files. The computer has no flexibility in the way that it interprets these commands; it recognizes one format and one format only. A user can't be "close enough" to the required format and hope to activate the appropriate function. It just doesn't happen.

Natural language—the kind that people use every day—handles inconsistencies with regularity and is very forgiving of grammatical abuses. People rarely speak in accordance with the rules of grammar: they interrupt themselves, they pick up thoughts in the middle of a sentence, they use slang, and they don't always define their subjects or objects. For instance, how many times have you been talking with someone and then waved in the general direction of an object and asked, "Could you get that?" If you're in a kitchen, you may be pointing towards a counter covered with appliances, but the listener knows that you are referring to the drink that you left there a minute ago. If the phone is ringing, the listener realizes that you want it to be answered. How does the listener know this? Simple. Context.

Context is something that has a direct bearing on the things that we say in conversation. It affects the way that words are interpreted and defined. The word "run," as an example, has 179 definitions in *The Random House Dictionary.* That's right, 1-7-9. This doesn't count compound words like runaway or runabout; this is "run" as a single word. This means that if I put "run" into the middle of a page by itself, it potentially has 179 different meanings. Any of these meanings could be correctly applied to the word as it stands alone, since there is no context with which to give it a specific definition. But if I create a context, then "run" takes on singular significance. Talking about baseball, run becomes a term that relates to scoring. Talking about women's nylons, a run is a tear in the fabric. In music, a run is a succession of rapidly played notes. Computer programmers run software applications. And of course, when moving faster than a walk, run defines a type of human activity involving quickly moving feet.

Once a context is established, we can easily define words that potentially have a variety of meanings. Context can be established in a number of ways. In conversation it is based primarily on the subject matter being discussed. This means that a listener establishes context from sentences prior to the use of a particular word. If people are talking about baseball, this provides a context for defining "run" as a description of scoring during a baseball game.

Misunderstandings arise from lack of context. Oftentimes people enter into discussions in the middle of a conversation and make ridiculous remarks about something totally unrelated to that conversation. Such encounters go something like this: Steve is telling Sally about his recent emotional conversion to Buddhism. After describing this event, he says "And I hope someday to be able to experience nirvana." At this point, Bill butts in, having only heard this last sentence. He remarks "Nirvana? I think their new album is awful, but the first one was pretty good." Bill then is informed that he has no clue as to what is being discussed, and he goes off to offend someone else's delicate sensibilities. Social blunders like this occur because new entrants to the conversation have not picked up the proper context. When corrected, people invariably say, "Oh, when I heard you mention X, I thought you were talking about . . ." They do not get the context because they have not been given enough information about the topic.

If Bill had been in a record store, however, he probably would have been able to enter a conversation that mentioned "nirvana" with a high degree of certainty that it related to music. This context would come not from previous discussion, but from the location where the conversation took place. Visual cues can also provide context, as can events (e.g., getting stuck in traffic, watching a parade, going to a concert). Humans, then, do not necessarily require words to set up a context. It can be established nonverbally. Two people crowding together in a doorway during a rainstorm have a context for understanding any conversation that comes up between them because of the shared experience of the rain. If one says, "Ever seen it come down like this?" then the other knows that the reference is to the rain, even though neither of them has actually spoken of rain before.

Such is the beauty of language, and as you can see, context is everything when it comes to language. We can abuse and abbreviate language as long as we have a context that fills in the gaps.

Unfortunately, computers exist in a world without context.

Computers cannot determine the context of a situation or of a particular word. They have to be given a specific definition by a programmer or user. One cannot hope that a computer can figure out context from conversation or location; computers are isolated from the world. The fact that they are also inflexible in their operation means that one cannot expect a computer to "get the idea" of what a word might mean. They just don't have enough intelligence. Let's use a business example to illustrate this.

Suppose your boss pops into your office and tersely says, "I need that expense report immediately." You know exactly what he or she means without having to define any of the six words in that command. You have just come back from a business trip, and you have incurred expenses. Your experience in the real world has taught you that if you want to get your expenses back, you need to fill out an expense report. This report is the document your boss is referring to. You know that the request relates to your most recent trip and not one you took last year, even though that wasn't specified. You also know that the boss wants your particular expense report and not someone else's; again, this was not explicitly stated. "Immediately" refers to the next few minutes, which means that you should probably put away the crossword puzzle that you're doing and finish the expense report. The boss did not tell you to drop everything and complete the report, but you are well aware that in your office "immediately" means as soon as possible. Again, you didn't have to be told this; you knew it from past experience.

There is no way to put all of this into exactly the same context for a computer. It needs more information from your boss than just the words that were used. If you were to try to retrieve expense data from your computer with the same phrase your boss used—"I need that expense report immediately"—the computer would want to know a number of things: which expense report in particular? whose expense report? when is "immediately"? Does "immediately" supersede other processes that are currently in operation? *You* don't need to be told this, but the computer does. It has no appreciation for the nuances of determining context based simply on language. It needs to be spoon-fed a context.

While MIT researchers remained devoted to the problem-solving aspects of intelligence as the 1970s dawned, two organizations intent on solving this natural language problem were founded at Dartmouth College and Yale University. The Dartmouth natural language work would eventually result in the first commercially offered AI product, while Yale would produce a natural language aficionado whose sense of hyperbole and self-importance would ultimately rival Marvin Minsky's.

⤽

Natural language differs from spoken language. While natural language is a component of spoken language—people use natural language when they speak—the ability to hear something is substantially different from the ability to understand something. We use natural language in written documents (although the absurd wording of legal documents probably doesn't qualify as natural), and comprehension does not depend on the ability to hear.

Since people normally use typewriter-style keyboards when they work on computers, the issue of understanding speech is often overlooked as a possible way to interact with computers. Unfortunately, many people don't use computers because they don't like to type. This is especially true of business executives, many of whom can't type. They are, however, quite comfortable with using dictating machines or secretaries who do their typing for them. Based on such facts of life, computer makers contend that the keyboard is the single biggest obstacle to getting everyone in the world to use computers. If people could speak to computers in the same way that they talk to each other, the reasoning goes, then they would be completely comfortable and willing to use the machines.

The attraction of using the human voice to control manufactured devices is not limited to computers. Vendors of home appliances, electronics equipment, automobiles, military vehicles ranging from tanks to jets fighters, and a host of other manufacturers would love to give their customers the ability to use their devices simply by talking to them. This would remove some of the hesitation that people have when trying to perform such basic tasks as programming their VCRs or setting the radio stations on their car stereos.

But computers don't have ears, which is certainly a big drawback in trying to hear. How, then, to get these machines to respond to voice commands?

AI researchers came up with the idea of "voice recognition," a technology that mimics the way humans act when they hear something. It is not hearing in the traditional sense; the researchers did not try to outfit computers with a literal recreation of the human ear. Instead, they began working on a scheme whereby a voice command would trigger a specific activity within the computer's memory, much like a keyboard command would. This was—and is—done by assigning keyboard equivalents to voice commands. It works like this:

A microphone is connected to a computer. The microphone records directly to a computer's disk drive, much like a stereo microphone records directly onto a cassette tape. During a "training session" for the computer, the user speaks specific words into the microphone. As the computer disk records these words, the user types in a keyboard command that corresponds to the spoken words. For example, many PC applications can be saved and closed by hitting the "F10" key on the keyboard. A user may decide to use the phrase "I'm finished now" to indicate that he or she would like to end a session. After recording this phrase onto the computer disk, the user then hits the F10 key to indicate which function "I'm finished now" relates to. Then, when the user is actually working with the application and says this phrase, the computer matches the spoken words to the words stored on disk. Upon finding them, it "realizes" that this is the signal to close an application. It then performs the function as if the user had hit the F10 key.

While this sounds straightforward and relatively easy on paper, it is extraordinarily difficult to achieve in practice. For one thing, the human voice takes up a lot of memory in a computer. Enabling the machine to recognize all possible combinations of words and phrases would take more disk space than most users have access to. Even more daunting is the fact that computers are inflexible, as I have pointed out before. For a computer to recognize the words that a person says, those words have to be spoken exactly the same way that they were spoken when the original recording was done during the training session. The variation in people's voices makes this a rare occurrence. Most people speak in different tones at different times during a day: lower and slower in the morning and late evening, faster and higher during midday. Other things, such as stress or a cold, severely affect an individual's speech patterns. Faced with all of these possible variations, the computer must be trained a number of times just to be able to make sure that it recognizes a specific word in all of its permutations. This eats up even more disk space, which limits the number of words that can be accurately recognized on a regular basis.

Not only this, but different people have unique voice patterns. One person saying "go" generates a range of frequencies (tone and pitch) and amplitude (loudness and volume) that is peculiar to that person and no one else. Thus, different voices do not sound similar to the computer—even though they may be saying the same word—because the computer must match these voice patterns exactly to the recordings from its training session. In fact, the computer may find that a second person's voice saying "go" may be closer to a different pattern in its memory and actually trigger some operation that is completely different from the intended one.

As with all early attempts at mastering a particular AI technology, there is an apocryphal story that accurately demonstrates the barriers that researchers faced in getting machines to hear. This particular tale, though, comes from the commercial world rather than the inner sanctums of the university labs. Computer manufacturers were among the first to realize the benefit to users of a voice-activated computer. This in itself is quite surprising, given that the computer industry has a well-established tradition of not caring what its customers want. IBM and Texas Instruments jumped on the bandwagon, and IBM in particular saw the long-term benefits of voice recognition. According to legend, IBM had a particularly nasty experience with its first voice system. (It is a legend because no one seems to be able to verify the story, or is even sure that it happened at IBM, but it sounds good anyway.) A meek lab researcher in IBM's Thomas Watson Research Center managed to develop an early software system that could respond to roughly a dozen vocal commands without screwing up. At the time, a dozen was considered a lot of commands because of the limitations of memory and processing power. So impressed were the executives at the Watson Center that they decided to show their new voice system to a general meeting of all IBM divisions at the company's headquarters in Armonk, New York. And, in a rare show of giving credit where credit was due, they allowed the meek researcher himself to give the actual demonstration.

It is conventional wisdom in the computer business that research people, along with software hackers, should not be allowed out in public. They best serve their organizations by staying in their labs noodling around with the nuts and bolts of computers. Another reason for this is that "lab rats" don't always have the greatest of interpersonal skills. However, the presentation of the voice system was an auspicious occasion, and the gentleman who had done the work was being brought out into the light of day to get his fifteen minutes of fame. On the eventful day, the assembled IBM execs waited patiently while the system was set up. The researcher, who had never made a public presentation, was reluctantly led to the podium and instructed to demonstrate his new technology. Scared to death at speaking in front of so many powerful IBM pinstripers, the researcher began his spiel by explaining the background of his work, and then he turned to speak into the computer's microphone. Unfortunately, as his anxiety level rose, so did the pitch of his voice. Command after command was uttered into the computer, and one by one, the computer failed to recognize any of them. The researcher's voice was so strained that his voice didn't even remotely resemble the patterns that he had previously recorded into the computer. His system did not respond to a single command during the entire demonstration.

As I said, this is an apocryphal story, but it is believed that the poor researcher was sent back to the lab for all eternity, his career and his technology destined to be a footnote in some book about artificial intelligence. Whatever the truth of this particular tale, voice recognition was creating interest in the AI community, and it would become one of the military's best-funded technologies during the 1970s.

~

Two other technologies are worth mentioning at this time for their relationship to artificial intelligence. The first is robotics. While many people feel that creating robots is obviously related to AI, this is not quite the case.

Robotics, which is the study and development of robots, has dealt primarily with creating machines that imitate the physical movement of human limbs and appendages, specifically arms and hands. This activity does not necessarily require any overt application of intelligence. A hydraulic arm that directs a welding gun into the same position over and over again is not relying on smarts. It is not making any decisions; it is simply following orders to point and shoot. This is what is typically known throughout the manufacturing industry as a "no-brainer," and it is one of the reasons why unions and management are always at each others' throats over pay scales for humans. Management claims that it is a low-skilled job (although it is tedious and potentially dangerous), while the unions claim that it is a "high-level" job that is crucial to ensuring the quality of a final product. Regardless of which side is right, robot arms themselves can do this job 24 hours a day, 365 days a year with little chance of screwing it up. The same is true of robot jobs like hoisting car fenders onto an assembly line or removing finished products from that same assembly line.

It is only when robots are used for more than mundane tasks in manufacturing that they enter the realm of AI. This is evident in situations where mobile robots are used to transport materials or inspect hazardous sites. In cases like these, robots often need to be equipped with an expert system to help them navigate through treacherous terrain without the assistance of humans. They must be able to recognize obstacles in their path and make decisions about getting around these obstacles. Expert systems and even neural networks can provide the robot's computer control mechanism with a rudimentary intelligence that gives it this decision-making capability. But by and large, robots do not wander around free and untethered like their TV counterparts on "Lost In Space" or "The Jetsons." In the majority of their environments, they are bolted to the floor, repeating the same dull task over and over without complaint or the need for a coffee break.

The second technology that relates to AI also relates to robotics. It is known as machine vision, and it is used to give computers and robots the ability to "see" in the same way that voice recognition gives machines the ability to hear. The principle behind machine vision is quite simple. Photographs of a given product are programmed into a computer's memory. These photographs are flawless representations of the product and are used as the standard by which all subsequent products will be measured. The computer is then equipped with a camera of its own, which is aimed at a whole group of products, usually on an assembly line. As newly manufactured products come down the line, they stop in front of the camera and have their pictures taken. The new picture is in digital form—taken by a digital or video camera—so that the computer can compare the new picture with the one in its memory. As it examines every minute detail of the new product, it compares these details with its master image. The process takes just seconds, and if any flaws are found, the computer signals to a human attendant. Proper action is taken and the line moves on.

This particular technology has been especially useful in manufacturing sectors involving microscopic products, such as semiconductors. Computers can scan every last nook and cranny of a semiconductor in less time than it takes to talk about it, while a human requires several minutes to perform the same function. Plus, any job that requires visual matching creates eye strain and cannot be done for more than several hours at a time because the eye suffers from fatigue, making the operator prone to errors. Machine vision systems don't get bleary eyes and don't need sleep and are perfect for these types of jobs.

Like robots, machine vision systems can have intelligence added to them. Again, this involves neural nets or expert systems, and the resulting intelligence is used in complex situations when the system must make a decision, or more appropriately, a value judgment. This might mean picking off-color objects out of a group (such as a food processing line for oranges or grapefruits) and directing a robot arm to grab the offending and/or offensive object.

Neither robotics nor machine vision garnered as much attention at the mainstream AI labs as did more "mentally oriented" projects, for the same reason that technologies like voice and machine translation were ignored; they were just too boring to bother with. Universities in traditionally "industrial" states like Michigan and Ohio became the leaders in these technologies, although Carnegie-Mellon in Pittsburgh began to take an interest in intelligent robots and would dominate the field in the late 1980s. That, however, was a whole decade away. Marvin Minsky also had a personal interest in vision technologies and started a group to work on robots that could see. This would result in little machines that scooted through the hallowed halls of the MIT AI Lab picking up empty soda cans. That, too, was some years away, although Minsky was dabbling in the field—as he dabbled in everything— by the early 1970s. In the meantime, machine vision and robotics were second-class citizens that didn't interest many of those at the forefront of AI.

The idea of intelligent robots and computers with sight did pique the curiosity of that erstwhile benefactor of AI, the U.S. Department of Defense. In fact, the Pentagon had a lot of new ideas about what it wanted from AI as the sixties came to a close. It decided to get serious about the demands that it would place on the AI labs and became so demanding that for the next ten years, AI researchers would be jumping through hoops to prove that money spent on AI research was money well spent. The seventies were about to begin, and as far as AI research was concerned, it belonged lock, stock, and barrel to the Pentagon. Though many of them didn't like the arrangement, most researchers understood that the DOD was the golden altar at which they had to worship in order to keep their AI projects up and running.

By the end of the decade, the researchers would sacrifice their own AI labs on that altar in order to create something new: personal fortunes.

12

AI's Rude Awakening
DARPA Pulls Some Plugs

To many people, the 1970s were one thing, and one thing only.

A cruel joke.

From fashion to politics, the 1970s were an ongoing abomination of bad taste and bad judgment. Leisure suits. Watergate. Mutton chop sideburns. H.R. Haldeman. Yoko Ono. Mood rings. Pet rocks. Iran. Jimmy Carter. "Three's Company." "Dallas."

Perhaps the group that felt the most poorly served by the seventies were the adolescents of the sixties, who gradually began to realize that their dreams of changing the world were not going to come true. The world went on as it had for centuries, and free love and drugs gave way to dysfunction, disillusion, and group therapy. It was a bitter pill, but the children of the sixties were forced to choke it down.

Another, less vocal, group that watched its dreams dissolve in the harsh light of the 1970s was the AI research community. The AI optimists of the 1960s began to realize a horrible truth—that they were not going to create their beloved thinking machines any time in the near future. All those promises of the 1960s were turning out to be just so much overblown hype. It wasn't going to take ten years to accomplish the goal of machine intelligence; it was going to take twenty or thirty or forty or maybe even fifty.

Part of the problem, as previously mentioned, was the failure of computers in general to keep pace with the forward movement of the AI community in particular. Another problem was that computers were beginning to intrude on people's personal lives as they never had before, and more and more people realized that computers were capable of making mistakes. This awareness was engendered by corporate America's immediate and intense love affair with IBM and its room-sized mainframes. Companies that could cough up the requisite seven figures worth of cash were buying (and leasing) computers as fast as IBM could make them. The need for "computer personnel" increased as well, giving more people the opportunity to enter the "fast-growing field of computer programming, maintenance, and repair." At the time, this was an alternative to the "fast-growing fields of refrigeration repair and/or cosmetology."

The first onslaught of computer science departments showed up at universities around the country in the 1970s. Schools trained their students in programming techniques and computer operation in preparation for the business world, while completely ignoring the esoteric theories of AI. The business culture and the AI culture had little in common at that point. The business world, of course, did not want the kind of geeks that were fostered in places like MIT. It wanted men in shirts and ties that could program accounting applications on IBM mainframes—people rooted in the real world. They wanted more traditional humans of the kind offered by Purdue or UCLA or Notre Dame. Renegade hackers were not the kind of people that rose to the top of corporate America (Bill Gates notwithstanding, but we'll deal with him later).

These computer science departments taught languages like BASIC and FORTRAN—nice, traditional computer languages. Most of the teachers had never even heard of LISP, even though it was already the foundation of a huge body of work at both MIT and Stanford. As such, a decade's worth of students from America's heartland were being readied for computer work with little or no knowledge of artificial intelligence. It would turn out to be a sad state of affairs. When these people went on to become administrators in large corporate computing centers during the 1980s, they simply would not be able to grasp the potential of AI and would stand in the way of those renegade hackers who tried to sell them expert systems and LISP machines. It was a blood feud in the making.

Mr. and Mrs. America were also running up against computers, and not always in favorable situations. Banks and credit card companies began using computers quite extensively in the 1970s for maintaining accounts and for processing functions such as the generation of billing statements. Since everyone was still getting used to computer operations, including the people hired to maintain them, there were many bugs to work out when huge tasks like these were turned over to the computer. The humans in the data processing (DP) centers were often as confused as the next person when the computer issued refund checks when it should have been sending invoices, or credited an account with thousands of dollars when it should have debited it by a few cents.

Such billing errors became the cultural fodder of many TV sitcoms and newspaper stories. Hapless Harry and his wife couldn't get some company to fix their bill, which was screwed up due to computer error. Mayhem and zaniness ensued until the matter was resolved and everyone could "blame it on the computer." Computer screwups still happen today, but by now we're all used to them. In the 1970s, though, there was a certain novelty and freshness to these mechanical mishaps.

The AI labs were left out of this loop, primarily because they wanted no part of it. They had bigger fish to fry.

It had been easy to talk about the potential genius level of computers when the machines were mostly hidden from sight and not doing too much to attract attention to themselves. Now that computers were showing up everywhere and displaying their limitations to the average American, it was a little more difficult to believe that these were the same machines that were going to think and act like humans within a matter of a few years. Skepticism about the pursuit of AI rose another notch.

The AI lab response was to pull out of the limelight. Like the groundhog that sees its shadow and then barricades itself back inside its den until winter is over, the AI researchers decided to back off their predictions and their big claims and let the waves of skepticism pass them by. They could not afford to have their projects subjected to the harsh light of scrutiny just as they were beginning to rethink the ways that they were going about achieving machine intelligence. This was especially true in light of how little in terms of tangible results had actually been accomplished in the first decade of research.

The 1960s had produced lots of activity but little to show for it. There was Edward Feigenbaum's DENDRAL application for use with mass spectrometers at Stanford. There was Richard Greenblatt's chess program. There was Daniel Bobrow's STUDENT application for solving mathematical word problems at MIT. Finally, there was Joseph Weizenbaum's ELIZA psychologist/natural language program. While all of these were first steps in the direction of working systems, none of them was really ready for use in business or by the general public. Rather, they served to show the possibilities for AI in the future.

Unfortunately, this was not much to show for ten years of work, especially during the ten years when Newell and Simon said that computers would be able to do the things that humans did, including create art and music. Dozens of other projects were undertaken during the 1960s, many of which resulted in doctoral theses, but they didn't spur progress in the manner that the programs mentioned above did. Even programs like Greenblatt's MacHack chess player were eyed with suspicion by an increasingly computer literate world. When held up as an example of artificial intelligence, skeptics asked if there was anything that it could do besides play chess. When the answer was "no," the skeptics scoffed and proclaimed the program to be nothing more than an idiot savant. In this case, the skeptics were right. The AI community was beginning to understand that no one program could be as intelligent as a person. On the other hand, specific programs could mimic singular activities or specific areas of expertise. One program might be a chess master, another might be an aircraft mechanic, another might be a financial advisor, and still another might be a doctor. From this perspective, the possibilities were endless, and a lot more realistic. Instead of trying to create the ultimate thinking machine, researchers turned their talents to creating specialized systems.

While this sense of timing appears to be the result of an amazing revelation, it was in truth driven by something much more substantial: The Department of Defense.

~

In every war movie or TV show you can think of, there is a clichéd scene that involves a hard-nosed sergeant reading the riot act to a new recruit. The sergeant is screaming into the recruit's face, spittle flying, while the recruit listens to an age-old admonishment: "You may have thought you had it easy before you got here. Your mother took good care of you and picked up after your sorry butt every day of your life. You never did nothing on your own. Life was a piece of cake. You never had to prove yourself. Well, that's all gonna change. From here on in, your butt is mine! I'll make something out of you!"

This could easily have been a scene from the Pentagon's new attitude toward AI researchers in the 1970s. "Play time is over. Now, let's see what you're really made of."

The U.S. military is the biggest single source of money for research into new technologies. This has been true for decades and will probably continue to be true for the immediate future. During wartime, the DOD hands out money to research groups like candy at Halloween. The Vietnam War provided the perfect environment for such handouts in the 1960s, when the United States was flush with cash and not yet concerned about deficit spending. MIT's Project MAC in 1963 came about as a result of wartime funds, as did much of the subsequent work in AI at Stanford and Carnegie-Mellon. At the time, there really was no rhyme nor reason for every handout; some of it was for pure research, some of it was political, some of it was for the creation of specific projects, and so on. In many cases, the military didn't need anything right away—it was investing for the future. Project MAC was a perfect example of this.

When the 1960s gave way to the 1970s, the military was a lot less popular than it had been a decade before. The Vietnam War had disenchanted just about everybody, including many in the Nixon administration and in the Pentagon itself. The war wasn't being won, and the money seemed to be going down a sinkhole. Nothing positive was coming out of Vietnam, either in terms of research or national pride.

Rumors swept through the research community around 1968 and 1969 that (DARPA) was going to cut back on its seemingly unlimited largesse. This was one of the things that prompted Minsky and Papert to publish *Perceptrons*, their attack on neural networks. If money was going to be tight, they wanted to make sure that someone else lost their funding, not them. They were lucky. Frank Rosenblatt and his neural nets were given the thumbs down by the DOD, and MIT kept its expert system funding. Kill or be killed obviously didn't apply solely to battlefield situations.

DARPA had another reason for wanting AI researchers to toe the line, and this reason's name was "Shakey."

Shakey was a mobile robot created by the Stanford Research Institute (SRI) as part of a project begun in 1966. SRI was an organization spun off from Stanford University to capitalize on government and commercial projects, especially those that required a working prototype of a planned product or technology. SRI won the DARPA contract to build a mobile robot that could navigate its way through an obstacle course and perform tasks such as stacking blocks. Though this was what Shakey would be initially trained to do, the DOD hoped that it would eventually be sophisticated enough to perform military functions like traversing enemy territory and searching out enemy locations such as trenches and bunkers.

SRI researchers, many of whom had been AI students at MIT and Stanford, approached the problem with typical AI zeal, only to find that a "moving" intelligence created a set of programming headaches that they had not anticipated. Shakey was built on a platform that consisted of a computer, a TV camera, a drive motor, and wheels. The entire boxlike structure was prone to shuddering as it moved from room to room, hence the name "Shakey." The shakiness of the robot was not its major weakness; its inability to recognize whether it had successfully completed a task was. If Shakey failed to make its way through a door before encountering a stack of blocks, it would move about as if it had gone through the door and attempt the block-stacking procedure anyway.

Two versions of Shakey, known as I and II, were created between 1969 and 1972. The second version improved on the first, but the machine was still incapable of doing more than one task at a time before moving to the next one. This meant that Shakey had to be programmed to move forward through a door and accomplish that program before moving to its next task. Instead of being a machine aware of its surroundings, Shakey was a machine comprised of singular instructions that didn't necessarily all relate to each other, or even to Shakey's environment. It was more like a circus animal that did specific tricks at specific points in a show. Move forward. Move through the door. Turn left. Turn right. Pick up block. Move block. After five years of work, DARPA expected more from its spy of the future. The agency was not pleased and suspended Shakey's funding—permanently.

The AI community felt that Shakey had gotten the shaft, but as with ALPAC, no one screamed too loudly. Many felt that there was a political motive to shutting down Shakey while others believed that DARPA didn't understand the complexity of the problem. But if DARPA was unaware of the complexity involved, then the AI community had itself to blame. As each proposal and request for funding went out of the labs, the AI researchers had to promise bigger and better results than those that they had promised in their last round of proposals. New proposals were usually submitted before the completion of the previous project in order to ensure a continuous flow of money. This meant that researchers were asking for new moneys based on the successful conclusion of the previous phase even while that phase was still being worked on.

In retrospect, the AI researchers were digging themselves in ever deeper with each new request for money. Yet, this was how the game was played. It must have appeared to all involved that by the time a day of reckoning came, everything would all be in order and all the goals would be met.

Shakey was the first project to fall prey to increased monitoring by DARPA. Pie in the sky predictions and rampant optimism had been exposed as smoke and mirrors, and DARPA was less than overjoyed. It adopted a policy of setting specific performance requirements in its grants. No longer was the AI community to be allowed to run wild and free with any brilliant and potentially marvelous idea that it came up with. DARPA wanted results. If it didn't get results from its AI prodigies, it would cut off the kids' allowance.

The first program it funded using this more stringent policy was called SUR, or Speech Understanding Research. Begun in 1971, the goal of SUR was to create a 1000-word voice recognition system that could perform in real-time, or as close as possible, with an error rate of less than 10 percent. This meant that the computer systems to be created from SUR would have to be able to respond to commands using any combination of 1000 words as soon as the words were out of the speaker's mouth and be able to recognize those words at least 90 percent of the time. Real-time means instantaneously, but computers need a little bit of time to process commands, so "near real-time" became an operative term.

Three primary projects were developed under the auspices of SUR (although a total of five were funded). The first two were at Carnegie-Mellon University, under the supervision of a young second-generation AI researcher named Raj Reddy. Born in India, Reddy had attended Stanford in the 1960s and had been one of John McCarthy's original thinking machine disciples. After graduation, though, Reddy went to Carnegie-Mellon, where his interest in robots, vision, and speech were more acceptable and respectable than they were in Uncle John's lab.

Upon winning the SUR contract in 1971, Reddy and his group began working on a voice system called HEARSAY. HEARSAY was designed to recognize spoken commands for moves in a game of computer chess (chess fascination in the AI community was hardly limited to MIT). The system was taught the meaning of words in a typical chess game and could recognize them as they were spoken. Unfortunately, its ability to recognize words outside of the chess domain was limited, but it managed to achieve a high level of accuracy in understanding continuous speech. Continuous speech describes the manner in which most people speak—running words together, slurring, stumbling over them. Single utterance speech, which is better for the computer, requires users to speak slowly, one . . . word . . . at . . . a . . . time in order to better define particular sounds.

Reddy wanted to teach his voice system to do more than just recognize words as part of a matching exercise. He wanted the machine to "understand" the words and figure them out based on their relationship to other words in the sentence, using context and syntax. To this end, he incorporated basic expert system and natural language techniques into HEARSAY to assist the system in determining precisely what a word was and what it meant.

After the initial success of HEARSAY, Carnegie-Mellon researchers expanded the focus of the system by applying what they had developed to business problems. Its next project was called HARPY, a combination of HEARSAY and another voice system called DRAGON, which was being developed by a CMU researcher named Janet Baker. Although DRAGON itself didn't make the final cut in the SUR project, Baker would eventually leave Carnegie-Mellon to form a company called Dragon Systems to sell commercial versions of her work. In the 1990s, her company became one of the leading voice vendors in the world, and IBM chose to sell Dragon Systems' voice products rather than those its own researchers had developed internally.

HARPY merged the work done for HEARSAY and DRAGON into a system that could be used to retrieve information from databases. HARPY was still only applicable to a single task (as HEARSAY had been with chess), but it was able to recognize the voices of more than one person, including both male and female voices, after recording voice samples during a short training session. This made it "speaker independent," meaning that it would recognize the voice of anyone who used the system.

Reddy and his group still needed to create a system that could be used for more than one application, and they came up with HEARSAY II. Like its predecessor, it could only recognize one person's voice, but it was able to understand a greater variety of words in different domains. Not limiting the domain (or applying constraints, as the AI community calls it) made HEARSAY II less efficient and more susceptible to making mistakes than HARPY, but it was notable for being able to execute more diverse commands.

Back up in Cambridge, Massachusetts, another SUR project was underway, only this one wasn't at MIT. A company called Bolt Beranek & Newman had won a piece of the SUR pie and was creating its own voice recognition system. Known simply as BBN, the company was a defense contractor that had worked on top secret and proprietary technologies for the Pentagon since its founding in 1949. Its location relative to MIT—they are less than five miles apart—made it a perfect post-graduate employer for those students who decided not to stick around academia for the rest of their lives. In many ways, BBN fostered the same kind of work environment as MIT, except that BBN's paychecks were bigger and hackers couldn't use the main computer to write chess programs. (They did put ELIZA on the computer, though, which we will discuss later on.) BBN was the perfect place to go after life in the lab.

It was only fitting that BBN should get into the AI business, considering all the activity at MIT and all the alumni that it was hiring to work on its defense contracts. The company was initially interested in natural language, but it soon moved into expert systems and voice recognition. It began work in 1974 on a voice system called "Hear What I Mean," or HWIM. Like Raj Reddy, the researchers at BBN wanted the computer to understand what it was being told, giving it a level of human intelligence far above simple recognition. HWIM was designed as a travel system to be used by a travel planner who would need to retrieve database information about such items of interest as expenses and schedules. It was a large domain to tackle, and BBN planned on having HWIM recognize multiple voices without prior training. Thus, HWIM could be used by anybody who happened to walk up to the computer, and it would not even need to take samples of their voices in order to work properly. By 1976, HWIM was working with about 50 percent accuracy, which was considered quite good in light of the fact that it didn't need training.

Then, in 1976, DARPA yanked the plug on all the SUR projects.

Despite the fact that all three projects had created systems capable of recognizing one thousand spoken words, and that the two Carnegie-Mellon systems regularly operated with 90 percent accuracy, DARPA said enough was enough. SUR was originally planned as a five-year project, but like most projects that demonstrated success, it was expected to be renewed for several more years. Time was up in 1976, and even though success was evident, DARPA still canceled the project.

Like any government project that was canceled in the AI community, opinions ran rampant as to the real cause of the shutdown. With the war in Vietnam over, some felt that the DOD had to take stock of its losses and rebuild its basic arsenal—missiles, tanks, planes, troops, etc. If this was the case, then technology investigation would definitely be cut because it was not an obvious manifestation of the arsenal. Others said that DARPA just wasn't pleased with the results; it had expected speaker-independent systems that could understand one thousand words in any environment and domain, whether it was chess or travel planning or battlefield management or aircraft maintenance. The idea of any limitations on the speaker system simply may not have been acceptable to the Pentagon.

One last group believed that DARPA wanted to make an example of the AI community. For more than a decade, the reasoning went, the agency had pumped millions of dollars into AI projects, and in all those years it had never gotten exactly what it wanted from any of the labs. If this latter statement were indeed true, it may have been sour grapes since DARPA had never been too specific about its requirements until the SUR project. The AI community, for its part, had never felt too badly about playing in the expensive DARPA toy box without creating anything usable. DARPA administrators may or may not have believed that they were being taken advantage of, or they may have felt that their money was never going to result in anything of any value to the military. They had given the AI community everything it wanted, including a huge national computer network for sharing ideas called ARPAnet (Advanced Research Projects Agency network), and they had gotten nothing in return, or so those who felt that ARPA was out for blood surmised.

No matter what the rationale, DARPA killed SUR and with it a great deal of voice recognition research, just as ALPAC had killed machine translation research. And, not so coincidentally, other AI projects found their funding cut to fractions of their previous levels. The military money didn't dry up completely, but it did slow down to a trickle. Now all AI researchers had something to worry about, not just those in specialized areas. This happened at the end of 1976 and the next few years suddenly looked like they might be pretty bleak. The 1970s really were proving to be the end of the age of AI innocence.

This came at a bad time for the hackers who had always found refuge in the AI labs. First of all, their mentors seemed to be losing interest in the original goals of AI. The first generation of AI pioneers were phasing themselves out of the day-to-day quest for machine intelligence. Marvin Minsky was involved in any number of projects, many of them related to AI, but he had acquired a keen interest in the appeal and affect of music on the human mind. Much of his AI work was limited to throwing out random idea bones and seeing how his pack went after them. Seymour Papert had chosen to follow his interest in teaching and was getting involved in Boston-area schools to teach a primitive computer language called LOGO. John McCarthy was seldom seen on the Stanford campus, choosing to sequester himself at off-campus labs as part of a personal pursuit of AI. Alan Newell and Herb Simon were Carnegie-Mellon icons, but they spent most of their time involved in areas not directly related to the technical side of AI.

Conversely, the new generation was chomping at the bit to do something with all of this AI work. Raj Reddy and many of his partners at CMU knew there was more to AI than waiting around the lab for the next round of funding. Edward Feigenbaum was already working on a new expert system that he expected would be better than DENDRAL. This one, called MYCIN, was used to detect blood diseases. Feigenbaum was also the undisputed head of Stanford AI due to McCarthy's reluctance to deal with administrative issues. He, for one, was not going to wait around for DARPA to come knocking again. Of all the AI researchers, Feigenbaum best understood that there was life beyond DARPA, and even life beyond the lab.

At MIT, the mood was somber. The last major publicized breakthrough at the AI Lab had been a natural language program called SHRDLU, developed in 1970 by a student named Terry Winograd. SHRDLU, named for a nonsense word found in MAD magazine, was a computer simulation of a robot arm that could respond to such normal commands as "Put the white block on top of the green block." More significantly, it could determine that, say, the white block was under the blue block, which needed to be removed in order to gain access to the white block. Then it could give explanations for its actions: "The blue block was removed from the white block so that the white block could be placed on the green block." The computer had been programmed with information on all of the objects, their size, their color, and their positions, and from there, the machine could make decisions based on what it "knew" about the blocks. All of this happened on the computer screen itself; there was no vision system or actual arm being utilized.

With SHRDLU, Winograd had demonstrated basic language understanding in his system, along with a strong set of reasoning capabilities. He had done this by making the computer determine what each word in a sentence meant before taking action. "Block" had to be representative of a particular object, as did its color modifier, and the action being undertaken had to relate to those objects. It was messy and complicated, but it worked. Yet like the majority of AI student programs, SHRDLU soon became just another footnote to the lab's research, destined ultimately for the "Where are they now?" files.

After SHRDLU, not too much of note came out of MIT during the 1970s. The university stayed out of DARPA's indulgences in second-tier AI projects, and for the most part worked on projects of interest to Minsky, Papert, and the new generation of hackers. But it, too, was affected by the cutbacks that began after the 1976 SUR debacle. Hackers began to worry about their precious research projects and the pursuit of AI. Who was going to fund it? More to the point, who was going to fund them?

Russell Noftsker, the man who had been hired as a lab administrator about the time that Hubert Dreyfus was getting his chess clock cleaned, was particularly interested in one long-time project within the lab. Although Noftsker had left MIT in 1974, he visited frequently during the late seventies and watched Richard Greenblatt's attempts to make a new computer, the LISP machine, with considerable interest. Without substantial DARPA money, though, Greenblatt wouldn't be able to properly complete his construction of the machine, which had the potential to create better AI programs than any computer invented up until that time. Greenblatt's computer was truly revolutionary, and Noftsker felt that there must be some way to capitalize on its potential. He had the feeling that there might even be a market for the machine in the real world, out in corporate America. The machine could be the basis for a whole new type of business—the selling of artificial intelligence. Noftsker decided to give it some serious thought.

Three thousand miles away, Edward Feigenbaum was considering whether or not his medical-based expert systems might be useful to companies in the medical industry. The expert systems themselves could even be the basis for a new business venture—a business that sold artificial intelligence. Feigenbaum decided to give it some serious thought.

It would take time, but things were going to change. Drastically. The AI lab geeks were about to be set free.

13

Europe and Japan Make Plans for AI

The United States can rightly lay claim to creating the first AI labs and the first AI programs. The true legacy of AI's origins, on the other hand, lies with the Europeans, especially the British. Machine intelligence was the brainchild of many people, but Alan Turing was its rightful father. He put forth most of the concepts involved in creating a thinking machine, and his writings on the subject hold up as well today as they did half a century ago.

Turing committed suicide before the term "artificial intelligence" was even invented, and he was never to see any applied work done in the field. Nevertheless, many of his associates were greatly influenced by Turing's initial exploration of AI, and in the decade after his death they began to pursue AI with all the seriousness of their American counterparts.

Chief among these practitioners was Donald Michie. An intense man with a dry wit, Michie had worked with Turing at Bletchley Park during World War II. Fascinated by the potential of the computer, Michie went on to become a professor of computer science at the University of

Edinburgh in Scotland. During the 1960s and 1970s, he was Britain's earliest and most vocal proponent of AI and spent much of his time trying to drum up government support for the small Edinburgh lab that he established in 1966. It was the first such lab in Europe, and today is one of the world's largest academic centers dedicated to applied AI.

Michie also built one of the first expert systems in Europe, a fact that was all but lost amid the attention given to American labs at the same time. However, another reason that Michie's work may not have received the proper degree of attention and respect may have been due to the man himself. Michie's continued appeals for government support of AI irritated people both in government and in research, and his personal style could be somewhat grating. Making a lot of noise about the way things should be done is not looked upon favorably in the United Kingdom, unless one is doing it from an approved forum like the soapboxes in Hyde Park or a seat in the House of Commons.

As a result of—or perhaps in spite of—Michie's personal crusade for AI research, other labs did manage to come to life throughout Britain in the late 1960s and early 1970s. Institutions of higher learning such as the University of Manchester, Imperial College, and Essex College set up AI centers like their American counterparts at MIT, Stanford, and CMU. These schools began to investigate the theoretical aspects of AI and developed an occasional working system to justify the basic level of government funding that all the sciences were entitled to. Most importantly, they began working with a new AI language, called PROLOG. It became readily apparent in the 1970s that a lot of Europeans didn't like to use the LISP language for their AI explorations, partially because it was an "American" product. Matter of national pride, and all that.

PROLOG, which stands for PROgramming in LOGic, was originally developed in 1970 at the University of Marseilles by a researcher named Alain Colmerauer. Colmerauer believed, as did LISP inventor John McCarthy, that traditional computer programming languages were inadequate and inappropriate for representing human logic in a machine. Colmeraurer's primary interest was in creating a better means to work with computers via natural language, and he determined that strict mathematical logic might be the proper middle ground between man and machine. The result was PROLOG, which was based on the Horn Clause within predicate calculus. Unlike LISP, all of PROLOG deals with the logical description of problems, along with associated facts and relationships. (LISP deals first and foremost with the qualities of specific objects and the relationships between objects; it is not necessarily designed to be structured according to existing rules of logic.)

In programmer terms, and especially as far as the hackers at MIT were concerned, LISP was more elegant than PROLOG. LISP was more flexible and also allowed developers to develop user-friendly interfaces for interacting with the computer. PROLOG, the hackers sneered, behaved much more like a strict professor, following each statement to its logical conclusion—and backtracking if necessary—in order to establish a mathematical solution. There was no "creativity" in it.

While the American AI community quickly dismissed the use of PROLOG, the language captured the fancy of Europeans. Colmeraurer's language found its way back to Edinburgh via a researcher named David Warren, and PROLOG soon became the preferred language for building expert systems on the continent. Not only was the language ideal for AI programs in the minds of the European AI researchers, but it had an appeal simply because it was not LISP. Damned if they were going to let the Americans shove their LISP language down the whole world's throats. PROLOG also migrated to Hungary, of all places, where it was immediately put into practice at the Institute for Computer Coordination in Budapest. In 1972, the Eastern Bloc had just begun to investigate AI as part of a Russian program to create thinking machines. Though its computers were sadly lacking in processing power, the Russian government and military were intrigued by any technology that involved using computers in conjunction with mental processes. For a while, it was even rumored that the Communist party had attempted to use mental telepathy to control the operation of their computer systems.

Other AI labs sprouted up in Europe at various universities during the 1970s, notably in the United Kingdom, France, Italy, Germany, Spain, and Sweden. Much of this work was government-funded, but unlike government work in the United States, it did not have a predominantly military bias. Because of the close relationship between European governments and European corporations—a relationship that does not exist in the United States—a small group of industrial giants began getting involved in AI. France, in particular, began fostering an awareness of the potential of expert systems among its largest companies. Two of the biggest French multinationals, Schlumberger and Elf-Aquitaine, both took an active interest in the possible use of expert systems in the petroleum industry. Within just a few years, these two would be instrumental in helping American AI researchers set up their own companies.

One country that stayed on the AI sidelines during the 1970s was Japan. The country had only just begun to build a reputation for building quality electronics, including mainframe computers, after years of international snickering at labels that read "Made In Japan." Companies like Hitachi and Fujitsu were aggressively trying to woo international customers to their brand of "IBM-like" computers and were beginning to manufacture their own semiconductor chips. AI, curiously, seemed of little interest to Japanese firms or the Japanese government in the early 1970s. Most observers and analysts felt that the Japanese were waiting to see if the United States or Europe had any commercial success with the technology. Should that success occur, then Japan could be expected to rush into the market, produce its own improved versions of various expert systems or natural language programs, and carve out a comfortable market share for itself. No one expected Japan to get involved in AI at the research level; its "copycat" mentality didn't lend itself to innovation or breaking new ground in any technologies.

Conventional wisdom dictated that the Japanese would sit and wait, as they always did, until the precise moment when they could assimilate someone else's technology for their commercial benefit. Until then, Japan would have no interest in AI.

Wrong. Japan wanted artificial intelligence—badly. In fact, it wanted AI so badly that it would break hundreds of years of cultural tradition and try to develop AI on its own. AI was so important to the Japanese that for the first time in its history, it would not be content to wait until someone else had done all the legwork. Japan wanted thinking machines before anyone else got them.

≈

If early AI projects in the United States were always at the mercy of DARPA, at least U.S. researchers knew the score when it came to dealing with a huge, faceless, government bureaucracy. Things could change for the worse at any time and there would be no one in particular at whom to point an accusing finger. You had to blame the whole organization. Bad DARPA decisions were thus open to interpretation, and funding cuts could be rationalized away as bureaucratic maneuvering or politically motivated stupidity.

DARPA pulled the strings that made the AI community dance in the early 1970s, and then, as we have seen, it cut those strings, leaving a thrashing marionette to fend for itself in the mid-1970s. It was nothing personal (for the most part); that's just the way it was. When the same thing happened in Britain, however, one man, and one man alone, was to blame.

Sir James Lighthill was a respected British scientist, having established his reputation in the 1960s as a physicist. He was also a Lucasian Professor of Mathematics at Cambridge University, a position held over the years by such notables as Isaac Newton, Stephen Hawking, and Charles Babbage. In 1972,

Sir James was asked by the British Science Research Council to evaluate the state-of-the-art applied research as it existed throughout Britain's scientific community.

Lighthill was not impressed. In a study written up in 1973, and known derisively thereafter as "the Lighthill report," Sir James found little in the British Isles to his liking. In particular, he found that the whole idea of artificial intelligence, with its expert systems and natural language interfaces, along with its claims to mimic human behavior, was nonsense of the first order. With a lack of compassion, understanding, and sensitivity that would have made the ALPAC authors proud, Lighthill recommended that all AI funding throughout the United Kingdom be cut off immediately, before further funds were flushed down the loo.

Like their American counterparts, who were getting used to such pronouncements, U. K. AI researchers were stunned. Speculation ran rampant, most of it built on the notion of political backbiting. It was surmised that Lighthill and other members of the scientific elite were tired of Donald Michie and his endless flag waving for more AI funding. Lighthill's contention that there was no benefit to be derived from any AI activity made it all the more suspect, given that British institutions such as the University of Edinburgh were keeping pace with MIT and Stanford. In the wake of the Lighthill report, the AI lab at Edinburgh was reorganized and many of its researchers let go. With the exception of Michie, who chose to ride the storm out, the Edinburgh researchers headed to America. While this exodus proved to be a benefit to the AI labs in America, Britain suddenly found itself without any AI researchers. No researchers translated directly to no research. So, as of 1974, Britain's AI programs went into deep-freeze.

Only Donald Michie kept the home fires burning, but even his efforts were not enough to prepare the United Kingdom for the surprise that the Japanese had in store.

❧

In 1978, Kazuhiro Fuchi, a researcher for Japan's Ministry of International Trade and Industry (MITI), took stock of the artificial intelligence projects underway in both the United States and Europe. He saw that progress was being made toward making thinking machines, but it was haphazard at best. Fuchi also knew that in its own inimitable way, Japan would follow these countries into the search for machine intelligence. AI would be the next frontier of computing, with the potential to change the world.

His particular concern, as part of the Japanese government, was that increasing friction between Japan and the United States over computer-related issues would hamper efforts to access the work being done in U.S. AI labs. Tensions had been mounting for several years between the two countries, especially as Japan stepped up production of computers that competed with IBM's mainframes. In addition, Japanese manufacturers were concentrating on churning out microprocessors by the millions—the microprocessors that were the heart of computers and the computer industry. They were going to do so more cheaply and in greater quantities than U.S. companies like Intel and National Semiconductor that maintained an unchallenged position as suppliers to the world. When Japan produced these semiconductors for mass market consumption, the animosity between the United States and Japan was sure to rise.

Despite its follies and foibles, false starts and dead ends, the possibilities inherent in AI were crystal clear to Fuchi, and he knew it was only a matter of time before Japan committed itself to the technology. Tradition dictated that the Japanese wait until either the United States or Europe established a market for AI. At that time, it would be worthwhile for Japan to take advantage of the time that the Westerners had spent laying the groundwork. Fuchi, however, was not one to follow traditional Japanese methods. Born in Korea in 1936, he had already risen to the top of MITI as head of Japan's Electrotechnical Laboratory. He was known as a brash researcher and administrator who had little time for all of the niceties and constricted business practices of the polite Japanese businessman. One aspect of Japanese tradition that Fuchi especially had little use for was the practice of copying the innovations of other countries. Japan, both culturally and industrially, had been accused time and time again of being unable to create its own technology, relying instead on the brain power of others to come up with new ideas and products. This had been Japan's modus operandi since the end of World War II, and it didn't seem to bother most Japanese, who saw nothing wrong with taking someone else's idea and making it better.

Kazuhiro Fuchi believed that Japan had the ability to create its own technologies and to lead the world in the development of new scientific breakthroughs. The country and its corporations had simply never attempted to break out of the copycat mold, perhaps because the proper opportunity had never presented itself. In Fuchi's eyes, artificial intelligence was the opportunity that Japan had waited for. Instead of following along in the wake of the Americans or the Europeans, Japan could finally take the lead in an exciting new technology. It could be the first country on Earth to create thinking computers.

On April 19, 1979, Fuchi organized the first meeting of a national committee to evaluate Japan's plans for high technology up to the year 1990. The committee was established as part of the Japan Information Processing Development Center, known as JIPDEC, and included 35 people from both the Japanese computer industry and academia. The general consensus of the assembled group was that any country seeking to dominate the world's computer market by the year 1990 would have to be a leader in artificial intelligence. The production of thinking machines, and not the "problem solver" software programs that the United States had been toying with, was the key to capturing the future of computing. This put a definite emphasis on hardware over software. Japan had already proven itself a master of building superior hardware at a low cost; why shouldn't it be able to build hardware that could think?

To a certain degree, this hardware mentality mirrored the thoughts of the MIT hackers who were working on the LISP machine, a computer designed specifically for AI development. But while the LISP machine would run AI software programs, Fuchi wanted to put more of the actual intelligence inside the hardware. Regular computers could run AI programs, and had been doing so for the last decade, although not particularly well. While LISP machines would make these programs more efficient and easier to build, the Japanese envisioned a computer that had natural language and expert system capabilities built right into the machine even before any software intelligence was added.

Over the next two years, Fuchi's group would hold some eighty meetings, hashing out a plan for a cohesive national effort to develop artificial intelligence, involving Japan's largest corporations, research centers, and government investment. This was not to be a bunch of isolated labs scattered throughout the country in the manner of MIT, Stanford, and Carnegie-Mellon University, but a single unified project with a specific goal.

In October 1981, at a conference in Tokyo, Kazuhiro Fuchi would announce a Japanese high technology project unlike any the world had ever seen. The government of Japan, he would declare, had set a national goal of making artificial intelligence a reality by the year 1992.

With those words, Fuchi would change the face of AI. It would no longer be toyed with and experimented with in the privacy of university labs. AI was something that had to be worked on seriously, with a distinct goal and a specific deadline. No more chess games or half-assed programs that appeared to be intelligent, no more diddling around with theory or philosophy. Japan was going to make all of the prior work in AI look like child's play by coming up with the real thing.

In Japan's eyes, the quest for artificial intelligence was to become a matter of national pride. It was time for everyone else, especially the United States, to put up or shut up.

14

The Loss of Innocence in the Labs

Welcome to the Real World

When corporate America began its love affair with the computer industry in the 1970s, attention was focused on two geographic locales. The first was Route 128 in Massachusetts; the second was Silicon Valley in Northern California. It is no mere coincidence that these areas sprouted up in the neighborhoods of MIT and Stanford.

On Route 128, companies like Digital Equipment and Data General were challenging IBM's dominance in computing with smaller machines called minicomputers. These computers were smaller not only in size, but in price, making them attractive to those businesses that did not have Fortune 500-size budgets.

The frenzied activity of Silicon Valley was taking place on a strip of land running from the southern part of San Francisco to San Jose. Companies like Hewlett Packard,

Intel, and Apple had caught the fancy of the press, the stock market, and aspiring entrepreneurs all over America. Along Route 128 and in Silicon Valley, the rush was on to bring computers into every business, and ultimately every home, in the United States. The progress of companies in these regions was notable both for how fast they were growing and for their contribution to America's newest and strongest "post smokestack" industry, the computer business.

While these areas attracted all the publicity, two small blips appeared on the computer industry radar, just off the beaten path. In the town of Waltham, Massachusetts, a former Dartmouth professor decided to take the fruits of his academic work and take a stab at running his own company. Artificial Intelligence Corporation was founded in 1975 by Larry Harris, who had been a professor of computer science at Dartmouth. Harris' principle area of interest was natural language, and he had determined that certain applications that ran on IBM mainframes were constrained (limited) enough that they would support the use of natural language. Since ubiquitous mainframe-type applications like order entry were fairly rigid, they wouldn't pose the level of complexity that might be found in more flexible applications such as manufacturing control or process monitoring. It was easier to address a computer in natural language when it only had a few choices instead of lots of them.

Harris developed a natural language package that he called INTELLECT. He targeted it directly to large corporations that used IBM mainframes for basic business tasks. At a price of more than $50,000 per copy, INTELLECT was not cheap software, but Harris could sell a few copies a year and make a go of it. Thus was born the first AI corporation, and it was only fitting that Harris should call it Artificial Intelligence Corporation.

That same year, a second blip showed up, this time in Rhode Island. Leon Cooper and Charles Erlbaum, both of whom were professors of physics at Brown University, founded a small firm called Nestor, named for a Greek hero in the Trojan War. Cooper, who had won a Nobel prize for physics, worked with Erlbaum at Brown University to refine the development of neural networks, a technology that had largely been abandoned when Minsky and Papert eviscerated it in their 1969 book, *Perceptrons*. Neural nets were computerized reconstructions of the human brain. Unlike other AI systems, which sought to mimic intangible aspects of the brain's functions—such as reasoning—neural nets sought to emulate the workings of the brain by modelling the physical structure of the organ. It was based on the concept of linking hundreds and even thousands of neurons together so that complex problems like pattern recognition could be tackled in the same way that the brain addressed them. The idea was that different "neurons" could work on different parts of a problem simultaneously, thereby increasing efficiency and reducing processing time. Cooper and Erlbaum, however, saw some potential in applying neural networks to computer problems such as recognizing handwritten characters and man-made objects. They formed Nestor to provide consulting services to clients who might be interested in such a technology.

In 1975, neural networks were not considered part of AI, basically because the AI community didn't like neural nets, thanks in large part to Minsky and Papert. To anyone you might happen to ask, AI was strictly expert systems and natural language. If the AI researchers were in a good mood, they might acknowledge some of the work in voice recognition and machine translation as being part of AI, and if they were feeling really generous, they might even give a nod to robotics and vision systems. But neural networks, never. Or at least not until 1985.

In the revealing light of history, Nestor qualifies as one of the first two commercial AI ventures, even though it was not considered AI at the time. Though the two Brown profs were about as far removed from the AI research community as was conceivably possible, they did set up a company based on AI-based technology before anyone else except Larry Harris. It is noteworthy, then, that Cooper and Erlbaum founded Nestor as early as they did, even though they would toil in relative obscurity until a 1988 article in *Forbes Magazine* pegged them as a company to watch. By that time, Cooper and Erlbaum had been in business thirteen years and had already sold off part of their company to well-known corporate raider Saul Steinberg.

Back in Waltham, Larry Harris had the good sense to lay claim to the term artificial intelligence as the name for his company, preventing anyone else from using it to promote their products. A small company in Seattle formed Artificial Intelligence, Inc. about the same time, but there was no danger of confusing the two. Artificial Intelligence, Inc. was a company that sold computer systems to veterinarians. It had no interest in thinking machines, and the name was chosen, according to a company representative, "only because we liked the sound of it."

From 1975 to 1979, Artificial Intelligence Corporation, and to a lesser degree, Nestor, were the only commercial companies dedicated to selling an artificial intelligence product. Much of Harris' business came via the numerous papers and articles he published in trade and technical journals. AI was a tough enough concept to explain, let alone to advertise. He did manage to land some major accounts, notably Transamerica, which found INTELLECT to be such a useful tool that the company helped to fund some of Harris' later projects.

While natural language researchers at MIT must have been aware of Harris' fledgling AI company, it certainly didn't induce any of them to strike out on their own. No one at MIT really gave the idea of running a company much thought, at least not until Russell Noftsker came back to the AI Lab.

Noftsker had been a fresh-faced 24-year-old when he was hired at MIT to be the administrator of the AI Lab in 1965. He had already received his engineering degree from New Mexico State University and had come to the East Coast to work for Philco, a government contractor that was working on the Air Force's secret SR-71 Blackbird spyplane. Once Noftsker was settled into his Philco job in Lexington, Massachusetts, a friend cajoled him into taking a part-time job at the MIT AI Lab, where he could work on truly cutting edge computing projects. Noftsker agreed, and started spending a lot of time at the lab in his off hours.

The amount of time he spent at the lab, along with the amount of work he was doing, was reported back to Minsky, who was taking a short sabbatical at Stanford. Hearing of Noftsker's efforts, Minsky called Russell from Stanford and offered him the job of running the lab in his absence. Noftsker, who to this day believes he was not the best-qualified person for the job, eagerly accepted the work and became the AI Lab's general manager on Minsky's three-thousand-mile say-so.

Noftsker's luck occurred as Project MAC ramped up into full gear. Just as John McCarthy was ceding administrative control of his Stanford AI lab to Edward Feigenbaum in 1965, Minsky hired Noftsker to do the same for him. Russell was not there to be a hacker, though; he was there to ride herd on the hackers. Minsky would still be their spiritual leader and mentor, while Noftsker, with the official title of chief engineer and general manager, would be their nursemaid. His duties involved regulating who had access to which computers at what time, and managing—as best as possible—the myriad projects that DARPA was putting money into. Given that the lab was operational almost twenty-four hours a day every day, this was not an easy or enviable task. Noftsker had to deal with the egos and schedules of post-pubescent men who slept on the floor of the lab in order to be close to the computer. One of his first decisions as lab supervisor was to give Richard Greenblatt a real job. Greenblatt would have lived in the lab whether he got paid or not, but Russell put him on the payroll in order to make it official and to make full use of Greenblatt's programming talents.

Noftsker spent the next nine years at the lab—from 1965 to 1974—overseeing the formalization of grants and projects that DARPA was giving to MIT. Minsky came up with the ideas for the funding proposals, and Russell committed them to paper, submitted them to DARPA, and then oversaw them once DARPA approved them. It was not an easy job, given the frivolous way that researchers in academia spent money, but Noftsker was pleased to be working with Minsky and Papert, both of whom he had read about frequently ever since his high school days.

As with any organization that is developing varying amounts of research, little of which can actually be measured, Project MAC ran into accounting problems in 1973. Specifically, money for Project MAC (which had metamorphosed from a project to a place, and was now called the Laboratory for Computer Science, of which the AI Lab was a major component) appeared to be working its way into related projects, such as Seymour Papert's LOGO project. LOGO was a programming language designed for children, which kids could use to create their own simple computer programs. Beneficial as the project may have been, it wasn't part of what DARPA had in mind when it gave its money to Project MAC. When DARPA conducted a review of the financial status of the AI Lab, the LOGO project turned up as an unlikely recipient of government funds. The discrepancy had occurred in large part due to Papert's involvement in both projects.

LOGO, however, was for kids, not for war, and the military bean counters at DARPA were incensed. They immediately demanded some sort of explanation or retribution for the wayward LOGO money. Although it is not clear today what was demanded in the way of specific atonement, MIT had to make some real show of penance in order to make amends with DARPA, and that meant offering up some human sacrifices. Instead of settling for scapegoats, MIT offered up its prize possessions, Minksy and Papert. Though they admitted no real wrongdoing, Minsky and Papert took the blame and resigned from the lab. Incredibly, Minsky's resignation was accepted, as was Papert's, and they were both removed from the administration of the lab that Minsky had founded.

Although DARPA had pried Minsky's creation from his own grasp, MIT accepted his recommendation that the lab directorship be turned over to one of his stellar students, an AI researcher named Patrick Winston. Even though the lab was no longer under Minsky's direct control, Winston's appointment ensured that it was under the guidance of one of his primary disciples. Given the change in command, Noftsker felt it only right to tender his resignation to Winston, who would be free to rehire or replace Russell. Winston, as a hacker with an allegiance to Minsky, did not care for Noftsker and believed that Russell was responsible for the DARPA accounting screwup—at least that's how Noftsker perceived it. Noftsker recalls that Winston told him in no uncertain terms that he didn't want Noftsker around anymore because he "hated his guts." Winston, however, remembers it somewhat differently.

He says he felt no animosity towards Russell and that he accepted the resignation because Russell was overqualified for the job.

At any rate, Russell decided it was time to get as far away from the AI Lab as possible. Without further encouragement, he moved to California.

After doing some consulting in Los Angeles, Noftsker founded a company called Pertron Controls, which manufactured computer-controlled welding systems. His work with the company took him back to the Boston area on a regular basis, and he frequently checked in on his former colleagues at MIT. After four years, Noftsker parted ways with Pertron in 1978. As he was looking for new career opportunities, he was drawn instinctively back to the AI Lab. Little had changed in the four years that he was gone, with one exception: Richard Greenblatt had working models of a LISP machine.

Since his first exposure to the LISP language, Greenblatt had proven himself a wizard at writing LISP code. Despite his proficiency, there was a major drawback to LISP in that it was so different from languages like FORTRAN that it strained the resources of the Digital Equipment computers that the AI Lab used. LISP simply didn't perform as well as hackers like Greenblatt knew it could. In order to really take advantage of LISP, a better computer needed to be developed.

Conventional computers and their software programs are designed to produce finite and predictable results every time they operate. This is ensured by running very rigid applications with very rigid parameters. These applications include inventory management, general ledger accounting, forms processing, and other programs that perform a multitude of standard business functions. While these programs are running, the computer is utilizing data sequentially, one piece at a time. Metaphorically, it takes one piece of data, does something with it, drops it off, and then runs back for another piece of data, much like a relay race. Only it happens so fast that humans never perceive the individual steps. To us, it looks like it's happening all at once.

Computer data is "coded" numerically (imagine the dots and dashes needed to create an individual letter in Morse code; the same mind-set applies), and so are the operations that manipulate the data. Everything relates to sequences of numbers. For the computer to do anything—even for it to display a word on a screen—programmers must define each piece of data and how it is to be handled at defined points in a process using this numerical code. A traditional computer and traditional computer program cannot do anything that is not predefined.

LISP, however, treats data as symbols. It does not rely on predefined procedures; indeed, part of the appeal of a LISP program is that the computer has a number of options to choose from while performing a function. In this way, a LISP program is similar to human thinking in that humans make decisions based on a number of different options. People do not go through life in a preordained manner, working on one piece of problem at a time before moving on to the next step. This would be too robotic, too structured—too computerized. For instance, a conventional computer program attempting to do two simple tasks would operate like this:

> Lift right foot.
> Move right foot forward.
> Lower right foot.
> Chew gum.
> Stop chewing gum.
> Lift left foot.
> Move left foot forward.
> Lower left foot.
> Chew gum.
> Stop chewing gum.
> Lift right foot . . .

And on and on. Ultimately, enough lines of code would be executed so that the program would describe an ongoing process of walking and chewing gum at the same time.

With a symbolic language like LISP, walking could already be defined as lifting, moving, and lowering feet in alternate succession. Chewing gum could also be defined as a continuous action. Components of the task do not need to be so literal in their specification, and might be programmed into the computer as

> Walk, chew gum—simultaneously.

Though oversimplified in this example, there is a certain flexibility and even "abstractness" in the symbolic command that obviously runs counter to the way that financial and personnel departments like their computers to run. LISP is too dynamic and too flexible for traditional application areas. As a result, computers that deal with information in a predefined order have trouble dealing with LISP and its symbolic representation.

A good deal of this has to do with memory management. Because of the strict manner in which conventional computers handle data, memory is used for one individual and sequential command after another. Once a procedure is accomplished, the computer has no need for the piece of data in that procedure again. If the same procedure comes up again, the computer deals with it almost as a new event. In symbolic processing, memory management is more complex. The computer needs to have access to the attributes of the symbols that it is handling on an ongoing basis. It cannot just define "walk" and discard all the associated characteristics that are involved in walking (raise foot, lower foot, etc.) because these characteristics are called out of memory to help provide continual direction for the entire length of time that "walking" is performed. Thus, the computer must be able to define what walking entails throughout the course of the procedure, and it must shuffle this information around its memory as the procedure continues. Using LISP and symbols, then, is a tradeoff in that the programmer does not have to specify every single program step, but does have to budget the computer's memory more efficiently.

Such memory gymnastics slowed traditional 1960s and 1970s computers—especially mainframes—down to a crawl. Having a computer spend hours trying to run through an entire LISP program drove people like Richard Greenblatt crazy. He knew that LISP was a better language for representing human thought than any of the more conventional languages like FORTRAN, yet his lab's computers weren't up to the task. No computers were. This made Greenblatt and the other hackers feel like concert pianists ready to perform their greatest work, only to find out that the only available instrument was a toy piano with plastic keys.

In order to use LISP to its fullest, the hackers in the AI Lab needed a computer that could handle the idiosyncrasies of LISP. Greenblatt and his fellow hackers began developing a machine called CONS (named for a LISP function) in 1973. They programmed LISP functions directly into the hardware, especially those functions related to memory management, so that the computer could continually free up its memory as a program was being run. On traditional computers, this memory management had to be written into the LISP software programs themselves, because the computers had no innate capabilities for doing so. The LISP-based computer also handled other chores that were difficult to recreate on mainframes and even minicomputers, such as maintaining a graphical interface (like those subsequently found on the Macintosh). By the time Greenblatt completed his first real prototype in 1976, nearly everything about LISP that was missing from traditional computers was built into the CONS machine.

Greenblatt had not done this for the purpose of improving computing around the world. He had done it so that hackers would never have to worry about slothlike program performance ever again. The machine was designed for hackers to give them a more friendly computing environment. In a sense, it was a gift from the ultimate hacker to all those hackers toiling away on what were considered substandard machines. The LISP-based CONS machine would make the hackers' lot in life much better by providing them with the best tool they could imagine.

Even though Greenblatt's CONS machine was created for hackers, enough people were impressed with it that it was sold internally at MIT to other research groups. Projects outside of the AI Lab that needed strong computer power actually purchased LISP machines for $50,000 each. The machine gained greater fame when Greenblatt and his colleagues demonstrated it during an international conference on artificial intelligence at MIT in the summer of 1978. The machine's built-in capabilities were so impressive that it even managed to arouse DARPA's jaded interest. The MIT AI Lab was given enough money by DARPA to build half a dozen of the computers, which DARPA believed might help speed up some of the LISP-based programs that it was still funding.

With funds from both DARPA and other groups at MIT, Greenblatt oversaw the construction of an improved LISP machine called the CADR (again, named for a LISP function that meant nothing to non-hackers), a computer that looked like a cross between a small refrigerator and a Macintosh. (I use the Macintosh references here because most people are familiar with the Macintosh's white screen with black letters, while most terminals and PCs have darkened screens with colored or white letters. The Macintosh, interestingly enough, had its origins at Xerox, which, as we will see, wanted to create a LISP machine of its own.)

It was at this point that Russell Noftsker reinserted himself into the life of the lab. He was intimately familiar with the potential of LISP from the years he had spent supervising the AI Lab's hackers. Unlike the hackers, though, he saw that there was a use for LISP—and a LISP machine—outside of the hacker world. If the government, along with large corporations, could be made to see the potential of artificial intelligence, they would have to have the proper equipment to run it on. And if the equipment were available, then they could be made to see the potential of AI. It was an unusual catch-22: if corporate America wanted AI, it would buy the machine, but it had to have the machine to want AI.

Noftsker approached Greenblatt in 1979 about the possibility of forming a company to sell the CADR machine. Making such an overture to the grand poobah of hackers required a fair degree of ballsiness on Noftsker's part. If there was anyone at the lab who would seem to be the least predisposed to entering into a business venture, it was Richard Greenblatt. The lab was his home, his world, his domain, his kingdom, his universe. It existed for the benefit and propagation of computer hacking, and he was the hacking master. What did he need a business for? Everything he needed in life was on the ninth floor of 545 Tech Square, Massachusetts Institute of Technology, Cambridge, Massachusetts, United States of America, 02139.

Greenblatt may have thought that Noftsker's suggestion about leaving the lab involved a lot of risk, but it was Noftsker who was taking the really big risk by asking Greenblatt to become part of a real world business venture. Richard may have been brilliant, but he was not a person who would make a good impression on investors or potential customers. In the roughly fifteen years that Greenblatt had been associated with the AI Lab, stories of his personal follies had not only become legend, they had become stranger than fiction. Primary among these legends was Greenblatt's disdain for personal hygiene. The odor that resulted from weeks without a bath or shower produced an aroma around Richard that resembled a crowded subway car full of unwashed humanity. Since very few of the hackers in the lab gave cleanliness a second thought, the fact that Greenblatt managed to be singled out for his personal stench is indicative of a higher plane of body odor. The more inventive hackers in the lab created an odor scale for describing how bad Richard's aroma was, an especially useful conversation tool for those rare social instances when they might be talking to someone not actually affiliated with the lab. This scale consisted of "Blatts," short for Greenblatt. For instance, flatulence was a microBlatt. A skunk was a milliBlatt. A sewage treatment plant was a miniBlatt. Richard himself was just a "Blatt." From there, the possibilities were endless, with mega and gigaBlatts only hinting at odoriferous nightmares not yet encountered.

It was the discovery of a megaBlatt, in truth, that may have saved Richard's life on one occasion. Sometime during the early development of the CONS machines, Greenblatt elected to walk around the lab without his shoes. The odor from his socks, which certainly had not been washed since the last time Richard himself had been, caused undue consternation in the hacker ranks. When told to put his shoes back on, Greenblatt complained that his feet had swelled up, and that his shoes wouldn't fit. Upon further investigation, it was determined that Richard had sliced his ankle on an exposed piece of metal from the innards of the CONS machine. The slice had resulted in a deep wound, which Richard had neglected to treat; the wound had since become viciously infected by the inordinate amount of bacteria on his unwashed body. The infection had swelled his foot to many times its normal size, although Greenblatt was too busy to pay much attention to it. Hence, his shoes would not fit. He was dragged bodily by his fellow hackers to the local emergency room, where doctors found the first stages of gangrene in his leg. Their diagnosis was that if left undiscovered for several more days, the infection would have necessitated the amputation of Greenblatt's foot. He was treated and released, and began subjecting himself, on doctor's orders, to a semi-regular regimen of soap and water.

Despite his lack of interest in Western standards of cleanliness, however, Greenblatt could be an extremely clever and articulate man with an incredible memory when he wanted to be. From his physical appearance and hygienic traits, it was easy to dismiss Richard as someone who was incapable of interpersonal communication, or who could only mumble when he opened his mouth. The reality was that there was substantially more to Richard Greenblatt than met the eye.

This, then, was the man Russell Noftsker wanted to start a company with. Richard had the brains—and now a proven product in his CADR machine— that Russell believed could form the basis of a viable commercial endeavor. Surprisingly, Greenblatt was willing to listen.

It wasn't that Richard was interested in going into business, or even contributing his talent to the marketplace. Instead, he was intrigued by the potential for getting his computer—the ultimate hacker tool—into the hands of other hackers. If that required selling his machine, well, maybe that was the only way to go. He was quite aware of the fact that MIT was not in the business of selling hardware, and some other way had to be found to get these machines out into the world. Yet Richard wanted any LISP machine business to be formed on his terms. Perhaps inspired by the "build it in your garage" mentality of Apple's Steve Wozniak and Steve Jobs, Greenblatt wanted to set up an organization that was run by hackers and sold equipment primarily to other hackers. He liked the idea of creating an informal company that was an offshoot of the AI lab; a bunch of guys making just enough money off their work to keep developing new products and ideas. This was the way it should be done, according to Greenblatt. No hacker in the truest sense of the term wanted to be like, say, Bill Gates, a guy who had alienated the entire hacker community in 1975 by making profits off his and other people's programming tools.

Russell's idea of a company built on the CADR machine was substantially different than Greenblatt's. He wanted to get venture capital investment, set up an organization with engineering and marketing departments, and move the machine into as many user sites as possible. If they were going to do it, Noftsker countered, they would have to do it with an all-or-nothing approach. There would be no half-baked middle ground where the company was staffed by part-timers who still owed their allegiance to the lab. It would be a business, and employees would be committed to making the business work.

Greenblatt held his ground, stating that he wouldn't let the CADR machine out of MIT under those circumstances. The two men were at an impasse. In both of their plans, a new company would require the participation of other members of the AI Lab. In fact, any LISP-based venture could only succeed if it utilized the considerable talents of the LISP hackers at MIT. Noftsker and Greenblatt decided to let the hackers have their say about the future of the CADR machine. Without explicitly saying so, they were also asking them to decide the immediate fate of the AI Lab itself.

~

Noftsker's business proposal created a substantial dilemma within MIT's hacker community. On one hand, leaving the AI Lab meant entering the real world. This involved schedules, responsibilities, clean clothes, and bathing—all of which were distasteful to the hackers. On the other hand, things were changing dramatically within the lab in early 1979. Some of the old-time hackers had actually gone on to real jobs at places like BBN and Digital Equipment. A few had even gotten married. Many of those that remained at MIT were in their late 20s and early 30s, and they began to have sneaking suspicions that there was more to life than sleeping next to a computer in the lab. Noftsker was offering a way out that meant they could leave together as a team. They would leave with dignity, with their heads held high, and still be spending most of their time hacking. It also meant that they would have some loose affiliation with the AI Lab. After all, the CADR machine and its LISP operating system would have to be licensed from MIT.

The most difficult part of leaving for the hackers would be the prospect of dealing with people. Since 1960, the hackers had lived in a vacuum that protected them from society. The only people they had to deal with were their landlords and the pizza delivery kid. As a group, they hung out together, shared the same ambitions, lived in the same apartments, and professed loyalty to a common love—the computer. Their world was each other and the computer; it literally involved no one else. Going along with Noftsker meant working with people—salesmen, secretaries, and others—who did not have the same mind-sets as they did, people who would not understand their devotion to creating new software programs or the thrill of developing an incremental coding step that helped to make a machine think.

The twist on this was not that the hackers feared "real world" people. They were not afraid of ridicule or even social shortcomings. Remarkably, the hackers felt that outsiders were not worthy of being part of their society—

the computer elite. They really believed that their work would change the world, whether the world deserved it or not. Hackers weren't pursuing AI for the benefit of mankind, of course; they were it doing to prove to themselves and to each other that they could do it. That alone was reason enough to justify their work and their behavior. They were hackers because they loved computers, but they also wanted to tame and to conquer the machine. That they had chosen to refer to Project MAC among themselves as "Man Against Computer" was proof of their ideology. Going into the real world would be an entirely different contest. For the hackers, it would become "Man Against Man."

It was a distorted way of looking at a business venture, but their arrogance can be explained away by putting their lives in perspective. Hackers literally knew nothing about the concerns of the everyday world. Vietnam had passed them by without any of them burning a draft card or marching through the streets of Boston. Civil rights were of no concern to young white males who never went outside the lab, and thus rarely met anyone of another race. Religion, politics, sports, entertainment, and the daily news were all lost in the twenty-four hour, nonjudgmental world of the computer.

❧

In the end, the hackers sided with Noftsker.

They gathered together on a frigid day in February 1979 to work things out among themselves. In a conference room on the eighth floor of Tech Square, a dozen hackers sequestered themselves with Noftsker and Greenblatt for seven hours to try to reach an agreement. Greenblatt stuck to his ideal of what a hacker company should be: no one would draw a salary until each machine was shipped, they would make every machine by hand, and he would be in charge. He insisted on these three main points, but they were the three points to which Noftsker would not give in. As Russell recalls, "We begged and pleaded and haggled and placated, but couldn't get him to change his mind. Finally, to end the meeting, I just said 'This isn't going anywhere. We will give you a year, Richard. If at the end of the year you haven't decided how to get these things produced, then the rest of us will feel we gave you your time and we'll do it the way we want to.' I don't think Richard responded right there, but everybody else agreed to it, so Richard understood it."

While Greenblatt basically agrees with this scenario, he claims there were other issues that weren't resolved to his satisfaction. He says that there was concern as to whether Noftsker would deliver on all his promises, or as Richard says, "whether Russell could be trusted." He says he was also concerned about the quality of other people that Russell wanted to bring into the company from outside of MIT.

Despite Richard's objections, the hackers left Greenblatt to fend for himself. None of them wanted to starve, and Greenblatt's plan didn't involve having a lot of cash with which to run an enterprise. Russell Noftsker, on the other hand, promised to find some venture capital that would help them to live comfortably while creating the ultimate fully equipped lab right across the street from the MIT campus. It would almost be better than MIT, if such a thing was possible: hours would be flexible, computer time would be available, and they would be getting paychecks.

This was not to say that they were against Richard Greenblatt. But with government funding at a premium, and diminished AI Lab interest on the part of Minsky, just how secure was the future of the lab? It was like asking what would become of the Catholic Church if God decided he wasn't interested in salvation anymore. The reason for existence would be questionable.

Still, no one could bear to leave Richard in the lurch. According to Noftsker, "Every one of us, to a man, regretted not having Richard's participation. This is completely aside from the fact that the computer was known as 'Greenblatt's machine,' which was the way he promoted it. We knew that he had been a principal proponent of the design of this thing, and that he had carried the ball on it in the early days. We felt like we were cutting him out, but we just couldn't work with him. But I made a deal for him that I didn't do for anybody else. I structured it so that Greenblatt could have the same percentage of stock that the other founders got if he would join up with us as a technical contributor, in a role that didn't give him authority over anyone else. I told him I would leave that offer on the table right up to the point when we signed a deal with the VCs [venture capitalists]. That role, and the founders' stock, was available to him for over a year after the date of incorporation." Greenblatt never even considered taking Noftsker up on the offer.

Richard started off slowly, his unfamiliarity with the outside world causing him to wander about aimlessly in a search for some business support. In fact, he really didn't even do much wandering. Greenblatt didn't know where to start at all.

He lucked out early on. Someone showed up on Richard's doorstep out of the clear blue and offered to help him get his business off the ground. If not for a series of coincidences, Greenblatt might still be putting LISP machines together by hand in the AI Lab today.

❧

Alexander Jacobson was a consultant with Control Data Corporation (CDC) in the late 1970s. At that time, CDC was considered second only to IBM in its ability to create large mainframe computers. Even though its primary customers were large corporations and research labs, the company began working on a project called PLATO, which would allow the mainframes that it had sold to schools—primarily as administrative machines—to be used as educational tools by students sitting at terminals. PLATO was a new venture for the huge company, and it brought in a number of outside consultants to assist in the development of the project. Alex Jacobson was one of them.

Jacobson is an extremely intense, wiry man, given to both quick laughter and bursts of shouting. He is an almost hyperactive speaker, quick to make his opinions heard on almost any subject. His outspokenness doesn't sit well with many of his AI colleagues, yet there is a certain amount of insight to his arguments that is lacking from most people in the AI business. First and foremost, Jacobson appreciates the fact that he is in business, and not in a playpen. That mentality seems to elude a large number of his peers.

As a consultant to Control Data on PLATO, Jacobson realized that one of the major problems with the program was that it was difficult to access. It was simply too computerlike for use by students. Discussing the problem with a friend in 1978, he decided that natural language might be a good way to handle the problem. He pitched the idea to CDC, which listened to it enthusiastically. After hearing his pitch, Control Data execs also thought that natural language might be useful in other areas of the company, such as in providing a better interface for its customers. CDC told Jacobson that if he wanted to develop such a program, it would provide seed money to fund the venture.

Jacobson set about finding hackers that could develop a natural language application from scratch. Unlike most AI companies, which would be built around the nucleus of Stanford and MIT, Jacobson opted to get started right where he was—in Los Angeles. Among the people he enlisted at the outset was Chuck Williams, a professor at the University of Southern California, who had been using LISP to develop an expert system of his own design. Williams brought in several other LISP hackers, and the whole group commenced to create Jacobson's natural language program. The problem, as every LISP hacker knew at the time, was that mainstream computers were not quite up to the task. As Jacobson recounts it: "We were using a DEC-10, which we planned on using during the course of all of 1979, to work on this LISP program. Within one month, we had exhausted the entire machine. The LISP hackers just looked at me and said, 'We told you this was going to happen. We need a better computer.' So the next thing I did was go to see Richard Greenblatt."

Jacobson's hackers had heard about Greenblatt putting together his CADR machine in the AI Lab, a hardwired computer that was being assembled literally piece by piece at MIT. If they were going to get their LISP program up and running the way they needed it to, the hackers told Jacobson, then someone ought to go talk to Greenblatt.

In the fall of 1979, about eight months after Greenblatt's confrontation with Noftsker, Jacobson caught a flight to Boston and met Greenblatt at MIT. By that time, the AI Lab had produced nearly thirty of the LISP machines, although each one was still built by hand. Jacobson had an offer for Richard. "I told him that we had money from Control Data to buy some computers and we wanted to buy one of his LISP machines. Richard said that he couldn't sell them out of the lab, but that he was in the process of putting together a commercial enterprise that would sell the machines. He told me that they would be available after the first of the year. I waited a few months and went back to see him in February of 1980. In all the time since I had last seen him, about five months, Richard had not done a single thing on his business since I had seen him last."

Alex Jacobson and his hackers needed the LISP machine, but it was obvious that Greenblatt wasn't going out of his way to get a LISP machine company up and running. In the meantime, Russell Noftsker and the AI Lab renegades were tired of waiting for Richard to do something, since they had promised to give Greenblatt his head start. Jacobson took Richard aside and decided to give him a shove into the real world. Alex offered to help Greenblatt put a business plan together and get his company off the ground in return for a seat on the new company's board and the option to buy the first couple of machines that it produced. Greenblatt agreed.

Upon returning to Los Angeles, Jacobson started looking for a businessman to team up with Greenblatt in the new company. He was introduced by some colleagues to F. Stephen Wyle, a young executive who had just left a company called EMG Hydraulics. Although only a year older than Richard Greenblatt, Steve Wyle had already spent a lot of time in the business side of the computer industry. He was on the board of directors of his family's Wyle Laboratories, one of Silicon Valley's prominent technical research labs, and had been active in that company's international operations. He had also spent considerable "extracurricular" time with EMG, a firm that he had cofounded. But Steve was more than a prodigal son eager to seek his fortune outside of the family business; he had received his undergraduate degree from Carnegie-Mellon University, one of the esteemed havens of AI.

Wyle listened with interest to Jacobson's description of AI and the hand-built machines sitting on the ninth floor of MIT's Tech Square. He and Jacobson went back to Boston in April 1980 to talk things over with Greenblatt, and after a few meetings, the three agreed to go into business together. Wyle and Richard would run the company, to be named LISP Machine, Inc. (LMI), and Jacobson would get a seat on the board for insti-gating the start-up process.

Greenblatt and Wyle agreed to pay MIT $85,000 as a prepayment for the use of the CADR machine, which from that point forward would be known simply as a LISP machine (although LMI would sell its first few computers as "CADR" models). The agreement was non-exclusive, which allowed MIT to sell the rights to the LISP machine to other companies in the future. That gave Noftsker and his associates the ability to use the machine even after Greenblatt and Wyle got their business going.

Greenblatt originally built the first few machines out of his corner of the AI Lab before moving to a small space on Blackstone Street in Cambridge. Wyle, at this point, had agreed to give in to Richard's desire to run a down and dirty operation. He himself decided not to move to Cambridge, and set up LMI's physical headquarters in Culver City, California. This location would be the site of administration, sales, and marketing, while Cambridge would be dedicated to engineering and development.

The moment that Control Data's order for the first LISP machine was in place, LISP Machine, Inc. was officially in business. Now a part of an actual capitalistic enterprise, Richard set about filling customer orders and began toying with the idea of a commercial "dream machine" version of the LISP computer, one that could be used by more than one hacker at a time. The concept of programmers sharing data—long a computer hacker dream—might ultimately be realized in a multi-user LISP machine from LMI.

Wyle and Greenblatt worked out of their respective sites in Cambridge and Los Angeles through most of 1980, bootstrapping the operation with money from the Control Data order, which had been expanded to two ma-chines. In accordance with Greenblatt's wishes, new orders were the sole source of all the money infused into the company. This was achieved by get-ting 80 percent of each order up front from the customer and using that money to buy the materials needed to build each machine. In effect, it was a made-to-order business, with most of the money demanded at the time of the order. In retrospect, it was a bit like paying for your car before it even got to the assembly line.

LMI got little support or recognition from the AI community at MIT, which was anxiously waiting for Russell Noftsker. While three or four hackers pledged their allegiance to Richard, fourteen of the lab's other LISP hackers had already agreed to work for Noftsker as soon as he was ready. When it became clear to Noftsker that Richard had not done anything between the meeting in February and December of 1979 other than have a preliminary meeting with Alex Jacobson, Russell began the process of incorporating his company, which was to be called Symbolics. He admits that it wasn't quite a year to the day since the fateful conference room meeting, but he felt that by the time Symbolics actually got running, Greenblatt would have had more than enough time.

Noftsker had met a lawyer named Robert Adams during his last days at Pertron, and Adams liked Noftsker's plans for Symbolics. Adams agreed to write the company business plan and shop it around to the venture capital community in return for a piece of the company. The two of them thus became the company's actual founders, and they both put up their California homes to get an initial credit line for their new business. By March 1980, Symbolics was a real company, so to speak, with a small office in a garage in Woodland Hills, California.

Noftsker was busy throughout 1980 arranging licensing agreements with MIT and investigating manufacturing options while Adams tried to get some investment money. But after nearly a whole year of trying to get venture funding, Symbolics had not raised a single dime. As 1980 drew to a close, the fourteen AI hackers who had agreed to sign on with Russell were getting impatient.

&

Greenblatt already considered many of his ex-hacker pals at Symbolics to be traitors to the LISP machine cause, even as he himself was trying to get his own LISP company off the ground. They, in turn, must have looked at Richard with a kind of sadness, believing from the get go that they were going to overpower him with money and manpower. On the day when Symbolics opened its doors for business, the assumption went, the AI Lab would virtually be deserted, all the hackers flocking to the new company in a mass exodus out of MIT's most prestigious research facility.

Even though Richard Greenblatt would not be going with them, he still had something of his own to attend to, a new place to call home. There was some consolation in that. However, there were two men who would remain at the AI Lab, both of whom would be disgruntled and angry at the loss of talent that MIT had sustained. The first was a hacker named Richard Stallman, who couldn't believe that any self-respecting MIT hacker would go to work for "a corporation."

The second was a man who found out too late that the computer world wanted more than a philosopher king. His decision to remain and hold court over the theoretical musings of the AI Lab would eventually be his public downfall, and he would come to be considered an "artificial intelligence exile" as AI became a real business.

Looking back on the way things were going in 1980, one would have thought that Marvin Minsky would have been better prepared.

15

Edward Feigenbaum and the Art of Combining Technology with Showmanship

The AI community on the East Coast was thinking "hardware, hardware, hardware" in 1979 as it put together its business plans to commercialize artificial intelligence technology. Edward Feigenbaum, head of Stanford's AI Laboratory, was—then as now—a contrarian. He was thinking "software, software, software."

Born in 1936, Feigenbaum was only nine years younger than Marvin Minsky, but they were worlds apart. Minsky was first generation AI, while Feigenbaum almost single-handedly spear-headed the second generation of AI. Feigenbaum was a disciple of Newell and Simon, then an associate of John McCarthy, and then a researcher in his own right, able to stand up to his predecessors' achievements as a true inno-vator. His influence was substantial enough in the AI community that when it came time to christen Feigenbaum as one of the leaders of AI, the commu-nity suddenly realized that it had spread itself too thin in giving out the du-bious title of "Father of AI" to everyone who had come down the pike. But Feigenbaum was clearly deserving of some kind of "father" title, especially since he had been the foremost proponent of developing expert systems. A new moniker had to be developed because that's the way the AI community honored its best and brightest. Ed Feigenbaum became the "Father of Ex-pert Systems."

Feigenbaum is an unassuming-looking middle-aged man, hardly the type that seems capable of stirring up trouble in the U.S. government or the world's AI community. Even when he speaks passionately, he never gets loud or boorish in the way that Minsky can. He is fond of plain brown and gray suits and a plain tie, a wardrobe that sets him apart from the AI pack by its subtle nod to the business community. His reddish hair is thin on top, and he al-ways wears wire-rimmed glasses. One might say that in appearance he could be any nondescript mid-level corporate executive. As he gets older, he and Hubert Dreyfus actually bear a passing resemblance to each other, a fact that probably dismays them both.

One thing that is a dead giveaway to the fact that Feigenbaum is not re-ally a corporate man is his pipe. Ed is never seen, or photographed, without it. Lit or unlit, the pipe has become a Feigenbaum trademark. He uses it to point with and he uses it to emphasize his statements. In a way, it is his stage prop. And if anyone in AI ever knew the value of a prop, it is Ed Feigenbaum. Every showman worth his salt has a good, recognizable prop.

He came to Stanford in 1965 at the request of John McCarthy, ostensi-bly to handle the administration of Stanford's new AI lab. McCarthy didn't want to deal with administration, and Feigenbaum was anxious to get out of Berkeley, where he felt that his work on machines and their capability to mimic reasoning functions were not appreciated. Stanford offered an oppor-tunity to expand his horizons in AI.

Yet Feigenbaum had acquired one skill at Berkeley that would set him apart from almost everybody else in AI (excluding Minsky): he had an uncanny knack for raising money. Ed, along with another researcher named Julian Feldman, managed to get $70,000 from the Carnegie Corporation in the early 1960s to look into the potential of artificial intelligence. This amount of money, broken down into lots of roughly $23,000 per year, was an unheard of sum for researchers at the time, and it set Feigenbaum apart from virtually all his peers. Though the funds were used primarily for research, part of the money went into compiling the book *Computers and Thought,* which Feigenbaum and Feldman coauthored. It proved to be the first volume of papers ever compiled about artificial intelligence, and it would establish a trend for Feigenbaum whereby he would use the power of the printed word to get what he wanted.

Even though Berkeley has a reputation for being among the most liberal colleges in the United States, Feigenbaum found that his work in AI was stifled by his older colleagues. This environment prompted him to eagerly accept McCarthy's offer for the position of computer science lab administrator at Stanford in 1965. Within months after bringing Feigenbaum on board, McCarthy had moved himself off the campus, and Feigenbaum was running the show. One of the first things that he did as lab overseer was establish the Heuristic Programming Project (HPP), a concentrated effort to build AI computer programs based on the expertise of human individuals.

Feigenbaum was among the first AI researchers to appreciate the netherworld of human experience as a critical component of intelligence. He encountered this when he set out to create DENDRAL, the system for analyzing mass spectrography. The rules from a text book or the laws of science paled when they were put into actual practice, because there was more information that had to be programmed into the computer than simple facts. Feigenbaum's heuristics were a first step in this direction, but heuristics were not easily identifiable nor easily discovered.

During the 1970s, Feigenbaum realized that heuristics needed to be extracted from experts in much the same way that teeth were extracted from unwilling dental patients—in a long and arduous process. Experts did not always have reasons for what they did, they "just did them." But in order to encode this knowledge of the experts into a computer program, the knowledge had to be made clear and had to have a structure that was translatable into computer code. The dilemma Feigenbaum faced was how to get this information out of the experts and into a computer.

At first glance, such a problem would probably have to involve two people. One would be a psychologist who would extract the data (heuristics) from the expert in a series of interviews, while the second person would turn this data into a computer program. Feigenbaum believed that these two people could be made into one, a combination psychologist and hacker—a superhacker, as it were. This person would become well-versed in the same field of expertise as the expert being interviewed (a biologist, say), and then after interviewing this leading expert, would have enough understanding of the subject matter to be able to program this expertise into a computer.

The need for a person with these capabilities became abundantly clear during the creation of Feigenbaum's second—and perhaps most famous—AI project, called MYCIN. Feigenbaum enlisted the aid of his computer science colleague Bruce Buchanan along with Edward Shortliffe of the Stanford Medical Center, and the three men sought to create a system for diagnosing infectious blood diseases. Like DENDRAL, the mass spectrometer analysis program, MYCIN had its roots in medicine—hence Shortliffe's role. Most of the work was done by Buchanan and Shortliffe, with Feigenbaum in the role of supervisor.

MYCIN acted like a specialist examining a hospital patient who had developed an infection, perhaps after undergoing surgery. When patients do develop infections after surgery, their attending physicians may not necessarily be experts in infectious diseases. In those cases, a specialist needs to be brought in. However, medical specialists, or any experts for that matter, are not always available at the moment they are needed. Expertise is scarce, by its definition, which is why so few people are truly considered experts or specialists in their fields. In the case of a patient who had contracted some infectious blood disease, MYCIN would act as a computer "clone" of the blood specialist and assist the attending physician in determining what the disease was and what the resulting treatment should be.

Diagnosing blood diseases entails understanding the patient's medical history, knowing the patient's current condition, and having an extensive knowledge of the combinations and permutations of the diseases themselves. Trying to put all of this information into a computer as a set of rules would be overwhelming because it would require that every single possibility that could be encountered in a patient be written as a rule. Seemingly trivial variables would have to be taken into consideration. One rule might state, "If the patient is male, over the age of fifty, and has a heart condition, then look for signs of . . ." while another might state "If the patient is male, under the age of fifty, and has a heart condition, then look for signs of . . ." For the computer to be aware of every possibility (age, sex, health, allergies, prior conditions, etc.) would involve thousands and even hundreds of thousands of rules.

The Stanford team realized that trying to build an application with thousands of rules would not make for an efficient program. By the time the computer sorted through all these rules, the patient might already be dead and buried. They came up with a different scheme, one which bore more resemblance to the way a human specialist might make an actual diagnosis.

Experts and specialists have facts and heuristics that they rely on in their work, but they do not necessarily use the facts as part of a rule. They do not, for instance, literally think that "If Waldo is fifty-six years old, and he has a heart condition, then I should check for signs of disease X." Rather, the knowledge of facts is separate from the rules of diagnosis, and the two are brought together for every situation that the specialist encounters. Facts are established, and then a diagnosis is made. Should the patient be a healthy young woman under the age of thirty, a whole different set of rules is used by the specialist than those used in diagnosing Waldo. Facts relating to the actual diseases remain the same in both cases, but the particulars of the woman's case require a different interpretation of those facts.

With this sort of duality in mind, Shortliffe and Buchanan decided to create an AI system that had two parts. One part would be the facts about blood diseases: how they were caused, what their symptoms were, how to treat them. The second part would be a rule system that would take these facts into account, and then work with them to arrive at a diagnosis. They consulted texts and disease specialists to come up with the facts, such as, "Aerobic bacteria can enter the body through the gastrointestinal (GI) tract" and "E. coli is an aerobic bacteria." Structuring information this way was the straightforward part of building the system (if any of it can be considered to be completely straightforward, which it cannot). When it was completed, this set of facts would be called a knowledge base. A knowledge base is similar in concept to a database, where data is stored as a group or list of specific items, as in an address book. Instead of numbers or addresses or ingredients, though, the list contains pieces of knowledge.

The more difficult part of creating MYCIN was in producing a way for these facts to be used as parts of rules. They chose to fashion a question-and-answer session by which the computer would get all the facts of the case, and then it could make decisions by invoking only those rules that applied to that case. What takes place, then, is a session in which MYCIN asks the physician questions about the patient until there is enough information to make a diagnosis. The following is an example of the way that MYCIN performs its diagnosis. The capital letters indicate the response that the doctor types into the computer at MYCIN's prompting. Note that MYCIN refers to itself in the first person, using "I" and "my," which adds a slightly disconcerting human touch to the session.

1. What is the patient's name?
   WALDO

2. What is the patient's age?

   56

3. What is the patient's sex?

   MALE

4. Have you been able to obtain cultures from the site of Waldo's infection?

   YES

5. Have you identified the type of infection from the culture?

   YES

6. What is the type of infection?

   PRIMARY BACTERIAL

7. This infection will be referred to as Infection-1 from Culture-1. From where was Culture-1 taken?

   PATIENT'S BLOOD

8. Do you suspect that Waldo may have an infection at a site from which you have not taken a culture?

   NO

9. What is the suspected entry site of bacteria into Waldo?

   SKIN

10. Has Waldo exhibited abnormal neurologic signs, such as coma or seizures?

    YES

11. Has Waldo ever undergone neurosurgery?

    NO

12. Based on this information, my diagnosis is that Infection-1 is related to meningitis. The following questions will be used to determine the cause of the infection. Has Waldo been exposed to infectious diseases recently?

    NO

13. Does it appear that Waldo acquired the infection in the hospital?

    YES

14. Is Waldo a burn victim?

    YES

15. Based on this information, the following bacteria are the most likely causes of Waldo's meningitis. In order of likelihood, they are E. coli; pseudomonas-aeruginosa; diplococcus-pneumoniae; enterobacter. The following questions will be used to determine treatment. Does Waldo have any clinically significant allergic reactions to medication?

NO

16. How much does Waldo weigh, in pounds?

165

17. My recommendation is to treat Waldo with 3 grams of ampicillin and 100 milligrams of gentamicin, in combination.

MYCIN's actual session would involve more detailed questions than shown here, and it would also give reasons for its decisions. The decision to list E. coli bacteria as the most likely source of infection might be because E. coli is a major cause of meningitis, and that it is oftentimes a cause of comas in people who have not exhibited other obvious coma-inducing infections or injuries. It would tell the physician that based on its application of rules to facts (Waldo developed the infection in the hospital, Waldo did not have neurosurgery, Waldo was in a coma, etc.), this was the most likely scenario it could derive from the information it had obtained.

Buchanan and Shortliffe's structure for allowing the computer to produce rules from its knowledge base came to be known as an inference engine. Together, the inference engine and the knowledge base served to act as a complete software application that behaved like a human expert. Beyond that, though, it became apparent that MYCIN's knowledge base could be stripped away from the entire system and leave an inference engine that would work with other knowledge bases. The MYCIN knowledge base only had information about infectious blood diseases, and had no knowledge of any domain other than infectious blood diseases. It was still an idiot-savant; if you were to ask MYCIN how to repair a fuel pump, it would probably prescribe a dose of penicillin. The inference engine, however, could stand on its own and accept new knowledge bases in any field. With a new knowledge base, the inference engine might become an expert in inventory management or oil refining or even some other medical specialty.

When stripped of its knowledge base, MYCIN became a shell that the Stanford AI researchers called EMYCIN, for "Empty MYCIN" or "Essential MYCIN." It was like pulling the body and interior off of a car, leaving just the frame, transmission, and engine. Depending on which body parts were added, the frame could become a Firebird or a Trans Am (which is exactly what General Motors does—produces two different cars from the same basic frame). The possibilities now existed to create more expert systems with less work, because the frame, or shell as it was called by the AI group, was already designed. Just add a knowledge base, and you had an instant computer expert.

A major obstacle that still caused a bottleneck in creating knowledge bases was getting the basic information out of a particular expert. As mentioned before, experts usually know more than they can verbalize; it's hard to verbalize a lifetime's worth of knowledge and experience. Using manuals and reference works helped with some of the basics, but these items did not contain the heuristics that were so important to Ed Feigenbaum's definition of what an expert did. A Stanford student named Randall Davis, who had done some work on MYCIN (and is alleged to have come up with the term inference engine), developed a program called TEIRESIAS, which could be used with an inference engine to help an expert state facts and conditions. It had its own interview-type interface, which prompted the expert to talk about the specifics of his or her work. As the interview progressed, TEIRESIAS (by comparing new data to previously input information) could verify that the expert did not contradict himself or herself, and it tried to ensure that the expert provided all the essential details of a specific scenario.

But who was to run this interview process, getting all the specific information into the newly formed knowledge base? Certainly not the expert—very few of them were, or are, computer literate to the degree that they could do any actual programming themselves. If not the expert, then who? Feigenbaum's super-hacker, of course.

Over the course of creating these expert systems in the mid and late 1970s, the super-hacker who was part Freud, part Phil Donahue, and part Richard Greenblatt evolved at Stanford. It was not just one person, but a group of people who knew all the aspects of programming in LISP and extracting data from human experts. They were called knowledge engineers. The best of them had, or would have, degrees in computer science and psychology or philosophy, disciplines that were needed to deal with both men and machines. Feigenbaum began promoting the concept of knowledge engineering—and the talents of individual knowledge engineers—in his teachings, speeches, and papers. There was a limited market for such talents in 1979, of course, just as there was a limited market for stripped-down inference engines. All in all, there was a limited market for AI in general, with customers confined to research institutions and the government.

Feigenbaum knew that he had the basis for a commercial enterprise. The inference engine, or expert system shell, could be a product, while knowledgable engineers could be consultants or service personnel that would develop expert systems. However, no one was much interested in commercial AI in 1979.

No one except the Japanese.

❧

During 1979, a number of AI researchers from the United States were asked to speak at forums and seminars throughout Japan. Paid nice fees and expenses, these researchers, including Feigenbaum, were more than happy to discuss their work in a public forum, even if it was a Japanese public forum. Japanese researchers themselves made frequent trips to the United States to visit labs and sit in on computer conferences. All the while, they were accumulating and assimilating information that would be used as the foundation for their big push into AI.

Look back at the mind-set of Japan, Inc.—the catchall term for the united front of Japanese government, academia, and industry—as it existed in 1979. It was making great inroads into most markets that relied on manufactured goods, except for computers. The dominant force in computing was IBM, an American company, and IBM did not look as if it would lose its market share any time soon. Since the commercialization of computers in the late 1950s, an inestimable amount of money for those computers had gone directly to IBM. Worldwide, investment in IBM machines and IBM-related products totaled billions, if not trillions, of dollars. The Japanese, determined as they might be, were practical enough to realize the futility of trying to completely dislodge IBM by coming out with their own brand of copycat computers.

There had also been some recent nasty legal problems between IBM and various members of Japan, Inc. over theft of trade secrets, which made many of Japan's computer makers a trifle queasy about just how far IBM would go to protect itself in the marketplace. But if Japan was going to become a big player in the world's computer market, it had to find a way to get around IBM. The question was how.

Computing offered Japan the best opportunity for maintaining long-term growth, and possibly leadership, in the world market. The country had always been short on natural resources, and its leaders realized that smokestack industries like steel production would ultimately strain both those resources and its crowded population. The information industry, with its computers and software and telecommunications, would be a much more efficient market for the Japanese. The information age was already in full swing, and it was abundantly clear that information was the key to the marketplace of the future. As Japanese people and organizations became more cognizant of this fact, they would not be content to be the rulers of the factories; they would want control of the information market. Computing offered the best path into the future for Japan as a growing economic powerhouse.

Artificial intelligence was a new enough form of computing that no one country or company had established a real head start. No one had commercialized it to a notable degree, at any rate. AI also promised to be the next and perhaps most important advanced technology to involve computers. Best of all, from what the Japanese had gleaned by picking the brains of U.S. researchers, AI was an area of computing that actually disdained the use of IBM's ubiquitous computers. It appeared that the development of thinking machines would necessitate a new generation of computers that were vastly different than those that IBM was churning out.

If AI was to be the wave of the future, and IBM computers were ill-suited for AI development, then that conceivably meant that IBM's existing machines would not be part of the wave of the future. Might it not be possible, then, to obsolete IBM's installed base by creating the perfect AI computer?

As Kazuhiro Fuchi and his colleagues met to discuss the future of computing, a plan based on building an AI computer began to take shape. In essence, Japan would leapfrog all the computers currently in use by inventing the next generation of computers. The history of computing had already gone through four generations as of the late 1970s. The first generation of computers were built using vacuum tubes, the second generation used transistors, the third generation used integrated circuits, and the fourth generation of computers was built on very large scale integration (VLSI) of microprocessors. In essence, the fourth generation, which was just beginning to produce personal computers, was using microchips that were so complex that they were really computers in and of themselves. These microprocessors had found their way into everything from cars to refrigerators, and they were the state of the art in 1979. It was this technology that Japan wanted to leapfrog. To do so, Japan Inc. would have to develop a new type of computer based on a new type of component. Such a component, in preparation for the onslaught of AI, would have to have intelligence functions built right into it. It would have to be capable of enormous processing power since effective AI would require more computer power than was currently available. The next generation of computer, the fifth generation, would involve a complete rethinking of the way that computers were designed.

Fuchi decided to give his computing project a name that would leave no doubt in anyone's mind about what he and Japan intended to accomplish. He called it The Fifth Generation Project.

Although Japan had made no formal announcement about its computing plans, word began to leak out of Japan to the American and European AI labs. Snippets of data filtered through the computer science community, although nothing of substance was revealed. The Japanese were up to something, and that was about all anybody knew. It raised the curiosity of U.S. AI researchers, especially Feigenbaum, who had given talks in Japan about his own work in expert systems. No one was surprised, but no one was alarmed, either. It seemed to be a matter of course that Japan would eventually get into AI since every other industrial country was exploring it. If Russia and Hungary could establish AI research centers, then anybody could, especially Japan. It wasn't a big deal.

Yet.

The Stanford Computer Science department under Feigenbaum had worked closely with the Stanford School of Medicine for most of the 1970s. This relationship had helped to spawn the DENDRAL and MYCIN expert systems. There were other joint ventures, one of the most significant being a project begun in 1975 researching molecular genetics, especially cloning. This program was called MOLGEN (for molecular genetics), and its aim was to apply artificial intelligence techniques to the analysis of DNA. Biotechnology had just begun to attract attention from the medical and research communities, and MOLGEN's research was funded in part by the National Institute of Health. Specifically, MOLGEN helped biologists in gene cloning experiments by advising them which steps to take relative to cloning a specific DNA sequence. It did this by establishing a cloning goal that the biologist wanted to achieve, and then, based on its knowledge of molecular biology, MOLGEN developed experiment plans for the biologist to follow in order to complete the clone.

In 1980, three primary participants on the medical side of MOLGEN decided to make use of the AI methodologies that they had learned while developing MOLGEN. Laurence Kedes, Douglas Brutlag, and Peter Friedland approached Ed Feigenbaum with the intent of starting a company that could sell its "biotech-meets-AI" expertise to other genetic researchers around the world. The idea was to put genetic engineering software on a large computer and have customers access it as they wished. This would involve computer timesharing, the multiple-user practice developed by John McCarthy at MIT, and later perfected at Stanford. Researchers could pay a basic fee or license to this new company to gain access to the computer, and they would then become "customers." These customers from all over the world could dial up the computer and use the software at their convenience just by logging on to the system with the proper passwords. They would be billed according to the amount of time they spent on the computer, and which programs that they accessed. The programs would enable users to "prepare oligonucleotide dictionaries, dinucleotide and codon usage tables, and align two sequences using the Smith-Waterman improvements to the Needleman-Wunch method," along with other similarly scintillating functions. This may seem beyond the scope, or interest, of the man on the street, but the Stanford researchers knew there were plenty of scientists eager to get their hands on this information.

Feigenbaum agreed to join the three men, and in September 1980 they formed IntelliGenetics. They moved into a small office complex just down the road from Stanford, allowing the men to come and go from IntelliGenetics to their "day jobs" at the university. The company rented space on two mainframes, one at UCLA and one in Paris, and purchased its own DEC 2060 mainframe to give research customers as much access as possible. Feigenbaum served primarily as an advisor to the other three, though he was given a hefty amount of stock and a place on the board of directors. IntelliGenetics wasn't an AI company in the pure sense of selling AI products or tools, but as far as Feigenbaum was concerned, it was a good start. IntelliGenetics had provided an entreé into the medical market based on his work in AI, but there was still a market for the tools and services related to building expert systems. And after all, he was "The Father of Expert Systems." Who better to propagate the world of science and industry with expert systems companies than the acknowledged parent of the technology?

And if one AI company was good, wouldn't two be better? That idea was circulating around Stanford's computer science center in 1980. IntelliGenetics was partially an AI spinoff, but it owed more of its expertise and clientele to the guys over in the School of Medicine. A real, pure-play "nothing but AI" company selling AI software and expertise could be a viable enterprise on its own merits. They could take the technology out of Stanford and sell it on their own, just like Greenblatt and Noftsker were planning on doing with MIT's technology.

It just so happened that during 1980, Feigenbaum and some of his students were putting the finishing touches on a compendium of all the AI work done in the United States (and parts of Europe) since the early 1960s. Having established a good reputation with the publication of the first-ever book on AI, *Computers And Thought*, it was only natural that Feigenbaum enhance that reputation and follow up with another book, even if it was almost twenty years later. There was certainly more to write about, or at least to edit. The new book was a review of both the work and the techniques used to develop programs and projects, ranging from Newell and Simon's General Problem

Solver to Stanford's own MOLGEN. The title of the work, *The Handbook of Artificial Intelligence*, was an understatement of the grandest kind. Ultimately encompassing three volumes and more than 1500 pages, it was more of an encyclopedia than a mere handbook. Impressive in its scope, the book served as a single source for exposing AI researchers to specific and diverse methods of creating expert systems, natural language interfaces, voice recognition programs, and a host of other minutiae that could not be found elsewhere. *The Handbook of Artificial Intelligence* was not intended for the casual reader.

The tail end of the *Handbook* project was in sight just as IntelliGenetics, LMI, and Symbolics were filing their incorporation papers. *The Handbook* did have a slight bias toward West Coast research—unavoidable perhaps, given the location of Stanford—although a number of its reviewers and editors did come from CMU, the University of Texas, and other colleges with growing AI research groups. The physical act of putting the publication together also seemed to create an epicenter for people interested in exploring the commercial possibilities of AI. A large number of the contributors liked the idea of putting together an AI company. They also liked the idea of doing it all together, perhaps as one big group of AI guys. Maybe it could be a company with the biggest concentration of AI researchers in the world!! Dozens of AI researchers just selling AI products and services!! It sounded like something from Junior Achievement: a bunch of friends and associates forming a company to work on in their spare time.

It also sounded preposterous, at least on paper. But they did it anyway. And Ed Feigenbaum led the charge.

Chapter **16**

Symbolics, Xerox, and Vulture Capitalists

Investment in the First AI Start-Ups

Of all the AI companies started prior to 1981, only Russell Noftsker did everything according to the book. He had a product, the LISP machine from MIT. He had skilled employees, fourteen of them from the very heart of AI land. He had a plan, to sell these machines to research labs around the country, especially those involved with DARPA. Best of all, he had plans for investment money, lots of it.

Unfortunately, he was not getting any of the latter.

Noftsker knew, as did everyone else in the AI Lab, that Richard's start-up would be half-hearted. That meant that Richard's promised one-year head start, from February 1979 to February 1980, didn't amount to much. It would take at least that long for Richard to tear himself from the lab and figure out how to do anything commercial.

After Richard joined forces with Alex Jacobson and Steve Wyle to form LMI in early 1980, Noftsker and Bob Adams got busy taking their business plan to nearly everyone in the venture capital industry.

Venture capital is the necessary evil of the high-technology business. Most researchers who realize that they have a potentially profitable product do not have the skills to start their own companies. This is simply a fact of life, like spring following winter. Researchers live to create, they do not live to sell or to administer. Minsky and McCarthy were typical manifestations of this personality trait; that's why they hired Noftsker and Feigenbaum to run their labs for them.

Part of starting a company involves getting funds with which to actually make the company a reality. Unless a researcher, or any entrepreneur, has someone ready to buy his or her products the moment the company sign is nailed up, then start-up funds are needed. In a high-tech company, this money goes to acquiring the basics: office space, employees, and necessary supplies like computers, software, testing equipment. Richard Greenblatt was fortunate in that Alex Jacobson and Control Data were ready to give him money for his product as soon as he had one to sell. This arrangement, however, is an extreme rarity in the computer business, so most entrepreneurs turn to venture capitalists.

Without generalizing too much, venture capitalists are either MBA students or former successful businessmen who want to put money into brand-new business ventures. They do not use their own money—they use someone else's. Funds are raised by the venture capital firm from outside investors who are trusting these MBAs and businessmen to use their money wisely and hopefully turn a profit from it. In this way, the venture capital firm serves the role of a quasi-banking and financial management firm. From there, the venture capitalists scour the countryside looking for entrepreneurs and start-ups that need money to build their companies. Using their investor-generated funds, the venture capitalists put money into these start-ups in return for a certain percentage of the new companies' stock. They are banking on the prospect that these start-ups will someday go public on the stock market. When that happens, their investments can be sold as stock on Wall Street and they can gain a nifty return on the investment. Actually a nifty return is not what they want. They want a monstrous return on their investment. This is then passed on to the venture capitalists' own backers—with a tidy sum reserved for the venture firm itself, of course.

By bringing in venture capitalists, which I will refer to from here on as VCs, entrepreneurs have to give up a portion of their company. When a company starts, the guy who starts it is either the 100-percent owner or an equal partner with other founders. If there are four founders, say, each person usually gets a 25-percent stake in the company. The VCs only give investment money, however, in return for shares of the company. The single individual who goes to the VCs may find that he has to give up a good chunk of his ownership for that money. For the sake of argument, let's say the VCs want 20 percent for their investment (the numbers vary; you wouldn't believe how many people sell off almost 100 percent of their ownership to get VC money). In the case of the single individual, then, he or she only retains 80-percent control of the company. In the case of the four individuals, each person's share is diluted to 20 percent from 25 percent, making the VC an equal partner.

VCs almost universally require a seat on the board of directors as part of their investment. That means that they put a representative of their choosing—usually one of the freshly scrubbed MBAs—on the governing body of the new company. Thus, they get some say in how the business is run. This is where problems occur. VCs want a return on their investment. That's about it. Entrepreneurs, especially those of the scientific variety, want to create a product that conforms to their vision of something revolutionary and useful. They also want to get rich, but they have an underlying personal concern and passion for the essence of the company. The last thing entrepreneurs want to hear while they're trying to build a product is, "When are you going to make a profit from this damn thing?" Nonetheless, that is exactly what they hear when they bring VCs on board. This is also why VCs are viewed as a necessary evil.

Over time, most companies need more than one infusion of capital. This requires going back to the VCs several times for additional money, and more often than not, it means getting more VCs involved. The more money that VCs give, the more the ownership of the company is diluted, especially as it pertains to the founder(s). Having more than one venture firm involved also means having more than one VC on the board telling the entrepreneur how to run his or her business. To achieve that personal "dream," though, the entrepreneur must keep giving away parts of the company until it can stand on its own. By the time this occurs, the founder may have a very, very small portion of the company's stock in his or her own name. The VCs will have the bulk of the company, despite the fact that they didn't do anything other than put in money and nag the founder. In this light, entrepreneurs of all shapes and sizes are inclined to refer to venture capitalists as "vulture capitalists"—not to their faces, of course, but in private conversation. Some do say it in public if the VCs kick them out of their own companies, which happens a lot.

Noftsker was well aware of this when he decided to raise money to get Symbolics off the ground. He also knew in 1980 that the VC community was gaga over high-tech stocks. The first round of small computer companies to go public in the 1970s, from minicomputer makers like Data General to the newer personal computer companies like Apple Computer, had returned huge rewards to investors. They had paid off so well that even founders and employees who had seen their original holdings diluted by venture money managed to make out like bandits. In Silicon Valley, entrepreneurs and VCs liked to claim that on the day that Apple went public, sixty of the company's employees became millionaires.

In that climate of substantial monetary reward, VCs were anxiously looking to make their next big kill. There appeared to be something in Noftsker's plan to commercialize this "new AI stuff" that could have a singular appeal. If done properly, AI could revolutionize the high-tech market. That alone carried potential long-range ramifications. Plus, Noftsker was talking about building machines—hardware—something that VCs understood better than software. Software often had vague descriptions and was intellectually abstract until it was actually put to use. Hardware could be touched and viewed; it had physical bulk and weight. The VCs could literally see where their money was going.

Noftsker needed substantial amounts of start-up cash, known as seed money. Not only was he ready to bring fourteen hackers on board all at once, each of whom expected to get paid, but he was going to have to physically manufacture his LISP machines. Parts would have to be ordered and purchased, and a minifactory where the computers could be assembled would have to be set up. People would have to be hired to do the assembly, and still more people would have to be hired to administer the entire business operation. Then it would need salespeople. Symbolics would have plenty of expenses from the moment it began operations.

Despite all of the potential, not one investment company offered to put any money into Symbolics. Noftsker couldn't understand it. The line from all the VCs was simply "thanks, but no thanks." The search for start-up money was falling flat on its face.

Jack Holloway, one of the hackers who had worked on the LISP machine with Greenblatt at the AI Lab, decided to rewrite the Symbolics business plan. Holloway had been instrumental in getting the hackers to side with Russell's concept of building a company, and served as their de facto leader. He felt strongly about raising the necessary funds in order to ensure that Symbolics would be as well capitalized as the hackers had been promised it would be. Adams' business plan wasn't going anywhere, so Holloway took a stab at it.

Noftsker and Adams had begun to differ on the stategic direction of the company, as well as on the issue of who would really be in charge. As Symbolics moved ever so slowly forward, it became apparent that the two couldn't both have it their own way. Infighting was considered bad form, and something had to give.

The revised Symbolics business plan looked better on paper than its predecessor, but still no one took the bait. Completely frustrated, Noftsker cornered one VC who had previously rejected the plan and demanded to know what was going on. If people liked the basic plan, what was preventing them from investing in it? The VC, Eugene Pettinelli of American Research and Development (ARD), told Noftsker that the company had to have a unified management team in place because it was readily apparent that Adams and Noftsker weren't seeing eye-to-eye. With such internal friction there wasn't a VC in existence who would even dream of investing in Symbolics. (Russell also claims that one of Adams' business references was casting aspersions on Adams' management capabilites to potential investors.)

Flabbergasted, Noftsker asked Pettinelli whether ARD would invest in Symbolics if the management problem were resolved. Pettinelli admitted that ARD might consider it.

While Pettinelli went back to take another look at Symbolics' business plan, the company was setting up initial operations in Woodland Hills, California. The first thing it did was hire some hardware engineers to redesign the original AI Lab version of the LISP machine. Even though Greenblatt was selling carbon copies of the lab machine, Symbolics felt it could improve on the design to make it more powerful and more manufacturable. One of the people it brought on board for this job was John Blankenbaker, who is credited with creating one of the first commercial personal computers in the 1970s. The company also put one of the MIT crew, Henry Baker, to work as a salesman. Noftsker moved Baker out to L.A. from Cambridge and began paying him, making Baker the first Symbolics employee to draw a paycheck. Baker started spreading the word about Symbolics' computer to various government and corporate research labs, making hundreds of phone calls per month to people who had never even heard of Symbolics. In most cases, most of them did not know what a LISP machine was.

Throughout 1980, the company made manufacturing plans and continued to operate out of its garage office in California. In this way it was oddly similar to LMI, in that company administration and sales were in southern California, and engineering was in Massachusetts. By the beginning of 1981, Symbolics had signed on nearly twenty people, some of whom were starting to collect regular paychecks. In addition to the credit line Noftsker and Adams had received by putting up their houses as collateral, they also eked out nearly

$250,000 from friends, family, and business associates. This money paid for a few salaries, engineering and design plans, manufacturing preparation, and basic expenses.

Things were still tight, though, as Pettinelli was holding up on any investment money until Noftsker and Adams resolved their management plight. Noftsker was not having an easy time convincing Adams to step down gracefully, and it got to the point that the two were not speaking directly to each other. They conducted their negotiations via other Symbolics employees who ran back and forth between Noftsker's and Adams' offices.

Facing a situation with Adams that vaguely resembled his impasse with Richard Greenblatt more than a year before, Noftsker resorted to an ultimatum. This time, Russell simply threatened to shut down the little company and cease all operations. Symbolics would just disappear without ever really getting started. As a result, all of the friendly and familial investors would be out their $250,000. Not coincidentally, Adams had a number of associates who had put up a significant portion of that money. When Adams still wouldn't budge after this threat, Noftsker called the informal investors and told them what he was going to do. The company couldn't get going, he said, unless Bob stepped aside. If he wouldn't step aside, then the company couldn't get any more money anyway, and there was no use in going on. They could kiss their cash goodbye.

The next day, Adams returned to the negotiating table, livid with Noftsker. Adams had apparently received phone calls of the "strong persuasion" variety from his investor friends, and was coerced into working out a compromise. By the end of the day, Noftsker had to allow Adams to keep more of Symbolics' stock than he would have liked, but at least it got Adams out of the company. In June, 1981, Adams resigned from Symbolics, was given $40,000 in unpaid back salary and expenses, and given the right to buy one of the company's first computers at cost. The way was clear for Gene Pettinelli and ARD to invest their cash.

As always, there was last-minute haggling. The investors wanted Noftsker to move the manufacturing from L.A. to Cambridge, even though production was about to begin. There was a fair degree of logic in that, but things were too far along to try to establish a new manufacturing site. Noftsker held his ground, and Pettinelli finally handed over $1.5 million to Symbolics. The investment was comprised of money from three different investment firms: $600,000 came from ARD, which was the lead investor; $500,000 came from Alan Patricof Associates; and $400,000 from Memorial Drive Trust. The first Symbolics machine rolled out of the factory two days later. Symbolics was now officially operating according to plan, even if it was a year later than originally planned.

The MIT hackers deserted the lab en masse and joined Symbolics full-time during the summer of 1981. They immediately began working on improvements to the MIT LISP software system to make it more efficient for the new LISP machine they were building. As part of the company's licensing agreement with the AI Lab, Symbolics would give these improvements back to the lab on a regular basis. Developers from Symbolics would work with MIT's remaining hackers to perform routine software upgrades that would improve the software at the lab. But the only real hacker left in the lab was Richard Stallman. And Stallman hated Symbolics.

Stallman had come to the AI Lab in the early-1970s. There were—and are—many people affiliated with the AI Lab that believed that Stallman may have been the most brilliant person to ever set foot in the confines of Tech Square. He was a bit too young to have been weaned on the early Minsky days, so he fell under the tutelage of the second generation AI researchers like Richard Greenblatt. Despite his youth, Stallman's hacking abilities nearly rivaled those of Greenblatt, especially when it came to LISP. Upon graduation—he also received a degree from Harvard in physics—he was hired by Noftsker to work in the lab as a full-time hacker. (Coincidentally, this occurred only months before Noftsker left the lab.) Stallman was as much the consummate hacker as anyone in the lab, but he possessed an extreme sociopolitical outlook on hacking. He believed that the fruits of his and all other hackers' labor should be free. Software should be available to anyone who wanted it, no matter who they were, and no matter where they were. Software, like music, should be available to the masses without a price tag.

When Russell Noftsker put forth the idea of starting a company based on selling the LISP machine, most observers believed that no one would be more reticent than Greenblatt. They were wrong. Stallman was much more reticent than Greenblatt. Beyond that, he was outraged. In Stallman's mind, no one had the right to sell the LISP machine; it belonged to MIT. Even worse, as far as he was concerned, the licensing agreement that Noftsker had with MIT involved the use of the LISP operating system for the machine, which all of the hackers past and present in the AI Lab had contributed to in some fashion since day one. Symbolics wouldn't just be selling computer hardware, it would be selling the life's work of dozens of hackers without their consent. From the way Stallman carried on, Symbolics might as well have been Satan, stealing the pure soul of the AI Lab.

When Richard Greenblatt left the lab to work with Steve Wyle, Stallman held his tongue. He didn't like the idea of LMI making money from the LISP machine, either, but he seemed to hold to the notion that Richard was forced into it by Noftsker, that Greenblatt had no other choice. Stallman sided with Richard reluctantly, letting his hacker peers know that he could never forgive them for siding with Russell. He secretly began working for Greenblatt, doing some hacking for LMI on the side.

Before long, Symbolics officials claimed that Stallman was actually taking the code that they were giving back to the lab, and that he was forwarding it to Greenblatt. Symbolics hackers even monitored Stallman's activities by using a little known feature that enabled networked LISP machines to watch what other LISP machines were doing. In essence, a hacker on LISP machine A could literally watch the screen activities of LISP machine B. After a few of these spying sessions, it became clear to Symbolics that Stallman was forwarding LISP code to LMI.

Several Symbolics executives approached MIT's administration and presented their evidence. Do something about Stallman, Symbolics' executives demanded. In order to keep its relationship with Symbolics on an even keel, MIT warned Stallman to stay away from the various LISP projects, but stopped short of denying him access to the lab's computing facilities. One more infraction, however, and Stallman might never again be allowed to get near an MIT computer.

This was too much for Stallman. Symbolics had not only raped the AI Lab and stolen all of its employees, thus destroying the hacker culture, but now it had tried to stop him from hacking. In a fit of rage, Stallman allegedly sent an electronic mail message out from the AI Lab that said, in effect: I will wrap myself in dynamite and walk into Symbolics' offices, and I will blow the whole the company up.

Stallman was fanatical, but this supposed threat was potentially more dangerous than anything else he had ever done. The message caused a brief flurry of excitement and speculation on the part of Symbolics' employees, but ultimately, no one took Stallman's outburst all that seriously. Despite his vehemence, Stallman never did get the dynamite.

Though this incident has been confirmed by several Symbolics executives. Stallman himself has no recollection of it. "I fought Symbolics with all my might for two years, but I didn't do it with threats," he says. "I am sure I never made such a threat to Symbolics. On the other hand, I can't be sure I never said that to anyone. I had some heated arguments with Symbolics employees, and we sometimes lost our tempers. Perhaps this story is based on one such event. I was definitely upset enough about the destruction of the AI lab."

Richard Stallman's refusal to leave the sanctity of MIT to go to work for any business enterprise marked the end of the hacker era. Basically, he alone remained to carry on some semblance of the hacker world at MIT. Geeks, dweebs, technoheads, and nerds they may have been in the past, but hackers would be prime candidates for technical positions in AI companies for the next ten years. Sadly, even the term hacker would metamorphose into something slightly sinister, connoting a rogue programmer who was only interested in terrorizing unsuspecting computer users with viruses and self-destructing programs. The nail had been hammered into the hacker coffin.

Stallman eventually left the lab to start an organization called the Free Software Foundation. Today, he writes programs in a language called GNU—which he gives away for free—and turns up occasionally in magazines where he carries on about such injustices as prohibitions on copying music from CDs. He is physically best described as the lone survivor of a nuclear war: he shambles about shoeless, long hair straggling down his back, eyes wide as if in perpetual shock.

For all intents and purposes, the capitalism of the 1980s passed him by. Yet in 1990, the MacArthur Foundation gave Richard Stallman $240,000 as part of its "genius fellowship" program. He was allowed to do with this money whatever he wished.

A man who thinks everything should be free given nearly a quarter of a million dollars of free money. Some things just defy explanation.

❧

With all the activity going on in the MIT and Stanford AI Lab spin-offs, it would have been easy to believe that artificial intelligence was a phenomenon born on the wings of companies like Symbolics, LMI, and IntelliGenetics. But other companies, big companies, had gotten wind of AI and were not ignoring its potential. They had secretly begun to use AI internally, and some of them were just as far along in their efforts as the new "pure-play" AI start-ups. They were just biding their time, watching.

Bolt Beranek and Newman, for one, had become more than a finishing school for hackers tired of life in the AI Lab. The company had successfully bid on several military contracts in the 1970s to develop natural language and voice recognition systems for the DOD. It had even adopted the LISP language from MIT, evolving and adapting the language to its own use in a form that it called InterLISP, for Interactive LISP. BBN had no problems attracting hackers looking to be part of the real world, but it did find that keeping them confined to the corporate mold was a trifle difficult. A revealing incident that shows how the company could "take the boy from the Lab, but couldn't take the Lab from the boy" involved Daniel Bobrow, the Minsky protege who had developed the STUDENT natural language program in the mid-1960s.

Bobrow left MIT in the 1960s to go to BBN and continue working on his natural language ideas. Along with other hackers, he spent some of his free time diddling around on the computer. Unbeknownst to the management of BBN, and anyone else who wasn't a hacker, a version of the ELIZA psychiatrist expert system had been loaded onto the company's mainframe. Bobrow later recalled a tale from BBN that showed just how unprepared the corporate world of salespeople and administrators was for AI.

Apparently, one Saturday morning when none of the hackers were around, a BBN sales vice president entered the computer room in hopes of giving a computer demonstration to a prospective client. On the keyboard of the computer was a note indicating that "all messages were to be entered into the computer, followed by a period." The sales VP thought that the note meant that the machine was a direct link to Bobrow's house. (At the time it was common practice to give senior programmers their own computer terminals for working at home.) Before using the computer, the VP wanted to clear the demonstration with Bobrow.

The note, though, had absolutely nothing to do with Bobrow. It was an instruction sheet left by a hacker who was providing explicit instructions on how to operate ELIZA; specifically, that each query or answer had to be followed by a period in order to trigger a response from the ELIZA program. Unaware of this, the VP thought he was communicating with Bobrow on that Saturday morning. The conversation went like this (VP's comments in capital letters):

> DO YOU THINK THAT I CAN USE THE COMPUTER THIS MORNING. (typed in by the VP)
> Why do you ask? (ELIZA's standard opening reply)
> I MIGHT BE ABLE TO MAKE SOME ADDITIONAL SALES.
> Why aren't you sure?
> MY PROSPECTIVE CUSTOMERS HAVE NEVER SEEN A DEMONSTRATION OF THE SYSTEM.
> Does this mean very much to you?
> OF COURSE IT DOES.
> You seem very positive about that.
> THIS IS RIDICULOUS. (The VP quickly realized this was a rather stupid conversation.)
> What do you mean this is ridiculous?
> IS THERE ANY REASON WHY I CAN'T USE THE COMPUTER NOW.
> Tell me more about your prospective customers.
> (This was too much for the VP) PLEASE DIAL ME UP ON 491-1850

After this last exchange the VP failed to get any response from ELIZA, because he had not typed in a period. Irritated by what he thought were Bobrow's strange and somewhat belligerent responses, and then downright angry that Bobrow didn't call him back right away, the VP decided to call Bobrow directly at home. When he asked why Bobrow was being so difficult, Bobrow had no clue as to what the VP was talking about. According to Bobrow, "The VP angrily read me the dialogue that 'we' had been having, and couldn't get any response but laughter from me. It took a while to convince him it really was the computer."

So much for intelligent man meets intelligent machine at BBN. Although the company offered the hackers more slack than they would have found throughout most of corporate America, many of them wanted even more freedom. There were too many regulations, and since BBN was doing a great deal of classified government work, there were certain restrictions on what they could and could not do with their beloved computers. A certain sense of "playfulness" was missing.

Another factor that may have led to their discontent was BBN's lack of interest in building a LISP machine. As Greenblatt was getting his first version of the CONS computer assembled, a number of BBN's hackers believed that they could do what Greenblatt was doing, only better, because they had BBN's corporate resources to help put the machine together. The primary obstacle to this goal was that BBN's administration didn't want to build its own LISP computer. It might be a hacker's dream, but BBN had to create systems for customers in order to turn a profit, and no one was ordering a LISP machine. Chances were pretty good that most of BBN's customers had no idea what a LISP machine might actually be.

Chagrined, the BBN hackers cast about for a better corporate climate. There was only one other company in the United States, and perhaps the world, that offered a place where hackers could explore and tinker to their hearts' content in the 1970s. That company was Xerox, and Xerox was hiring. The hackers decided that Xerox's technical center in Palo Alto, California, was the one place where they could hack away and still get regular paychecks. Xerox also offered something that BBN could not: a new computer workstation of its own design called Alto, a machine that could be used by individual hackers. In one fell swoop, all of BBN's hackers loaded up their cars and bolted to California in 1978, leaving BBN as decimated as the MIT AI Lab would be four years later. Today, there is still a huge amount of resentment at BBN towards the AI group that left en masse.

Xerox is the strangest high-tech company in the Fortune 500. It has struggled for years to shrug off the stigma of what it considers the burden of being a "copier company." No matter how hard it tries to change popular perceptions, people still think of Xerox as a corporation that makes copy machines, and the whole world still refers to the process of paper copying as "making a Xerox." Xerox the company hates this because it has accomplished so much more in its high-tech labs than just the fine art of xerography. In fact, it created many of the most significant components in today's personal computers. Everybody thinks that IBM and Apple did this. They didn't. Xerox did.

In 1970, Xerox took a huge step to broaden its world beyond copy machines. On a grassy knoll just up the road from Stanford, the company created a research lab that it called the Palo Alto Research Center, or PARC. The single intent behind the lab was to do research and generate ideas, nothing more. Xerox wanted to see what happened when the world's best technical wizards were put in an environment where their wildest thoughts and proposals could run free. No guidelines, no deadlines, no budgetary constraints. Xerox's mandate to the people at PARC was, "Think and build. If anything useful comes of it, we'll find some way to make use of it."

In this spirit of technological abandon, Xerox started hiring people from all over America. Most of these researchers came from Stanford or the Stanford Research Institute (Stanford's business spin-off), but many came from Cambridge, including MIT and BBN. Specifically, John Seely Brown and Daniel Bobrow from BBN came to PARC, bringing many of their peers with them. They all wanted to do AI at Xerox because it was the best of all worlds: unlimited freedom to hack away, lots of money, dozens of like-minded individuals, and California sunshine.

Over the course of the 1970s, Xerox created several computer components, including the mouse, the basic windows interface, pull-down menus, and the stand-alone workstation. Unfortunately, Xerox didn't know what to do with these things. Its marketing people were too busy selling copy machines.

The Xerox Alto, the company's workstation, would be a model for personal computers and workstations that would follow it, but Xerox never found a market for the machine. Instead, it was used internally. Many of the former BBN hackers had access to this computer for their AI work. The fruits of Xerox's computer work only entered the real world when Steve Jobs of Apple eventually "appropriated" many of the technological innovations he had seen at PARC for the Apple Lisa and Macintosh computers.

Most importantly to our story, Xerox had a finished version of a LISP machine at the same time Richard Greenblatt did. The researchers at PARC knew the importance of the LISP machine, but Xerox executives did not. Even though these executives wanted to create a computer company, they just never "got it." Market opportunities whizzed by (and out of PARC) like air from a leaking balloon. In the 1980s, Xerox looked on disinterestedly as

Symbolics and LMI sold LISP machines as fast as they could build them, until someone woke up and said, "Hey, we've got one of those at PARC." The company jumped on the bandwagon as fast as it could, but by that time Xerox was the third man in a two-man race. Those PARC guys never could get a break.

∾

The Xerox LISP machine was developed out of the same need that drove Richard Greenblatt. A hacker's paradise should have a heavenly tool, and a LISP machine was that tool. The BBN refugees had wanted to build one soon after they saw Greenblatt's CONS machine, and that desire was only heightened in the PARC playpen. Instead of using the MIT LISP language, called MacLISP, they built their machine on the InterLISP version used at BBN. To avoid confusion with their former employer, the Xerox hackers called the slightly modified language InterLISP-D (the "D" was considered sufficient to separate the language from original InterLISP in the minds of knowledgeable hackers). They built a LISP computer in 1978 similar to Greenblatt's second generation CADR machine and dubbed it the Dorado. It was actually based on Xerox's own Alto workstation, but it was a substantially less powerful machine than Greenblatt's. The Dorado was used internally at PARC solely for the benefit of PARC hackers. Beyond that, it never saw the light of day—at least not in its original form.

The PARC group developed a number of AI projects as 1980 rolled around and worked on a new language called Smalltalk, which seemed to have the potential for building expert systems in a LISP-like way, but it was easier for traditional programmers to use. In addition, John Seely Brown, who led the exodus out of BBN, rose to prominence at PARC, eventually becoming its director. But unfortunately, beyond these individual achievements, the story of Xerox's involvement in AI is checkered at best. When it finally decided to compete with Symbolics and LMI, it set up a marketing group in Pasadena, half a state away from Palo Alto. It unveiled two different LISP machines based on the Dorado with the unfortunate names of DandeLion and—get this—DandeTiger. New salesmen, people who hadn't been selling copiers, were hired to sell the stupidly named and hard-to-explain machines to Fortune 500 companies. If that wasn't humiliating enough, and it probably was, these salesmen were stuck three hundred miles from the source of Xerox's LISP research and training in a city known for little other than the Rose Bowl. It's remarkable that all this marketing mismanagement occurred within the same company that popularized the copy machine.

Xerox would have the distinction in 1985 of making the biggest sale of LISP machines ever, one thousand machines valued at $20 million. As we will see, it trumpeted the fact all over the computer trade press, lording the sale of these machines over Symbolics and LMI. It was somewhat less vocal when the buyer reneged on the deal a year later. Delivery of the machines was never taken.

As I said, those PARC guys never could get a break.

In 1978, as the AI research labs were experiencing their first tinglings of commercial angst, and Xerox was completing its first LISP machine, a large French corporation was dipping its toes into the AI water—or more accurately, into the AI oil.

Schlumberger is one of the world's largest industrial concerns. Its primary business is oil and all the things associated with oil: exploring, drilling, refining, etc. Schlumberger maintains two large research facilities in the United States, one in Connecticut and one in Palo Alto. The facility in Palo Alto was originally set up under the auspices of Fairchild, a semiconductor company owned and controlled by Schlumberger. Because of the fact that this lab existed in Palo Alto, and was a research facility, and was investigating new technologies, it was inevitable that the Fairchild center should come into contact with Stanford's AI programs. There is a fair degree of incestuous business behavior in Palo Alto (Cambridge as well) that permits competitors and allies to keep tabs on what everyone else is doing in Silicon Valley. This is due in equal parts to the transitory nature of employees, the meetings of venture capitalists, the brotherhood of Stanford alumni and professors, and plain old gossip. Little escapes anybody's attention in Palo Alto. Sometimes competitors know what Company X is going to do before Company X's employees do.

The Schlumberger-Fairchild lab took note of Stanford's work in expert systems, as well as the work that was going on at the Stanford Research Institute, now called SRI International. The researchers at SRI, who had fairly liberal access to the goings on at Feigenbaum's lab, were themselves much more interested in building business systems than any other organization in the late 1970s, with the exception of BBN. SRI and BBN can even be considered corporate counterparts to Stanford and MIT, even though BBN's affiliation with MIT was a much looser arrangement than the one between SRI and Stanford. Still, they both served as "feeder" systems of AI technology out of the labs and into the real world, especially into DARPA.

In 1978, SRI developed an expert system with a decidedly unmilitary bent called PROSPECTOR. The goal of PROSPECTOR was to help geologists interpret mineral data and predict the location of mineral deposits. Like earlier expert systems, it would use facts about minerals and apply rules to them in order to create a plan for narrowing down the possible site of a particular mineral. Created by Richard Duda and Peter Hart, the system was designed to be experimental, but in a strange twist of fate, PROSPECTOR actually proved that it could work in the real world. Duda and Hart had programmed the experience of nine geologists into PROSPECTOR and proceeded to apply the wisdom of their computer expert to a mining site at Mount Tolman, in Washington state. Since World War I, geologists had believed that a substantial vein of molybdenum was located in the Mount Tolman area. All the indications were there (that is, the presence of certain other related minerals), but after more than sixty years, no one had found any such vein or deposit. When PROSPECTOR was put to the task, it began by inquiring about the location of geological faults in the area, as well as magnetic anomalies and the discovery of other significant metals from the previous molybdenum dig failures.

When it processed all this data, PROSPECTOR decided that the molybdenum was there all right, but not in any of the locations that the geologists had already dug up. Instead, the molybdenum was under the waste pile that held the rubble from the earlier excavations. PROSPECTOR said that the miners had dumped their trash on the very vein they were looking for.

With some skepticism, the miners removed the waste pile by the geologists and excavated the land underneath it. It wasn't too long before the startled miners found something completely unexpected: a molybdenum vein. PROSPECTOR had done what human experts had not been able to do.

This was artificial intelligence's first commercial success, and it was big. Very big. Though many outside AI considered it to be a one-time achievement in an uninteresting field (mining isn't exactly one of your glamour fields), there were those who immediately saw the potential of AI for other commercial endeavors. Schlumberger was one of those companies that saw the light as if a veil had dropped from their eyes.

That same year, 1978, Schlumberger looked into how expert systems could be applied to its core business of oil exploration and drilling. One of the company's main concerns was its lack of experts in the domain of oil well analysis. On the face of it, this specialization involves making decisions about where to dig oil wells. While wildcatters in post-depression America may have chosen well sites in Oklahoma and Texas by using divining rods or tasting the sand, modern companies like Schlumberger can hardly afford to be so unscientific. Instead they bore holes into the ground or ocean floor and take readings about the content of the earth using a tool called a dipmeter. The dipmeter data, in technical terms, analyzes the bore hole for evidence of subsurface tilt, which is an indication of the flow of underground strata. Based on the results of the dipmeter operation, a specialist must decide if there is enough evidence to warrant a complete drilling operation. This involves an extreme familiarity with the way that mineral layers have built up and moved over the eons, and what one might expect to find in specific strata formations. It is not an easy job, especially since a wrong interpretation could cost a company millions of dollars.

Schlumberger decided that it needed more efficient analysis of its dipmeter data because it only had a small group of people capable of dipmeter interpretation. One individual in particular had become the company's primary expert, and he was even hired out as an external consultant. But this man, and the handful of other experts, could not be expected to be everywhere at all times. After all, they were only human, and a human cannot be on job sites at different points around the world for 24 hours a day, 365 days a year. In the global business of oil exploration, this was a serious shortcoming, and Schlumberger believed that the only way to overcome it was to create an expert system that acted as a clone of its dipmeter analysts.

In 1979, right after Schlumberger acquired Fairchild, it set up an AI group at Fairchild's northern California facility. PROSPECTOR creators Hart and Duda were brought in to run the group, which was called FLAIR, for Fairchild Laboratory for Artificial Intelligence Research. With help from local Stanford experts, FLAIR created an expert system called the Dipmeter Advisor. A working version of the program, called a prototype, was developed in 1980 and put to work in selected Texas oil fields. Acting like a human specialist, the Dipmeter Advisor started telling the company where to drill its wells.

Schlumberger viewed the expert system as a program that would give it an advantage over its competitors. There were only so many dipmeter specialists in the world, and now Schlumberger could clone them simply by installing a computer at its drilling sites. For this reason, it was reluctant to share its newfound computer expert with other companies. Dipmeter Advisor became the first expert system developed specifically with the intent of becoming a corporate tool that could help improve corporate efficiency. It was, in a sense, Schlumberger's very own competitive weapon. Though it would talk publicly about the Dipmeter Advisor, Schlumberger was not about to let anybody else get their hands on it.

The Dipmeter Advisor, like PROSPECTOR before it, garnered its fair share of publicity and trade press write-ups, but very few companies had the faintest idea of how to go about building anything similar to it. Precious few organizations had the resources to even attempt building it, since estimates ranged upwards of $3 million for the development of the Dipmeter Advisor. This included hardware, software, consulting services, and the time and effort of all those involved in the project, including the time spent interrogating the company's dipmeter experts—time that they otherwise could have spent making money for Schlumberger. There were other large companies that had all of the required resources to build an expert system, such as time and money, but for the most part they did not know how to go about tackling such a project.

Digital Equipment Corporation was one of the few companies that intimately knew what it took to build an expert system. DEC's computers were the favored machines at most AI labs, especially those at MIT, Stanford, and CMU. Even though DEC was headquartered down Route 128 from MIT, and its founder Ken Olsen had graduated from MIT, the company had fostered a close relationship with all of the labs during the 1970s. In practice, then, no one lab was especially favored over the other (although DEC salespeople might tell a different story because of their personal relationships with MIT).

In 1978, DEC was on its way to becoming the world's second largest computer company, after IBM. Control Data, Honeywell, Sperry, and Burroughs (the latter two now known as Unisys) were all stumbling drastically by overestimating the need for extremely large computer systems such as mainframes. They were losing market share to minicomputer makers like Data General, Hewlett Packard, and DEC. Fully aware of its growing presence in this latter market, DEC unveiled a general-purpose computer called the VAX that appealed not only to scientists and engineers, but also to small and medium-sized businesses. (VAX stands for Virtual Address eXtended, for those of you interested in such things—a reference to its design.) DEC was going to throw its entire marketing and sales weight behind the VAX, which it would offer in an infinite number of variations to meet each customer's needs.

It was this "infinite variety" concept that plunged DEC into the AI world. A typical new VAX system used from 10 to 200 orderable parts from among 8,476 available items of hardware, software, accessories, documentation, and services. This involved the configuration of cables, disk drives, memory units, power supplies, software, processors, terminals, and a host of other necessities and accessories in a list longer than most rural phone books. Since DEC was offering custom systems, there was no one standard configuration of the VAX. Orders could potentially involve millions of different combinations of parts and accessories.

Seeing that DEC was staking its immediate future on the VAX in 1978, it could not leave customer configurations of the computer to chance. Its previous machines, such as the PDP series, had been configured by humans who laid out each order based on customer requirements. As DEC grew and the number of orders increased, configuring by hand promised to become an overwhelming administrative chore. For each order, certain components had to be matched with compatible components based on the applications that the customer was going to run. Even space limitations in the customer's computer room had to be taken into consideration. Sending out a VAX that met all the customer's needs but was too big for his office would not be a good example of customer service.

DEC clearly had to find a way to handle and configure all of its orders without completely swamping its human configuration experts. They had to have some automated help or they would never get any VAXes out the door; the logistics and time involved with configuration were just too immense.

A former Carnegie-Mellon University professor working at DEC recommended that management look into building an expert system to handle the configuration of VAXes. This connection led DEC to CMU's AI group, instead of to the more obvious and more convenient MIT AI Lab. There the company hooked up with John McDermott, an associate of Raj Reddy, the man who had worked on the HARPY voice-recognition project. McDermott was a professor of computer science who felt that AI research had sweated too long over trivial non-real-world problems (writing chess programs comes to mind). Under the direction of DEC's Dennis O'Connor, McDermott was hired to create an expert configuration system.

Although DEC was familiar with AI technology, many people inside and outside of DEC thought that the company was taking a huge risk. No corporation had ever taken on an AI development project that would affect the entire operation of the business. If the configuration system was put to work and failed to properly configure customer orders, then DEC could easily find itself up the proverbial creek without paddles. In addition, this wasn't going to be an isolated expert system that some specialized users kept to themselves in some remote corner of the company. This expert system was going to require acceptance from executives, engineers, and salespeople throughout DEC. The impact of the system would be felt by everyone. It was Dennis O'Connor's job to make sure that everyone in the company supported the AI project.

DEC named the program XCON, for eXpert CONfigurator, and began development in December 1978. For five months, McDermott immersed himself in the configuration process, learning all he could about the ins and outs of putting together a VAX order from scratch. Interestingly, he wrote the program in a language called OPS, which was Carnegie's own answer to LISP and PROLOG, but was optimized for use on VAX machines. The OPS language was the converse of Greenblatt's plans for his LISP machine, which was in its final stages at this time: Greenblatt built a machine optimized for a specific language, while CMU researchers optimized a language for a specific machine.

McDermott delivered a prototype of XCON to DEC in April 1979, and then set about "knowledge engineering" the prototype with information gleaned from the human configurators. By the end of that year, McDermott had built a system with 750 rules describing the various ways that a VAX order could be configured. In January 1980, DEC installed XCON in one of its manufacturing plants in Salem, New Hampshire, where it was used to assist the human configurator at that facility.

This is the *Reader's Digest* condensed version of the story. While XCON has been used successfully for more than a decade by DEC, and now contains (by some estimates) as many as 20,000 rules, McDermott did not create the perfect expert configurator on his first attempt. Midway through 1979, for instance, McDermott tested XCON's skill in the lab and found that it developed accurate configurations more than 90 percent of the time, a percentage that was better than some humans achieved. When it was tested in an actual facility, however, it managed to achieve an accuracy level of only 80 percent, which was not acceptable to DEC. In the isolation of the lab, McDermott had failed to take into consideration certain real world problems that affect the actual configuration process (for example, factory delays, unavailability of parts). Going back to the lab, McDermott reworked XCON until it could perform at near-perfect levels, which was consistently between 95 and 98 percent. Humans performed with less precision, at a rate closer to 90 percent.

DEC also had to contend with something unexpected among the users of XCON: fear. Like blue collar workers who had worried that robots on the assembly line would take their jobs away from them, white collar workers at DEC began to worry that the expert system might alleviate them of employment. This was not the case (nor was it with robots), and DEC management worked diligently to ensure that people did not fear the use of the system. Human configurators would always be necessary for those specialized product orders that XCON had no expertise in, and the system itself would always need constant upgrading to reflect the change in VAX products. New products would be handled by humans until XCON got up to speed on them, and even then it would have to make use of expertise developed by the humans.

The initial fear of white-collar worker displacement, however, would prove to be a major stumbling block for expert systems as the technology started making its way into the marketplace.

DEC put XCON into use permanently in 1981. Since then, the company claims it has saved millions of dollars per year by using XCON. The system is integral to its daily business, and observers say that if XCON were somehow rendered inoperable, DEC as a company would grind to a halt within one working week.

Another benefit to building XCON was that DEC itself learned a lot about the development of expert systems. A select group within the company, notably those associated with Dennis O'Connor, had gained enough experience in the process that they were almost as well-versed in AI as their Carnegie-Mellon colleagues. DEC used these people full-time to care for and maintain XCON, and with them in place, the company sent John McDermott back to CMU. McDermott, too, had personally learned a lot during the creation of XCON, which he referred to in the academic community as R1. This designation came from the experience he had gained at DEC, because, as he claimed, "Three years ago I wanted to be a knowledge engineer, and today I are one." Both DEC and McDermott knew that there was life beyond XCON. DEC wanted to use expert systems in other areas of its business, and McDermott wanted to apply his substantial knowledge to other projects.

This is how the emerging AI business stood in the summer of 1981. LMI had sold approximately a dozen LISP machines. Russell Noftsker and his AI hackers had formed a strong hardware company with lots of financial backing. IntelliGenetics was happy with its medical business, but was investigating even more opportunities for selling AI tools, like inference engines. Stanford researchers wanted to form one big happy AI company. Randall Davis, who had worked on MYCIN and the Dipmeter Advisor and developed TEIRESIAS, wanted to capitalize on his well-publicized AI expertise. So did Raj Reddy and John McDermott at CMU. Alex Jacobson had a team of LISP hackers and some start-up cash from Control Data. DEC figured it had enough AI expertise to possibly start a new business. A handful of others around the country had the same inclinations.

All each of these individuals and organizations needed was one big push to send them out into the marketplace.

Japan, Inc. was only too happy to oblige.

17

The Fifth Generation

Japan Challenges the World

On Monday, October 19, 1981, the government of Japan sponsored the first International Conference on Fifth Generation Computer Systems in Tokyo. The three-day conference was hardly international; it was primarily presented by and for Japanese researchers. Only a handful of speakers came from other countries, Edward Feigenbaum being one of them.

The conference was the culmination of three years of political and technical work for Kazuhiro Fuchi. Though the plans for The Fifth Generation Project were already set in stone, October 19 was the day that made it all a reality. In effect, the conference served as the high-technology version of a debutante ball. The Japanese were playing the role of the formerly shy young girl who was now ready to make her entree into the world, confident and poised. In a series of bold speeches and presentations, complete with graphs, charts, and time lines, the Japanese outlined their mission for the coming decade. It was their moment in the spotlight.

By 1992, they claimed, Japan would build an intelligent machine. This machine would be a revolutionary new computer, and the Ministry of International Trade and Industry had pledged the equivalent of millions of dollars to ensure that it got built. The project would begin the following April with the establishment of a computer research center called the Institute for New Generation Computing (ICOT). In addition to the government's role, eight major Japanese firms had already agreed to support the program with both manpower and resources.

These basic facts seemed straightforward, but there was much that was underlying the obvious. In various presentations, mention was made of the importance of The Fifth Generation Project to Japan both economically and culturally. In case anybody missed the point, program chairman Tohru Moto-Oka made it crystal clear in his opening address.

"Our society is about to enter a transition period in various meanings of the term. It is an age of changes in internal and external environmental conditions such as the energy situation, and together with building a wealthy, liberal society, and overcoming the constraints of resources and energy, we must at the same time make international contributions as an economic power.

"In making our way through this new age, informationization and the information industry which centers around computers are expected to play a big role. In the 1990s when fifth generation computers will be widely used, information processing systems will be a central tool in all areas of social activity to include economics, industry, science and art, administration, international relations, education, culture, daily life and the like, and will be required to meet those new needs generated by environmental changes. Information processing systems will be expected to play a role in the resolving of anticipated social bottlenecks and the advancing of society along a more desirable path through the effective utilization of their capabilities . . .

"Japan, which has a shortage of land and a population density about 40 times that of the United States, cannot attain self-sufficiency in food, and her rate of self-sufficiency in energy is about 15 percent and that of oil about 0.3 percent. On the other hand, we have one precious asset; that is, our human resources. Japan's plentiful labor force is characterized by a high degree of education, diligence, and high quality. It is desirable to utilize this advantage to cultivate information itself as a new resource comparable to food and energy, and to emphasize the development of information-related knowledge-intensive industries which make possible the processing and managing of information at will.

"Such an effort would not only serve to help our country meet international competition, but would also enable us to make international contributions through knowledge-intensive technology . . .

"Although we have mainly followed the lead of other countries in computer technology up to now, it is time for us to break with this outmoded tradition and center our efforts on the development of new computer technology based on our own conceptions, so that we can provide the world with new technology with a view to promoting international cooperation."

This was unusual prose from a Japanese scientist. To hammer the point home, Kazuhiro Fuchi added his own admonishment, this one intended to stir up the Japanese researchers in the audience.

"The various researches described (at this conference) must be aggressively carried forward. These are intended for development through the eighties and for perfection in the nineties, but at the same time it must be remembered that their basic components were developed in the seventies. While the route to knowledge information processing is an advance to a new age, it can also be viewed as representing the inheritance and development of the legacies of the past from the viewpoint of research efforts. In this sense, the route to knowledge information processing represents a practical philosophy and an inevitable direction for development of information processing technology. The question is rather whether to stand still or proceed, as there are no other paths to choose from."

Many of those in attendance were not Japanese; they were Americans and Europeans who had come primarily out of curiosity. What they heard over the course of the three days shocked them to the point of speechlessness. The Japanese were going all out to be the world leader in artificial intelligence, and they had the human and monetary resources to back it up.

The Fifth Generation Project was not confined to AI, although that aspect of it drew the most attention. The Japanese also planned to do considerable work in the area of relational databases and parallel processing, and ICOT wanted to develop hardware architecture for both of these computing concepts. The United States had actually already done considerable work with relational databases in the 1970s, but it had approached the idea from a software perspective. The Japanese, true to form in this respect, had opted to make it a hardware effort.

The eight companies that joined with MITI to establish ICOT were Toshiba, Hitachi, Oki, Mitsubishi, Matsushita, Fujitsu, NEC, and Sharp. Each of them pledged to give a handful of researchers, four or five, to ICOT free of charge. ICOT insisted that these not just be any researchers; they had to be among each company's best and brightest. Furthermore, as stipulated by Fuchi, none of the researchers could be over thirty-five years old. This would give him a group of young, talented individuals who had not been thoroughly ingrained with the idea of progress through consensus, which was the Japanese way. Fuchi wanted people who could come up with ideas of their own and not be afraid to develop them.

In return, the companies would reap the rewards of the technologies developed at ICOT. They could commercialize this technology for their own benefit, and they would get their young researchers back after three years (at which time a new crop would be recruited). As far as the government was concerned, this was a good deal for the companies, because MITI was funding the entire bill. In practice, the companies would look on it as considerably less than a good deal and would be none too happy about the practice. But, for the sake of appearances at the conference, they were willing to go along with the party line.

The Japanese government made a big deal about funding The Fifth Generation Project. Although the amount was not specified at the conference, it sounded like the amount was going to be in the range of zillions of dollars. Not even close. The actual budget would be between $20 and $40 million per year (in yen, of course), which was less than any of the eight participants spent on their own individual R&D projects. In th United States, IBM alone was spending more than $1 billion per year on corporate R&D, which was twenty-five to fifty times the amount of money that The Fifth Generation was getting.

❧

Go back and read Tohru Moto-Oka's speech. Note that he stresses the need for international cooperation in achieving the goals of the project. In all likelihood, the researchers at ICOT fully expected to be joined in their venture by foreign parties. The Ministry of International Trade and Industry had a completely different expectation. They would not allow any other interested organizations outside of Japan to become full participants in the project. This was not stated, yet it would become abundantly clear within the next year.

Also note that both Moto-Oka and Fuchi make mention of "knowledge," relating it to knowledge-intensive technology and knowledge information processing. This struck a responsive and sympathetic chord in Ed Feigenbaum, who realized that these people were pursuing the same AI goals that he was. Knowledge engineering, knowledge acquisition, knowledge bases, knowledge information processing—it all had to do with representing human knowledge in a computer. This was a project Feigenbaum could fall in love with.

In truth, Japan, Inc. was interested in knowledge, but what it really wanted was a knowledge machine—something along the lines of a LISP machine, only better. It wouldn't be used to process a computer language, it would be used to process knowledge. Rules and heuristics would be programmed right into the hardware. It would be a quantum leap beyond the LISP machine, which only had LISP functions programmed into it. If someone wanted to use these LISP functions for an expert system, that was fine and dandy, but that didn't make a LISP machine inherently intelligent. The ICOT computer would be inherently intelligent.

To show just how little the Japanese researchers thought of their American counterparts and their AI software efforts, they chose to use PROLOG for the development of this computer, not LISP. Though there was lots of hand waving and hemming and hawing over why ICOT chose PROLOG, the real reason boiled down to one simple fact: PROLOG was not invented in the United States. To choose, LISP would have been to admit that the Japanese were following in the footsteps of U.S. researchers.

With these components in place, ICOT was scheduled to open for business in April 1982. It would have a ten-year run, according to MITI, ending sometime in late 1991 or early 1992. That was surely enough time to change the entire nature of computing. And, out of respect for the work that he had put into developing The Fifth Generation Project, Kazuhiro Fuchi would be the Institute's director. He would leave his post at the prestigious Electrotechnical Laboratory. While this might have seemed like an obvious reward for a job well done, it had sizable risks. Like Dennis O'Connor at DEC, as well as a growing number of AI proponents in other American companies, Fuchi was putting his career in jeopardy if this artificial intelligence stuff didn't work out. In Japan, you cannot go back. You go up, or you go out. Fuchi was determined to go up.

❧

Reaction to the announcement of The Fifth Generation Project was swift and knee-jerked. Every major industrial nation, particularly the United States and Britain, saw the project as a direct challenge to their technical superiority in computing. The governments of these countries realized that they had to mount their own counterattacks to the project or Japan might just eat them alive. Bureaucracies being what they are, however, getting these counterattacks going was easier said than done. Britain commissioned a study on "new generation" technologies in a move to reverse the specter that had hung over the United Kingdom since the days of Sir James Lighthill and his report. The United States, being a more hands-off kind of country, encouraged private enterprise to get its act together in response to the Japanese threat. Many people and politicians went so far as to recommend the formation of various technology consortiums (or consortia, if you prefer). Consortiums, they cried, were the only way to compete.

A word here about technology consortiums. They never work.

Any consortium, including ICOT, requires that participants put their own needs, desires, and greed aside for the greater good of a common cause. A consortium expects to get complete, unwavering, and unquestioning support from its members—kind of like a cult. In return for this, the consortium promises to come up with better technology than any of the individual members could ever come up with on their own. This is done by pooling the best resources of each participating organization—namely, the best researchers—and forcing them to work together to develop brilliant inventions and technical breakthroughs. The idea is that if you put enough of these people into the same place for a long enough period of time, and you throw enough money at them, a synergy will occur. This is "The Beatles Method," based on the fact that John, Paul, George, and Ringo came up with some of the world's most popular music while working together, but on their own they were somewhat less endearing. The sum was basically greater than the parts.

Unlike The Beatles, the researchers that are sent to work at consortiums are employed by companies that compete with each other. The researchers' companies usually continue to pay their salaries during their tenure at the consortium. This ensures that their allegiance is first and foremost to the company, appearances to the contrary notwithstanding. These people are oftentimes privy to company secrets as well, which they are not to share with other members of the consortium, since the other researchers' companies are competing with them in the real world (consortiums do not count as the real world). The researchers are thus prevented from sharing their best ideas with the consortium. Those best ideas belong to the company.

Let's imagine for a moment that two researchers are working on building The Ultimate Black Box, whatever that may be. As part of the consortium, they are supposed to build the best Black Box ever invented. Researcher 1 asks Researcher 2 what he thinks the Black Box should be made out of. Researcher 2 thinks about this for a moment, mentally noting who signs his paycheck, and answers, "I can't tell you that. My company is building its own new version of the Black Box, and we think we've got the best material available for it. I'm not going to tell you what that material is, because you'll go back and tell your company my secret. So let's talk about something else."

This situation does not lend itself to the harmonious outpouring of information and expertise that the consortium founders envisioned. Yet, it is typical of the kinds of obstacles that consortiums face when they bring individuals from competing organizations together. Reality, plain as it may be, does not stop people from starting consortiums.

ICOT hoped to break this consortium pattern by creating an environment totally out of sync with the Japanese notion of technology development. The young researchers were to abandon all notion of loyalty to their companies and forget everything they had ever been taught about conforming to the ideals of a group. They were to innovate, free-associate, and generally act un-Japanese. If you've got an idea, they were told, run with it. Don't wait for a committee to agree upon its merits.

Seeing as how these were Japan's most scientific young minds, each of these researchers had to have gone to the country's best schools and universities. Thus, they had grown up in a society where suicide was a popular alternative to not getting into the "right" school. It is possible that some of these same researchers, forty in all, had had to deal with those same suicidal tendencies only a few years before. Now they were informed that that mind-set was to be discarded: Lighten up, think, create. Don't worry about the fact that the rest of society wants you to conform. While you're at ICOT, you'd better not conform at all.

The personal and professional difficulties that this produced should be obvious.

෨

After the fallout had settled from the Japanese bombshell, the world took stock of The Fifth Generation and its implications. By mid-1982, when the hysteria that immediately followed the announcement had died down, The Fifth Generation Project looked somewhat less frightening than it had several months earlier.

It appeared in retrospect that Japan had been hoping to score a worldwide public relations coup by being the first nation out of the chute to commit itself to AI research. Despite all the fancy charts and diagrams, which showed intricate (though abstract) plans for building an AI research effort based on a knowledge machine, there was very little of substance that the Japanese had actually put into place. The ideas were there, but the people and the tools, and even the money, were not.

In a way, this scenario was similar to the Noftsker/Greenblatt race. Like Noftsker, Japan, Inc. had put the world on notice that it was going to get into this business, like it or not. Like Greenblatt, the United States and Europe had a window of opportunity to take advantage of in order to get its act together before the Japan juggernaut began its work. Unlike Greenblatt, the United States and Europe did not blow their head start.

The media had taken hold of The Fifth Generation Project with a vengeance, latching on to it like a deranged pit bull. With headlines like "Japan's Challenge To The World!!", "The Second Computer Age Begins," and "The Future Belongs To Japan!!", the U.S. media whipped up the passions of a country long used to leading the world in technology. Suddenly, there was a popular interest in artificial intelligence from sectors where there had previously not been any interest. The Reagan administration, in particular, worried about the threat to the American high-tech industry. Politicians in Washington were approached by William Norris, the CEO of Control Data Corporation, who pitched the idea of creating a consortium to develop the exact same "new generation" technologies that Japan was planning to target. The politicians agreed that something needed to be done and resolved to find a way around antitrust laws to help Norris's proposal become a reality.

Large corporations in the United States also took The Fifth Generation Project seriously. It was apparent in 1982 that Japan was already primed to unseat Detroit as the car capitol of the world. It had already taken market share from U.S. television, camera, and stereo manufacturers. The Japanese seemed unstoppable, and if they created a whole new type of computer, including computer systems that acted as clones to human experts, then they would be free to pick and choose which industry they conquered next. The teeth-chattering of executives throughout corporate America could be heard loud and clear.

Computer vendors, including IBM, Control Data, Sperry, Burroughs, Honeywell, and Texas Instruments, along with manufacturing concerns like Boeing, Westinghouse, Lockheed, TRW, and financial institutions including American Express, Transamerica, Cigna, Citicorp, Travelers, and Chemical Bank, all opened their eyes to the potential of AI in the harsh glare of The Fifth Generation Project. The technology could be used internally by these companies to increase efficiency, as well as to counter any Japanese threat. Each of them had the financial and personnel resources to start their own small AI groups to research the technology, much like Schlumberger and DEC had. It was the beginning of the 1980s, and most of them had more cash than they knew what to do with, coupled with bloated management layers just waiting to do something productive.

Not surprisingly, General Motors and Ford Motor Company were two of the first corporations to begin looking for ways to put AI to work in their organizations. The Japanese had made significant inroads into their core vehicle businesses, and although one could not say that Japan, Inc. was eating Detroit's lunch, they were certainly grabbing food off the plate. GM and Ford had other technical businesses, however, which could be affected by Japan's new computing strategy, and they had no intention of being caught off guard as they had been with the automotive side of the business.

General Motors had a technical center in Warren, Michigan, where much of its basic research and computer-oriented technology development resided. It was also the home of GM's programmers (these people were not called hackers—ever), but a quick look into the Warren Tech Center showed that very few people were completely up-to-date on artificial intelligence. After all, AI had only been making big headlines since late 1981 and early 1982, after The Fifth Generation Project was announced, and most corporate researchers were largely unaware of what was going on in specific labs at MIT, Stanford, or CMU. It might take several years for GM to get into the AI game without skilled people, and GM knew that it didn't have several years. Thus, the company would have to go out and purchase the expertise from one of the major AI labs. Maybe it would even invest in a little AI start-up if the prospects looked good. But where to find a ready-made AI organization?

The answer came as if by divine inspiration. Weren't there twenty guys out at Stanford who were looking to form a big AI company? There sure were. Wouldn't that company be a great investment? You bet it would.

General Motors was about to enter The Match Made in Hell.

Chapter 18

The Exodus Begins
Researchers Plead the Fifth

For AI researchers who needed a reason to start their own companies, the aftermath of The Fifth Generation was as if the gates to the asylum had been left open—or the dam had burst, or all bets were off, or the chains had been loosened, or any other quaint metaphor you care to choose. The fact was, a significant interest in the field of artificial intelligence had been awakened.

One company that formed in anticipation of this interest was called Teknowledge. It was founded in July 1981 by those twenty Stanford-based researchers who had been planning to form one big happy AI company led by Ed Feigenbaum. Incorporation papers for the new venture—the name of which was created by the merging of "techno" and "knowledge"—were filed literally just weeks before the Japanese Fifth Generation Conference. The researchers rented space in Palo Alto a few short blocks from the Stanford campus, just as IntelliGenetics had done.

Unlike IntelliGenetics, which sold licenses to its cloning expert system software, Teknowledge had no product to sell. What it did have was the combined talents of its founders, a group of nineteen men and one woman whose names read like a 1981 "who's who" in AI research. They included Ed Feigenbaum and Peter Friedland, both of whom were founders of IntelliGenetics; Bruce Buchanan and Edward Shortliffe, the MYCIN alumni; Frederick Hayes-Roth, a RAND researcher who had worked on the HEARSAY-II project at Carnegie-Mellon; Avron Barr, a research associate at Stanford who had been managing editor of *The Handbook of Artificial Intelligence*; Randy Davis of TEIRESIAS fame; Douglas Lenat, a former student of Feigenbaum's who had taught at both CMU and Stanford; Penny Nii, Feigenbaum's wife and one of the first knowledge engineers; and a host of other primarily Stanford-based researchers including James Bennett, Harold Brown, William Clancey, Robert Englemore, Michael Genesereth, Jerrold Kaplan, Ingeborg Kuhn, Thomas Rindfleisch, Carlisle Scott, William van Melle, and William White.

Shortly after getting started, the technical founders decided that to make this a real business, they needed real businessmen to run it. This had not been attempted in the AI business to that point, although Stephen Wyle's role in tiny Lisp Machine, Inc. came close. Most founders in the AI business chose—and would continue to choose—to run their own businesses, feeling that they had a much better understanding of the technology than anyone that could be brought in from the outside, especially some "suit," as business executives were disparagingly called.

Teknowledge's founders had a different idea. They would create a corporate image from the first day of business, giving them an edge over potential rivals, as well as over the labs from which they had emerged. Three months after its inception, the founders hired Lee Hecht, a self-styled entrepreneur, to be president and CEO of Teknowledge. Hecht was the epitome of the well-heeled businessman—a natty dresser and smooth talker who was involved in lots of ventures, oftentimes as a director or board member. That was a whole different world from the one that the AI researchers had lived in.

Hecht had had an unusually varied career path, one which included stints at Stanford and U.C. Berkeley as a visiting lecturer on the development of new businesses. But he had little experience in actually running an advanced technology company of Teknowledge's intended scope; most of his businesses had been little-known cash management companies, and one was a motion picture production company. This track record appealed to a group of researchers who knew little about running businesses. The techies were so taken by him that Hecht's arrangement with the founders of Teknowledge allowed him to keep his position as president at one his cash companies, Middlefield Capital Corporation, an investment firm he had started prior to joining Teknowledge. Thus, he was president of two companies simultaneously.

The plan was for Teknowledge to sell knowledge engineering services to the government and to large corporations. Knowledge engineering, as Feigenbaum and crew had pointed out, was a critical component of making viable expert systems. It was also a technology that was homegrown at Stanford. Neither MIT nor CMU put as much stock in it as did the West Coast AI contingent. Teknowledge decided that from Day One it would be the "largest knowledge engineering center in the world." This was a verifiable claim, since no other organization had an actual center devoted exclusively to knowledge engineering. It quickly became the corporate slogan.

Teknowledge was unusual by the standard of the other start-ups in AI. Its founders knew that they were at the forefront of technology, and they exuded an air of savvy, professional cynicism, and smugness that didn't exist anywhere else in AI, including Noftsker's business-oriented Symbolics. Teknowledge adopted a regal purple as its corporate color, splashing it over marketing brochures, product literature, and eventually the walls and carpets of its offices. To add to the air of business, many of its employees wore ties, and some, like Hecht and Hayes-Roth, sported well-trimmed beards and moustaches—personal accoutrements that were not often found in high-technology companies. Plus, they all bathed.

In its first year of business, Teknowledge's business consisted almost entirely of renting its employees out as consultants. They gave executive briefings, seminars, and extended courses on AI to anyone willing to pay for the information. These were almost entirely educational in scope, but the company charged thousands of dollars for each course. Teknowledge also got involved in some contract research whereby its "AI professionals" would assist in the early design and creation of expert systems for large corporate customers. It kept them busy but it wasn't making anybody rich. Part of getting involved in a start-up is wanting to get rich, and people at Teknowledge definitely wanted to get rich.

๛

In the few months leading up to The Fifth Generation Conference in October 1981, IntelliGenetics, Lisp Machine, Inc., Symbolics, and Teknowledge were doing "okay." This is different than doing great. None of them were making a killing in the marketplace because the primary marketplace was the one from which they all emerged: the research labs. There was only so much money that could be extracted from the labs, which in turn were relying on DARPA. The companies all hoped to have bigger markets, but prior to The Fifth Generation, the labs (and DARPA itself) were about the only customers that understood AI technology.

Even after The Fifth Generation made the headlines, there was still no overwhelming feeling outside of the AI companies themselves that AI was "the next big thing." It was an important technology, certainly, and it had to be explored. Like any new technology, though, the mass market had to get used to the idea of just what to do with AI. It wasn't as though Fortune 500 CEOs were reading about AI in *Business Week* one morning, and then saying, "We've got to have this! Let's get some this afternoon." That's like waking up one day and deciding you want to be hog farmer, so you go and buy a whole farm without consulting *Consumer Reports* or *Hog Farming Daily*. Preparation was necessary. There was a learning curve in AI that involved getting familiar with the concepts and the practical applications of the technology. Just hearing the words "expert system" or "artificial intelligence" was not enough justification to go out and spend hundreds of thousands of dollars on a largely untested technology. Unless, of course, you worked for a venture capital firm. Those people spent hundreds of thousands of dollars on largely untested technologies every day.

This fact escaped the founders of AI start-ups. They thought that as soon as they opened for business the world would beat a path to their doors. To them, the benefits of the technology were obvious. Never mind the fact that many of them had been deeply involved with AI for more than ten years, and that the rest of the world was only getting around to hearing about it, let alone investigating it and learning its value. This stuff was important, damn it, and the world should understand that.

Much of the slow learning curve had to do with the products of AI. Teknowledge, for instance, wasn't really selling products; it was selling consulting services. Consulting is an easy enough business to understand, except when it is based on unknown concepts like knowledge engineering. IntelliGenetics' medical software was straightforward, but it had a very specific and ultimately limited market because it only had value to medical researchers on the cutting edge of DNA research. There are not nearly as many of these people as there are, say, accountants or short order cooks, so the total number of potential customers worldwide was probably in the low hundreds.

As for LISP computers, both LMI and Symbolics had to literally teach anyone not directly involved in AI research the difference between their machines and regular computers. If artificial intelligence was a new term for prospective customers, "LISP machine" itself was a downright comical term. No matter who the prospect, it was inevitable that they first and foremost thought that lisp was a speech impediment. Getting past this to describe a programming language unlike any other was a big challenge for the "lithp" vendors.

Up until September 1981, in fact, Symbolics did not sell any computers. It was literally in start-up and development mode from April 1980 to September 1981. For that year and a half it had no product, and as a result, no revenues. It introduced its computer, the LM-2 (for LISP Machine 2, as in son of MIT's original LISP machine), the month before The Fifth Generation conference convened. The company made its first sale in the late summer of 1981 to the Fairchild AI Lab, which had created the Dipmeter Advisor.

LMI, despite the preconceptions about its inability to get off the ground, actually sold a dozen of its machines in 1980, its first year of business. Wyle and Greenblatt priced the machines at around $100,000 apiece, which means that they took in a million dollars their first year. Not a bad start for a couple of guys and a handful of employees who had started up without any outside venture capital and got no support from the locals.

Of those original LMI machines, two went to Control Data via Alex Jacobson. Another computer company, Texas Instruments, also took two that first year. (Symbolics had lost this particular sale to LMI in part because its own machines weren't ready.) At the time, it seemed like an innocuous purchase; it was natural that a large semiconductor manufacturer like TI would be interested in new technology. Yet, TI had bigger plans in mind than merely buying some start-up's AI product. It was tired of being an also-ran in the computer hardware business, and it wholeheartedly believed that AI was the answer to its dreams of bigger things.

Texas Instruments had made a name for itself as a pioneer in the manufacturing of transistors in the 1950s. Since then, it had built a huge business out of developing specialized computer microprocessors, primarily for use in military equipment and calculators. Along with Intel, Fairchild, and Motorola, TI was among America's premier semiconductor vendors.

As a point of information, there is a longtime tradition among semiconductor manufacturers of wanting to get into the hardware business. After all, these are the companies that provide the real guts for computers. IBM and its ilk just assemble those guts into machines. It makes perfect sense that the component makers would want to make their own hardware out of their own components, thereby eliminating the middlemen and creating a new business endeavor for themselves.

Coincidentally, there is a similarly long-standing belief among computer industry veterans that computer makers would never tolerate any attempt by the component makers to encroach on their business. As legend has it, there has been an implicit threat in the nice, symbiotic relationship between hardware vendors and the semiconductor suppliers for the last few decades.

The semiconductor makers manufacture their microchips, and the computer makers manufacture hardware. This is the basis of the nice part of the relationship. Computer vendors pay the semiconductor companies big bucks for these chips, which they buy by the millions each year. Since the computer makers are such good semiconductor customers, they have made their suppliers aware of one condition for continuing to do business. That condition is: we buy your products in massive quantities, and you don't compete with us. This is a fairly reasonable expectation on the part of the computer vendors. No company wants its supplier to go into business against it. This would cause all sorts of problems the next time the hardware manufacturer wanted to buy microchips.

Far from being just a business understanding, the story goes, this agreement carried a hint of malice. There was no way that the computer companies were ever going to let their suppliers compete directly with them, and they would work to ensure that this remained the case. The first instance of "enforcement" occurred in the 1960s, when a couple of the component manufacturers thought they had enough clout and power to try developing computers on their own. Getting wind of this, the big computer companies devised a plan. These companies, collectively known in the industry as the BUNCH, decided to withhold orders for parts from any component manufacturer that tried to market a computer. This is known in polite circles as a "squeeze play." It works quite simply. Component manufacturer X decides to build a computer. The BUNCH find out about this, and within one week, all the BUNCH orders for parts from Company X are cancelled. Since components are Company X's main line of business, and the new computer product is just a sideline, Company X sees that it is in danger of losing a lot of money in its core business. Company X, in a thoughtful re-evaluation of its operations, immediately kills its computer plans. All of its BUNCH orders reappear as if by magic.

No one can prove that such backroom dealing actually occurred at the BUNCH companies. No one will admit it, either, since the Justice Department frowns on such allegedly monopolistic behavior. The belief was widespread in the computer industry, nonetheless, and an ongoing reality seemed to support this belief: not one single computer offering from a semiconductor company was even close to being successful. They all died slow and agonizing deaths.

In the late 1970s, Texas Instruments took a chance on introducing its own personal computer. It was designed to compete with products from Apple, Commodore, several of the BUNCH companies, and IBM (IBM was never included in the legend of BUNCH steamrolling because it manufactured most of its own components). While every other little computer maker seemed to be making a bundle from PCs, the TI personal computer was barely able to dent the burgeoning PC market. No amount of effort could move the machines despite TI's best efforts. By 1980, the TI computer was already a loser. When it eventually killed the machine in 1983, Texas Instruments would take a loss of almost $600 million on its foray into computers.

The signs of this failure were already on the wall when TI bought its first two LISP machines from LMI in 1980. In talking with members of the AI community, TI was well aware of the need for better computers to run expert system and natural language programs. But the first generation of commercial LISP machines were cobbled together with available components and special hand-built parts. It was conceivable, from TI's perspective, that this AI business might eventually need its own custom-developed chips. Anticipating a long-term interest in AI, TI set up a research group of its own in Texas to explore ways that it might make inroads into commercializing AI.

Best of all, from TI's perspective, there were only two companies selling LISP computers, Symbolics and LMI. There was no BUNCH group to contend with. The two little LISP start-ups might be easy pickings compared to the BUNCH.

~

Though the pre-Fifth Generation activity in the United States was concentrated primarily in Palo Alto and Cambridge, there were other cities where researchers mulled over the commercial possibilities of their work. Alex Jacobson, for one, had decided to stay put in Los Angeles when he formed his company. Larry Harris had chosen Waltham, Massachusetts, but his work had been done at Dartmouth College in New Hampshire. The University of Texas at Austin and Yale University in New Haven, Connecticut, both were doing significant work in AI as the 1980s dawned.

But if there was a certain animosity between Stanford and MIT, the Left Coast and Right Coast of AI, there was a mutual disdain for AI research located anywhere else, with the possible exception of Carnegie-Mellon in Pittsburgh. Stanford and MIT shared the same roots, namely John McCarthy and his LISP language. They both had an affinity for CMU, partially out of respect for Newell and Simon, but also because of Feigenbaum's early years at that school. Outside of these three centers, anyone doing AI was really a second class citizen. Unfortunately, the media was to hold to that same tenet for years, rarely recognizing the AI work of labs or start-ups that resided outside this AI mainstream.

Jacobson found this out early on. Even though his new company, Inference Corporation, had started with a good-sized infusion of capital from Control Data, he was primarily cited in the popular press as a founder of Lisp Machine, Inc. The hackers and founders at Inference had come from southern California universities like USC and defense contractors like Hughes, but their lack of affiliation with the three major AI labs often meant that Inference wasn't accorded full pioneer status by the others in the AI community. The stigma was something that the company would battle for the next decade. (Perhaps this says something about why Inference in the 1990s is the only AI company that resembles its original incarnation. Over the years, guilt by association with AI labs came to haunt more than one company.)

One hundred forty miles southwest of MIT, in the hallowed ivy halls of Yale University, a natural language researcher named Roger Schank was certain that he could make a business out of his AI experience, regardless of his location. He had been working on various AI problems for more than a decade, and he didn't care if his lab was located outside of the MIT and Stanford corridors. He also didn't fit comfortably into either the East or West Coast AI contingents, partially because AI researchers in the mainstream were not particularly fond of Roger.

Schank is a heavyset man with long dark hair and a thick black beard. He looks like someone who would be more at home teaching rabbinical studies than the fundamentals of AI. Schank has perfected the art of glaring into the camera when photographed, presenting a menacing Rasputin-like face to the world. He must like this image; it would eventually grace the insides of numerous computer and psychology magazines throughout the 1980s.

In person, Schank is not quite the brooding dark lord of research that he might appear. As a matter of fact, he is fairly harmless looking, and his outlook on AI research can even be said to be somewhat tongue-in-cheek. According to Schank, "I think my mission in life—if I have a mission—is to put AI in perspective. I'd like to give people a sense of what's real and what's not, what's hype and what isn't. Most of all, I'd like to explain why AI is hard, because AI is hard. There is not an easy fix."

Roger attended Carnegie-Mellon in the 1960s, receiving his degree in mathematics. In his years there, Schank claims never to have met either Allen Newell or Herb Simon, despite the fact that they were the resident AI gurus. From CMU, he went to the University of Texas in Austin and received his doctorate before joining both the linguistics and computer science departments at Stanford in 1969.

Still in his early twenties, Schank undertook extensive research into natural language. He thought that most of the previous efforts at getting computers to understand language had gone wide of the mark. Researchers were focusing on words, and by extension, the syntax of those words within a sentence. As far as Schank was concerned, words had little to do with understanding language. It was all a matter of what he called "conceptual dependency." This theory holds that memory and language understanding rely on an individual's ability to conceptually represent and remember stories, lessons, conversations, etc. in his or her mind. This understanding, in Schank's view, was language-free and had almost no relationship to actual words. Roger even went so far as to tell the AI community that "One task in AI, strangely enough, is to get the computer to forget about the words."

The AI community didn't like being told what to do, especially by a non-pioneer, and especially when it *was* focusing on the words. Schank's ideas ran against the grain of then-popular natural language theory, which held that syntax was one of the most important components of language understanding. Not surprisingly, Schank found little support at Stanford. He left the West Coast for Yale University, where he became a professor of computer science and a professor of psychology in 1976. While Yale offered him a less hostile research environment than Stanford—to this day, neither the CMU nor Stanford AI communities claim Schank as one of their own—it also put him in direct contact with the substantial resources of Yale's famed psychology department. Schank quickly gathered a group of students around him to work on his conceptual dependency theory.

Roger seems to have formed his own cult of personality at Yale. Numerous people from both the psychology and computer science departments rallied around Schank's efforts in the late 1970s, and in 1980 he was named chairman of the computer science department. His students accorded him the same kind of status that Minsky was given by his MIT students, and indeed, there are parallels between the two men. Both tend to say whatever they feel at a particular moment and are unapologetic for their words or behavior. Both believe that AI has more to do with unknown facilities of the mind than logical computer programs or mathematical equations. Both also had a great deal of their work advanced through the activities of their students, whom they relied on to handle much of the programming and detail work.

Like Minsky, Schank was given his own Artificial Intelligence Lab at Yale, which he oversaw as director. Unlike his "competitors" at the other university labs, Schank chose very common, almost mundane problems for his research, things that were easily understandable to people who were not versed in AI. As a result, the acronyms for his natural language programs were almost too trite for the academic community: MARGIE, PAM, SAM, CYRUS, and FRUMP. (MARGIE, for example, supposedly stood for "Memory, Analysis, Response Generation in English," which is a big stretch for an acronym. In truth, Margie is the name of Schank's mother.) When demonstrating his programs, he used storybook characters with names like John and Mary and placed them in familiar settings like restaurants.

According to Roger, in order for a computer to understand the activity in a restaurant, it would have to be aware of what he called a "restaurant script." This script would serve the same purpose as a movie script: it would contain character roles, props, and scenes. The character roles would be "played" by waiters, waitresses, customers, and cashiers. Props would be objects such as tables, chairs, menus, silverware, and food. Scenes would be the actual activity that incorporated characters and props. John and Mary entering the restaurant would be one scene, ordering their food would be another, and actually eating would be another scene. The computer needed to be aware of the components of a script to truly understand any dialog pertaining to the restaurant (for example, "John had the clams on a half shell") before it could make any real sense of the scenes. Simply assigning values to the words, in Schank's opinion, would limit the computer's capability to adequately understand all the events that might take place in the restaurant. That's why programs like ELIZA could be tripped up or fooled within minutes of their operation; they had no conceptual knowledge of the environments they were discussing. They only knew about specific words.

Schank's most notable success was with a program called CYRUS. Although CYRUS allegedly stood for Computerized Yale Reasoning and Understanding System, its job was to interpret news stories about Cyrus Vance, the secretary of state under Jimmy Carter. In keeping with AI tradition, though, Schank concocted the technical sounding acronym, because "In this case, we knew the name had to be Cyrus; it was just a question of figuring out what CYRUS could be an acronym for." CYRUS was an intelligent system that compiled a personal and professional history of Vance. From this information, it could then answer questions about the man without having every word in the news stories defined. In essence, it would have a conceptual understanding of what Vance did, where he went, whom he met, and what he was involved in—from Vance's point of view. The program did this in a number of ways. It extracted basic grammatical structures from each sentence in the news stories and assigned value to the words (like other natural language programs), but then it made inferences about what the sentence meant in relationship to the other sentences in the story. It was this overall "meaning" that Schank concentrated on, and not just the strict definition of each word.

CYRUS acted as if *it* were Cyrus Vance. It could answer questions such as "Whom did you meet with on September 28, 1978?" or "When was the last time you were in Egypt?" The program allegedly was able to answer questions about situations not actually detailed in the news stories that formed its database by making inferences about particular situations and the "scenes" that were involved in those situations. When asked if Mrs. Vance had ever met Mrs. Menachem Begin, the program answered in the affirmative, providing a time and date. Though no news story actually stated that Mrs. Vance had ever met Mrs. Begin, CYRUS made this inference based on a news story that reported that the Vances and Begins had attended the same state dinner. With a conceptual understanding of what state dinners were all about, the computer basically guessed that the respective spouses would have met on that occasion.

Schank's work on language understanding also crossed into the realm of expert systems. As far as he and the other Yale researchers were concerned, natural language and expert systems were part of a larger technology that they called advisory systems. Schank used this term to address the fact that experts depended upon conceptual understanding of their specialties in order to actually function as experts and were not just walking textbooks. While Feigenbaum chose to refer to this facility as heuristics, Schank avoided that word. In practice, though, it was almost impossible to differentiate between the two terms. Schank stuck with his preferred names, as did Feigenbaum, and eventually expert systems would compete with advisory systems, even though they were essentially the same thing. Schank wasn't going to let Stanford's terminology dictate Yale's.

While much of the AI community found Schank to be a little too cute and too glib for his own good, it had to recognize that he was making important contributions to the study of human reasoning and perception as it applied to computers. Schank himself certainly realized this, and in 1979 he formed a company called Cognitive Systems in New Haven. The company didn't do much of anything until 1981, when Schank decided the time was right to do some ardent commercializing. Cognitive went into full start-up mode in 1981, seeking investment and hiring technical and administrative staff, employing many of the Yale students who had worked on Schank's various projects. Schank himself did not leave his post at Yale; after all, he was chairman of his department, and as previously stated, he had a mission.

A quick cross-referencing of dates will show that Cognitive Systems commenced its real business operations in the same year that The Fifth Generation was announced. With the wave of AI companies that were founded in the wake of The Fifth Generation, universities across America—including Yale, Stanford, MIT, CMU, and the rest—ran into a situation that they were not prepared for. Their leading researchers were starting companies and still keeping their academic jobs. This raised the possibility of divided loyalties. At the same time younger researchers, such as grad students or non-tenured professors, were quitting the schools entirely to go work for their mentors. This created an increasing brain drain that led from the universities directly to the start-ups. The lure of bigger paychecks and less-restricted research was siphoning the talent pool from the universities.

In public, both Roger Schank and Marvin Minsky would eventually decry this practice, claiming that no one would be left to do pure research in the academic labs. In private, however, they were hedging their bets by getting involved with their students in various start-ups. This kind of schizophrenic behavior would catch up with both men in just a few short years. Schank, in particular, would incur the wrath of his boss, Bart Giamatti, then president of Yale. Giamatti was not one to tolerate potential conflicts of interest among his employees, a fact that was demonstrated to the world when he became commissioner of baseball in 1989. Giamatti, it will be remembered, is the man who banned Pete Rose from baseball for his extracurricular activities—for life.

Even though it was a different ball game, Bart didn't think too much of Roger Schank's extracurricular activities, either.

Chapter 19

The Fifth Generation Again
The Book, Not the Movie

At the end of 1982, there were roughly two dozen artificial intelligence companies in the United States ready to sell their services to a waiting world. The only problem was that the world wasn't waiting for services, it was waiting for products.

1982 was actually rather anticlimactic for the AI business after the initial excitement of the Japanese announcement wore off. The potential customers of AI realized that they had plenty of time to investigate the technology because there were no actual products to be bought. This didn't count LISP machines, but no one was quite sure what to do with those things anyway. They could be used to run AI software, but where were customers going to get AI software? Teknowledge would design it for them, but that was a service, not a product.

It was this reality that led Texas Instruments, DEC, Boeing, General Electric, GTE, and a host of other large industrials to create their own internal AI organizations.

They could conceivably build their own AI software programs by the time any of the little start-ups finally got their acts together. And the roots of a national consortium, called the Microelectronics and Computer Technology Corporation (MCC, for short), had been planted in Austin, Texas. It, too, would focus on AI—once all the antitrust hurdles were cleared. Products were sure to flow from one of these big corporate environments.

This emphasis on products was anathema to academic researchers. Artificial intelligence was not about products, they argued; it was about research. It was about exploring links between human thinking and machines. Anything that was a product represented a finite manifestation or conclusion of a particular area of research. In effect, it was a dead end to that research, because once products were given over to customers, the researchers had no control over what was done with the technology. And since all the problems of creating machine intelligence were not even close to being solved, researchers didn't want their babies taken from the playpen too early.

Scientists, engineers, and researchers of all stripes are never quite ready to give up the fruits of their work when the time comes. Even in corporations, development personnel are constantly at war with marketing and manufacturing departments over decisions as to "when the time is right." If marketing says it needs the completed product on, say, April 1, it expects to get the product on that date. If the engineers agree with the date, they rarely plan on delivering it then, regardless of what they promise. When marketing comes in asking for the finished product, the engineers will inevitably say, "It's almost done, just give us two more weeks." Marketing gives in, two weeks go by, and engineering once again begs off, asking for more time. This happens over and over again, in businesses ranging from software development to auto manufacturing. Engineers and scientists can always find something to improve in a design and want free rein to fiddle with it until they are satisfied. Unfortunately, they are never satisfied.

The founder of a successful computer company once told me, in figurative terms, that there was only one way to deal with product developers and design engineers. "Tell them you want the finished product next Friday. When they agree to that demand, as they always will, leave them alone until the day before the scheduled completion. Then, on Thursday afternoon, go into the corporate development lab and shoot all the engineers. The product will be as ready then as it is ever supposed to be, and you won't have to listen to the engineers bitch and moan about it not being ready, because they will be dead."

This is not to be taken literally, so don't try it in your company. What this gentleman was saying is that engineers have to have their fingers pried from their babies, like over-protective mothers. The best way to deal with this is to just snatch the product away from them and then go on with the business of selling the product and making money. Companies that do not do this are forced to delay product introductions or keep stalling customers until their products are finally set free by the technodweebs in the corporate lab.

Over-protectiveness is exacerbated in academic labs, where real live products are rarely expected. Useful technology, however, is always expected. The companies or government organizations that put up money for research grants are not giving these funds out of the goodness of their hearts; they expect some return. That return is usually supposed to be some software or hardware technology that can be molded by the organization into a viable product.

As it gradually became apparent to the AI start-ups that products were going to be part and parcel of their future customers' expectations, they made a philosophical break with the university labs. Selling AI could not be about selling "technology;" it had to be about selling solutions to customer problems. Customers didn't want pie-in-the-sky theory; they wanted tangible results. As a result, the start-ups began to turn their lab-derived knowledge into products. Watching this, the lab minions, who believed that AI was a technology to be nurtured in the loving care of a university environment, felt betrayed.

This sense of betrayal was heightened as people left the labs to help the start-ups produce various AI technologies, such as expert systems. Suddenly, there were fewer and fewer people to work on the basic research necessary to uncover the secrets of AI. Marvin Minsky, in particular, was seething over what he viewed as the capitalistic rape and pillage of the universities by commercial AI enterprises. "None of the artificial intelligence groups in industry are doing really basic research," he bemoaned. "They do not make machines that learn. They do not work on the simplest problems of common sense. In general, they are not working on the kinds of things that ten years from now would produce a new wave of intelligent systems... The big laboratories at MIT, CMU, and Stanford University have fairly good equipment, but none has the amount of equipment per person that is needed to pursue basic research at full speed with high morale. One consequence is that the computer-starved students are more easily tempted by industry. High salaries are another temptation, and that is a problem that I see no way to solve." Though Minsky was scoffing at the notion of industry doing anything worthwhile in AI, he did manage to leave himself an out should things change. "I am thinking of starting a private research institute to do basic research in artificial intelligence, feeling that something has to be created that is in between the universities and the companies."

But Minksy's ideas and control over AI were already in a free fall. From the end of 1982 forward, Minsky would be considered out of touch by the commercial AI community. He had already contradicted himself a number of times during his career, making bold statements that put his reputation on the line. In 1967, he had stated "Within a generation, the problem of creating artificial intelligence will be substantially solved." As AI progressed into the 1980s, he was no longer sure of that. Too many people were mired in the "brain as logic machine" school of thought, creating expert systems and trying to formalize thinking processes—endeavors that Minsky sneered at. ("In the laboratory we regard the term 'expert system' with a certain amount of scorn," he said.) Businesses were wasting their time with problems like those that his old partner John McCarthy championed, and Minsky wanted no part of it. With the way they were going, Marvin said, AI might take another century to become a reality. This curmudgeonly behavior endeared him to no one.

Minsky's stated plans for a private research institute were hardly what he prophesied, either. Instead of a halfway house for industry and academia, Minsky started a commercial endeavor to create the most powerful computer in the history of the world. Far from being an altruistic organization, the company, called Thinking Machines, got its funding from CBS founder William Paley and DARPA. That's CBS, as in NBC, ABC, and CBS—television networks. The computer that Minsky's company was going to build using this money was called the Connection Machine, and Thinking Machines planned to price this computer at a very capitalistic $3 million. In doing this, Minsky was trying to straddle a barbed wire fence between AI in the marketplace and AI in the lab, and his reputation was getting pretty scratched up.

Roger Schank, too, was perching himself on this industry versus academia pedestal. He freely admitted to the schizophrenic nature of his pursuits, but seemed to relish the position he was in. He publicly told anyone who would listen that the AI well was drying up, and that there were only so many researchers to go around. On the other hand, he said, "I think that Cognitive Systems will succeed because our people were all trained by me. They have been working with me for years. We know we can build these things (AI products). Why do I think I can do it and other people cannot? Because ultimately, the hard part of artificial intelligence is having qualified people work for you. There are not very many. Fortunately, I know a few."

This devil-may-care attitude of Schank's irritated a lot of people. Schank was telling industry that they were only entitled to—or able to take—just so many people from the university labs. At the same time, he was claiming that he had all the best people in AI anyway, so he was going to be one of the few successful new AI entrepreneurs.

His competitors in the fledgling AI business were not the only ones to take issue with Roger's attitude. A. Bartlett Giamatti, Yale's president, found this attitude to be indicative of Schank's lack of regard for his professorial duties, which Yale was paying for. Giamatti didn't like the idea of any Yale professors working on projects in which they had financial interests because such projects took time away from their teaching and research responsibilities. This shoe certainly fit Schank's foot. Roger countered Giamatti's argument with the proposition that Yale should support its professors and create a high-tech center around New Haven, an area akin to Palo Alto and Cambridge. The argument fell on deaf ears, and New Haven remains an idyllic section of Connecticut without the slightest pretension to being a technology center.

Schank continued teaching, and he continued to spend time working as Cognitive System's president. He even got involved with two other minor ventures, Compu-Teach and Intelligent Business Systems, thus pushing Giamatti's patience to the limit. Rumors abounded that Giamatti wanted to take some decisive action in regards to Schank's recalcitrance, perhaps even going so far as taking the AI lab away from him. But it was not to be. Giamatti would be gone by the time Yale finally got around to ridding itself of Roger Schank.

❧

Much of the rhetoric spewed forth by Minsky and Schank, along with other hard-core lab techies, was done in public forums such as conferences. The AI research community had created a formal annual conference for itself under the auspices of a new organization called the American Association for Artificial Intelligence. The organization and the conference were both known as AAAI and were always referred to as "Triple-A-I." The first AAAI conference was held in the summer of 1980 at Stanford, and it provided a forum for a few hundred interested researchers to come and present papers and discuss new AI techniques with each other. It was a very familial affair, limited to the AI cognoscenti and not tainted by the presence of commercial enterprises. The AAAI Conference did allow researchers in certain AI companies to come and speak, but businesses per se were not allowed to come and advertise, or market, or sell, or do any of those other scurrilous things that companies normally do at trade shows and conferences.

The AAAI "shows" helped propagate the growing schism between the burgeoning number of AI start-ups and the lab researchers. The researchers looked down on the commercialization of lab efforts, while start-up companies shook their collective heads at the researchers' inability to see the need for practical applications of AI technology. A number of researchers, like Ed Feigenbaum, Richard Greenblatt, and Randy Davis, were caught somewhere in the middle. Though they were involved in companies, they maintained close ties with their labs, so their commercial shortcomings were routinely overlooked. It was the people like Russell Noftsker, Alex Jacobson, and Stephen Wyle that the lab researchers considered to be the real technology charlatans.

It is amazing that this factionalism was already running rampant in an "industry" that had barely thirty companies in 1982, none of which was doing any significant business. Things were downright slow, all things considered. Interestingly, they all basically had the same customers: the U.S. military (primarily the Army and Air Force); NASA; defense contractors like Mitre, Fairchild, Martin Marietta, and BBN; technical labs like MIT, Lawrence Livermore, Sandia, Oak Ridge, and Los Alamos; and several large corporations in the aerospace and manufacturing industries, including Rockwell, Grumman, Lockheed, General Dynamics, and Sperry. That was the total extent of the customer base. Given that this was not a huge marketplace, the AI companies weren't exactly gutting the academic brain pool. They were hiring researchers from the lab, yes, but they really hadn't skimmed off the bulk of talent that was still available. That wouldn't happen for two more years.

Going into 1983, the AI start-ups needed more sustained public interest in their services and in the products that they were planning to create. They needed something on the order of another Fifth Generation announcement, but with more staying power. Not that The Fifth Generation was forgotten by 1983; it was just that it was taking awhile to get off the ground in Japan, and it would probably be several years before any visible results emerged from ICOT. At that time, The Fifth Generation was primarily a set of conference papers, and it was sort of old news. The bloom was off the rose, as it were. Few people, with the exception of Ed Feigenbaum, were still all that worked up over the Japanese project.

At that point, no really one knew just how worked up Feigenbaum really was. But everybody in AI was about to find out. So were government politicians. So was DARPA. So was Japan.

So was Merv Griffin.

෴

Ed Feigenbaum had already established himself as a pioneer in the field of building expert systems by late 1982. He had been America's representative at the 1981 Fifth Generation Conference, and he had developed two of the most significant books on the topic of AI. Both *Computers And Thought* and *The Handbook of Artificial Intelligence* had done quite a bit to ensure Ed's continued legacy and his reputation.

But The Fifth Generation struck a new chord with Feigenbaum. The whole concept of a knowledge industry or knowledge society fit quite nicely into his technological belief structure. In a way, The Fifth Generation, or at least its ramifications, epitomized Ed Feigenbaum's "special purpose."

During 1982, the year following The Fifth Generation announcement, Feigenbaum began working on a new artificial intelligence book. Instead of being a compilation of papers or programming techniques, this one would be a personal narrative of Ed's impressions on the importance of The Fifth Generation to America's own artificial intelligence efforts. He enlisted the aid of Pamela McCorduck, a technology writer and longtime Feigenbaum fan, to help him actually put words to paper. The result was a hardcover book entitled *The Fifth Generation*, which was published in 1983. Before we look at the singular impact of this book on the AI business, we need to take a moment and look at the book itself.

The Fifth Generation (the book, not the project, although the pro-Japanese bias of the book makes it easy to confuse the two) was based on Edward Feigenbaum's concern that the United States was not doing enough to combat the international threat posed by Japan's desire to be the first nation to create thinking machines. In its 275 pages, Feigenbaum outlines in great detail what the Japanese are planning to do in AI and how they are going to accomplish their goals. The essence of the entire book can be condensed down to two statements: "The Japanese are going to hold the key to the future of computing—which is artificial intelligence—unless the United States does something about it. If the United States doesn't do anything about it, then we should get used to being farmers."

Two sentences aren't enough to fill a book, so Feigenbaum and McCorduck created a written potpourri of their personal feelings about artificial intelligence and Japan. *The Fifth Generation* is ostensibly about the importance of artificial intelligence to the world, yet McCorduck and Feigenbaum are the primary characters. It is more a look at "Pam and Ed's Excellent Adventure" than a scholarly study of the implications of The Fifth Generation Project. The two authors actually have more page references for themselves in the index than any other individual, whether it be Kazuhiro Fuchi or Marvin Minsky. Actually, I shouldn't include Minsky here—he's not even listed in book's index. McCorduck is Feigenbaum's sidekick on a trip through Japanese culture, and they never fail to divulge their innermost and unspoken thoughts as they meet the leaders of The Fifth Generation Project. With phrases like "McCorduck smiled to herself, but said nothing…" or "Feigenbaum felt obliged to remind the Japanese… ," the authors attempted to create the impression that they alone had the inside track—and a quasi-gossipy one at that—on both the Japanese and the development of artificial intelligence.

Side by side with technical descriptions of expert systems are odd references to cultural trivia. Gratuitous citations of dead writers and obscure economists are tossed into the book, people like Hortense Calisher, George Ball, and Edgar Guest. (Don't know who these people are? That's okay, nobody else does either, that's why they're gratuitous references.) One example: "Those who disagree with McCorduck invariably begin by quoting Santayana on the virtues of studying history: if you don't know history, you're condemned to repeat it. She smiles politely. Some appropriate attention to the rise and fall of Troy is worthwhile. An afternoon with the odes of Pindar can be wonderfully refreshing." This is a book about artificial intelligence?

Actually, no. It is a book about the authors, with a healthy dose of fear tossed in. Their prologue takes on a grave tone right from the opening pages: "We are writing this book because we are worried. But we are also basically optimistic. Americans invented this technology! If only we could focus our efforts, we should have little trouble dominating the second computer age as we dominated the first. We have a two- or three-year lead; that's large in the world of high technology. But we are squandering our lead at the rate of one day per day. America needs a national plan of action, a kind of space shuttle program for the knowledge systems of the future. In this book we have tried to explain this new knowledge technology…we have also outlined America's weak, almost nonexistent response to this Japanese challenge. The stakes are high. In the trade wars, this may be the crucial challenge. Will we rise to it? If not, we may consign our nation to the role of the first great postindustrial agrarian society."

America as a nation relegated to farming? Never, cried those who read the book and agreed with Feigenbaum.

Yet Ed saw no other future for an AI-less America. The Japanese would overcome the myths about their culture to finally take their rightful place at the head of the world's economy. (It's funny that he should fall for this, given that he states that his wife, who is Japanese, thinks that The Fifth Generation Project sounds very un-Japanese.) Throughout the book, people talk about the Fifth Generation as a fait accompli, as if the Japanese have shattered all the myths just by making an announcement. It fails to concede the fact that nothing tangible had been done by 1983, and that saying something is very different from doing something. In fact, Feigenbaum gives the Japanese every possible consideration, which he does not extend to the United States. He claims that all our beliefs about Japan are simply myths, and that they will have no problem dispelling these myths when the time comes. Supporting evidence for this contention is weak, at best.

The book played up the importance of expert systems—Ed's forte—even though that was only one component of the overall Fifth Generation project. Each and every chapter seemed to confirm that the Japanese were attempting to do exactly what Feigenbaum had been working on for decades. The uninitiated must have been amazed at the similarities between The Fifth Generation Project and Feigenbaum's own work.

At the end of the book, Feigenbaum offered six possible American responses to the Japanese. One, we could maintain the status quo, and basically do nothing. Two, "We can form industrial consortiums to meet the Japanese challenge and as citizens insist that the Justice Department take a reasonable stance regarding joint industrial R&D. This might take an act of Congress." Feigenbaum admitted that Americans have little consortium experience, however. Three, we could enter a major joint venture with the Japanese, "and the joint venture could be powerful internationally." Four, we could concentrate on knowledge-based software (a la expert systems) while conceding the hardware to the Japanese. Five, "We can form a national laboratory for the promotion of knowledge technology…which has at least a fighting chance to achieve brilliance." And six, "We can prepare to be the first great post-agrarian society. We absolutely shine in growing things."

Of these six, Feigenbaum and McCorduck favored door number five, which should come as no surprise. It was exactly the kind of proposal that someone who had a lot to gain would make. Critics in the AI community—and there were many—decried this type of self-serving prose, noting that Feigenbaum was teaching at a university that taught knowledge technology and had just founded two companies that sold knowledge technology. Very few people in the AI community liked The Fifth Generation. Many researchers and new entrepreneurs were incensed that Feigenbaum was setting himself up as an industry spokesman by trying to set a national charter and direction for AI research. For instance, how could he say that the nascent MCC consortium wouldn't work when he claimed in the same breath that the Japanese consortium was almost sure to work? (When the MCC was started, it actually had more funding than ICOT, a fact that was ignored in the book.) He wondered how America could ever fund or afford such research, where it would get resources, and how it would work. Conversely, he accepts The Fifth Generation line of patented responses to these questions as if they were sent down on holy tablets from the mountain.

Yet somehow the book caught on. Despite its barely literate prose (one AI researcher called it "unctuous"), its two-sentence message captured the hearts, if not the minds, of a large segment of the American population, especially those who commuted to the Pentagon every day. A new conventional wisdom grew up around Ed's treatise on The Fifth Generation: Here was another international threat from Japan, every bit as dangerous as Pearl Harbor had been forty years earlier. And the book was a physical, tangible manifestation of that threat. Unlike the actual Fifth Generation Project announcement, which involved a lot of speeches and technical papers, here was a book that could be waved about, thumped on tables, and passed from office to office. It was an actual symbol of The Fifth Generation, one that the Japanese had not come up with on their own.

Feigenbaum's book itself was perhaps the single grandest paradox of the ongoing high technology war between the United States and Japan. He claimed that the Japanese would set the agenda for the future of computing on their own terms and with their own innovation, yet it took a book by an American computer researcher to make sure that the Japanese got the recognition they wanted.

The popularity of the book at the time, and the seriousness that it was allowed, garnered Feigenbaum a whole new popularity. The Fifth Generation became such a topic of conversation that Ed was invited to discuss the book and share his views on "The Merv Griffin Show" in the spring of 1983. "Nightline" it wasn't, but being on Merv in the early eighties gave guests a certain celebrity cachet, and Ed was never one to argue with the benefits of being a celebrity.

While AI researchers derided *The Fifth Generation* as "that book by Ed 'Chicken Little' Feigenbaum," its publication had one immutable and irreversible effect: It scared the living daylights out of the technologists in Washington. A sense of urgency that had been missing the first time the government became aware of The Fifth Generation now took hold. This was war, albeit a technological one, but it could impact economies, futures, jobs, and companies. Feigenbaum had been explicit in his warnings, and now everyone knew what the perils and pitfalls were. They didn't have to imagine it—Ed had laid it out for them.

DARPA began making plans for sinking more money than it ever had into artificial intelligence. Congressmen made plans to allow the MCC consortium to become the biggest organization of its kind in the United States. American researchers, fueled by renewed government interest, made plans to immediately leave their labs and start new companies. In the aftermath of *The Fifth Generation*, America began its artificial intelligence efforts in earnest. Everything else was a precursor, and from 1983 forward, AI would be a serious business.

For all its faults, *The Fifth Generation* jump-started the entire American AI industry, and for that alone it deserves a certain level of regard. Almost overnight, dozens and then hundreds of AI companies sprouted from out of nowhere, like algae in an untreated pool. During the year after the publication of the book, anyone could start an AI company. If you put AI into your business plan, and couldn't get money, you were considered a moron. Everywhere in corporate America, there was investment money to be had, from companies like General Motors, Ford, Lockheed, Procter & Gamble, Raytheon, Westinghouse, NYNEX, US West, Honeywell, and plenty of others. Getting it was as easy as asking for it.

A footnote needs to be inserted here, a seemingly trivial fact that will soon become evident: Almost everything in Feigenbaum and McCorduck's book turned out to be completely wrong.

Chapter **20**

Promises and Politics

Selling Out and Signing Up

Richard Greenblatt and Stephen Wyle had outgrown their little makeshift facility on Blackstone Street in Cambridge. It was time to move. Greenblatt would rather die than leave Cambridge, so there was no chance that he would go to Los Angeles and work there. Instead, he and the other Lisp Machine, Inc. engineers moved into larger quarters on Massachusetts Avenue in Cambridge, with offices that flanked the entrance to the MIT campus.

LMI was now feeling the pinch of Symbolics' superior cash reserves. Even though LMI had sold more machines than Symbolics had in 1981, Russell Noftsker and company wasted no time in recapturing the head start that they had given Greenblatt. In 1982, Symbolics sold nearly forty of its LM-2 machines, at a pricey $125,000 apiece. LMI, on the other hand, had barely matched its own first year sales. By the end of 1983, it had sold a grand total of twenty-three computers.

LMI was severely hampered by its piecemeal strategy of building everything by hand. The company's primary processing board, a wire-wrapped circuit board, had to be custom built by a company not too far from Cambridge. The lead time on getting these boards was nearly six months per order, and since Greenblatt and Wyle were only buying parts after they received a customer's up-front money, the delay was substantial. Symbolics, on the other hand, was popping machines out of its California assembly plant, and LMI began losing sales because of its lack of inventory. Considering that individual LISP machines sold for more than $100,000, each sale substantially affected the company's income. Though there were fewer than seventy commercial LISP machines, all told, in sites around the world, representing approximately twenty-five customers (since almost all customers bought two or three machines at a time), the machines added up to a market worth more than $6 million. LMI couldn't afford to lose too many sales if it wanted to stay in business.

As of late 1983, Symbolics was preparing to introduce its completely revamped version of the original MIT LISP machine. It had told its customers to get ready for this new computer, which would make the original obsolete because it featured a completely redesigned processor better suited for running complex applications. Greenblatt had heard of the machine, but he dismissed it as hype designed to get customers to hold off on purchasing his own machines while they waited for Symbolics. Yet the pressure was on, and LMI realized it could not continue to churn out copies of Greenblatt's five-year-old machine.

When their own customers started talking about Symbolics' new machine—even though no one had seen it—Greenblatt and Wyle knew they had to do something. According to Greenblatt, "We finally fell for the Symbolics' hype, and we chickened out. We stopped committing money to wire wrap boards, because we believed we couldn't compete with the new machine's design." LMI decided instead to come up with a new design of its own. But the problem of the six-month delay time came back to haunt the company almost immediately. Symbolics' new machine was late in shipping, and that meant that the life of the existing CADR machine was extended for several months as customers sought an interim solution. Since LMI had decided not to order any more processing boards, it was now caught between a rock and a hard place. While it thought that it had a six-month overlap to work on its next computer, there was suddenly a spark of life left in the old machine. LMI couldn't afford to turn down these orders, but it also couldn't afford to redirect the resources it had committed to working on a new computer. In order to develop a new computer and take advantage of orders for the old machine, Greenblatt had only one option. He was going to have to get some outside investment.

This prospect severely dismayed Richard. Outside money would mean the end to his bootstrap operation. It would make his company beholden to someone else. It would also mean that Lisp Machine, Inc. would become, in essence, the very thing he didn't want. It would make his company just like Russell Noftsker's.

LMI had no choice. It could sink into obscurity, or it could swim with a flotation aid from some investor. Not only did LMI have its own financial dilemma, but things in general were getting very strange in the computer hardware business. Once upon a time, it had been a world completely dominated by mainframes and minicomputers. Then in the early 1980s, PCs had shown up. But now there was suddenly a new class of machine that seemed to fit somewhere between PCs and minicomputers.

Built by companies with celestial names like Sun and Apollo, these computers were called "workstations." They were gaining popularity in the engineering community because of their exceptional graphics, extraordinary power, and the fact that they were designed with the needs of individual programmers in mind. LISP machines were also a type of workstation, but of a much more specialized type. LISP machines were used for building AI programs and complicated graphics simulations. Sun and Apollo, on the other hand, were selling their machines for every conceivable purpose—everything from computer-aided design to financial modelling. Both Greenblatt and Noftsker thought there might eventually be some overlap with generic workstations and LISP workstations due to similarities in their level of power and programming capabilities, but in 1983 the two computer types didn't compete. In fact, as the LISP machine evolved, the AI companies believed that it might just outshine the generic workstations, which didn't have all the bells and whistles that the AI Lab had spent years developing. Nonetheless, these upstarts were probably worth watching.

So, in order to stay alive and continue playing in the hardware game, LMI swallowed its pride and held out its hand. Right away, an investment company called Genesis Capital ponied up $650,000 for LMI. Another $100,000 was provided by a French investment firm, and Steve Wyle's father put in $100,000. The total investment was $850,000, which gave the new investors 30 percent of the company. Wyle and Greenblatt kept the other 70 percent, as well as control of the board of directors.

As Greenblatt recalls sadly, "From that point, the top was off the cookie jar." Another company wanted a piece of the action that LMI was now handing out, and it wanted a big piece. That company was Texas Instruments.

Texas Instruments had purchased two of LMI's first machines, and it was itching to do something more in AI. The company's chief technical officer, George Heilmeier, liked the prospects of AI. His background was well-suited to exploring new technologies; he had been one of the earliest developers of liquid crystal displays, those ubiquitous gray-white screens found on digital watches, calculators, and laptop computers. He had also been director of DARPA during a couple of its "down" years, from 1975 to 1977. In fact, some of DARPA's artificial intelligence funding had been cut during his tenure.

Heilmeier returned to the commercial world when he joined Texas Instruments in 1977. After seeing the kinds of work that had come through DARPA's doors, he was ready to get TI involved in exciting new technology growth areas. Although AI hadn't necessarily looked like a winner in the mid-1970s during his DARPA stint, it was certainly beginning to look a lot better in the early 1980s. In the uproar of the post-Fifth Generation brouhaha, Heilmeier decided that TI was going to ride the AI tidal wave. One of the ways it was going to do this was to get involved in the LISP machine business. This hardware might also prove to be the way that TI could finally sneak its way into the computer manufacturing industry. First, though, Texas Instruments began by inviting itself into LMI's manufacturing operations.

When Lisp Machine, Inc. decided to stop handmaking its first generation of computers, it was determined to take a more conventional approach for its new machine, which was to be called the Lambda (yet again, another arcane LISP hacker reference). A computer company called Western Digital was building a workstation that it was attempting to sell to the mass market in the same way that Sun and Apollo were. Western Digital's underlying technology was called the NuBus, a type of hardware processor that had been developed at MIT. Although NuBus was an MIT computer technology, it hadn't been created in the AI Lab. It was the product of a completely separate computer group, but Greenblatt was familiar with the technology.

MIT licensed NuBus to Western Digital (after courting Zenith and Heathkit, the maker of Radio Shack's do-it-yourself gadgets), which began manufacturing NuBus machines. It occurred to LMI that it could buy the NuBus computers from Western Digital and put its own LISP processing boards into the machines. This would effectively make a NuBus machine a LISP machine. Best of all, the Western Digital computer ran UNIX, an operating system that provided for extensive data sharing between users on different machines. It could provide a basic foundation for allowing LISP hackers to work simultaneously in the same environment.

LMI and Western Digital teamed up in 1983, and LMI began swapping out the factory-installed Western Digital processor boards to create Lambda LISP machines. Problems quickly raised their heads. Western Digital was ill-prepared to market its own version of the machine, and LMI soon realized it was selling more of the Western Digital machines than Western Digital was. As it turned out, LMI was Western Digital's biggest customer. This meant that Western Digital was in deep trouble, because LMI was selling its machines in small handfuls, not in the quantities of dozens or hundreds that were necessary to make a workstation company successful.

Texas Instruments liked what it saw at LMI and also saw the problems at Western Digital. In what was to become a strange three-way agreement, TI bought the workstation group from Western Digital. Along with this take-over, it acquired the NuBus rights as well as the manufacturing rights to the computer that was the basis of the Lambda. Thus, TI became the supplier of Lambda machines to LMI, even though it was a major customer of LMI's.

Here the tales of Texas Instruments' further involvement with LMI diverge. Greenblatt claims that this unique arrangement via Western Digital led to an investment by TI into Lisp Machine, Inc. Since the "top was off the cookie jar," this was not as bruising to the ego of the LMI founder as it might have appeared. However, Greenblatt is hesitant to be specific about details, and he admits that the investment was a "sad situation."

People outside of Texas Instruments and LMI have more detailed stories to tell. In particular, Noftsker claims that the TI investment was prompted by a recommendation from Symbolics. Henry Baker, Symbolics' salesman, could not convince TI to buy any of his LISP machines, and in fact, TI was such a good customer of LMI's that it accounted for more than a third of all LMI's sales. Since it appeared that this situation was certainly not going to change after the Western Digital deal, Baker tried to find a way to take the wind out of LMI's sales. According to Noftsker, and with Noftsker's consent, Baker allegedly told the men in charge of TI's artificial intelligence group that as the primary customers of LMI, they were also the primary funders of LMI's development work. If they were paying for this development, Baker queried, why weren't they given equity in the company? Surely TI was giving enough of its time and resources to LMI to justify a piece of the pie. TI loved the idea and bit on Baker's hook.

Regardless of how accurate the non-LMI version of the story is, Texas Instruments immediately acquired 25 percent of LMI. This deal had all sorts of weblike conditions and cross-licensing arrangements, which included giving TI up to forty-five days of Richard Greenblatt's consulting time. If Richard hadn't wanted to get into a big company situation before, he was in it up to his eyeballs now.

Symbolics viewed its recommendation as a way to link LMI's fortunes to Texas Instruments in a move that would surely hog-tie LMI, its only competitor. Noftsker says now that he regrets giving the nod to this ploy. While the investment served to muck up LMI's operations over the long term, it also gave Texas Instruments a quick entry into the LISP market. TI was hundreds of times larger than Symbolics, and it could afford to throw its weight around once it chose to. TI also had lots of friends and former employees in the military and in large corporations who were loyal to TI, and were always eager to throw business the company's way. Noftsker hadn't counted on this, and his suggestion to throw Texas Instruments into Lisp Machine, Inc.'s arms would backfire nastily. Noftsker would eventually find himself losing sales to TI from the one customer that he thought was pledged forever to Symbolics—the MIT AI Lab.

 ❧

While the hardware business was in the process of getting messy in late 1983, the software side of AI was just getting started. All those university researchers with pent-up entrepreneurial pangs decided to put down their pocket protectors and go for the gold.

In Pittsburgh, the relatively anonymous members of Carnegie-Mellon University's AI projects ventured carefully out into the commercial world. Led by four of the school's leading AI lights, they set up the aptly named Carnegie Group to sell expert system and natural language services. The four founders were the principal scientists and directors of four different CMU computer labs. They included John McDermott, principal scientist of the Computer Science Department, who had successfully created Digital Equipment's XCON system; Raj Reddy, director of the Robotics Institute, who oversaw much of the military's voice recognition work during the Speech Understanding Research project in the early 1970s; Mark Fox, the head of the Intelligent Systems Laboratory; and Jaime Carbonell, director of the Natural Language Processing Project, who had been Roger Schank's student. Together they decided it was time to capitalize on their combined expertise. As Reddy said at the time, "If someone is going to get rich out of the technology developed here, it ought to be the people who developed it." This left no doubt as to the plans of Carnegie Group's founders.

Carnegie Group started with the same basic business plan as Teknowledge. It would provide consulting services to big customers and to the government, and its products would come later. The primary thing was to get the company started and to find investment money. Like Teknowledge, Carnegie's founders were not inclined to go shopping around for VC money. They wanted big bucks from big companies that were also willing to be clients or development partners. People like John McDermott had worked intimately with DEC, and he knew that large corporations were eager to latch onto AI technology.

When Carnegie Group was incorporated, the cornerstone of commercial pure-play artificial intelligence was complete. Symbolics and LMI sold hardware. IntelliGenetics, Inference, Teknowledge, and Carnegie Group all sold software or consulting. These six companies became the de facto "AI pioneers" of the business, and in some way, shape, or form, almost all the companies that would enter into AI in the future would either do business with them or be related to them. Other companies that appeared to be AI pioneers, namely Cognitive Systems, were just far enough off to the edge of the map that the press never quite got a good enough look at them. These six, though, were to be AI media darlings and prime industry motivators for the remainder of the decade.

They were also the last to have to scramble for investment money. For the next three years, almost any business plan with the term artificial intelligence in it was welcomed by the VC community. Not that the technology was any more viable than it had been just months before, because it wasn't. But the amazing amount of post-Fifth Generation press generated by Feigenbaum's book got everybody on the AI bandwagon. Like piranhas, the VCs wanted to be part of the frenzy. More insistently, they wanted to be the first ones to get their pound of flesh, figuratively speaking.

There was one other thread that served to complete the commercial AI web. This was the formal incorporation of America's technology consortium, the MCC. Since raising his first concerns about Japan right after The Fifth Generation announcement, Control Data chairman William Norris had actively solicited support for a national consortium from both the Reagan Administration and CEOs of other large technology companies. Over the course of 1982, Norris received enough tentative thumbs up from these parties to lay the groundwork for his proposed Microelectronics and Technology Consortium. He even found a man to run it, Bobby Ray Inman.

Bobby Ray Inman, as his name may suggest, is from Texas. He is a short, rather squirrely looking man in the Ross Perot mode, but without the big ears and the irritatingly folksy banter. When Norris approached Inman with his plans for a consortium in 1982, Inman had acquired extensive government experience, but very little practical business experience. This was of no concern to Norris, who needed someone with government ties and influence to make sure the consortium didn't run into antitrust problems. It is hard to imagine anybody who fit this description better than Inman. Bobby Ray was a retired admiral of the U.S. Navy who had gone from the military directly to the deepest and darkest corridors of the U.S. intelligence community. He served as director of the National Security Agency for four years in the late 1970s before becoming deputy director of the CIA in 1981. In Washington parlance, this made Bobby Ray a "spook," the polite term for a member of the nation's undercover community. But Inman was more than your every-day spook; he had held executive positions at the NSA and the CIA, which meant that he was also privy to America's most important national secrets. If anybody knew which skeletons were in the closet, or where the bodies were buried, it would be Bobby Ray. Norris could hardly have picked a better front man for the MCC.

In addition to snaring Inman, Norris got the attention of a number of large U.S. firms with his "us against them" rhetoric. Specifically, ten companies promised they would join MCC if Norris could make it a reality. They were mostly computer and semiconductor manufacturers, including Motorola, National Semiconductor, Allied Signal, Mostek, and Control Data. Most importantly, Norris was given a waiver on the United States' rigid antitrust code by the Justice Department at the insistence of the Reagan Administration. (This would become a legitimate clearance in 1984 when Congress passed the National Cooperative Research Act, HR 5401).

MCC and Bobby Ray set up camp in Austin, Texas, near the University of Texas, and began work in 1983. As the Fifth Generation Project had, there were a multitude of programs that MCC would undertake, the most visible of which was AI. The programs were divided into five categories. The first was Advanced Computer Architecture , a ten-year program focusing on par-allel processing and AI. The second was called Packaging, a six-year program designed to advance the state of the art in semiconductor packaging and interconnect technology. Third was VLSI/Computer-Aided Design, an eight-year program for improving CAD technology as it applied to propagating other technologies. Software Technology was fourth, a seven-year program to improve software productivity and development by quantum leaps over what previously existed. The fifth program, actually added later than the others, was formed to conduct research into supercomputers.

Member companies had to put up $125,000 apiece in order to join MCC, and then they followed an ICOT-like plan. Each company signed up for whichever programs it was interested in, and then it "donated" researchers to those programs. Additional fees were charged depending on the programs that the companies got involved in, and MCC used this money for expenses as well as for hiring outside program directors that would not be affiliated with any particular member corporation. This hiring process helped keep projects from being biased towards any one member company. In return for all of this consorting, the participating companies each got one share of equity in MCC, and were entitled to the first use of any new technologies developed by the particular programs.

Notably missing from MCC were IBM and AT&T, which were both a little gun shy from coming under Justice Department scrutiny just prior to the incorporation of MCC. IBM, however, did set up a research facility in Austin, evidently to take advantage of all the brainpower that was heading in that direction.

The AI group of MCC immediately settled on LISP as the language it would use for its development projects. Scouting around for computers to complement this work, it decided on Symbolics. This gave the LISP machine company a large new source for revenue. Better than that, MCC member companies got acquainted with the Symbolics machines via their researchers and started ordering the computers for their own labs. Without really trying, Symbolics became "the" machine of America's response to The Fifth Generation.

It is important to note that Ed Feigenbaum's *The Fifth Generation* cast aspersions on Bobby Ray Inman's ability to make the MCC work even before the consortium really got running. In fact, after a discussion of Inman's career, the book stated flatly, "We need some new American heroes." Feigenbaum made it quite clear that Kazuhiro Fuchi's personality was better suited to making a large national project work than was Inman's. The MCC was not the CIA, Feigenbaum argued, and Inman might not be able to handle a technology enterprise the way he handled politics.

Once again, Feigenbaum was tilting at windmills. Without giving away the ending of our story, even a "spook" like Inman would end up looking a lot better than Fuchi by the time The Fifth Generation was over—at least until Bill Clinton asked Bobby Ray to be his secretary of defense.

ᕝ

The MCC was underway, and AI projects and public interest clicked up another notch. Back in Cambridge, Randy Davis of TEIRESIAS fame had gone from working on knowledge engineering at Stanford to a professorial position at MIT's Sloan School. Davis had already lent his name to the list of twenty founders of Teknowledge and was now ready to lend it again to a Cambridge start-up. Along with others from MIT, Davis created a company called Applied Expert Systems, or Apex for short. The goal of Apex was to sell expert systems to financial institutions. Like IntelliGenetics, it would create a single product and sell tons of copies into a large niche market—in this case, the financial planning market. No consulting, no services, just one expert system that helped financial planners do their job better than ever before. It was a simple, straightforward concept. There were more than twenty thousand certified financial planners in the United States, and Apex was sure that each of them could benefit from a personal computerized assistant.

In Palo Alto, Peter Hart and Richard Duda—who had set up the Schlumberger-Fairchild FLAIR lab after creating PROSPECTOR—also decided it was time to head out on their own. Hart, in particular, wanted to start a company that would sell expert systems that could be used by mineralogists. He met with Sheldon Breiner, a businessman who ran a company called GeoMetrics. Hart talked to Breiner because GeoMetrics, which Breiner had founded, sold geophysical instruments that were used in the mining and drilling industries. Although he had many years of experience in those businesses, Breiner had little interest in creating software for mineral exploration. He did, however, like the idea of applying expertise to more lucrative and mainstream industries like finance, especially banking and insurance. If Hart could direct his expertise to that field of business, Breiner would definitely be interested.

It didn't take Hart long to come around to Breiner's way of thinking. Hart bailed out of FLAIR, where he had approved the purchase of the first Symbolics machine, and entered the world of financial expert systems. In no time at all, Breiner and Hart wrote a business plan, culled research people from SRI and Stanford, and raised more than $3 million in venture capital. The company was named Syntelligence (*syn*thetic in*telligence*) and by the end of 1983, it was creating expert systems for use in the financial industry, just as Apex was.

The financial industry, which includes banks, stock brokers, insurance companies, investment companies, portfolio managers, money managers, accounting firms, and Wall Streeters of every shape and size, was of singular interest to the fledgling AI industry. It held the allure of big bucks and exciting possibilities, since computers were beginning to play an important role in the day-to-day control and operation of everything from interest rates to the New York Stock Exchange. Financial firms had a lot of excess cash in the early 1980s, and they were looking for ways to make even more. The potential of computing, especially intelligent computing, promised additional returns by making better use of complex economic data than the average human could.

Apex and Syntelligence believed that they could get a slice of the financial industry's increasing largesse beginning in 1984, and they went to work on systems that would hopefully make financial institutions drool. Though they were the first companies to target this market, they had no products to sell just yet, and they had to hurry. Other start-ups would see this same financial industry opportunity and crowd in on their game. Specifically, a man named Phil Cooper was getting ready to barge in to the financial expert system market with a company called Palladian. By the time Palladian was through with its competitors, it would be immortalized in a Harvard University case study. It would also be one of the biggest farces in the brief history of artificial intelligence.

21

Customers Rave About AI

This is the shortest chapter in this book because it deals with early customer success stories in AI.

The reason for the brevity is simple: Throughout the early years of AI, not one user or customer dared to talk about AI. With the exception of Schlumberger and Digital Equipment, every company or organization that purchased any form of AI, be it hardware, software, or consulting services, kept mum about its work in artificial intelligence. This is not a generalization or an exaggeration. Schlumberger's Dipmeter Advisor and DEC's XCON were the only publicly known commercial projects up until the end of 1984. The press used these examples in countless articles, citing them over and over again in any mention of the promise of AI.

Those first customers—the labs, defense contractors, and industrial giants listed earlier—viewed AI as a strategic weapon. They weren't about to divulge corporate secrets involving AI to the outside world. A tight lid was kept on this information so that it wouldn't leak to competitors. The reverse side of this secrecy was that it also served as a safeguard in case a project failed, in which case the company might come under attack from the press and, God forbid, Wall Street.

Vendors like Symbolics, LMI, and Teknowledge were expressly forbidden—by their customers—from discussing their sales or development efforts. This effectively cut off the best means of promotion that the AI companies could utilize. After all, success breeds success, and a few good stories would encourage potential customers to sign on as bona fide clients. The AI vendors begged and pleaded with their existing customers to act as references or press sources so that they could tout the benefits of their wares. They met with only steadfast refusal.

Symbolics, in particular, could not discuss its clients' work because many of them were involved in classified or high-level military work. It was forced instead to refer to "selected customers" or "work undertaken by some customers." There were some generic areas of work that did appear in sales literature or press releases that was indicative of AI endeavors: diagnostic systems for machinery, scheduling programs for manufacturing and logistics, industrial process monitoring, and equipment maintenance applications. These ran the gamut from use in fixing army tanks to monitoring the flow of petroleum through refining plants.

While no one was publicly talking, word of mouth did help sales since the military-industrial complex is a fairly close-knit microworld. While companies in the military-industrial complex keep information from the taxpayers who fund their work, they actually do a fair amount of behind-the-scenes sharing of information. One piece of information that was making the rounds in late 1983 was that LMI was not delivering its computers on time, and that Symbolics was making the best LISP machine on the market. Another juicy tidbit was that the new AI software start-ups were willing to make deals with big companies whereby they would give equity in exchange for some cash and a decent-sized development contract.

Both of these items were true. It was not, however, the kind of information that AI vendors wanted to talk about. They wanted to talk about their customers. But their customers had them, to put it colloquially, by the short hairs. "Breathe a word about us," the customers said, "and you'll never do business with us again."

That's the entire story of the early AI success stories. To make any money, the AI companies were going to have to rely solely on good executive leadership, pure salesmanship, and the power of the press. Since the first two were almost nonexistent, it's a good thing that the latter was a sure bet.

22

Money, Not Time, Heals All Wounds

Looking for New Investment

From the outside, Symbolics looked like it could do no wrong. It had found a new corporate customer in MCC, it had a large number of DARPA orders, and it was whipping its major competitor in the marketplace.

On the inside, the reality was much uglier. Everything was going wrong at Symbolics.

As far back as the summer of 1982, the company had planned on introducing its new LISP machine, the 3600. It gradually let customers know about this superior machine, which would be a vast improvement over the MIT CADR that had inspired both its own LM-2 machine and LMI's CADR. Symbolics was giving its customers the hype that Richard Greenblatt claims he fell for, which eventually forced him to get outside investment. Greenblatt's assessment of the new product introduction plans as hype was quite astute; Symbolics was nowhere near ready to ship the 3600 by its planned target date of July 1982.

The engineering group in charge of creating the 3600 was overseen by John Kulp, the vice president of research and development. Kulp had been one of the founders and had worked on creating high-level software at MIT for the original LISP machine. He was also on the company's board of directors. Unfortunately, like most of the other founders, Kulp had a negligible amount of real world business experience. Running a new R&D project that was to result in an actual product by an actual point in time was not necessarily a concept he was familiar with, but the same was true of almost everyone in Symbolics' engineering-oriented organization. The 3600 group in particular, though, was too loosely structured and too isolated from other corporate groups—like marketing and manufacturing—to be fully cognizant of, or accountable for, timetables and deadlines.

It became clear to Kulp in early July that the 3600 wouldn't be ready by the promised date. Various custom-designed components simply were not working, and the machine was not fully operational. Kulp told Noftsker that his group needed another month to finish the machine. The setback would cause the company to miss some anticipated revenues from sales of the 3600, so Noftsker began to work on ways to stretch the company's cash reserves, which were disappearing at a phenomenal rate. General Instruments had put $500,000 into the company as an investment earlier in the year, bringing the amount of money Symbolics had raised to $2 million. But Symbolics was hiring people left and right, and it was already up to more than 100 employees by mid-1982. Each of these people cost the company money, since they weren't generating much revenue just yet. At the urging of some of his investors, who wanted to cut costs wherever possible, Noftsker had already moved all of Symbolics' administrative functions back to Cambridge, leaving only the manufacturing operation in California. The new headquarters offices were located on the eastern perimeter of the MIT campus, less than half a mile away from Greenblatt's new LMI offices on the western perimeter of the campus.

Noftsker devised a plan to get the company through the last few months of 1982, at least until the 3600 could ship and start generating revenues. His plan would get the company through until November, when the revenues from the 3600 would probably start rolling in and salvage the company's cash position. Russell knew that Symbolics would eventually need another round of venture capital, but he didn't want to go out and solicit investments if revenues were down. Low sales would give the VCs a reason to lower the valuation of the company and get more equity for their investment. The founders' stock, and that of the original investors, would be severely diluted if he tried to get money during that period when 3600s weren't shipping. The VCs would have him over a barrel and would get equity at a cheap rate.

Noftsker figured that if he cut back on major expenses, his cash might last the three months from August to November. Beyond that, he had nothing. The 3600 had to be shipping by November in order for the company to survive.

Kulp came back to Russell in August and told him that things were worse than he had originally thought. The 3600s wouldn't be ready by the new August date. In fact, they wouldn't be ready until November. The timing could not have been worse. For Noftsker, the new 3600 ship date and his financial drop-dead date were a little too close for comfort—perhaps even a little too close for coincidence.

Russell came to believe that someone was trying to wrest control of the company from him. Maybe it was one of the VCs who wanted better equity terms and was trying to back him into a corner. Maybe it was someone internally who wanted more executive power. Whoever it was, Noftsker was determined to fight back. His company was barely two years old, and he wasn't going to let some political infighting ruin his plans for success.

November 1982 rolled around and the new 3600s were not ready, as John Kulp had predicted. Symbolics was literally out of money. Noftsker had no choice: He went back to his VCs to plead for more cash. His past experience, though, told him he couldn't do it without showing that the company was making progress with the 3600. Asking for more money while the 3600 sat dormant in a Chatsworth, Calfornia factory would be laughable. He might as well give the VCs the entire company on a silver platter and then just slink away into some corner. Noftsker had to find a way to make the 3600s work so that he could show something positive to his financial backers. Kulp had told him it wasn't going to happen, no matter what.

Noftsker was desperate enough to try something extremely reckless by business standards. Symbolics employed a talented teenager named Howard Cannon as one of its primary developers. Howard had been something of a mascot around the MIT AI Lab when he was a new student, although his ability to hack in LISP was nearly equal to that of Richard Greenblatt and Richard Stallman. The bespectacled, short, and portly Howard worked closely with Greenblatt during his years as an undergrad, but he sided with Noftsker during the AI Lab schism that led to the formation of Symbolics. Howard quit MIT without receiving his degree (which the university has offered to him time and time again since) and joined up with Russell. He was the youngest member of Symbolics, but one of its most exceptional members. Howard's affinity for and knowledge of the internal workings of the computer were unparalleled within Symbolics. His talents even led him to create his own programming language, called Flavors. Today, Flavors, and Howard Cannon, are considered the forerunners of a popular form of computing known as object-oriented programming.

In November 1982, however, Howard was an eager kid who got paid to work at Symbolics. Though something of his mascot status carried over to Symbolics, no one ever questioned his formidable computing skills, and Howard became somewhat of an icon within the company. Like a prize jewel, Howard and his skills were a tangible asset to Symbolics.

Noftsker took Howard aside and made a deal with him. "I told Howard that if he would take the 3600 prototype out to Chatsworth and get just three 3600s to work so that we could ship them to customers by the end of the year, I would buy him the Porsche of his choice." That was a pretty outrageous promise to make to someone who had had his driver's license no more than a couple of years.

With visions of the ultimate sports car dancing in his head, Howard caught the next plane out of Boston to Los Angeles. He took several processor boards with him to California and then rented a car to drive from LAX to Chatsworth, about forty miles north of the airport. En route, Howard was involved in a severe car accident that apparently resulted in the rolling of the rental car. The processor boards, the key to Symbolics' survival, were tucked in the trunk of the car and flung about in the accident. Remarkably, neither Howard nor the boards sustained any damage, and Howard continued up to Chatsworth to work on getting the three 3600s operational.

During this time, as an interim step, Noftsker and several other executives put up some cash to help Symbolics make it through another few weeks. Scrambling about for more money, they also offered additional equity to any employee who wanted to buy into a temporary stock plan. A Cambridge VC firm, Memorial Drive Trust, offered to provide bridge financing in conjunction with the executive and employee plans, and the entire group came up with $2.6 million worth of cash. Amazingly, Howard Cannon did the impossible: He got three 3600s up and running, and the Chatsworth factory shipped the machines to the Fairchild AI Lab.

All of this activity occurred just a little too late. Symbolics found itself facing the end of the year with three 3600 sales recorded on its books, $2.6 million in promised equity, and absolutely no money in the bank. Promised equity is different than cash on hand, and Symbolics found that it could not meet its payroll for the last pay period of the year. The money was all gone.

One of Symbolics' second-tier founders, Robert Strauss, had recently come into a large amount of money from the sale of another company that he had founded. Flush with cash, Strauss himself offered to put up the cash to meet the year-end payroll. It was just enough to tide Symbolics over until the investment money showed up. When those funds arrived shortly thereafter, they supported Symbolics' operation until the spring of 1983, when the company began collecting revenues on the sale of the 3600 machines.

Howard Cannon still owns the Porsche 928 that Symbolics gave him for hacking services above and beyond the call of duty.

ᵔᴥ

Despite the last-minute rescue of Symbolics, Russell Noftsker was not out of the woods. His timely—some might say miraculous—shipment of the 3600s still did not alleviate the fact that Symbolics was going through cash faster than it could make it. The board of directors met in January 1983, shortly after the payroll fiasco, and ordered Noftsker to downsize his operation. There was no way that Symbolics could recoup its losses unless it got rid of some its employees, the investors argued. They also wanted to cut development of future products, including a computer that would have its own LISP microprocessor chip. Noftsker and most of the Symbolics executives agreed to the personnel cutbacks, but balked at the thought of killing the microprocessor project. After heated arguments, the board capitulated, reluctantly, and allowed the company to limit its cutbacks to layoffs. But, the investors warned, they would definitely kill the microprocessor project if Symbolics couldn't reduce its operational burn rate after making the layoffs. "And, if improvements aren't made," one board member screamed, "we'll fire you all and start over again from scratch!"

Commanded by the VCs to reduce staff, each vice president had to lay off individuals within his own organization. Noftsker and the company's legal counsel, Andy Egendorf, came up with a precise plan for who would go and who would stay. One of the areas they were going to spare was a small team of LISP hackers in Palo Alto who were developing a product called Portable Common LISP. Portable Common LISP would allow other workstation vendors like Sun and Apollo to run LISP. Once this happened, Symbolics believed that it could sell its own software programming tools to organizations that were purchasing the more generic workstations.

However, without consulting Noftsker or Egendorf, John Kulp, who was in charge of this operation, eliminated the entire Portable Common LISP group. Though they were to have been spared in the original plan, Kulp opted to wipe these hackers out in order to save huge amounts of cash. Not at all pleased with being summarily dismissed, these ex-employees went out and formed their own company, which they called Lucid. In the process, they took the LISP product they were developing with them. In retrospect, Noftsker believes that letting these employees go was the single biggest mistake that Symbolics ever made.

Unfortunately, no one had much chance to worry about it at the time. Everyone was scrambling to cut costs in their own divisions. Plus, Noftsker had promised the board that he would get shipments of the 3600 up to at least seven per month, with 100 in the pipeline by the end of 1983. By June of that year, with all the cutbacks achieved, the company was on target with its projections. Believing that he had now shown the board his skill as a manager, Noftsker wanted more money from them to expand the sales operation. The VCs, however, wanted him to cut back even more, especially in the sales department.

One person who was inclined to side with the VCs was John Kulp. Kulp, who had already given Noftsker two of his biggest headaches at the company—the delayed shipment of the 3600 in August 1982 and the firing of the Portable Common LISP group early in 1983—was becoming a constant thorn in Russell's side. (To this day, Noftsker believes that Kulp was intent on setting him up for a fall as far back as mid-1982.) Most of the Symbolics executives were concerned that Kulp might join up with the investors at a summer board meeting and take control of the company. They didn't want that to happen, primarily because Noftsker was close to signing up with two new investors, and any management change would jeopardize the deal.

Four company executives—Noftsker, Minoru Tonai, Andy Egendorf, and Jack Holloway—spent the week before the board meeting hammering away at Kulp, convincing him to buy into their strategy and not cave in to the board. They even threw Kulp a bone and promised to let him make the new business presentation to the board. Kulp agreed, and when the directors saw that he had sided with Nofstker and the others, they decided not to press their agenda, which included terminating more R&D projects. They were still insistent, however, that the company continue to cut staff and reduce its operating expenses.

Noftsker and the others appeased the board with what amounted to lip service and continued to ship LISP machines. Sales and shipments were going according to plan, which encouraged the investors that Noftsker had been soliciting to come up with a new round of funding. At the end of 1983, Paine Webber and Hambrecht & Quist, two of the leading venture firms in the high-tech business, came up with $16 million worth of private financing to help Symbolics expand its operations and continue development of its LISP processor.

In December 1983, with a lot of cash at his disposal, Noftsker wanted to ramp up the sales operations. The board balked and told him to wait until early 1984. The last thing the board members wanted was Russell going out and adding more people to the company when they wanted him to reduce personnel—even though Symbolics had closed the year with more than $10 million in sales, up from $1.8 million in 1982. Though this represented the sale of more than one hundred machines, cash was seeping out of the company like blood from a severed artery. The board became increasingly disenchanted with Noftsker, viewing him as a man who liked to watch the blood flow.

❧

Life wasn't any easier on the software side of AI. IntelliGenetics, too, was in a bind. The Stanford spin-off had begun life as a small company selling access to AI-based cloning software. By the end of 1983, it was a mid-sized company selling the same basic cloning service and not much else. In its first full year of operations, 1981, the company had been in start-up mode and made no money while it went about setting up its computer timesharing system. In 1982, IntelliGenetics made $131,000 from genetic researcher customers who accessed its cloning software via this timesharing system. In 1983, the same system brought in almost $600,000. Not bad income, until you realize that the company had grown to forty employees. Of those, eleven were in management.

The problem with selling services of any sort is that you get paid by the hour or the day or the project. This is an extremely time-intensive and personnel-intensive way to make money. In IntelliGenetics' case, this money came from billing the actual time that clients were logged onto its computer systems to use its cloning expert. A product, on the other hand, gets built once and can be sold many times over. The economies of scale are far more impressive in a product-oriented business than in a service-oriented business. That's how Amway and all those other pseudo-entrepreneurial product organizations manage to attract so many followers. They sell basic products such as soap or cosmetics, and even people with nonexistent IQs can understand that all the "business" effort goes into moving this product out the door. More products equal more revenues. That's a simple equation, and it's easy to implement. Conversely, you don't see anyone trying to create consulting-based versions of Amway.

The management team at IntelliGenetics was familiar with the concept and set about trying to reorient itself in a product direction. The first product idea it came up with was putting its cloning software on a workstation computer and then selling the software and the hardware bundled together as one item. The software normally ran on a mainframe, which could cost as much as several million dollars, and that was certainly not something that the average medical researcher had in his or her budget. Workstations were cheaper, with costs ranging from about $30,000 to $80,000. (LISP machines, with their $100,000 price tags, were at the very high end of the workstation market.) IntelliGenetics put its software on Sun Microsystems workstations and then sold the whole package as BION, a dedicated medical research computer system.

BION seemed like a good revenue generator, since the company sold it for $60,000, but IntelliGenetics was not a hardware company. It relied on Sun to manufacture the hardware, and then it had to turn around and sell BION as both a hardware and software solution. As any company in high technology can attest, it is extremely difficult for one organization to be in the business of selling both the hardware and the software. The two businesses require different forms of expertise, and maintaining a hardware inventory is substantially more costly than maintaining a software inventory. With hardware, you need to keep monitors and keyboards and disk drives and power supplies and cables and processing units in stock. With software, you have a bunch of floppy disks and some shrink-wrapped instruction manuals.

Looking around for a software solution, IntelliGenetics went back to the drawing board, specifically Edward Feigenbaum's drawing board. As we have seen, before Ed became an entrepreneur and world-famous author, he had been instrumental in the development of MYCIN, the blood diagnosis expert system. The stripped-down version of MYCIN, known as EMYCIN, was an expert system without the knowledge base plugged in. It was comprised of only the inference engine and rule structure of the expert system. In this reduced state, called a "shell," EMYCIN could serve as the basis for the development of other expert systems. People could use it however they chose, and it could be sold time and time again as a stand-alone software package.

Bingo.

IntelliGenetics created its own version of the EMYCIN shell and called it KEE, the Knowledge Engineering Environment. The product development was overseen by Tom Kehler, a technologist from the Texas Instruments AI group who had joined IntelliGenetics as employee number ten the previous summer. KEE was written in LISP and designed to run on the new Symbolics 3600 machines, which had replaced the original LM-2 machines. Interestingly, KEE also ran on another machine that was little known outside of Palo

Alto, although it was well-known throughout Palo Alto. It was the internally developed Xerox Dorado LISP machine, come to commercial life as the Xerox 1108. Xerox wasn't quite sure how to market the computer, but it was making the 1108 available to developers so that they would create software for it. By default, IntelliGenetics became one of the first developers for the 1108, since it was also one of the first developers of AI software. Xerox didn't have a whole lot of choices for developers anyway.

KEE was introduced toward the end of 1983, just as IntelliGenetics was running out of money. The company was three quarters of a million dollars in the hole—money that had gone almost equally into R&D and salaries. To raise quick working capital, it sold equity to Computers Services Corporation, known as CSK. For $1 million, IntelliGenetics also gave CSK the rights to sell KEE in one international market—Japan. Thus, CSK, itself part of a Japanese corporation, would be marketing knowledge engineering software—software developed by U.S. researchers—into the heart of The Fifth Generation.

Think about this. IntelliGenetics took investment money from a Japanese company. It also agreed to give that Japanese company the rights to its AI software for sale in Japan. Japan was trying to develop AI software so that it could dominate the future of computing. Ed Feigenbaum was one of the most vocal opponents of The Fifth Generation. But Ed Feigenbaum was a founder of IntelliGenetics. So, given that Ed Feigenbaum had worried publicly about the Japanese AI threat, and that he was a founder of IntelliGenetics, it is not surprising that more than a few eyebrows were raised when his company sold part of its technological soul to the Japanese in exchange for cash.

Ed had already found himself in another conflict of interests when the development of KEE got underway earlier in 1983. IntelliGenetics was founded as a medical software and services company, not necessarily an AI company. This distinction allowed Feigenbaum to help start Teknowledge, which would be selling AI services and expert system consulting. With the introduction of KEE, that distinction became blurred. IntelliGenetics would now be selling AI software used for developing expert systems. In effect, it would be an expert system company, as Teknowledge was. To make matters even stickier, Teknowledge was also getting ready to announce an expert system software product of its own. Teknowledge knew, as did IntelliGenetics, that its basic services were not enough to sustain a growing business. It needed products and so did its customers. To capitalize on its proclaimed leadership in knowledge engineering, Teknowledge was developing an expert system package that allowed users to build their own expert systems in much the same way that KEE did. Teknowledge's product, called M.1, would be a personal computer software package. It would have nowhere near the power that KEE did, since KEE ran on LISP machines. In fact, M.1 was sort of a beginner's package, even though Teknowledge was going to sell it at the very unaggressive price of $12,000. KEE cost five times as much—$60,000. Though the products might not be identical and would not have the same capabilities, M.1 and KEE would compete with each other in a marketplace that did not know how to tell the difference between any types of AI software.

With Teknowledge and IntelliGenetics both in the expert system software market, Feigenbaum had to withdraw from active participation in the two companies. He was actually never all that active from a day-to-day perspective, but lending his name to the companies gave them each a certain cachet, and he was active on the board of directors of both companies. He withdrew from those boards in August 1983, and then became a consultant to each company. Ed also kept his founders' stock, which amounted to ownership of over 500,000 shares, or 16 percent, of IntelliGenetics alone. In addition to all of this, he really wasn't qualified to be part of the management of a company, since he had absolutely no business experience. This fact would elude IntelliGenetics five years later when it hired him back as its chairman.

The million dollars from CSK didn't hold IntelliGenetics over for very long—its burn rate was nearly as extreme as Symbolics'—and the company decided to do what no other AI company had yet done. It went public. IntelliGenetics filed a prospectus with the Securities and Exchange Commission to offer its stock on the public market in December 1983 with an initial public offering (IPO).

IPOs are the dream of every entrepreneur. They make the founders rich and move the company into the realm of the big time. Shares of the company from the date of the IPO are traded on one of the major exchanges, and the company gains credibility and higher visibility for its business. In the high-tech industry, this involves getting listed on the NASDAQ, or over-the-counter, exchange. The offering itself serves not only to make wealthy men and women of the company's founders and senior executives, but it also gives investors a chance to get in early on a company that may pay long-term dividends or climb to a high stock value. If the stock goes public at $6 and grows to $20 or more, investors can make out like bandits.

The returns from an IPO are not guaranteed, although sizable growth in the first few weeks and months of the stock's listing are almost as certain and inevitable as Elvis sightings at convenience stores. The huge rush to purchase shares creates a groundswell that carries the stock along without much regard as to the company's real value. It's pretty much a mob mentality.

The caveat for potential buyers of IntelliGenetics stock was that no other company selling artificial intelligence had ever been traded publicly. Few investors could honestly claim to understand the technology, but the buzz was that it might be the next big computer technology. That alone, and nothing more, got the stock market interested in AI. IntelliGenetics, for instance, had never turned a profit in its three years of business. It had no real competition, and it had no real products, so it was hard to find any precise way of measuring the company's value or its prospects. But Wall Street is a creature that lives and dies by the rumor and gossip mill, and the positive chatter on AI would prove to be extremely beneficial to IntelliGenetics.

The IPO took place in December 1983, and IntelliGenetics raised nearly $9,000,000 to further its development of the KEE expert system package. On paper, Ed Feigenbaum made $3,000,000.

∼

While Symbolics had a comfortable supply of cash by late 1983 to tide it over for the foreseeable future, Lisp Machine, Inc. was in a much more precarious position. Like Symbolics, it had found itself badly wedged between an old and a new product line. Unlike Symbolics, sales of its computers were slowing and the prospects for revival didn't look good. LMI found itself hemorrhaging cash so fast that it could find no way to staunch the bleeding other than to get a new infusion of capital. Texas Instruments' investment, only half a million dollars, had barely lasted through the summer of 1983, and the relationship was proving painful for LMI. At the questionably gentle prompting of TI, Greenblatt and Wyle brought in a TI executive, Frank Spitznogle, as the new president of LMI. Spitznogle had spent more than a decade with TI, and he was brought into LMI's Los Angeles headquarters to get the company's somewhat slipshod operation into shape. Reports of malfunctioning machines were beginning to affect LMI's sales, and Spitznogle's job was to do something about it.

Realizing that continued product development was going to cost a lot more money than LMI had in the bank, Spitznogle and Wyle raised $5.4 million in November 1983 from the venture capital community, including companies such as Citicorp Venture, Montgomery Partners, and New Venture Partners. This new investment substantially diluted Texas Instruments' 25 percent stake of LMI, but the money was a requirement if LMI was going to survive through the next few months. The company was already developing its multiuser versions of the Lambda, which would service more than one programmer at a time.

These new computers, the Lambda 2x2 and the Lambda 4x4 (for two and four users, respectively) were also joined by LMI's first software development project. Many of the company's customers, notably Texaco, were using the Lambda for monitoring various industrial processes, such as petroleum refining. Texaco was interested in putting an expert system on the Lambda that would take control over specific aspects of the refining process. Since refining was a twenty-four-hour a day process, an expert system might be useful in assisting human process engineers with frequently occurring and routine functions of the job.

LMI saw the synergy that could be achieved by developing a process control expert system and selling it to customers with the Lambda as a complete package (similar in concept to what IntelliGenetics was doing with its BION workstation). It hired some new software engineers and began work on PICON, an acronym for Process Intelligent CONtrol. Lisp Machine, Inc., however, as its name implies, was founded as a hardware company, with Richard Greenblatt overseeing the development of new hardware features. A software project was not in the original business plan, nor was it something that Greenblatt took a great liking to. The other executives, however, saw that they needed some way to better differentiate themselves from Symbolics, which was rapidly eating away at their hardware sales. Work commenced on the new software, and PICON became the first nail in Richard Greenblatt's professional coffin. Four years later, it would come back and be the final nail as well.

❧

The entire calendar year of 1983 was one of transition for the small group of AI start-ups, which numbered almost forty by the beginning of 1984. While they were mostly expert system companies—some selling toy like programs that were capable of processing only a few dozen rules—there were also the two LISP machine vendors, along with several voice recognition and natural language start-ups. Prominent among the voice companies was Kurzweil Applied Intelligence, the third of three eponymously named high-tech companies formed by former MIT whiz kid Raymond Kurzweil. One of Marvin Minsky's students, Kurzweil was a tinkerer and entrepreneur unlike any other at MIT. Born with the same gift for self-promotion that was a character trait of people like Ed Feigenbaum and the great showman P.T. Barnum, Kurzweil had no problems talking up his technical prowess. Fortunately for him, he could usually back it up. At age thirteen, he sold a computer program to IBM. In college, he sold a computer program to publisher Harcourt Brace Jovanovich for $100,000. At age thirty, he invented a reading machine for the blind, a device that could scan written pages and "read" them aloud with a synthesized voice. Such creations earned him a great deal of popular acclaim, and in 1984 he told *Esquire* magazine (of all places), "I remember very distinctly, ever since I was five, knowing that I'd be a scientist, and knowing that I'd be a famous one, a very successful one."

One of the customers for his reading machine was pop musician Stevie Wonder, who raved publicly about the usefulness of the Kurzweil device. After selling the reading machine and the little company that manufactured it to Xerox, Ray had enough money to start on his next project—a music synthesizer that sounded like real acoustic instruments. Stevie Wonder had lamented to Ray that digital music synthesizers never accurately reproduced the sound of a nondigital instrument such as a grand piano or flute. Kurzweil went back to tinkering and in 1982, at age thirty-five, he developed a synthesizer that came closer to mimicking these natural tones than any other instrument then on the market. Though he priced the synthesizer at the high end of the price scale relative to his competitors, he won huge amounts of praise for creating a truly revolutionary instrument. Ray eventually sold his music company to piano manufacturer Young Chang.

Having learned about AI under Minsky (who has taken credit for inspiring Kurzweil), Ray decided to tackle the elusive voice recognition problem. Before getting started in 1983, he bragged to the popular press that he would have the equivalent of a "voice-activated typewriter" by 1985—only two years away. His "talkwriter" as he called it, would be a computer that would eventually replace both typewriters and Dictaphones in offices. People would simply talk to their machines, and they would respond. No one else was making these claims, but Ray Kurzweil was not noted for his understatement.

He was also not noted for his managerial skills. Both the reading machines and music companies had performed poorly in the marketplace despite offering the best products available. These companies were notoriously inept at determining pricing structures and developing customer-requested features. The sell-offs to both Xerox and Young Chang came about primarily because Kurzweil and his chosen management teams could not make a go of the businesses.

Xerox, however, was impressed enough with Ray to invest more than $2 million in Kurzweil Applied Intelligence, the voice recognition company. With unabashed self-confidence and his public relations team in tow, Ray set out to build the "talkwriter." It would prove to be a lot harder, and a lot longer in coming, than he or anyone else had ever imagined.

23

Pulling Products Out of Thin Air

As George Orwell predicted, 1984 finally showed up.

His tale of human alienation in some future world—where the government controlled every waking moment and men were slaves to machines—made for an extraordinary novel but a poor piece of prophecy. Like all apocalyptic predictions, Orwell was way ahead of his time. Then again, so were the AI companies.

Whether it was expert systems or natural language or voice recognition or machine translation, customers were having a hard time sinking their teeth into AI. High prices were one factor limiting the number of organizations that could actually afford to buy any sort of AI service. LISP machines sold for more than $100,000, although discounts brought that figure down to about $75,000. IntelliGenetics' KEE software cost $60,000, and that didn't count the cost of additional consulting that would be necessary to guide clients through the development of a complete expert system.

Symbolics could see that its customers were warming to the idea of LISP machines. While they had started with small orders of one and two, they were now beginning to order in quantities of half a dozen or more. This was especially evident in its DARPA contracts, where the military planned to install dozens of machines in specific locations over the next few years. Symbolics' executives could see the light at the end of the tunnel.

Its investors, however, could not. What they saw was a $10 million company that was out of control, spending-wise. In January of 1984, they once again warned Russell Noftsker to slow down on his expansion plans. Symbolics was up to nearly three hundred employees, and Russell still wanted to significantly increase the company's sales and marketing staff. His plan, as he recalls, was to "front-load" the sales organization, a process whereby a company overhires its sales personnel in order to achieve more sales over time. While this stresses a company's reserves at the outset, it eventually balances out when each salesperson begins pulling in orders and the sales staff more than supports itself. That's the theory, anyway. Symbolics already had eighty people in sales; Noftsker wanted twenty more.

Neither the board nor John Kulp agreed with this idea. It would entail spending money that could not be directly linked to revenues for several months or even several quarters. As far as they were concerned, Noftsker had to be stopped, and they had to put him out of their misery. He just wasn't listening to them.

The VCs had had enough. They called an emergency meeting on April 2, 1984 to inform Noftsker that he was being removed from the operating committee, and that effective immediately, they were looking for a new CEO. For the time being, they would assign John Kulp to take over operational duties. Russell would remain as chairman, but would not be involved in the actual running of the company. Shaken, Noftsker felt betrayed by his investors and by Kulp. He was, however, out of choices. He had pushed the board as far as he could, and he had no aces left up his sleeve. "I had to go along with what the board wanted, since you're supposed to do what your board of directors says to do—as if that's any excuse."

Above and beyond that, he personally resented their timing and their lack of tact. The day before the meeting, Russell's wife had been diagnosed with multiple sclerosis.

John Kulp's new job was to get the company back on track while Noftsker cooled his heels in accordance with the board's demand. Symbolics was beginning to rack up substantial sales with its 3600 computer, but it was also ready to introduce an updated and more powerful version of the 3600, called the 3670. Kulp, however, wanted to start selling the 3670 right away and discontinue the 3600. He commanded the sales force to stop selling the 3600 and concentrate all their energies on pushing the 3670.

The problem with this plan was that the 3670 didn't work and couldn't be delivered. Obviously not having learned from his own experience when the original 3600 delivery date had slipped the previous year, Kulp was in the same bind all over again. The salespeople began selling 3670s, but they weren't functioning properly, so the machines sat on the Chatsworth factory floor. Hence, no revenue could be realized from them. By the same token, the factory had dozens of leftover 3600s that were no longer being sold by the sales force—per John's orders. Kulp found himself in the unenviable position of having to tell the board that Symbolics was sitting on $6.5 million worth of 3600 inventory that it was going to have to write off.

If the board had been unhappy before, they were incensed now. With the unused inventory, almost everyone was convinced that Symbolics was going to go under, drowned in its own red ink. It was the investors' turn to panic. The board members sent a representative to Russell Noftsker's office and asked if he would return to take over the company's operations and at least get the inventory problem solved. He agreed—on the condition that the board drop its search for a new CEO. The investors, chagrined, bit the bullet and called off the search. But they insisted on continuing to look for someone who could serve as a chief operating officer. It wasn't a perfect arrangement, but it was the best that both sides could come up with—and it got Russell essentially what he wanted: Kulp was out and he was back in.

Noftsker's first order of business was to get rid of the remaining 3600s. He instructed the sales force to do whatever discounting was necessary to move the 3600s out the door during the summer. He also informed all customers that there would be a two-month delay in shipping some of their orders. He then shipped dozens of the nonworking 3670s to customer sites in order to put them down as sales on the company's books. When customers received the LISP machines, they were not in working order—which Symbolics knew—so a special team of customer service people and repairmen were put in place to go fix each and every machine.

There was a questionable amount of legality in shipping nonworking computers to customers with the foreknowledge that they didn't work. Even though Symbolics sent repair people out to fix the machines immediately—in good faith—it is doubtful that customers would have been all that pleased to learn the details of how they finally got their machines. But Symbolics was desperate, and as they say in the movies, "Desperate times call for desperate measures." Those desperate measures succeeded. By the fall of 1984, Symbolics' sales were on their way to a projected $40 million for the year. Heady with their turnaround success, Noftsker and his hackers prepared to go public.

❧

As product development flourished throughout the AI community in early 1984, the need arose for a forum in which to exhibit these products. Every industry has an annual convention of some sort where all the vendors in that industry unveil a slew of new products to waiting and willing prospective customers. From the movie business to the lawn-care business, these conventions are the highlight of the year for buyers and sellers alike. In addition to huge exhibit floors where vendors set up booths—complete with free giveaways and buxom-yet-brainless product demonstrators—there are often seminars located at the convention site where industry luminaries discuss new products or market trends. There are also panels and presentations that help members of the industry make sense of changing demographics and economic upheavals.

Most of all, however, there are parties. Tons of them. For many people, the convention is the one time during the year where they can schmooze and booze without worrying about the consequences. The hotels are usually right across the street or on the convention site, and someone else is always willing to buy dinners and drinks. Plus, the nation's largest convention centers are in cities where there is plenty of nightlife and extracurricular activity: Las Vegas, Chicago, New York, and Anaheim. While industry conventions hardly reach a level of outright debauchery (unless you want to include the Tailhook convention), a good time is usually guaranteed for all.

The only thing the AI industry had that resembled an annual convention was its AAAI conference. Unlike other business-oriented conferences, there were no exhibitors to speak of, and the atmosphere was largely academic. A typical AAAI from 1980 to 1983 made conservative Baptist conventions look like Sodom and Gomorrah by comparison. This was not a lively bunch.

However, AAAI was the only organized assembly specifically targeted to people interested in or working in AI. By default, then, it was the only environment where the new AI companies could talk to potential customers. If these companies went to a large computer industry show, like Comdex, no one would know who the heck they were or what they were trying to sell. The vendors had to start by making sales pitches to their own kind, and they wanted to do it at AAAI.

The academic organizers of AAAI were not too keen on the idea. They had consented to let various technical book publishers sell programming texts and educational materials from tabletops during their conferences, and had even allowed IntelliGenetics to demonstrate an early version of KEE at the 1983 conference. Other than that, they wanted nothing to do with the product-mad bastards who were derailing pure research in the AI community.

In 1984, the AAAI show was planned for Austin, Texas—an unlikely enough place for a conference, but AI activity was growing there, especially with the establishment of the MCC. A number of companies, including Symbolics, LMI, IntelliGenetics, Teknowledge, and several others pressured the governing board of the AAAI to allow them to demonstrate their products. It would all be on the up and up, they promised. No selling of products on the show floor, just demos and information distribution. They would also pay AAAI for the privilege of renting booth space.

Reluctant to the end, the AAAI gave its okay for a separate exhibit hall to be set up outside the conference area. Hours of demonstration would be limited, and the vendors were not to take any orders or do any active selling. It seemed like a simple and straightforward enough arrangement. Historically, such arrangements always are, as anyone who has ever made a deal with the devil could attest. The AAAI organizers had just sold their souls to the commercial vendors.

The summer of 1984 had the same importance for the artificial intelligence business that the summer of 1967 had for the hippie generation. Austin's AAAI conference was a coming out party of unprecedented proportions (although it would get even bigger over time). From August 6 to August 10, visitors swarmed to the heat of the newly dubbed "Silicon Prairie" to see artificial intelligence in action for the first time. This was not the secretive lab stuff that was discussed only in academic or military papers; this was AI that you could buy.

The vendors had helped to fan the flames of interest by pouring gasoline on the media's ongoing spark of interest in the technology. With their tantalizing press releases about the impending debut of a new breed of computer products, the AI start-ups had driven the appetite of the popular and technical press from mild drooling to rabid slavering. No magazine or periodical, however, gushed over AI with more eagerness than *Business Week*. On July 9, 1984, just a month before the AAAI conference, it put a picture of Ray Bolger's immortal scarecrow from the Wizard of Oz on its cover—with a LISP machine in its lap. The three-inch headline screamed "ARTIFICIAL INTELLIGENCE: IT'S HERE!" The capital letters and the exclamation point were key indicators that this was A BIG NEWS STORY! If the cover alone didn't convince readers that something major was happening, the magazine's seven-page article on the wonders of AI surely did. Interviews with the AI Lab's Patrick Winston ("It's like being at Kitty Hawk"), Apex's Randy Davis ("Three years ago, AI was considered flaky, now everyone wants in"), Allan Newell, Peter Hart, and the founders of Carnegie Group ("It's a gold rush") gave credence to the notion that AI was indeed "here."

With widespread newsstand exposure from the nation's premier business weekly, the traditionally intimate AAAI was deluged with humans from all around the world. Normal attendance at the conference had been around a thousand researchers; more than three thousand people showed up in 1984. People and companies came out of the woodwork like a swarm of locusts.

More surprisingly, commercial organizations that no one would have ever suspected of having an interest in AI showed up with actual products. Altogether, twenty-five vendors crowded into a small Austin exhibit hall to demonstrate—but not sell (heh-heh)—their AI goods. While some of these exhibitors, such as DEC and Data General, were really just gauging the mood of the crowd or reselling some pure-play products developed by the start-ups, there were certainly more types of hardware and software than anybody expected. Tektronix, a U.S. manufacturer of test equipment and scientific workstations, unveiled its "4404 Artificial Intelligence System," a computer that ran Xerox's Smalltalk programming language for creating expert systems. Xerox announced the opening of its AI Systems Business Unit and pitched its line of LISP machines, which had inexplicably gone from being called the Dorado to being renamed the DandeLion and DandeTiger. Interestingly, the head of Xerox's new AI group had previously been employed at the toy manufacturer Mattel, a fact that caused no end of snickering from Symbolics and LMI.

Teknowledge announced its M.1 expert system tool, and Symbolics dem-onstrated its new line of LISP machines, the production models of the 3670 that had gotten John Kulp into so much trouble. Alex Jacobson's Inference Corporation, which had abandoned its original natural language package for Control Data, introduced an expert system shell called the Automated Rea-soning Tool, or ART. The product, which was written in LISP, was designed to compete directly with IntelliGenetics' KEE. But IntelliGenetics wasn't called IntelliGenetics anymore; it was now IntelliCorp. Realizing that its future lay in selling expert systems, the genetics tag limited the image it wanted to present to the mass market. Just before the *Business Week* article appeared, the company's management approved a name change to IntelliCorp, which had a more general AI "feel" to it than the medically oriented IntelliGenetics.

Undoubtedly, the biggest surprise at AAAI was the presence of IBM. The company had quietly been developing AI tools in a number of its research centers around the world, primarily in San Jose, Paris, and Yorktown, New York. It showed attendees a number of its AI programs, all designed to work on IBM computers and not on LISP machines. Although the offerings were in a fairly rudimentary state, and IBM appeared to be testing the waters more than anything else, they did confirm that IBM was not totally out of touch with what was going on in the world of AI. The company showed both a version of LISP and a version of PROLOG that it had optimized for its mainframes. It also had an expert system that would help mainframe users operate mainframes more efficiently called YES/MVS (Yorktown Expert System for MVS—MVS being the name of IBM's mainframe operating system).

IBM was coy about its plans, though, and did not promise any sort of strong marketing effort for the products. The whole display was just an indication of what IBM might do if it really got serious about this whole AI business. There was a hint of "we could eat you up if we really wanted to...but we're not yet sure if we want to" in its presentation. Symbolics was the largest pure-play AI company in the business with revenues of $10 million: IBM was more than one thousand times bigger than Symbolics. Its annual R&D budget alone was more than ten times larger than Symbolics'. If IBM wanted to get serious about AI, it wouldn't have any problems competing with these little tikes. Or so it thought.

☙

The AAAI and the press helped take the edge off some of the reservations that the marketplace had regarding expert systems and their intelligent ilk. If IBM was looking into it, well, it couldn't be that weird.

One of the first corporations outside of the computer or industrial sectors to become convinced of AI's potential was American Express. The credit card and financial services company had long been known for investing in high technology, especially untested technologies that it might be able to utilize before the competition did. Because its various divisions and subsidiaries, such as Shearson Lehman and IDS, covered so much of the financial landscape, there was usually some competitive edge to be gained somewhere in the company via the application of new technology.

In early 1984, a Shearson Lehman vice president named Bruce Gras attended a technology seminar, which featured a track on artificial intelligence. The AI speaker, John Clippinger, had attended MIT and started a small consulting and market research firm in Cambridge called Brattle Research. In addition to his core business, Clippinger was also working with Symbolics to develop joint marketing deals whereby Brattle and Symbolics would collaborate on certain expert system projects.

Gras' position at Shearson was vice president in charge of new product development for the investment banking division. He approached Clippinger after the talk and asked him about the prospects of applying AI to the problem of interest rate swapping. In particular, Gras wanted to find a way to automate the process of matching up major borrowers who might want to exchange interest rates. It was a complicated process, one which relied on decision-making based on the knowledge of the changes in various interest rates as they applied to different financial products (mortgages, savings, etc.). Every time Shearson brokered an interest rate swap between two companies, it made a substantial fee that ran into the hundreds of thousands of dollars. During the course of a single year, Shearson did nearly $15 million worth of business in rate swaps. The problem was that it had too few experts who could regularly perform the rate swap deals. If there was a way to get even two more deals done per year, the company could add $1 million to its bottom line.

Clippinger told Gras that it might be possible to handle the process with an expert system. He suggested a meeting with Symbolics to discuss the possibility of creating a LISP-based application to run on Symbolics' LISP machines. As Clippinger presented it, Symbolics would provide the hardware, Shearson would supply the interest rate experts, and Brattle would manage the program development.

Gras went into sticker shock after his first meeting with Symbolics. The up-front cost for the hardware alone would be $100,000, and Shearson could expect to spend about another quarter of a million dollars in development and consulting costs before the application was fielded. This amount was much more than Gras had counted on, and he back-pedalled from the deal rather rapidly. However, Symbolics didn't want to alienate someone from American Express—especially someone who might come in handy later on—and it suggested that Gras come with them to check out a new little company about a half mile down the road. In the bad section of town.

If you've never been to Cambridge, it's difficult to explain just how strangely the city is laid out. Along the Charles River, MIT and Harvard take up all the acreage with the good views. Greenery, trees, parks, and bikeways predominate. Behind MIT, going away from the river, there are blocks and blocks of concrete and brick industrial complexes, ranging from old factories like the New England Confection Company (makers of Necco Wafers) to 1960s concrete structures occupied by the likes of Polaroid, on to brick office parks that began rising out of the ground just as AI was hitting its stride in 1984. All of this is joined together in a hodgepodge of confusing and meandering roads that more often than not dead-end into some MIT faculty parking lot. It's chaotic, but as a business environment where sharing ideas is crucial, it works quite well.

Barely six blocks away from the concrete and brick offices, moving even farther from the river, you come upon Cambridge's housing projects. The buildings of MIT are still visible from this distance, and the pepperminty scent of the Necco factory is faintly detectable in the air. But like most cities, Cambridge has an obvious line of demarcation where business ends and projects begin. Even though the two butt right up against each other, businesses—as a rule—do not set up shop in the projects area. Very few rules, however, applied to Gold Hill Computers.

Located in a building that had once served as an Armenian dance hall, Gold Hill was in the heart of the projects, with low-cost housing on one side and a fenced-in playground on the other. It was not the kind of place where you would want to walk in the dead of night without some sort of protection, perhaps something along the lines of an AK-47.

Gold Hill was founded by three transplanted University of Idaho grads who had migrated east to Cambridge: Stan Curtis, Jerry Barber, and John Teeter. The name of their company, unusual for its lack of techiness, was as obscure as the LISP terminology that hackers had used to name the CONS and CADR machines. The original Gold Hill was part of a forty-acre ranch that Teeter owned in Moscow, Idaho. Obscure—yes. Technical—no. But inventive nonetheless.

The three young men served time at various New England high-tech companies like Honeywell and Wang in the early 1980s. They banded together in 1982 to explore the entrepreneurial life after finding that none of them much liked the corporate world. Naming their loose-knit group Gold Hill Computers, they came up with a number of different computer ideas that were all investigated to some degree over the next two years. Teeter and Curtis were involved with the computer architecture groups at Honeywell and Wang, and they thought about developing add-in cards for the IBM PC. These cards would provide more functions to the PC, including parallel processing (which was—not coincidentally—one of the goals of The Fifth Generation). But other vendors unleashed a flood of multi-function boards in the early 1980s, a timing obstacle that effectively scratched Gold Hill's plans to enter the hardware market.

In addition to hardware, the company toyed with the notion of putting some of MIT's programming languages on the PC, notably LISP and Seymour Papert's LOGO. Gold Hill's version of LOGO, developed by Teeter and Barber (who was getting his Ph.D at MIT), attracted the attention of another software company, Digital Research. For those of you with long memories, Digital Research was the company that provided the first popular operating system for the IBM PC, a system known as CPM/86. Legend has it that IBM wanted to use Digital Research's CPM/86 for its brand new PC, but when IBM representatives showed up at Digital Research's headquarters, the company president had blown off the meeting to go fishing—literally. IBM decided to use Microsoft's MS-DOS instead, and the rest, as they say, is history.

At the time, though, Digital Research was doing a lot of software work, and it licensed the personal computer version of LOGO from Gold Hill. That contract gave the three founders enough capital to launch the company in earnest, and they moved out of Stan Curtis' basement into the Armenian dance hall. Their work on the PC won the hearts of many in the Cambridge software community, and Patrick Winston of the AI Lab especially liked the idea of running LISP on a PC. Barber had hacked up a version of LISP that he was able to make run on an IBM PC, but it was much slower than anything that ran on a LISP machine. Yet the founders of Gold Hill figured that more people would end up owning PCs in the future than LISP machines. This same logic also dictated that LISP software for PCs had to be a bigger market for products than the market for LISP machines. As of 1984, there were only about two hundred LISP machines in the world, and there were tens of thousands of PCs. Companies like IntelliCorp might be able to sell a few dozen copies of KEE at $60,000 a piece, but Gold Hill could sell thousands of copies of its personal computer LISP at around $500. What it lacked in price points, it could make up for in sheer volume.

They called their product Golden Common LISP. Golden signified Gold Hill, obviously, but Common LISP was a phenomenon working its way through the AI community. Since its initial creation by John McCarthy in the late 1950s, LISP had undergone many mutations and modifications. Depending on who was using it and where, LISP was altered and adapted to fit the needs of its individual users. The original MIT LISP, called MacLISP after Project MAC, had evolved—although Richard Greenblatt might say it devolved—into dozens of different versions. There was BBN LISP, which became InterLISP, which became InterLISP-D when the BBN hackers went to Xerox PARC. DEC's adaptation of the language for its computers was known as VAX LISP, and IBM's optimized version for its mainframes was called VM LISP. Symbolics' own specialized version of the language was called ZetaLISP.

While everyone and his brother was off creating some permutation of LISP, these variations were getting further and further removed from the original MacLISP. Many of them were incompatible with each other. Coding structures and operations in one LISP might not be the same as in another version, meaning that a programmer would have to learn different commands for each type of LISP. With so many deviations from the norm, it would be very difficult for anyone to master all the idiosyncrasies of all the LISPs. Each LISP was in danger of becoming its own separate and independent language. In an effort to stop this fragmentation of LISP and try to get everyone to adhere to certain formal structures, a number of prominent LISP hackers and their associated companies met to try to develop a standard, or common, LISP. Gold Hill bought into the idea right away, and adapted the Common LISP standard to run on IBM personal computers. People like Greenblatt may have sneered, but there was no getting around the fact that Gold Hill was intent on bringing the power of LISP to the masses.

In January 1984, with the street buzz running high regarding AI, the three Gold Hill founders formally incorporated their company. They solicited Winston, the AI Lab director who had written the definitive textbook on LISP, as an advisor to the company. They also brought on another AI Lab professor, Carl Hewitt, who had been one of Barber's MIT advisors. Hewitt was a quirky MIT professor in the Ichabod Crane vein who roller-skated back and forth from MIT to the Gold Hill housing projects, always with a smartly tied cravat billowing out behind him. Hewitt and Winston were two of the only people left at the lab from its glory days, since everyone else had gone off to find their fortunes elsewhere.

While Gold Hill was preparing to market Golden Common LISP, Bruce Gras and representatives of Symbolics showed up on its doorstep in the spring of 1984. Gras wanted to know if Gold Hill could help him save money on his interest rate swap idea. Was there any way to use personal computers as part of the expert system instead of requiring that every user have his or her own LISP machine? The answer was a barely conditional yes. Jerry Barber proposed a strategy that would allow PCs to be hooked into a single LISP machine. The primary knowledge base could be placed on a Symbolics 3670, and users could access the expert system with their PCs. Instead of using, say, four 3670s at $100,000 per machine, Shearson could buy one 3670 and three PCs, for a total hardware cost of less than $110,000. Gras loved the plan and signed both Gold Hill and Symbolics to contracts with Shearson.

John Clippinger hated the plan. He had been effectively cut out of the deal when Gold Hill was brought in, since Gold Hill would be doing its own program development. While Clippinger was none too pleased with Symbolics for proceeding without him on a project that he had delivered to the company, he was especially upset with Bruce Gras. Clippinger got the distinct impression that Gras was interested in the interest rate expert system primarily as a vehicle to further his own career. Something else about Gras didn't ring true, but Clippinger couldn't quite put his finger on it. Whatever it was, though, Clippinger believed that Bruce had a hidden agenda, and in the long run he was probably up to no good.

As Symbolics and Gold Hill were both to find out—in spades—John Clippinger was dead right about Bruce Gras.

❧

Work commenced on the interest rate swap program in mid-1984. The expert system, to be called K:Base, would consist of knowledge that was gleaned from experts at Shearson, and the system development would be overseen by Gras, who would in turn be directing the programmers at Gold Hill. Symbolics would also provide technical consulting to the K:Base project.

The procedures in interest rate swapping are extraordinarily intricate, which is why Shearson could charge so much for putting a deal together. An actual deal begins when a company comes to Shearson and says that it wants to swap its interest rate with someone else. Basically, this company wants to find another company willing to swap rates such that they will both benefit. This means that Shearson, as the dealmaker, has to find a second company that will find the first company's interest rates attractive. Company A, for instance, may realize that the fixed-interest rate of its investments is no longer as worthwhile as a floating-rate interest may be (for a myriad of possible reasons). It is Shearson's job to find Company B, an organization that wants to get rid of its floating-rate interest in order to lock into a fixed-rate interest. If both companies can come to terms, they can reduce the interest costs on their borrowed money and save huge amounts of cash over the life of their respective loans.

The trick is finding compatible partners. Locating the appropriate companies is not easy, because rates are interchangeable only if certain criteria are met. Citicorp, for instance, is not going to exchange its rate with Mom and Pop's Screen Door and Liquor Store. Beyond the obvious, there are the details of the loans that have to be matched up: total amount of the original loan, total amount of interest over the life of the loan, final due date of the loan, how often payments are made, how often floating-rate interests are reset, and a host of other concerns. These factors cannot be just matched up one-to-one, because each of them contains variables that change or are up-dated almost daily. Something as simple as a single payment—or a missed payment—of interest charges changes the entire equation of how these fac-tors relate to each other. Outside factors, such as the prime interest rate, which the borrowers have no control over, also affect the deal.

The complex interactions in interest rate swapping do not lend themselves to traditional computing tasks because they are not just matters of calcula-tion. In addition to finding companies that fit well into the basic criteria outlined above, the rate swap expert at Shearson has to anticipate market conditions and take advantage of those conditions at the most opportune time. A deal that closes later than expected can cost both Company A and Com-pany B lots of cash if the interest rates change.

Gras and Gold Hill came up with a program structure that had the essen-tial rules and heuristics of rate swapping, but these rules could be flexible if any new and pertinent information were added to the system. This allowed Shearson to take daily feeds of information off the financial wires and dump them into K:Base, which would then adjust itself according to that day's new data. Rules would change based on this new information, allowing a rate swap deal to evolve even as it was going through its review process.

Once the expert system was in place, the process worked like this: Gen-eral market data on selected financial components was fed electronically into Shearson's DEC VAX computers, which were already receiving that data on a daily basis anyway. The VAXes sent this data to a Symbolics 3670—where K:Base resided—which used it to update its files about the interest rate swap deals that Shearson was interested in. After processing this information, the Symbolics-based part of K:Base made some decisions about the best way to proceed with a planned swap. These decisions (perhaps "suggestions" is a better word) were sent to individual human experts at their personal com-puters, who could then manipulate the data even further to take full advan-tage of K:Base's recommendations.

One of the plans for K:Base, once it was fully operational, was for Gold Hill to strip the knowledge base out of the program, creating an expert sys-tem shell much like EMYCIN. Shearson, since it was not in the software business, was going to give the rights for the K:Base tool to Gold Hill, which could then sell it in the market against Teknowledge's M.1. Gold Hill even gave demonstrations of the program at the 1984 AAAI conference in Austin.

Accolades for K:Base came fast and furious. One magazine claimed that Shearson had already made $1 million from the program's expertise in the first few months of its existence. As details of the story unfolded in the fall of 1984, Gold Hill joined the ranks of media darlings in the nascent AI business. *Newsweek* even ran an article about the company in a special edition called *Newsweek Access*, and Gold Hill was featured right next to other start-ups expected to make it big, including Sun Microsystems and Thinking Machines Corporation.

Everything looked to be in place for making K:Base the next big expert system success story, the natural heir to the overplayed and overanalyzed Dipmeter Advisor and XCON systems, both of which had overstayed their welcome in the popular press. Bruce Gras took the opportunity to parlay his newfound fame into his next career move. He quit Shearson in September 1984 to join Symbolics as vice president of marketing.

The decision to bring Gras into Symbolics was Russell Noftsker's. He had been impressed with Gras' corporate background, and Gras had become intimate with the inner workings of Symbolics during the development of K:Base. Symbolics had no real sales or marketing leader, and Noftsker was convinced that Gras could bring the necessary expertise into the company.

Gras accepted Noftsker's invitation, and as soon as he had cleared his desk at Shearson, the K:Base program abruptly fell to pieces. Bruce had made no provision for anyone within Shearson to take over the management of the project, and suddenly K:Base was an orphan. No one knew what to do with it since Bruce had overseen every aspect of its development and implementation. Gold Hill tried to keep K:Base alive, but no one at Shearson had any idea how to manage it. Gras, for his part, was too busy helping Symbolics prepare for its public offering. He really couldn't be bothered with the expert system project he had started and offered little assistance to either Gold Hill or Shearson relative to K:Base. That was past history as far as he was concerned. Unfortunately, the press didn't pick up on the sudden shutdown of K:Base, and to this day the program is often held up as an early expert system success story. While it had started successfully, the lack of corporate and individual support shut K:Base down by the end of 1984. Shearson ended up calling the whole project a loss, with an estimated $250,000 gone down the drain.

Clippinger's suspicions that Gras was using K:Base as a stepping stone had proven to be true. But Gras' real character had yet to come to the fore. Symbolics was not the lead contractor on K:Base, and the company felt very little repercussion from the shutdown of the project. As far as it was concerned, Gras was now an employee of Symbolics, and his allegiance was to Symbolics. He had good business experience, and he was a positive addition to the company's management team. Bruce's value to the company was something it could be proud of, right up until the day Noftsker got an anonymous letter in the mail.

Symbolics started sending out its IPO prospectus in November 1984. By law, Symbolics had to list all the executives and all the officers of the company, along with any malfeasance that the company or its employees may have been involved in. Nothing in the prospectus indicated that there might be any problems with the company or its management. It had been so truthful that it even stated that the board was actively looking for someone who might replace Russell as chief executive officer.

Noftsker claims that just weeks prior to the IPO, he got an unusual letter in the mail. No name was signed to the letter, but attached to it was the page of the prospectus that listed Bruce Gras as an executive of the company. The anonymous letter asked, bitingly, how the company could file a legal prospectus when Bruce Gras was involved in a personal bankruptcy.

Bankruptcies are serious business in the public market. The tiniest hint of bad financial management can kill an investor's trust in a company, and bankruptcy ranks up near the top of the list of traits associated with bad management.

Noftsker nearly burst a blood vessel when he read the note. He immediately called a meeting with other Symbolics' senior management, and the entire group stormed into Bruce Gras' office. Russell asked Gras if he had ever filed for bankruptcy, and if so, why he had not made it clear to the other members of the executive staff. Bruce admitted that he had indeed filed for bankruptcy, but didn't think it was that big of a deal. That bankruptcy was all in the past.

So was Gras's career with Symbolics. Noftsker fired Gras right then and there as the rest of the executives looked on. Gras was ordered to clean out his office and vacate the premises immediately. As soon as Gras was out of the building, Russell quickly informed his board of directors, as well as the IPO underwriters, of what had just occurred. Gras had endangered the IPO by not disclosing his bankruptcy, but at least Russell could say that Symbolics had gotten rid of Bruce as soon as it had found out.

Unruffled, Gras went over to Gold Hill, where he signed on as a consultant. When his reputation caught up with him there, Bruce quit, claiming that he had bladder cancer. Citing this health problem, Gras immediately left his wife and kids and moved to Tibet. The last time anybody in AI heard anything about Bruce, he was rumored to be living in a monastery in Tibet. The only possessions he had kept with him were a portable computer and a copy of Golden Common LISP.

Russell Noftsker considers his hiring of Bruce Gras to be the stupidest thing he has ever done in his professional life. He is at a loss to explain it, but admits that he made a big mistake. Having Gras at Symbolics during the end of 1984 almost destroyed the company's IPO, and nothing but ill will came from the association. However, Russell's situation was not unique. It was hard for the AI start-ups to find good sales and marketing people, regardless of their alleged reputations. In the hard driving and thriving business environment of the 1980s, there weren't a lot of people willing to leave their existing positions for the risky and perhaps not-so-lucrative world of AI.

Like Symbolics, AI companies had to settle for whoever they could get in the way of administrative or marketing executives. Although Gras was at the sinister end of the spectrum, none of the people willing to join with the technical founders of the AI companies was ever going to qualify as a candidate for president of a Fortune 500 company. They just weren't of that caliber.

The AI vendors were going to have to dig deeper down into the barrel.

24

B-Teamers and B-Schoolers

Executives Come into AI

The founders of Teknowledge, IntelliGenetics, and Carnegie Group learned early on that they were not going to get high-profile executives from Fortune 500 companies to serve as their whipping boys. Until AI companies were selling millions of dollars worth of goods and services, it just wasn't going to happen. Big name executives weren't interested in AI technology—yet. So the AI companies had to go down to the next level. They had to settle for the B-Teamers.

B-Teamers are different than B-Schoolers. B-Schoolers are people right out of some university's master of business program, people educated at places like Harvard, Wharton, Duke, or Yale. These people are trained to be businessmen and women, regardless of the industry that they eventually wind up in. As products of the MBA world—business schools—they are not-so-affectionately called B-Schoolers.

B-Teamers, on the other hand, take their names from the world of sports. They are competent individuals, but they do not possess the stellar qualities of that all important first string, the A-Team. Much of their game time is spent on the bench waiting for an A-Teamer to get hurt, or for the score of the game to be so far out of whack that they can be sent in to play without seriously disrupting the outcome. In business, B-Teamers are the individuals that make up most of the corporate world: anonymous people who are destined to reach the level of middle management at Fortune 500 corporations, or perhaps senior management at smaller companies. Their forte is oftentimes nothing more than managing the status quo.

Since people who were A-Teamers saw AI as a big risk in the early 1980s, they were not interested in getting involved with the start-ups that could have benefited from their services. They were more than happy to watch the B-Team take the field in order to see if the B-Teamers got the bejeebies kicked out of them. If the B-Teamers performed well, the A-Team could step in and take the glory when the final score was tallied. If the B-Teamers got sufficiently bloodied, however, then the A-Team would just as soon pass on the opportunity to get their own bodies bruised. They'd stick to the sidelines instead.

To be fair, the number of A-Teamers is minuscule, probably numbering in the several thousands of people. That's a small fraction of all the executives in corporate America. Anyway, being a B-Teamer isn't anything to be ashamed of; after all, they aren't the C or D Team.

Now that they were in the limelight, AI start-ups had to capitalize on their newfound fame. The outside world was ready to be indoctrinated with the gospel of machine intelligence. The message could not be delivered by the software developers; they had too little appreciation or concern for social graces and communications skills. Thus, AI organizations started to bring on hordes of people who were not technical in nature: salespeople, marketing people, manufacturing people, and administrative people.

Every AI company had to begin life with technical people—the hackers, the nerds, the researchers, the dweebs—that had the core knowledge upon which to build a business. Overwhelmingly, they were people from academia who had never held a 9-to-5 job in their lives. The exception might have been some sort of high school employment—maybe as a busboy, mail room clerk, or grocery check-out clerk. I think we can safely rule out jobs such as part-time construction worker or piano mover.

When these scientific people went to start their AI companies, they figured that they alone knew best how to develop AI products. Yet knowing how to develop a product is an entire dimension away from knowing how to manage or sell that product. That's why, for better or worse, the world has salespeople. Technical people don't know how to sell, and salespeople don't know how to build. Such capitalistic dichotomies make the world go round.

In the first few years of AI, from roughly 1980 to 1983, when the migration from the AI labs produced a group of companies intent on selling a brand new technology, sales and marketing weren't all that important. The AI founders knew who their customers were because they had worked with those customers during their years in the labs. They were the government, the national R&D labs, and large corporate research centers, all of whom contributed money to the academic AI labs.

For a new AI company, the process of selling AI technology to customers basically involved talking to the same people that had already expressed an interest in AI. It was as simple as sending one hacker out to talk to another. Symbolics made its first sales to people like Peter Hart at Fairchild, people who had already cut their teeth on LISP at places like Stanford and SRI. Selling AI products or services was less a process of actual selling than it was a process of cajoling fellow techies into buying the latest and greatest result of technical evolution.

This sort of incestuous shifting around of products and services within a closed community reached its saturation point in 1984. A company like Symbolics or Teknowledge could only sell so much AI to its inbred relatives in the labs. It had to make a real go of selling products into the mainstream market, and that included reaching people who had little knowledge of the benefits of AI. The vast majority of the world—even the computer world— had never heard of LISP, and, as mentioned earlier, the world needed a significant amount of education to truly understand the technology. The AI companies couldn't send their technical people out to evangelize about the benefits of building software systems. Someone else had to do it.

As far as the technical people were concerned, this was the job of administrators and sales forces. They had better things to do with their time than deal with prospective customers who needed to be hand-held through lessons on the benefits of expert systems. Unfortunately, this same lack of respect for customers was shared by many founders, who often believed that if customers didn't understand AI, then they probably weren't worth the trouble. They blindly overlooked the fact that the number of people in the United States who understood AI in the early 1980s probably amounted to fewer than 2000 people out of a nation of more than 200 million, or roughly 1/100,000th of the population. You had a better chance of contracting cancer than you did of finding someone who understood AI.

Reluctantly facing up to this reality in 1984, AI companies began hiring "outsiders" who had some sense of corporate management and marketing.

The thing to do, the founders thought, was to get someone from the "business world" who would handle all the mundane chores associated with running a company. There was a historical precedent for this, from an AI perspective. The AI lab directors at various universities had always hired someone else to do their administrative chores while they attended to what they considered to be the real work. This mentality easily carried over into the AI start-ups, and the technical founders looked for people who could attend to their corporate dirty work for them.

Dirty work is a euphemism for conducting business. In the labs, the people hired to do administration were rarely accorded the same status as the hackers or researchers. They were primarily thought of as paper-pushers (Ed Feigenbaum being a singular exception). This attitude changed not one iota when it came time to create commercial organizations. The hiring of a president or CEO had the same minimal level of importance as the hiring of a lab administrator. The job was necessary to keep things running smoothly, but the administrator was a second-class citizen who was subservient to the will of the company's real braintrust, the technologists.

Finding executives who would accept this role was rather difficult, as one might imagine. Any qualified exec who had spent time in a big corporation like IBM or General Motors or AT&T was going to scoff at the notion of being the lackey for a bunch of egotistical hackers who wanted to change the world with their new computer systems. Besides, AI was not a proven technology, and could pass away as quickly as any other technical fad. With a track record of less than four years, it was a technology to be watched and to be considered, but not a technology to bet one's career on. There were absolutely no experienced corporate executives in the world who would be willing to risk their jobs, and their reputations, on something as young and untested as AI, no matter how much media attention it garnered. The A-Team would pass on the first round.

Greenblatt and the founders of Teknowledge chose B-Teamers when they hired Stephen Wyle and Lee Hecht, respectively. Hecht, in particular, had minimal experience dealing with high-tech companies; at least Steve Wyle had been with EMG Hydraulics and spent some time at his dad's technology lab in northern California. Hecht's primary businesses prior to Teknowledge were finance-oriented, not computer-oriented. But, he certainly walked the walk and talked the talk, and landed in the driver's seat at Teknowledge. Interestingly, as it turned out, Teknowledge ultimately became more of a cash management company than a technology company, but that story comes later.

Carnegie Group's four founders also went the B-Team route when they hired Larry Geisel as president for their new business. Geisel, like Hecht, had started his own finance-oriented concern, Summit Information Systems, which sold computer services to banks. Prior to that, he had been with a variety of companies at different executive levels. Interestingly, Geisel and Hecht had surprisingly similar visions for each of their companies, and both visions involved getting lots of money from big companies to help finance operations and research. They were also smooth talkers who tended to talk about the "big picture" of AI.

They weren't interested in selling AI to the labs and the government markets; those were ultimately too poor for the long haul. The real business opportunity was in industry, especially those Fortune 500 companies that needed to gain quick access to new technology. Geisel, for instance, referred to AI as "white collar robotics," and both he and Hecht were extremely conversant with all the business buzz words of the 1980s, from "top down management" to "mission critical applications."

They also had a financial funding perspective in their businesses that was diametrically opposed to the thought processes of someone like Richard Greenblatt. While Greenblatt and LMI fought long and hard to keep a big corporation like Texas Instruments from getting a stake in their company, Hecht and Geisel actively courted big companies. If TI forced Greenblatt to give it an equity share of his company based on TI's role in his development efforts, Carnegie Group and Teknowledge avoided any similar unpleasantness by making the offer to their customers almost from the beginning. Their spiel went something like this: "Hey, you're helping to fund this new technology. For a few dollars more, you can actually own a part of it. Why don't you kick in some extra cash and get in on the ground floor?" While Greenblatt hated this mentality, Hecht and Geisel embraced it like a lover. They became the leading proponents of a business arrangement known as "strategic partnerships," whereby customers took a vested interest in the AI companies from whom they were buying services and products. Between them, Hecht and Geisel would court some of the largest companies in the world and end up in bed with a most impressive array of "strategic partners."

Unfortunately, strategic partnerships often bear a passing resemblance to a form of corporate prostitution, where one company pays another for the privilege of getting—how shall I phrase this?—access to its assets. And one of the downsides to prostitution is that at least one of the parties is going to end up getting used.

IntelliCorp had bought its own B-Teamers, hiring a group of Texas Instruments middle managers like Tom Kehler to oversee its business development. Another former TI manager it hired was Gene Kromer, who became IntelliCorp's president shortly after the AAAI '84 conference. Interestingly, Kromer had been one of the TI execs that Symbolics' salesman Henry Baker had badgered into investing in Lisp Machine, Inc. at a time when Greenblatt and crew were desperate for cash. In an even more incestuous turn of fate, Kromer came to IntelliCorp to replace Tony Slocum, the company's first non-techie president who presided over the organization when it was still called IntelliGenetics. Slocum left IntelliCorp to team up with some Stanford researchers and several of the hackers that John Kulp had booted out of Symbolics in his massive, but short-lived, housecleaning effort. Slocum's new company, Lucid, was developing a form of LISP that would run on workstations from Sun and Apollo. If it could create this new LISP, known as Portable LISP, Lucid could make generic workstations behave like a LISP machine.

Lucid, like every other AI company, bar none, was technology-driven and not market-driven. There was no proven market for LISP anywhere in the world outside of the research labs and DARPA government projects. From 200-person companies like Symbolics to the tiniest one-man consulting firms, the AI business was comprised of companies waiting for a market to happen. They all had technology to sell, but did not necessarily have anyone banging down their doors to get at that technology. They existed in a state of being technology-driven, which is popularly characterized by the line "Build it and they will come."

Being market-driven, conversely, means that a company is selling products for which demand has already been established. Examples of the latter include driver's side airbags (people got tired of crushing their ribcages on their steering wheels during car crashes) and contraceptives (people got tired of unwanted pregnancies). Market-driven companies find a need and then build their products, while technology-driven companies build their products and then look for a need.

The concept of "Build it and they will come" works fine in the movies, but is hardly practical in real life—with the exception of mind-boggling anomalies like the Pet Rock and Madonna. Having a technology and no market requires that the market be made to understand just what it is missing out on. This entails educating the marketplace. Since technoheads are busy creating products (which they really don't care about selling; the glory is in the creating), and B-Team administrators are busy trying to fund the cost of this development, market education falls to the last major component of every company: sales and marketing.

Selling was a foreign concept to the men and women who came out of the AI labs. Their procedure for getting money was largely cut-and-dried and didn't specifically involve selling. The researcher wrote a proposal requesting funds for a specific project. The proposal was submitted to the proper authorities, usually the university administration or a particular government agency, and the money was handed over. Sometimes it wasn't; in that case, the researcher wrote a different proposal. No song and dance, no dog and pony show, no haggling over terms. You either got the money or you didn't. End of story.

AI start-ups could not simply ask for money like their founders did in the good old academic days. They had to go out and earn it. Earning it required getting money from organizations that needed to be convinced as to the reason why they should spend this money. These organizations weren't sitting around waiting to buy—they had to be sold. The techies weren't biologically equipped to perform this function. Enter the salesperson.

Having had little experience seeing a salesperson at work, and having little understanding of what salespeople actually did, the founders of Symbolics and LMI and Teknowledge and all the rest at first attempted to transform certain engineers into salespeople. This met with limited success, since the mentality of a salesperson is light years removed from the mentality of an engineer or a hacker. It is only by a quirk of evolution that they are even part of the same species.

Most salespeople claim that they can sell anything, including the ever popular "ice cubes to Eskimos." Artificial intelligence was another matter entirely. In order to sell AI, a salesperson had to understand it. It was not like selling regular computers—which were flying out the door in the mid-1980s—or any other item that could be understood by the average Joe in charge of corporate purchasing. Salespeople had to be familiar with the concepts of knowledge engineering, rule structures, and LISP programming.

The incentive to learn was high. A typical high-end PC software package, such as Lotus 1-2-3 or dBASE, sold for around $1000 in 1984. Teknowledge's M.1, which was also a PC software package, sold for $12,500, or more than ten times as much. A Sun Microsystems workstation sold for less than $30,000 during this period of time. The average LISP machine sold for more than $100,000. Economies of scale indicated that there was more money to be made per sale in AI than in any other segment of the computer business.

Still, there was reluctance on the part of computer industry salespeople to jump into AI, for the same reason that A-Team executives were unwilling to leap. Business in almost every area of high-tech was growing at a phenomenal rate, and no one wanted to leave their own guaranteed express train for the potential speed of the new and highly experimental AI gravy train.

The downside of even courting these people in the first place was that if they were actually induced to come aboard, these salespeople usually wanted large compensation packages from the start-up to help cushion any blow. This included not only generous commissions, but stock options. Founders were reluctant to give up too much of their stock, because the VCs and select members of the Fortune 500 were nibbling at it rather voraciously. So, rather than go with A-Team salespeople who might be a little too rich for their blood, the AI founders decided to go someplace else. Low-level or incompetent salespeople were not acceptable, because they probably didn't have the brain power to comprehend the rudiments of AI. And, it was very likely that they did not understand the basis of setting up sales organizations, or else they'd be A-Teamers, right?

AI founders determined that the best way to get knowledgeable salespeople who hadn't been tainted by the large commission checks at other companies was to go to the source of their sales and marketing knowledge. That source was the B-Schools.

Hiring MBA students, as Wall Street was doing, had a number of benefits. First, the B-Schoolers wouldn't demand astronomically high wages. Second, they had been taught business essentials, and could bring that knowledge to a small company that might be largely ignorant of those business essentials. Third, they would be eager to get in on the ground floor of the next big thing, and would work their asses off to make it a success. Thus, hiring a fresh-faced MBA student was like "buy one, get two free" in the minds of AI techies. And like B-Teamers, B-Schoolers didn't have the experience to argue back when they got bossed around by the founders.

❧

Putting salespeople into a primarily technical AI environment was like throwing gasoline onto a slow-burning fire. Technical people are usually private and very protective of their turf. Salespeople, by their nature and as part of their job description, are outgoing and gregarious. There was no basis for a relationship other than that they worked for the same company. Techies didn't wanted to be bothered by the salespeople, whom they found to be intrusive and rather boorish. Salespeople, on the other hand, wanted to know why the technodweebs were always acting as if they had something to hide.

Even Noftsker, primarily a techie himself, saw that there was an inherent problem in building an organization first and foremost around the technologists; they matter-of-factly saw themselves as the real heart of the company. "One of our biggest liabilities in the beginning was that we were bringing in far too many technical people and not enough business and marketing people," he recalls. "The technical people grouped together more tightly whenever anybody else was brought in. This caused the technical people to be an island, and the other groups did not fit together well with them."

Be that as it may, sales and marketing were going to be a requirement if the AI companies wanted to do more than sell products back and forth to each other. Sales and marketing would have to work side by side with engineering. It might be a forced fit, but it would be a fit.

Throughout 1984, all of the AI companies began expanding their sales and marketing staffs. It was this same expansion that got Russell Noftsker into trouble with his board of directors, since Symbolics had had salespeople—primarily Henry Baker—from the day that it was incorporated (Baker was a rare exception to the technical person vs. sales person stereotype: he had received his Ph.D. at MIT and then went on to teach in New York. He returned to Symbolics as a salesman to relish the entrepreneurial challenge). Primarily, though, other AI companies were just getting around to hiring their first real salespeople during mid-1984.

Teknowledge started its descent into the sales world by hiring three MBA students as its first three salespeople. One of the salesmen, Arthur Schwartz, had already worked for Arthur D. Little, a large international consulting firm, before attending business school at Wharton. This made him the exception to the new AI salesperson rule, which expected that these individuals would have had little real world experience. To add to his qualifications, he had helped to do the basic research for Applied Expert Systems' business plan during his stint at Wharton. Apex was just getting ready to begin operations and decided to hire someone from outside the company to do a feasibility study for its proposed financial expert system. Schwartz interviewed a number of bank executives to see if there would be a positive reception to Apex's plan to introduce a financial planning expert. The reaction was mixed; large companies liked the idea, small companies weren't sure they could justify the cost. That was as far as Schwartz' work with Apex went, as he told the company's founders that their business plan as written probably wasn't going to work.

Due to his interest in AI software, Schwartz hired on as the first of Teknowledge's three salespeople in the summer of 1984. His mission: to sell the M.1 expert system shell to corporate America.

Teknowledge, in its naivete, had no idea how to sell or even demonstrate the M.1 product. M.1 was written in PROLOG, which was not even close to being a standard AI language in America. Everyone in America was using LISP. This disparity existed because the product was developed by Steve Hardy, who was a British AI researcher working at Teknowledge. Even though it was written in PROLOG, it was still an expert system tool that could be used to create revenues, so Teknowledge decided to sell it right away. But because it was in such a hurry to get M.1 to market as quickly as possible— expert system shells were springing up all over by late 1984—Teknowledge didn't have time to develop a custom demonstration program to show off M.1's "expertise." Instead, it decided to use a simple program that Hardy had created mostly as a lark. The demo program was called The Wine Advisor.

The Wine Advisor was an expert system that selected the appropriate wine for any dinner menu. If the dinner consisted of shrimp appetizers and a veal main course, it would recommend a buttery chardonnay. If the meal was based on red meat—consisting of something like steak, potatoes au gratin, soup, and salad—then The Wine Advisor would recommend the appropriate red wine, perhaps a Beaujolais or a cabernet sauvignon. In an interview session, the program would ask the chef about the items to be served during the course of the meal, and then it would make a recommendation about the specific wine that was supposed to be served with that meal. The Wine Advisor con-tained the expertise that one would expect James Beard or Julia Child to have at their fingertips.

This was the only demo available that showed the capabilities of M.1. There were no others—no financial modelling packages, no diagnostic or repair demonstrations—nothing at all related to the daily operation of any business in the world with the exception of vineyards and cooking schools. Incomprehensibly, Teknowledge—either not knowing any better or not caring—decided to use The Wine Advisor as the program which would dem-onstrate the capabilities of M.1 to corporate America. The company's man-agement gave The Wine Advisor to the salesmen and instructed them to go win over the wallets (and presumably the tastebuds) of the Fortune 500.

Schwartz laughs as he recalls Teknowledge's sales program. "It was sur-real. They had no idea what a salesman really did—and neither did we. It was the only time I'd ever taken a job where I knew from the instant I walked in the front door that I'd made a mistake. There were these purple walls and purple furniture, and a picture of the founders on the wall, and no products, because M.1 only came out the week after we were hired. And here they were telling us to demonstrate this $12,000 piece of software to senior executives by telling them what kind of wine they should be having with their dinner.

"At first we just spent all our time on the phone, trying to get large companies with discretionary software budgets to buy a few copies of M.1, companies like GTE and NYNEX. And anytime someone was interested, we'd all fly to the customer site to pitch them on buying this software. No matter where the location was, we'd immediately hop on a plane and give them a personal demonstration.

"To try and make some better use of our time, the sales staff eventually decided to travel around and give these group presentations. We'd get all the prospects in a hotel conference room at one time, and then we'd demonstrate The Wine Advisor. We'd rent fancy hotels in a selected city, bring in lots of lovely food, put PCs around the room on these big pedestals, and try to wow them with this M.1 presentation. And we had a lot of interest from vice presidents, guys who were only two or three layers from the top of their companies. They would be excited about all the potential of artificial intelligence right up until we began showing them The Wine Advisor.

"One occasion that is indicative of what we were up against occurred when we set up a sales demonstration at the Boston Copley Plaza Hotel. We had sent invitations to a number of large companies, and got a respectable turnout, about thirty executives from corporations like John Hancock, Gillette, and Honeywell. And we proceeded to show them the "power" of M.1 with The Wine Advisor, giving it all the importance of the discovery of the obelisk in *2001*.

"As we're getting further into The Wine Advisor, matching Bordeaux with beef and sorbets with champagne, these executives started looking quizzically at each other, like 'What is this?' And one guy actually said out loud to us, right in the middle of the demo, 'You've got to be kidding.' They knew right then that they'd been taken for a ride. But then they figured that since they were already at the presentation, they might as well go along with the joke and have some fun. So these pin-striped management guys start shouting out things like, 'Put in a lobster dinner and see what happens!' And we would try to explain to them—with a straight face—that the rule structure didn't work that way, and that you had to follow a specific sequence of events during the interview process. By the time they left, they'd all had a great laugh. Of course, none of them even considered buying the product. The entire event was completely humiliating.

"We never had another replacement for the demo—ever. The executive staff would scream at us to close sales, and we would say 'Look, we're doing the best we can. This stuff looks silly.' Despite how absurd and obvious this was, they stuck with The Wine Advisor the entire time."

But M.1 did begin to sell. It most likely had nothing to do with The Wine Advisor, but with the fact that M.1 was a reasonable alternative to large scale systems that required LISP machines and expensive software. In fact, it began to sell well enough that Teknowledge sold a more primitive "test" product called T.1 that would allow potential users to get a feel for using M.1. Of course, it included the demo of The Wine Advisor.

Now that it had a budding sales force, Teknowledge brought out another product, called S.1, designed to compete directly with workstation-based expert system shells like KEE and ART. It had fewer bells and whistles than its competitors, required less intensive programming on the part of users, and could run on several different types of computers. Teknowledge figured that customers who had built successful small systems with M.1 on PCs would then expand those programs by moving up to S.1, which ran on workstations. This is called "migration;" a vendor hooks a customer into buying one low-level product and then has that customer upgrade to better products over time. (General Motors does this by trying to breed brand loyalty among image-conscious young adults who buy Camaros and Firebirds. After selling these cars, GM then hopes to be the vendor of choice when these individuals want luxury cars—for example, the Cadillac—in their more mature years.)

Migration was a sound strategy, and allowing customers to grow from M.1 to S.1 made a great deal of sense. Except for one thing: S.1 wasn't compatible with M.1. An expert system built with M.1 had to be completely rebuilt in S.1. This kind of defeated the whole purpose of migration, but the Teknowledge sales force slogged along, undeterred by the technical limitations put upon on them by Teknowledge's hackers.

Many AI companies just didn't know how to handle S&M, or sales and marketing. Some of them tried to hire outsiders who eventually were unable relate to the founders or the founders' ideals. Alex Jacobson at Inference went through what seemed to be dozens of senior S&M people during the 1980s. Carnegie Group also had an ongoing sea of S&M people who came and went with regularity. At Symbolics, where technodweebs ruled, S&M was constantly shifting in an endless series of combinations. This so amused the hackers at Symbolics that they created a small program to let the company know how funny they thought it was. The hackers built a screen-saver application especially for use on sales and marketing's computers. Screen savers are those cute little programs that put up fancy graphics or games on computer monitors to prevent the screens from getting a ghost image burned into them —

the kind of image you see on ATM machines where the greeting line is always on screen. In the hackers' screen saver, though, they created an S&M organizational chart. Every few seconds, the chart would change, switching names and duties to different levels on the chart. One moment the head of sales might be moved to a support position, or a telephone salesperson would be director of marketing. As these jobs and titles shifted around on the screen, the salespeople were left to watch helplessly because they couldn't figure out how to remove it from their computers.

To add insult to injury, most of sales was kept in a separate building from Symbolics' administration and technical people. In the frenetic building that took place in Cambridge's Kendall Square during the 1980s, an entire row of high-rise offices was linked at a six-way intersection. These high-rises were—and are—collectively known as Cambridge Center. Symbolics owned the entire building that made up Six Cambridge Center, but kept most of the salespeople in its original offices at Four Cambridge Center, just across the street. Bill Hoffman, one of the earliest Symbolics' marketing managers, remembers the first company-wide meeting he attended where both salespeople and hackers were in attendance. "All the sales and marketing people entered the room, looking fairly professional with suits or dress shirts and dress shoes. The hackers were already there. Most of them were sitting on the floor, and some guy was standing off to the side going through his tai-chi routines, flailing his arms and legs around. A lot of them had beards and were wearing t-shirts and no shoes. And Russell is presiding over all of this, wearing a suit with sneakers. If that wasn't a weird combination of people working together, I don't know what is."

For all of its weirdness, this first group of AI people to make their livings in the world of thinking machines was linked by an extreme passion for what they were doing. Whether it was Symbolics or LMI or Teknowledge or Inference or any other AI company, the founders had almost universally managed to get people who were consumed with what they were doing. This wasn't just selling disk drives or spreadsheet software or personal computers. This was artificial intelligence, a technology with the potential to change the world. As Hoffman recalls, "There was a real passion that I haven't seen in any other business. People really believed that they were involved in something so new and so advanced that it was going to make a huge difference in the world. Eighty-hour work weeks was the norm—by choice—and even 100 hours wasn't that unusual for some of the Symbolics people. We all did it because it was extremely exciting and it was the ground floor. No one had any doubts that AI was going to be the single most important development in computer technology. No doubts at all."

Then Symbolics got hit with a nasty dose of business reality. In October 1984, it was trying to sell a large number of its 3670s to MIT for use in various labs throughout the school. It seemed like a no-brainer; everyone expected that MIT would buy machines that it had helped to develop. Symbolics also wanted to close the sale by the time of its IPO—which was planned for November, the following month. Getting a significant order would help the company look good on Wall Street.

Just days before Symbolics' IPO, Texas Instruments announced that MIT was going to buy 400 brand new LISP machines—from Texas Instruments. Not Symbolics LISP machines, or LMI LISP machines, but Texas Instruments LISP machines. Four hundred of them. That was almost as many LISP machines as there were in the whole world.

The people at Symbolics were aghast. MIT was their alma mater, their birthplace. Texas Instruments was an intruder. This sale should have been theirs. How could it happen, especially so close to their IPO? After their initial shock, all they could figure was that MIT had finally turned on the company that had stolen its computer talent, and it was going to make Symbolics pay.

Chapter 25

Investors, Big and Small

Texas Instruments' proposed sale of four hundred LISP machines to MIT in October 1984 stunned the small AI community. The battle for LISP domination had largely been fought between Symbolics and LMI, and LMI was already losing. Xerox showed up from time to time, but had difficulties convincing customers that it was committed to the computer hardware business. In addition, its machines weren't nearly as powerful as the offerings from Symbolics and LMI.

Texas Instruments, for its part, had become fed up with LMI's manufacturing and reliability problems as the end of 1984 rolled around. It had also seen the growing interest in LISP machines as a way to set itself up in the hardware business without having to worry about a BUNCH backlash.

To get itself off the ground quickly, TI opted to build its own LISP machines based on the same NuBus architecture that LMI was using (from the three-way deal with Western Digital). It licensed the basic LISP design from

LMI, which would receive a royalty on the new computers, and it would also sell single-user versions so as not to obviously compete with LMI's multiuser Lambdas.

LMI was horrified, but it had no choice in the matter. TI was a major investor. At first, the new LISP machine from TI, called the Explorer, appeared to be some sort of cross-development or marketing effort with LMI. In reality, it was a calculated move on TI's part to take all of Symbolics' and LMI's business. To make that happen, TI priced the Explorer at less than $100,000, cheaper than any model from either of the two LISP pioneers.

Texas Instruments had announced its intention to build a LISP machine at the Austin AAAI conference during the summer of 1984, but it had no plans to start shipping the machine until the spring of 1985. Symbolics IPO concerned TI, though. The IPO would boost Symbolics' visibility in the market for the near-term, which might eclipse its formal introduction of the Explorer in the spring. Frantically, TI looked for a way to take the wind out of Symbolics' sails.

To this day, no one claims to know exactly what happened when TI jumped into bed with MIT, and those who do know aren't talking. The popular wisdom is this: With Symbolics' IPO less than a month away, TI decided that the best way to adversely affect Symbolics' plans was to hit the company where it lived, namely in Cambridge. MIT was already a customer of Symbolics, as was LMI, but Symbolics was the favored machine in the AI Lab. TI's NuBus architecture, also developed at MIT, had some support in other MIT computer science labs, but not as a computer for AI applications.

The director of the MIT Laboratory of Computer Science (with which the AI Lab is associated) was Michael Dertouzos. Like many of MIT's various directors, he had a penchant for the spotlight when it came to discussing new technologies in public, and he was a very visible figure at MIT. Before Symbolics' IPO—even before the Explorer had gone into production—Dertouzos was approached by TI about the possibility of buying the new Explorer. Dertouzos was willing to listen.

Many people claim that George Heilmeier, TI's technology head, had a close working relationship with Dertouzos from Heilmeier's DARPA days and was willing to make a deal with Dertouzos. The deal was this. Texas Instruments would donate (a code word meaning "give for free") two hundred Explorers to MIT on the condition that MIT apply to DARPA for money to buy an additional two hundred machines direct from TI. To make DARPA receptive to the deal, TI offered to sell the two hundred DARPA-authorized Explorers to MIT for a mere $28,000 per computer, a savings of more than half off the normal Explorer selling price. And in case DARPA didn't cough up the bucks for the remaining two hundred, MIT would still get the first two hundred machines for nothing. That possible loss was okay with TI, though; the deal would ensure that hundreds of MIT hackers would be learning their craft on Explorers and not Symbolics' machines.

It boiled down to one equation: If MIT asked for two hundred bargain-price machines from DARPA, TI would give it two hundred just for doing the asking. There was no way on earth that Symbolics and LMI could compete with that, and TI knew it.

A press release that was picked up by major publications, including *The Wall Street Journal*, identified the four hundred machines as part of a bona fide purchase agreement. No mention was made of the free machines in the press, and MIT's Dertouzos did nothing to clear up the "mistake."

Noftsker went ballistic. "That hurt us, and it hurt us bad," he says. "The IPO prospectus had just gone out, and this sale cast a lot of doubt on Symbolics. We knew the details of TI's offer, but anything we said would have been seen as griping over a lost sale." Instead, the company started leaking details of the TI-MIT deal to the analyst community, which finally confronted TI on the issue. Anxious to look good on its first big Explorer sale, TI re-released the announcement, adding specifics about the deal that included the "gift" factor. As with most retractions or corrections, however, the revised information didn't get as much play as the original version of the announcement.

The damage was done. Symbolics went public on November 16, 1984, with a share price of $6 that brought more than $12 million into the company. It made a number of the founders, and the investors, quite wealthy— at least on paper. But Symbolics was still smarting from the TI announcement and felt that it could have had an even better offering if TI had not been so devious. Symbolics executives instructed the sales force to get even with Texas Instruments.

The company developed a standard line for its potential customers designed to undermine TI's credibility. If it appeared that Symbolics was going to lose a sale to TI, the Symbolics sales rep would give the customer the details on the MIT freebie deal. "If TI is giving these machines away for free," the salesman would ask, "then how come you're not getting some for free? TI is treating you like a second class citizen, and you should demand a similar deal." Not surprisingly, the ploy worked. All of a sudden, customers started demanding that TI give them better terms and bargain prices—not to mention free Explorers—just as MIT had gotten. These customers, many of whom were defense contractors, were in a position to demand such consideration, since they were going to be buying more and more of the machines in the future. TI found itself over a barrel again, just as it had with the BUNCH companies in the past. Free LISP machines started rolling off the TI production line in April of 1985.

TI could afford to lose a few dozen machines at a time, although Symbolics could not. Neither company ultimately benefited from the strategy since Symbolics couldn't compete with TI's prices (free) and TI couldn't give machines away forever. But the big loser was LMI. TI had established itself as a LISP player almost overnight, and most of the market was aware of the relationship between TI and LMI. Why buy a Lambda, the reasoning went, when you could get the same basic machine for free from TI? With a big drop in revenues—its sales had fallen to less than a third of Symbolics—Wyle, Greenblatt, and former TI-exec Frank Spitznogle were back pounding the pavement looking for more investment money in October 1984. Just as Symbolics was preparing for its first public stock offering, LMI went out and raised $7.6 million in venture capital from some of its previous investors. It also added Control Data and Manufacturers Hanover to its growing list of equity partners. A company founded solely as a bootstrap operation, LMI had now accumulated $13 million worth of outside investment. Clearly, things were not going as planned.

❧

With media attention focused on AI, as well as on Texas Instruments' formal entry into the field, the prospects for returns on AI investment were more attractive than ever. This was true not only for the VC community, but for corporations with lots of cash that wanted to play in the new realm of artificial intelligence. As the second wave of AI start-ups was about to find out, there was plenty of cash to go around. Beyond that, companies like Carnegie Group and Teknowledge were more than willing to give up lots of equity in return for "strategic partnerships."

For Carnegie, a perfect strategic partner loomed in the form of Digital Equipment Corporation. Carnegie Group already had ties to DEC via John McDermott's work on the XCON expert system. DEC was interested in doing more XCON-like work, and was willing to send some consulting business Carnegie's way. Once that arrangement was in place, it didn't take long for Larry Geisel and the little AI company to convince DEC that it should invest in Carnegie's plans for the future, although those plans were a little murky. Carnegie founders Mark Fox and John McDermott wanted to sell expert system products and services, while Jaime Carbonell wanted to sell natural language programs. Instead of compromising, they decided to sell both types of AI, along with a programming language developed at Carnegie-Mellon University. (Carnegie Group had a licensing agreement with CMU much like Symbolics and Lisp Machine, Inc. had with MIT.)

DEC was eager to team up with Carnegie Group. Even though it had started its own AI group after XCON was installed, DEC's bureaucracy prevented the group from actively pursuing clients in the AI market. DEC was—and is—a sales and marketing nightmare, and the company's sales force didn't really understand how it was supposed to position this new AI group. Was it a service organization? Was it a product organization? Was it black, white, or gray? DEC management didn't have the answers, as it was using these internal AI resources solely to build follow-on systems to XCON. The AI group floundered, looking for some direction.

Carnegie Group was unhindered by such corporate agonizing. It was going to build big LISP-based systems for clients, primarily those in the industrial sector, which was CMU's claim to fame. The company's plan was direct, to the point, and unfettered by the kind of marketplace second-guessing that DEC was going through. (DEC had also just begun to explore the PC market, which would soon end disastrously for the company.) Sensing a long-term opportunity, DEC plunked down $2 million to acquire 10 percent of Carnegie. It also guaranteed Carnegie that it would spend additional money on various AI development projects. With DEC's cash, Geisel and his four technoheads were on their way.

Lee Hecht was doing the same wheeling and dealing for Teknowledge. Eschewing the traditional venture capital routes, he started raising money by aiming straight for his clients' bank accounts. Two of Teknowledge's earliest and biggest customers were French energy companies: Elf Aquitaine, a large petroleum corporation, and Framatone, a Paris-based nuclear energy concern. Both companies were intrigued—if not a little put out—by the public success of Schlumberger's Dipmeter Advisor expert system. Although Schlumberger is an international company, its roots are ostensibly French, which gave its nationalistic competitors even more reason to pursue AI. Looking for expert systems that might help to duplicate Schlumberger's success, both Elf and Framatone scouted around Palo Alto to find their own private AI developers. They didn't need to look any further than Teknowledge. By the time the 1984 AAAI Conference rolled around, Hecht and Teknowledge had received $2.1 million from Elf and $3.1 million from Framatone. The latter investment gave Framatone, and its computer subsidiary Framentec, the rights to sell future Teknowledge products in Europe. Elf and Framatone each took about 10 percent of Teknowledge in exchange for their money.

Having scored big with foreign investors, Teknowledge looked for some cash from U.S. investors. In April 1984, as it was preparing M.1 for its unveiling at the Austin AI conference, Teknowledge struck pay dirt with its most significant "strategic partner." General Motors decided to put $4.1 million into the company, along with a promise of substantial business from development work. This investment gave GM 11 percent of Teknowledge.

GM was already busy in the early 1980s trying to tap into the computer business. While its most notable and most high profile deal was its purchase of Ross Perot's Electronic Data Systems, the automaker was also putting money into other, more cutting edge, computer companies. It dumped millions into little-known start-ups like Automatix, Robotic Vision Systems, and View—companies involved in artificial vision and robot control. But its deal with Teknowledge was perhaps its most publicized investment for a number of reasons. GM was one of the first major US industrials to put up such a large amount of cash to get involved with artificial intelligence. Secondly, the investment gave immediate credibility to the entire field of AI, especially expert systems. Third, the press had been waiting for something of this magnitude to give it a basis for doing more features on—and analysis of—the AI business. *The Wall Street Journal*, for instance, began to run regular articles about AI after the deal closed.

While Teknowledge and Carnegie Group bragged about their strategic investors, naysayers snickered to themselves. So what if DEC and General Motors had put millions of dollars into AI? Four million dollars was a tiny drop in the bucket to a company like GM. The automaker probably spent more on postage in one year than it did on its entire Teknowledge investment. Whether this was true or not—GM does not break postage out as a line item in its annual report—the doors to full-scale strategic partnerships were thrown wide open. In the next two years, from the middle of 1984 to the middle of 1986, companies including Procter & Gamble, Lockheed, US West, Ford Motor Company, General Electric, and Raytheon would dump tens of millions of dollars into AI start-ups. Even Texas Instruments would continue to invest money in AI companies, but it would not give any more cash to LMI. It chose to cannibalize that company instead.

The investment from corporate America was massive in scope. The amount of money put into AI alone by these companies shows just how much cash flows in and out of major corporations. For our purposes, it helps to see a group of the investments all together to appreciate how much money was actually going into the little AI firms:

- General Motors put $4.1 million into Teknowledge.

- Procter & Gamble put $4 million into Teknowledge.

- NYNEX put $3 million into Teknowledge.

- FMC Corporation put $3.2 million into Teknowledge.

- Boeing put $1.6 million into Carnegie Group.

- DEC put $2 million into Carnegie Group.

- Texas Instruments put $5 million into Carnegie Group, half a million dollars into LMI, and an undisclosed amount into Brattle Research, the company that had been burned by Bruce Gras and Symbolics during the K:Base project.

- US West put an undisclosed amount of money into Carnegie Group and Syntelligence, the financial expert system company.

- Control Data put undisclosed sums in Inference, Lisp Machine, Inc. and an expert system developer called Software Architecture & Engineering.

- Ford put $6.5 million into Inference, and $6.5 million into Carnegie Group.

- Lockheed put a total of $6 million into Inference.

- General Signal put $5 million into LMI.

- Raytheon put $4.5 million into LMI.

- Xerox put $2.5 million into Kurzweil Applied Intelligence.

- Wang put $1.5 million into Kurzweil Applied Intelligence.

- Travelers Insurance put an undisclosed amount of money, estimated to be more than $1 million, into Applied Expert Systems.

- Microsoft put $2 million into Natural Language, Inc., a developer of natural language software.

These numbers, including guesstimates for the undisclosed figures, amount to more than $50 million that was invested in AI start-ups by corporate America. This doesn't even count the large amounts of cash that were given in exchange for exclusive licenses or joint development agreements. And it certainly doesn't include the amount of VC money that was spent, which would bring the total AI equity investment to well over $100 million. Most of this occurred primarily within a four-year time span from 1983 to 1987.

Carnegie Group, in particular, made corporate investments an art form. Each of its investors was usually given a 10-percent stake in the company.

This happened so often that analysts claimed that a dozen companies all owned 10 percent of Carnegie, meaning that it had given 10-percent shares to more than ten companies (the real number of corporate investors is closer to half a dozen). It was true, though, that Carnegie had given away a significant amount of the store in return for corporate cash.

But there was a big advantage in choosing corporate investors over VCs. Corporate investors, who were also technical partners, were usually content to let an AI company tend to its own affairs. Though they frequently had seats on the board, corporate representatives rarely interfered with their AI investments.

Venture capitalists *always* seemed to interfere. If the company wasn't performing to their specifications, VCs usually had no compunction about threatening to throw the founders out. They often held this threat, as well as the possibility of shutting down the company entirely, over the heads of the AI executives. The VCs were in the game for the short haul, with the desire to have the start-ups go public as soon as possible. The corporate investors, like GM, were most interested in getting workable technology out of the AI companies, thus they were in for the long haul. The investment payoff would be an added bonus when and if the time came to cash out.

The important thing to remember about these corporate investments, though, is that most of them were made by customers. Companies like Procter & Gamble and General Motors were looking to ensure an additional degree of protection over the AI work that they were paying for. Keeping companies alive in order to keep working on specialized development projects was always a part of the investment deal. If P&G was sinking several million dollars into Teknowledge as part of a development contract, a few million more to make sure the company survived was not going to hurt its bottom line. This money also ensured a certain loyalty and silence on the part of the AI companies. No one was going to endanger their investor relationships by talking about proprietary work to the press or anyone else. Money from corporate investors, just like money from the Mob, could buy silence.

It also tended to buy exclusivity. AI companies were bound by the 80/20 rule of economics: 80 percent of their sales went to 20 percent of their customers. This made for a very lopsided sales chart. Teknowledge, for instance, derived more than half of its revenues from its strategic partners, with 10 percent coming in directly from GM. Carnegie also did the majority of its business with its strategic partners, especially Texas Instruments and US West. Even when corporate investors weren't a factor, the 80/20 rule still applied. IntelliCorp found that it was selling 22 percent of its KEE expert systems to Sperry Corporation. Symbolics' primary customers were limited to a small group including Fairchild, Gould, Hughes, Boeing, and DARPA, all of which bought large quantities of machines relative to other customers.

IntelliCorp's relationship with Sperry is especially indicative of the pull that large customers held over their AI providers. Sperry, like TI, wanted to find a back door into AI, and offered IntelliCorp $4 million for the rights to market KEE as well as for consulting work. At the same time, TI and Sperry were negotiating a deal whereby Sperry would resell the Explorer LISP machine. The three companies had lots of points in common upon which to base this troika. Most of IntelliCorp's senior management came from TI, namely Tom Kehler and Gene Kromer, while IntelliCorp founder Ed Feigenbaum was also a member of Sperry's board of directors. Together, these men arranged a nice working arrangement which ultimately forced IntelliCorp to rely on Sperry for a significant part of its revenues.

Sperry was anxious to get involved with AI. It was not in the habit of investing in small companies, so it formed "strategic alliances" with these companies. These alliances usually involved purchasing products from the other vendors—namely TI and IntelliCorp—and packaging them together under a new name as a Sperry product. Sperry even spent $20 million to create a Knowledge Systems Center in Minnesota that would handle the flood of AI business it planned on getting throughout 1985 and 1986, and it offered internships to university students who had studied AI.

Sperry already had one major project in the works, an airline expert system for Northwest Airlines, then known as Northwest Orient. Sperry was the main provider of computer systems to Northwest in the mid-1980s, and it pitched the airline on the idea of using AI to help it optimize its passenger load on every flight. The system, called the Airline Revenue Optimization package (but simply called the Seat Advisor), would be built on Explorer machines using KEE, and would enable booking agents to get the optimum price for each seat that was sold on each airplane. Traditionally, airlines adjust their fares for a particular flight based on seat availability, departure date, and availability of seats on other airlines (this is why you might be told that there are no more seats left in a certain fare class). If, for example, there are few seats available on its own or competing flights and the departure date is only a few days away, airlines can charge near-bloodsucking rates to a passenger. If, however, a competing flight has lots of availability, the airline might ease off the fare a bit to induce the passenger to fly on its plane. This game goes on right up until the moment the actual flight leaves the ground, and the goal is to fill as many seats as possible for the most amount of money.

Each airline analyzes this data regularly to make adjustments to the fare schedule. It does not, however, monitor the data on a twenty-four-hour basis, simply because it is not cost-effective to micro-manage every seat in order to extract the best price. Thus, some fares might slip through the cracks between adjustment periods. With an expert system online, however, an airline might be able to make changes throughout the day and night without needing a human analyst to make the decisions. The expert system would be fed a continuous stream of data regarding seat availability and change the rates based on up-to-the-minute data. This would help to optimize fares, and would even lower fares on flights for which the airline needed to make up in seat quantity what it lost in dollar quality.

Sperry began work on the system, working closely with IntelliCorp. Ed Feigenbaum assumed a high profile in the project—something he normally did not do—because of his relationship with both companies. All systems were go for the Seat Advisor to become the next XCON and Dipmeter Advisor, a notoriety which was originally supposed to have gone to the K:Base project.

Unfortunately, like K:Base, the Seat Advisor fell victim to outside forces. Northwest Orient merged with Republic Airlines, creating a new entity known simply as Northwest. One of the big concerns and priorities of the merger was trying to unite the two companies' computer systems so that they would work together flawlessly. In an attempt to make this computer transition go as smoothly as possible, all extraneous projects, those not critical to the new company's survival, were jettisoned. The Seat Advisor was relegated to the level of lost luggage.

Sperry itself was in trouble, too. In the merger mania of the 1980s, the company looked like easy pickings for any suitor, especially since its computer business was falling prey to the rise in popularity of the PC. Even as it tried to make a name for itself in AI, it was trying to fight off corporate takeover offers. Both TI and IntelliCorp looked on anxiously; neither could afford to lose their wealthy benefactor to some junk-bond raider or greenmailer. For TI, the thought of Sperry getting gobbled up was especially disconcerting; Sperry had promised to buy $42 million worth of Explorers in the next several years as the basis for what Sperry called "the most advanced artificial intelligence package available today."

Like many other AI companies, TI and IntelliCorp were putting too many of their eggs in one basket, and this one happened to have Sperry's name on it. No one realized at the time that companies like Sperry and DEC and Boeing and General Motors and Control Data and Lockheed could only carry so much of the market on their own backs. The AI companies were depending on them for too much and failed to anticipate that each of these companies would run into problems of their own over the next few years. The start-ups were all too willing to let the good times roll, even if the good times were being provided by a total of roughly fifty companies and government organizations in the United States, as well as a handful in Europe and Japan.

There continued to be a problem in dealing with this select group of customers, a problem arising from the secrecy that surrounded AI projects. Even as more money was spent on AI, less information was available to the general public. The first wave of publicity in 1983 and 1984 focused on those systems that were almost common knowledge within AI, the Dipmeter Advisor and XCON, as well as academic programs like PROSPECTOR, MYCIN, and DENDRAL. These were, however, old news in 1985, and the press wanted something more. Unfortunately, the AI companies weren't allowed to give it to them. Their hands were tied and their mouths were gagged. No one was able to talk about anything, and the press became wary, and even a little angry. Had they been lied to? Was this AI stuff a scam? Where were all the success stories? There were two major public companies (Symbolics and IntelliCorp), there were hundreds of millions of dollars of investments and contracts, and there were lots of promises. But where was the meat of it all?

Chagrined, the popular press kept writing stories about the investments in AI, but was forced to spend more time talking about the actual technologies than about any actual applications. It was ground that had been covered before, but it was the only way to keep tabs on AI without getting more substantial information. More substantial information, however, was not coming. The press contented itself with the potential of AI, the deals between hardware and software vendors, and interviews with the fathers of AI—mostly Minsky and Feigenbaum, but also Newell and Simon, Schank, and even Patrick Winston. John McCarthy wisely kept out of the fray.

It was ironic that the press should turn to the AI academics for quotes and information about the commercialization of AI, since most of them really had nothing to do with it. Minsky, Feigenbaum, and Schank could all be counted on to give good quotes, but their grasp of AI in the real world paled next to their understanding of AI as an academic pursuit. Still, the press hounded them for their opinions instead of talking to people like Russell Noftsker and Alex Jacobson who were actually in the business of selling the technology.

Part of this was because the commercial founders were so reluctant to talk about their work explicitly as "artificial intelligence." Everybody knew that AI wasn't a reality; everybody, it seemed, except the press. The AI start-ups were fully aware that they were using the basics of AI research to create marketable products, but this in no way meant that they had created true artificial intelligence. Usually they referred to their products by their more generic designations—such as symbolic processing workstation or expert system shell—and avoided the AI tag. AI was something on the far distant horizon, and they all knew it. What they were doing was selling a piece of a future technology, in the same way that taking the Concord was like experiencing space flight. Even smooth talkers like Lee Hecht and Larry Geisel tried to avoid the hyperbole of AI, always referring to their products as "solutions" for real-world business problems.

These people were not immune to the excitement of being in the spotlight, though. AI was a hot topic, and they were in the AI business, whether by accident or predetermined plan. They acted like someone who has accidentally stumbled into the wrong party. Instead of the beer and pretzels that they were expecting, they got champagne and shrimp. Once they realized how good this particular party was, they were in no hurry to be ushered out and sent back to their original destination. It was a hell of a lot more fun in the glamour lane, even if they were there because of a case of mistaken identity.

But they were all that the press had as far as commercial AI went. Sure, Minsky could rag on the vendors for not producing real AI as it was meant to be, but he wasn't getting investments from GM and Ford. Business publications had to write about businesses, and that meant Symbolics and its ilk. It didn't help matters that these AI companies weren't talking about their customers. They just weren't cooperative in the way that marketing-oriented companies like IBM were. The press needed someone in the business of AI who could talk about the importance of AI to business. They needed a real sales and marketing guy, someone who could talk the talk and walk the walk, as they say in Hollywood. This certainly did not describe any of the techno-heads. It did, however, perfectly describe Phil Cooper.

The press was about to get the answer to its prayers.

26

Phil's Petting Zoo
Programmers Run Wild

Every industry has both infamous and famous executives. In the auto industry, it was Lee Iacocca. In finance, it was Donald Trump and Henry Kravis. In computers, it was Bill Gates and Steve Jobs. In circuses and sideshows, it was P.T. Barnum.

In AI, it was Phil Cooper.

Phil Cooper had gotten involved with AI through the successful sale of his first start-up company, Computer Pictures Corporation, in 1982. Computer Pictures had developed decision-support systems and graphics programs for executives who relied on information stored in large mainframes. The programs gave management the chance to make some sense of all those printouts they were being bombarded with by their data processing departments. Computer Pictures and its products quickly became popular with senior management throughout the computer industry. And even though it was a private company, Cooper had made sure that everybody—including the financial press—knew that Computer Pictures was a moneymaker.

In an industry dominated by hardware engineers and hackers, Phil Cooper was the consummate marketing man, his skills honed during a five-year stint at BBDO, Inc., one of the largest advertising agencies in the United States. Unlike many in the computer community, Cooper was a large, aggressive man who was not afraid to raise his voice to make his point heard, even when everyone else was whispering. And he knew how to generate interest in his ideas and products. When he let it be known that he might be interested in selling his stake in Computer Pictures after only two years in business, Cooper created a feeding frenzy among large computer firms that became eager to buy up his apparently successful venture. After some deft negotiations, he sold Computer Pictures to Cullinet Software, then one of the largest software companies in America, for an estimated $14 million. Cooper's personal take of that amount was more than $2 million. He served an obligatory one-year stint as a vice president at Cullinet after the buyout, and then went casting about for new ventures to capitalize on in the computer market.

He didn't have to look far. Throughout the computer industry, the word on the street in 1983 was that the next big thing in computers was going to be artificial intelligence, and anybody who could afford it should get into it now while the getting was good. Cooper liked what he saw of the technology, but wanted to know more. Aware that most of the AI development in the United States was coming out of MIT, Cooper enrolled in MIT's Sloan School of Management, where he focused on the application of AI technology to corporate management problems. He did well during his academic stint, becoming an Alfred Sloan Fellow by the time he completed his studies. At the age of 34, he started his next computer venture, Palladian, Inc., using his master's thesis as a business plan. Palladian was Phil's very own AI company.

Cooper had spent a lot of time during his year at Sloan in and around Cambridge, learning and living with the city's growing AI populace. Two things were readily apparent: One was that the technological future of AI was squarely in the hands of hardware manufacturer Symbolics. The other was that the people trying to run the AI start-ups were rank amateurs and geeks.

It was true that most of the AI companies were founded and managed by men who had no practical business experience. Almost without exception, they had come from university research labs or from large engineering groups within large computer companies like Digital Equipment, Data General, and Wang. They had good ideas, but they didn't know how to build big companies. They also didn't know how to get proper amounts of venture funding, so most of them were severely undercapitalized. Philip Cooper did know how to do these things, and instinctively, he found his opportunity.

In 1984, he incorporated Palladian. The name means knowledge or wisdom, the attributes of the Greek goddess Athena. Cooper's intent, he claimed, was to legitimize AI from a business perspective. His customers would be dealing with professional business people who understood business problems—not academics. Palladian would not be another group of rambunctious propeller-heads out of MIT hoping to run wild in the playpen of venture capital. Instead, Palladian was to be a real business, and it would be selling AI as a business solution, just as databases and transaction systems were sold as business solutions.

There were two very valid issues that Cooper wanted to address with Palladian. The most important was that to classify artificial intelligence as a stand-alone generic technology was to miss the point of the usefulness of intelligent machines. An AI application had to be designed to do something specific; it could not be sold as a panacea to solve all the problems of the computer world. This was where generic tools like KEE, ART, and S.1 were missing the boat. "You can't just go out and buy AI any more than you can go out and buy art," he told *Venture* magazine. "Just as in art, where you must buy a painting or a sculpture, or some real object, in AI you will have to buy an application." The other thing that Cooper wanted to accomplish with Palladian was something that had never been done in the computer business. He wanted his software to be so intelligent and easy-to-understand that users wouldn't even need manuals or documentation to run the programs. The programs would learn from the users and adapt themselves accordingly.

Before Cooper opened Palladian for business, he stacked his deck heavily with all the proper cards. Five of the leading management professors from the Sloan School signed on to be part of Palladian's board of advisors, including Stewart Myers, Sloan's renowned head of corporate economics, finance, and accounting. Cooper would be tapping the brains of the Sloan brain trust to create his expert system. It was their knowledge that would be engineered into Palladian's software. He then went and hired top AI researchers and programmers from MIT at salaries that turned heads even in the fiscally frivolous world of technology start-ups. And, most importantly, Cooper cushioned his company with a comfortable amount of investment capital. Eighteen million dollars worth. This was more money than either Symbolics or LMI had started off with.

Like all good entrepreneurs, Cooper had learned early on that the best financial principle for avoiding personal failure was to use someone else's money to fund your company. That meant giving away percentages of the organization to investors, but the payback would be worth it if you could hang on long enough to go public.

Cooper managed to solicit millions of dollars for Palladian from some of Wall Street's largest investment firms: Kleiner Perkins, Venrock (the Rockefeller family fund), Lazard Freres, and Morgan Stanley. These investors reviewed Phil's management success in creating and then selling Computer Pictures—at a hefty profit—and liked what they saw. Plus, they liked the fact that Cooper had assembled an all-star advisory board for developing a product in a hot new industry. It all looked fantastic on paper. Phil Cooper got his money and the green light from the money men, and Palladian was off and running.

The first order of business was to establish Palladian—and Phil Cooper—as a new type of AI entity; one concerned with addressing the needs of modern business. AI wasn't just for scientists and engineers, claimed Cooper. It was also for assisting corporate executives with the often cumbersome and even routine process of making business decisions and planning business strategy. Palladian was going to develop an expert system that would target those executives who were buried under the information overload that the computer revolution was dumping on them. With Palladian products, these same executives would have access to the smart machines that the engineers and scientists had for too long been keeping to themselves.

Cooper set up offices in Four Cambridge Center, the same building that housed Symbolics' sales staff. With Palladian's arrival, there were now about a dozen AI companies in the Kendall Square area, notably Symbolics, LMI, Gold Hill, Apex, and Palladian. The local media, and Phil, took to calling the area "AI Alley," a term that both denoted the concentration of AI companies as well as the scrappy nature of the new technologists. Having set up shop in AI Alley, Cooper immediately went across the street and introduced himself to Russell Noftsker. After all, they were neighbors. Cooper told Noftsker that Palladian would design its executive AI software to run exclusively on Symbolics' hardware, which meant that their companies' engineering teams would have to work closely to ensure complete compatibility. The men subsequently signed a joint development agreement, and Noftsker spoke publicly about the importance of Palladian's software at various investment seminars and conferences. "In a public speech during my road show for the IPO in 1984, I said that Palladian was an example of the kind of application that would help to develop the market for high-powered workstations," recalls Noftsker. That belief didn't last long. "The fact that I even mentioned Palladian at all is an embarrassment to me now," he says, regretfully.

On a personal level, both Noftsker and Cooper shared a unique interest in vintage aircraft, and together they invested in several airplanes, including a B-25 bomber. As individuals, though, the two men couldn't have been more different. Noftsker was soft-spoken and somewhat shy. Cooper was bombastic and loud, the product of the classical school of marketing and salesmanship. He also stood over six-feet tall, and resembled a bear in a three-piece suit. Noftsker was polite and would listen quietly at length to reporters' and customers' questions on any range of topics. Cooper, on the other hand, talked at people, or he simply didn't talk to them at all. There was rarely any in-between. In discussions and interviews, he would ignore questions, people, and issues if they weren't on his agenda of things that he wanted to talk about. During meetings, he interrupted other speakers as if they weren't even in the same room. Cooper also never hesitated to use his imposing size to make his point in face-to-face conversation. More often than not, conversation with Phil was best described as confrontation.

Surprisingly, for all his overt rudeness, the investment community and the media loved Cooper. He took to flying prospective clients, investors, and members of the press up and down the Atlantic coastline in the B-25, all the while dressed in appropriate attire—long silk scarf, bomber jacket, and goggles. It not only gave him the aura of entrepreneur as daring-and-bold character, but it also provided him with a nice hook to generate high-profile press coverage. The scheme worked—Cooper was depicted as a flamboyant businessman who had truly made it, and he could do no wrong.

Palladian's first product, the Financial Advisor, was released in August 1985 during the international AI conference held in Los Angeles (the successor to the Austin AAAI conference). The demonstrations of the $95,000 software product were impressive, and a number of potential customers were given evaluation copies of the Financial Advisor. Its appeal lay in the fact that the Financial Advisor was an expert system product with the expertise already built-in. Users of the product did not have to develop and then program the knowledge of financial experts; the expertise had already been supplied by Palladian's select and esteemed board of advisors. With this product, Palladian became the first company to sell pre-packaged expertise in the AI market.

Cooper's target audience was the largest industrial companies in the United States, beginning with the Fortune 1000. Chief financial officers and executives responsible for any capital-intensive ventures would be sure to want—and need—the Financial Advisor as a tool for evaluating the impact of financial and budgetary decisions. The product would be able to analyze financial data, make recommendations on specific methodologies, and pinpoint inconsistencies in any proposal that it reviewed. It could also gauge the investment return on new product introductions or strategies by performing risk analysis and determining break-even points that would squeeze the last dollar of profit out of any planned venture. In short, the Financial Advisor could do everything that a human financial executive could do, but the software could do it better and in less time.

To drum up sales, Cooper embarked on a non-stop PR campaign that focused on his goal of "business AI for businesses." He was quoted frequently in business and computer publications. His picture was printed in full-color in *USA Today* along with Symbolics' Russell Noftsker and the new CEO of Gold Hill Computers, Carl Wolf. The three men were heralded as the leaders of the new computer revolution. And Cooper's perceived business acumen became so substantial that he even convinced the MBA school at Harvard University, which was a Palladian investor, to develop one of its fabled business "cases" around Palladian—even though the company had been in business for less than two years. Interestingly, the Harvard case study was long on praise and short on specifics when discussing the company, focusing instead on Cooper's success with Computer Pictures and his ability to raise money "without a formal business plan."

Cooper's ability to raise money was matched only by his ability to spend money. The philosophy around Palladian was that money was a wonderful incentive, and the people who needed the most incentive were the hackers.

Like other AI start-ups, Palladian wanted to make hackers feel as comfortable as possible, almost as if they were living in the AI Lab but with better amenities. That began with big paychecks and stock options. Randy Parker, an MIT AI Lab grad who went to work for Palladian right out of school, recalls Phil's fiscal graciousness. "Other companies in Cambridge were offering normal salaries to software engineers, around $25,000 to $35,000, usually with no stock. I walked into Palladian, with no experience, and was immediately offered $40,000 and five thousand shares of stock. There is no way to turn that down when you're twenty-two years old."

Palladian's offices were divided into two separate sections of the 11th floor of Four Cambridge Center. One section was reserved for administration and sales and marketing, while the other was devoted to engineering. The two were separated by elevators and a reception area. But Phil's office was in the corner of the engineering section, nowhere near the other senior administrators. In order to get to Phil's office, one had to walk through the area where the hackers resided. In most companies, this would have been no-man's-land. At Palladian, it was Exhibit A.

The hacker domain resembled nothing so much as a fraternity playroom gone insane. One of the technical vice presidents kept several birds in her office area, which continuously squawked and scattered bird seed, bird droppings, and torn newspaper all over the floor. Another hacker kept a dog in the office. A pinball machine and popcorn machine were operational twenty-four hours a day. Each hacker had his own LISP machine, and Frisbees routinely crashed into cubicles and $100,000 computers.

The hackers were also well-fed, plied with late night pizzas and seafood. At the time, the only up-scale restaurant in Cambridge Center—amidst the Chinese food places and pizza parlors—was a seafood restaurant called Legal Seafood, located downstairs from Palladian. Legal became "the" place to take clients and have business meetings in Kendall Square, despite its unusual practice of charging for meals before they were served. Legal Seafood was not only the haunt of the administrators and the S&M crowd during the afternoons and evenings; the hackers were treated to its takeout menu during their late night sessions—which occurred essentially every night. Hackers were authorized to expense all their Legal dinners, and many of them were fed seafood every day courtesy of Palladian.

Providing this expensive food took on ridiculous proportions when one of the hackers found out that Palladian had an open tab at Legal. The hackers sent out for even more food than before because they didn't have to provide the up-front cash that would be expensed later. Only when Palladian's director of sales came screaming into the hacker enclave did they realize that the Legal tab was reserved for use only by the sales staff. Accounting had to sort out thousands of dollars worth of crabs and clams and shrimp and chowder to figure out how much the engineering department owed S&M.

Despite this brief setback, life at Palladian was extremely good for the hackers. Parker notes, "It was like being at the AI Lab, only better. You got paid, you got fed, you didn't have to spend any of your own money on pinball games, you got to hack as much as you wanted, and you had your own LISP machine. It couldn't have been any better."

Cooper could watch the hacker madness from his corner office, like a king watching over his prized subjects. "Phil would bring clients or investors up to his office, so naturally he would have to walk through all this hacker chaos," says Parker. "He would stop to make small talk with us as he wandered through, pointing out items of interest to the clients. It was as if he were showing off the bizarre environment where all these creative computer people were dreaming up new technology and new products. In effect, that's what he was doing. The hacker area was like Phil's very own personal petting zoo."

Cooper wasn't the only one catering to the hackers. Symbolics was a little tighter with its food budget, but hackers still had free rein over the company. In the basement of Symbolics' building, where all of its computers were kept, the hackers installed a life-size doll called Zippy The Pinhead, which was based on a popular underground newspaper cartoon. Zippy was situated in a lawn chair and placed atop several of the refrigerator-sized computers, where he dominated the impressive array of machines. Zippy was also given an employee badge, and his name was the code word that allowed all the hackers to gain access to any of the company's computers.

Carnegie Group, too, allowed its hackers their freedom of expression. Many of the company's software development areas were divided into theme rooms, including one which was exclusively decorated with Elvis memorabilia. Such levity did not extend to the West Coast AI companies, however, which were rather tame and almost overly corporate in comparison to their East Coast siblings and rivals.

Nowhere was the "anything goes" ethic more ferociously adhered to than at Gold Hill. Perhaps due to its less than respectable location, the company came to be something of the "Animal House" of AI Alley. The company didn't pay nearly as well as its AI neighbors, but it promised more fun and better food. The company's vice president of marketing, Gene Wang, routinely rewrote the words to pop songs and sang them at company functions, using female staffers as dancers and background singers. He rallied the troops with songfests and impromptu concerts, which were part and parcel of life at Gold Hill.

Even better, from a hacker's point of view, employees could work their schedules to get three square meals a day at Gold Hill. Twice a week, the company sent the building handyman, known only as Ralph, to go out shopping for food. Orders were taken for employee preferences as to breakfast food (bagels, donuts), snack food (Pop Tarts and Mystic Mint cookies predominated), lunch food (deli sandwiches), and dinner food (microwave pizzas, etc.). Randy Parker, who joined Gold Hill after his tenure at Palladian, remembers food was big on Gold Hill's list. "You would always come in early on Tuesdays, because Ralph went shopping that morning and would return with an entire shopping cart full of food. Then you would have all the munchie food to last you during the day between lunch and dinner. Towards the end of the week, when the good stuff had been picked over, Ralph would go out again and you'd realize that you were planning your arrival and departure at the office based on how good the food would be during a particular time. The refrigerator was always stocked regardless, so even if you stayed late, you'd get something worthwhile. I'd guess that with all that food, there were about six feeding sessions a day at Gold Hill. The food might have been more expensive at Palladian, but I'd have to give Gold Hill four stars for their kitchen."

Of course, all of these on-premise enticements served a useful purpose; they kept hackers at their desks for up to twenty hours at a time. Work was conducted twenty-four hours a day, and Palladian in particular had a technology vice president in the office around the clock. Of its three technical VPs, one would arrive at about eight and leave around six, the second would show up at close to noon and leave around ten, and the third would come in about ten at night and leave at eight the next morning. Thus, all their schedules overlapped, providing a nonstop executive-sanctioned work environment at the company. It wasn't scheduled to work this way; it was just the natural routine of each of the VPs.

In addition to feeding and entertaining the hackers, there was another endeavor on which AI companies decided to spend a lot of money during 1985: impressing each other. There was no better place to do this than at the annual AI conference, which in August 1985 was held at UCLA. The Austin show the previous summer had been a mere precursor to the S&M tide that descended upon southern California in 1985. Instead of being simply an American AI show, it was an international show, known formally as IJCAI (pronounced ish-kye), the International Joint Conference on Artificial Intelligence. And instead of attracting only the three thousand people who had visited Austin the year before, it drew nearly seven thousand people from around the world. Many of these people had come to see the AI companies exhibit their products.

The vendors literally stole the show from the academics. The fear that the AAAI council had had the previous year when they let a few exhibitors into the conference was now a nightmarish reality. Fifty-seven vendors took over the UCLA exhibit hall, many with demonstration booths the size of small buildings. In addition, hotel suites throughout the Westwood section of LA were used to hold private parties, conduct business, and give product demonstrations.

But it was the parties that made this AI gathering different than anything that had come before. As mentioned at the outset of this book, Symbolics rented a Malibu mansion to host its own party for anyone who could make it ("I think our transportation bill for buses and limousines that night alone was about $20,000," says Bill Hoffman). The night before Symbolics' party, Inference hired a yacht to take selected clients and dignitaries on a Pacific cruise out of Marina del Rey. Other companies like LMI took over restaurants or clubs to show everyone just how well they were doing financially.

The problem was that the finances were still coming primarily from venture money. LMI was losing money from its operations, as was nearly every other company at the conference. The exception was Symbolics, which had made a $1.1 million profit on sales of $40 million the previous year. But everyone wanted to make a big impression for one particular reason; Digital Equipment, Xerox, and Hewlett Packard were all announcing their plans to enter the AI market. Each of those companies was setting up an internal AI group to market products specifically dedicated to creating expert system applications.

Outside of Texas Instruments, these new entrants were the largest companies to jump on the AI bandwagon. Each of them was many times larger than Symbolics, and they lent another level of credibility to a technology that was still struggling to get legitimate attention from the business community. With these large computer companies drawing more people to the conference, all of the pure-play AI companies had to act as if they were playing on the same level.

In fact, they weren't. Hewlett Packard and DEC, in particular, were only paying lip service to AI, offering souped-up versions of existing hardware products and calling them "AI computers." They wanted to be serious about AI, but it wasn't their primary area of business, so they had literally thrown together some misfit operational groups and assembled them into "AI Business Groups." These companies were just hoping to ride the AI wave, as it were. The original companies, the AI pioneers, had a lot more at stake.

Dozens of little AI start-ups attended the conference as well, some with booths, some with hospitality suites, and some with nothing more than briefcases and business cards. They had very AI-sounding names, and just like the big hardware companies, they were trying to get any scraps that might fall off the AI table.

From the looks of things, 1985 was shaping up to be a great year for AI. Investment money was flowing like water, start-ups were multiplying like rabbits, and companies were buying products. Granted, it was the same old set of companies doing the buying, but the fact was that they were actually buying this time around.

These apparently wonderful indications of a growing industry failed to address the need to produce some tangible benefits. Even the customers who had already purchased AI products and services were still working on getting them up and running. In the warm glow of Southern California, nobody was worried about that—yet. They had plenty of venture capital to tide them over until the real sales started coming in. Then AI would take over the world. It was just a matter of time.

❧

A good chunk of AI's potential to take over the world still remained in the hands of the Department of Defense. DARPA specifically had received increasingly greater sums of money during the Reagan years as part of the President's plan to create a war machine so big that its mere existence would deter any potential foe.

The most visible part of Reagan's largesse was the Strategic Defense Initiative, known as Star Wars or SDI. This was the space-based weapons system that would provide a defensive shield for America against enemy missile attacks. In order for Star Wars to work properly, it would rely quite heavily on AI. But another, lesser known component of DARPA's computer plans was the Strategic Computing Initiative, or SCI, which is not to be confused with SDI. The SCI program was unveiled in October 1983, at about the same time MCC was getting started. It was a ten-year plan dedicated to pushing the state-of-the-art in AI and microelectronics. To show that it was serious about AI, DARPA allocated $600 million to the program for its first five years, significantly more than the Japanese had committed to The Fifth Generation. Unlike the space-based Star Wars project, DARPA's SCI plans called for the development of Earth-based artificial intelligence systems that could operate in the air, on land, and at sea. The ultimate goal of the SCI was the creation of four expert systems, one each for the Navy and the Air Force and two for the Army.

The first project was the development of an Autonomous Land Vehicle, or ALV, a driverless land rover that could navigate any terrain. The goal of the ALV program was to develop an intelligent battlefield tanklike vehicle that could act autonomously rather than being remotely controlled. Thus, it would require on-board computers and would rely on real-time sensors and artificial intelligence programs to interpret visual data. The project was assigned to the Army Engineering Topographical Labs at Fort Belvoir, Virginia, which would oversee nine different contracts totaling roughly $30 million, including a $17 million, five-year plum for Martin Marietta as lead contractor. (This project received the most publicity of any SCI project, and the nightly news still runs occasional footage of the ALV working its way down an abandoned road complete with obstacles and hazards.)

Project number two was the Battle Management Project, an expert system for naval aircraft carriers that could manage a complete tactical operation at sea. The system would be fed data from radar, other ships, naval offices, and airborne reconnaissance planes and make decisions about the best positioning and utilization of individual aircraft carriers during a naval battle.

The primary sites for the tactical management system were the Pacific Fleet headquarters at Pearl Harbor and the USS Carl Vinson. Litton Industries and Texas Instruments were the lead contractors, and they would work with a secretive AI firm called Advanced Information & Decision Systems. As a side note, Advanced Information and Decision Systems went by the acronym AI&DS, which was shortened to AIDS. Its name was a somewhat unfortunate liability as soon as the AIDS epidemic became a matter of public concern, and the company quickly changed its moniker to Advanced Decision Systems, or ADS, which was significantly less embarrassing.

The third SCI project was the Pilot's Associate, a microelectronic "copilot" that would make combat decisions faster than the human pilot. It has been estimated that in the heat of battle, a fighter pilot may be faced with several hundred considerations at any given moment, from altitude to fuel level to armature status. In order to relieve this burden, the Pilot's Associate expert system would monitor mechanical conditions of a fighter jet while the pilot was engaged in other activities—such as a dogfight—and take over control of such things as radio communications and navigation systems. It would also make recommendations about evasive or attack strategies as necessary. This project was headed up by the Air Force Wright Aeronautic Laboratory at Wright-Patterson AFB in Ohio. Contracts were awarded to two separate development teams, with a value of between $4 million and $7 million each. The first team was led by McDonnell Douglas and included Texas Instruments, which managed to get its fingers into most of DARPA's SCI plans. Lockheed led the second team, which consisted of General Electric, Goodyear, Carnegie-Mellon University, and Teknowledge.

The fourth and final project was the AirLand Battle Management system. AirLand would provide real-time battle information to ground-based Army commanders and help to simulate the outcome of possible maneuvers, make decisions, and suggest plans of action. Once those orders were executed, the system would be able to monitor the battle situation, feeding the information back into a loop for continued revision and improvement. This contract went to Lockheed, with support from MITRE Corporation, Advanced Decision Systems, and Roger Schank's AI company, Cognitive Systems.

In addition to these ambitious plans for SCI, DARPA still had enough money to explore new technologies just as it had in the late 1950s and 1960s. One of the biggest projects was a contract that it awarded to Texas Instruments (again) for the creation of a LISP microprocessor, called the LISP MegaChip. This chip would shrink the combined hardware components of an entire LISP machine down to the size of a postage stamp. Once it was that size, the chip could be programmed with an expert system and placed into, say, the navigational system of a missile, where it could make its own decisions about target location and detonation. Sounds kind of scary in retrospect.

Another contract was given to Thinking Machines Corporation, a startup founded by an MIT student, a Harvard professor, and Marvin Minsky. DARPA gave Thinking Machines several million dollars to build the world's most powerful and potentially intelligent computer. At the time of the award, Thinking Machines was a little company that was operating out of a house in Cambridge, but the DARPA contract gave it enough cash to move uptown to Kendall Square, just down the street from MIT.

Last—and at the time, least—DARPA was giving small grants to a variety of companies that were interested in doing some basic research into neural networks. This money went primarily to two defense contractors, TRW and Science Applications International Corporation, both of which had AI labs in San Diego, California. These two inconspicuous neural net groups would eventually mutate into a booming new AI industry by the end of the decade.

❧

It is impossible to recount the stories—or even list the names—of all the startups that dove into AI during 1985 and 1986, spurred on by VC interest and DARPA. A short list from the time reveals eight pure-play companies offering hardware, a dozen offering voice recognition products, another dozen offering natural language services, more than twenty that were offering AI programming languages, and more than forty offering expert systems. The names are a treat in themselves, however, so a quick look at them is worthwhile, if only for entertainment value: Advanced Information & Decision Systems, Aion, Airus, California Intelligence, Expert Edge, Exsys, IntelligenceWare, Intelligent Business Systems, Integrated Inference Machines, Knowledge Garden, Knowledge Systems, Logicware, Mind Path, Neuron Data, Prologica, Prologia, Reasoning Systems, Silogic, Smart Systems, Speech Systems, Verbex, Voice Control Systems, and Votan.

Other companies, whose main businesses were not based on AI, formed internal AI groups to take advantage of DARPA contracts for the SCI program as well as for other DOD projects. They included Hughes, Litton, Boeing, Bendix, Lockheed, TRW, Rockwell, McDonnell Douglas, Martin Marietta, General Dynamics, and Northrop. Each of these companies dedicated a sizable number of people—usually ranging from twenty to one hundred—to the creation of AI applications.

Still other organizations just began offering AI products as an adjunct to their normal businesses. Radian, a division of Hartford Steam and Boiler Insurance Company, bought an expert system shell developed by Donald Michie, called it RuleMaster, and put it out in the market. Sperry began offering its TI Explorer and IntelliCorp package as the Power Pack. Other nondefense companies even began developing their own expert systems without the assistance of AI companies. Most Fortune 500 companies were doing something with AI, although they weren't saying much about it. AI was still a dirty little secret that wasn't ready to be shared with the outside world.

While everybody kept looking to the defense contractors or the big industrials to say something positive—or just say something at all—about AI, substantial advances were being made in business areas that nobody had paid much attention to. There is no way that anyone could have predicted that companies like Campbell's Soup and Mrs. Field's Cookies would be the real leaders in the successful application of artificial intelligence.

27

Charley, Aldo, and IBM

Legitimizing Artificial Intelligence

Aldo Cimino was getting tired. So was Charley Amble. Both men had put most of their lives into their respective companies, and it was time to pack it in. Collect the gold watch and retire.

Leaving wasn't going to be that easy. Cimino, for example, had worked at Campbell Soup Company for forty-four of his sixty-plus years. He was the only person in the entire company who had worked on all of Campbell's product sterilizers, huge eighty-foot-high contraptions that cooked soup before it was canned. He was intimately familiar with the causes of breakdowns in these machines, and knew the best methods for repairing them quickly. No one else at Campbell Soup knew as much about the giant cooking machines as Aldo Cimino.

But Aldo couldn't stick around forever. Traveling around the United States to fix the cookers at various

Campbell plants was taking its toll, and Aldo couldn't continue to keep up the pace. Besides, it was time to do something else after forty-four years.

Charley Amble was in the same situation. After more than twenty years at General Motors, he too was ready to retire. During those twenty-some-odd years, Charley had become GM's resident expert on vibration analysis, a technique which helped to predict failures in machines. Working day in and day out at GM's Saginaw, Michigan plant, Charley would listen to the vibrations created by the machines that manufactured axles and steering gears. These same vibrations were also analyzed by sensors attached to a computer. After years of listening to the machines, Charley was able to tell when something wasn't operating correctly or whether it was starting to sound slightly irregular. Working with the computer sensor data, he could determine what was wrong with the equipment and give an order to have it investigated. Such preventive maintenance ensured that GM would not have to shut down an entire production line if one of the machines blew out unexpectedly.

Machine vibration analysis was—and is—a respected means of avoiding major manufacturing breakdowns. In order for any one person to become really good at it, though, that person had to spend years getting used to the peculiar sounds and idiosyncrasies of different machines. After all that time, he or she could detect vibration changes that would completely escape the notice of anyone else. This skill made experts out of a limited number of people, one of whom was Charley Amble. But like Aldo Cimino, Charley Amble was taking his knowledge and expertise with him on the day he cashed his last paycheck.

Neither Campbell Soup nor General Motors had anyone within their monstrously huge organizations who had the same level of expertise as Charley or Aldo. They couldn't force the men to stay, but they also couldn't afford to lose them. When a soup cooker went down or an axle machine broke down, each company was crippled for hours or even days until the equipment could be repaired. Neither one relished the thought of operating without the experience and expertise of these men at their beck and call.

This predicament showed how large industrial organizations relied on seemingly innocuous job experience to keep their operations running efficiently. Charley and Aldo couldn't just be replaced by any other people; no one else knew what they knew. Some other employees knew bits and pieces of what Aldo and Charley knew, but nowhere else was the knowledge about equipment as complete as it was in these men's heads. It also wasn't the kind of knowledge that could simply be written down in a book. There were too many heuristics and gut instincts that the men had acquired over the decades that couldn't be easily expressed in words and sentences.

Campbell Soup executives thought that maybe all the ballyhooed AI stuff could help them preserve Aldo Cimino's expertise after he was gone. As one big company to another, Campbell approached Texas Instruments to see if it could help out. Campbell was already using some TI equipment, and felt comfortable about working with the company on a risky AI project. Obviously, TI would have liked to put some Explorers in each one of the soup maker's production facilities, but Campbell wanted something simpler, more accessible, and less imposing for its production employees. A personal computer, perhaps.

TI's artificial intelligence group had been delving into every area of AI that it could. In addition to the Explorer LISP machine, it was also working on a cheap version of LISP called Scheme, a voice recognition product called Speech Command, and a microprocessor which would shrink the hardware of a LISP machine down to a single chip. And, fortunately for Campbell Soup, TI had just finished creating an expert system shell which would run on a personal computer, called Personal Consultant. It wasn't as powerful as KEE or ART, but TI knew it was as good as Teknowledge's M.1, and it cost about $11,000 less than that particular expert system software.

TI agreed to help Campbell Soup clone Aldo Cimino's expertise. If Campbell Soup would give TI access to Aldo on a continual basis, then it could knowledge-engineer his expertise into Personal Consultant. The resulting software would be like having Aldo on a floppy disk.

The soup maker readily signed up for the project. For his part, Aldo figured it might take a day or so to tell Texas Instruments' knowledge engineer everything he knew about soup cookers and how to repair them. Like most experts, he had never "brain-dumped" all the specifics of his job, and he really didn't think there was all that much to it.

Seven months later, TI produced Cooker, an expert system that knew what Aldo Cimino knew. Aldo sat with TI's knowledge engineer for much longer than the one-day session he had expected; the process took what amounted to two weeks worth of time. He provided as much detail as he could about his job, and then was prodded to describe what he would do in unusual and unexpected situations. The bulk of his expertise was programmed into Personal Consultant, and then it was boiled down to 151 rules covering most of the occurrences Aldo alone knew how to deal with. Giving the system the name Cooker, Campbell Soup installed the application in seven of its production facilities around the United States. With Aldo's expertise running on a PC at each site, resident repair staff could diagnose problems as if Aldo were looking over their shoulders. They would provide Cooker with details of a particular malfunction, and it would recommend the appropriate repair procedure. In this way, the repair personnel who were less experienced than Aldo increased their own knowledge of the cookers because the software gave them access to knowledge they did not yet possess. Aldo retired on schedule, yet his expertise remained on staff (or on disk) and is still consulted regularly by Campbell Soup.

GM did the same thing with Charley Amble's expertise. Taking advantage of its relationship with Teknowledge, GM put the AI company's knowledge engineers to work on preserving Charley's expertise. GM, however, wanted something that was bigger in scope than Campbell Soup's Cooker. It wanted to be able to address a multitude of problem areas that occurred in manufacturing and assembly equipment, conditions such as misalignment, mechanical looseness, structural weakness, resonance of components, bearing wear and failure, and gear malfunctions. As if that wasn't enough, GM also wanted to be able to detect these problems in all sorts of components, including gear trains, motors, belt drives, pumps, fans, blowers, bearings, couplings, and spindles.

Teknowledge had its work cut out for it. It worked on "Charley" for three years, eventually coming up with one thousand rules that encapsulated Charley Amble's expertise. The estimated cost for the entire project was $5 million, but GM figured that the expert system would save $500,000 in machine repairs in every plant in which it was installed. Installing it in ten plants would recoup the investment in one year. Not a bad return by anybody's standard. GM also considered the possibility of selling Charley to other manufacturers.

The press loved Cooker and Charley. Both expert systems had all the essential ingredients that made for good copy: human interest, efforts by industrial companies to modernize themselves, science-fiction technology, and success. These applications were less complicated to understand than previous expert systems, and they were being used in areas that everyone in America could relate to: cars and food.

One disturbing aspect of these applications, at least as far as the core AI community was concerned, was that neither of them involved a LISP machine or a large-scale expert system shell. GM and Campbell Soup had proven that creating a workable expert system didn't require everything that the MIT and Stanford crowd had claimed was necessary to make an AI program work properly. A simple program, done carefully, could be accomplished without LISP and all its attendant costs. A small—but very definite—chink in the armor of the AI purists had been discovered.

Teknowledge, in particular, was being beaten over the head with this fact by its strategic partners. Not one of them was pleased with the fact that

LISP-based systems couldn't tie into their main computers, most of which ran other languages like FORTRAN or COBOL or C. Information on the main systems often had to be re-entered into the LISP system, causing a duplication of data. When one was updated, they both had to be updated. It would be much easier, and more cost effective, if expert systems could be written in the same language as more popular computer programs so that they could share data.

These concerns came about just as the AI companies were staging a holy war with each other over the importance of LISP and LISP machines. Gold Hill's Golden Common LISP for personal computers had become extremely popular almost overnight, selling thousands of copies to rabid PC programmers in its first two years. Lucid, under the guidance of Stanford LISP guru Richard Gabriel, had introduced its version of Common LISP that gave general purpose workstations many of the capabilities of a dedicated LISP machine. Lucid's LISP allowed companies like Sun, Apollo, and even DEC to sell their computers head-to-head against Symbolics. Such prospects gave Symbolics and its investors night sweats.

To top it all off, lots of little PROLOG companies were entering the market. The most notable was a company called Arity, a spin-off of Lotus Development Corporation, the vendor of the popular Lotus 1-2-3 spreadsheet. Funded with nearly $1 million from Lotus, Arity wanted to bring PROLOG to PCs in the same way that Gold Hill was bringing LISP to PCs.

Complicating and confusing matters even further, Japanese companies participating in The Fifth Generation project were buying LISP machines from Symbolics. Even though PROLOG was the designated language of The Fifth Generation, ICOT researchers found that it wasn't as flexible for creating some of the more ambiguous human attributes as LISP was. Thus, some of them were sneaking around the party platform. One Japanese Fifth Generation member, Fujitsu, had even developed a LISP machine that it wanted to sell in the United States. Called the Facom, the computer failed dismally when it was introduced in 1984, but Facom was indicative of the fact that the Japanese were hedging their AI bets by utilizing both LISP and PROLOG in their quest for thinking machines.

The LISP language, though, wasn't providing any benefits to its namesake, Lisp Machine, Inc. Things went from bad to worse for LMI during 1985, and there appeared to be no relief in sight. The company had sold a mere one hundred machines during its four years in business, and its share of the market had dropped to less than one fifth of Symbolics' share. To add to the humiliation, nearly half of its machines had been sold to Texas Instruments, which was now actively competing with LMI. TI had even broken off its agreement with Western Digital to manufacture the NuBus computer, then known as the NuMachine, and tried to get LMI to take over the rights to it. LMI was using the basic NuMachine for its Lambdas, and TI saw no reason to continue its involvement with the NuMachine since it now had the Explorer.

LMI had grown to more than 170 people, located both in Cambridge and Los Angeles, and its sales were just over $10 million. It had not made a profit since its first year of business, and it was running through money even faster than Symbolics. Frank Spitznogle wasn't doing the turnaround job that he had been brought in for, and LMI decided it was time to hire someone else to run the company. Surprisingly, LMI enlisted one of the first and only A-Teamers in the industry.

Ward MacKenzie was an eighteen-year veteran of Digital Equipment, where he had been vice president of the Business Computer Group as well as manager of the third-party (OEM) division. This had given him substantial experience in dealing with all facets of the computer business and had made him a high-profile computer industry executive. When he was approached by LMI in late spring of 1985, MacKenzie was offered the chance to take over the entire show, including Steve Wyle's role as chairman.

MacKenzie had been considered as a possible candidate to replace DEC president Ken Olsen when Ken retired. But it looked like Olsen might never retire, and MacKenzie didn't want to stay in the same job with DEC for the rest of his life. It was a no-win situation. Taking the CEO position at LMI, however, would be a win-win situation. If he turned around the faltering LISP vendor, MacKenzie's executive stature was sure to go up a few notches. If LMI went belly-up, it probably wouldn't be blamed on MacKenzie because things were downright abysmal by the time he got there. Either way, it was worth the risk. Ward MacKenzie resigned from DEC and signed on with LMI.

His departure from DEC was noted in a number of computer trade magazines, a phenomenon that had not occurred when other people joined AI companies. It was obvious that MacKenzie had a lot of visibility in the computer industry, and his presence could be nothing but positive for LMI.

The first thing that MacKenzie did upon arriving at LMI was to begin looking for more money. Within three months, he raised $18.1 million for LMI, including more than $4 million from defense electronics firm Raytheon, and $5 million from General Signal. Considering how bad LMI was doing relative to its competition, it seemed as if MacKenzie must have raised the money on his reputation alone. This financing upped the amount of money that LMI had raised to over $40 million worth of venture capital and corporate equity funds. It now had more than two dozen separate investors and did not even remotely resemble the original company started by Richard Greenblatt.

To add insult to injury, Greenblatt was removed from most of the company's operations, as was Steve Wyle. In addition, the investors determined that Cambridge was a little too expensive for a company that was losing money hand over fist. Keeping the Los Angeles headquarters didn't make much sense in this light, either. Just as MacKenzie was brought on, the board of directors decided to consolidate the entire operation of the company and move it out to Andover, Massachusetts, a sleepy enclave about an hour west of Cambridge. People from LA were transferred to Andover or they were let go—with the exception of Wyle. Spitznogle, who still held his chief operating officer job after MacKenzie was hired, had to relocate to Andover, as did the entire S&M staff. As a consolation prize to Richard Greenblatt, MacKenzie allowed a small staff of hackers to remain in Cambridge.

By the end of 1985, LMI's sales were only $19 million, even though the original sales projections had been set for $40 million. The company started putting more money into the development of its PICON process control system, hoping to build revenues from software in order to offset the decline in hardware sales.

But a new and insidious problem was entering into the equation: customers weren't paying for their Lambdas, claiming that they didn't work.

～

Money was tight all over, and both Symbolics and IntelliCorp went back to the public market in 1985 to raise money with additional stock offerings. Sales were good, but burn rates were taking up too much of the companies' cash. Symbolics' sales for 1985 were $69 million with a $2 million profit, while IntelliCorp made $8.6 million in 1985 with a profit of $1 million—the first profit in its five-year history.

AI still hadn't reached the mass market, and the vendors were usually competing with each other for exactly the same pieces of the government and research lab pie. Some of the AI companies couldn't keep up any longer and simply ran out of steam. Verbex, a voice recognition company owned by Exxon, was quietly closed down after the oil giant failed to find a buyer for it. Silogic, an expert system company backed by Sumitomo, slipped into oblivion. Breit International, a self-proclaimed elite group of developers who had been trained at Martin Marietta, disappeared without ever introducing a product. Perq Systems, a hardware company formed to compete with Symbolics and LMI, never made it out of the starting gate.

One vendor that had been destined for the "where are they now?" files managed to pull off a major coup at the end of 1985. Xerox, the erstwhile AI also-ran, signed a deal with Applied Expert Systems for one thousand of its little LISP machines. These computers, formally known as the 1186 AI Workstation, were to be bundled with Apex's new financial planning expert, called PlanPower. Apex would install its LISP software on the Xerox machines, and then resell the entire package to banks and other financial institutions for use by financial planners. The value of the sale was $20 million, which Xerox called "the largest sale of AI workstations in history." Apex, which had yet to sell any of its PlanPower systems, was depending on Travelers Insurance, a major Apex investor, to fund the buy. In fact, a subsidiary of Travelers was going to help sell the package.

Xerox was ecstatic to be able to rub this news in Symbolics' face, but Symbolics barely noticed. Apex's product was competing with similar financial packages from Palladian and Syntelligence, and both of those companies had more experience in developing viable AI applications. Besides, if Xerox was involved, how serious could this deal really be?

Amidst this chaotic activity, and under pressure from its investors, Teknowledge decided it was time to separate itself from the AI pack. In December 1985, it announced that it was no longer going to support LISP or PROLOG, and that in the future all of its products would be written in the popular C language. Teknowledge's decision marked the first major corporate break from the rank and file of American AI. As far as Symbolics, IntelliCorp, and the other AI pioneers were concerned, it was blasphemy to think that a group of people with their roots in John McCarthy's Stanford AI Lab could even imagine doing AI work in some language other than LISP. The fact that M.1 was a PROLOG product was bad enough, but C? Teknowledge might as well have hired Hubert Dreyfus to run the company for all the wisdom behind that decision.

Teknowledge's decision was based on the need to develop a mass-market tool. It is doubtful that it arrived at the decision itself (many have speculated that General Motors forced the issue) since it didn't have any prior examples of this kind of foresight. At a deeper level, Teknowledge's change in strategy created a hairline fracture in the normally united AI community. So did Texas Instruments' obvious plunder of LMI. In the few years that the AI companies had been doing business, they all had a common foundation, and had formed a kind of "mutual admiration society." They sold products to each other and worked together to pitch corporate customers on buying their respective wares. Now that one of the pioneers had become a turncoat and denied a basic tenet of AI—"Thou shalt use LISP and only LISP"—things could never be the same. Like a hateful word between lovers that can never be taken back, the seeds of animosity had been planted. Soon, it would be every man for himself.

One source of amusement for the AI community as 1985 came to a close was a Doonesbury cartoon that ran on Sunday, November 24, 1985. There, in full color for all the world to see, the comic strip depicted one of its characters using artificial intelligence to embezzle cash from his employer. The system was so smart that it even booked a flight to Rio for the user when the money was transferred to the proper bank account.

Perhaps not so amusing was the fact that more people learned about AI by reading the Sunday funnies than they had ever learned from the companies that were selling the technology.

ᐧ

IBM decided that 1986 was going to be the year that it got serious about artificial intelligence. There was too much going on for it to ignore AI any longer.

Consider this: In March 1986, Teknowledge went public and raised $28.3 million. The buzz on Wall Street was so positive that the offering was oversubscribed by 500,000 shares. This happened despite the fact that Teknowledge had never turned a profit.

Borland International, an upstart PC software company started by a former French laborer named Philippe Kahn, was growing quickly by selling cheap versions of popular programming languages for the PC. In early 1986, Borland introduced a $99 version of PROLOG called Turbo PROLOG. At $99, almost any hacker or would-be programmer could afford to create programs with this language. If they couldn't, well, $99 wasn't too much money to have wasted. It certainly wasn't the thousands of dollars required to buy basic LISP programming tools or the tens of thousands needed for LISP machines. The product instantly became one of the best-selling programs in the PC software business.

Thinking Machines Corporation, a Cambridge company started by MIT student Danny Hillis and his mentor, Marvin Minsky, introduced a computer it called the Connection Machine. Designed specifically to be the most powerful computer in the world, the Connection Machine boasted 65,000 different processors and a price tag of $3 million. While this company had originally been planned as Minsky's halfway house between academia and industry, as of May 1986 it was a heavily funded corporation with backing from DARPA and CBS founder William Paley, who happened to be related to the company's president, Sheryl Handler. Thinking Machines was going to use its technology to handle the most difficult of computer problems, including machine learning and reasoning.

Texas Instruments had a contract from DARPA to develop the LISP MegaChip microprocessor, which meant that LISP machines could be compressed to the size of a single chip. At that size, they could easily be plugged into IBM PCs or other devices in order to provide them with intelligence. Symbolics, too, was developing a LISP chip, and had received $7 million in funding from Merrill Lynch to produce the microprocessor. (Xerox also had a LISP chip, but nobody seemed to care.)

Yet, there was plenty of disarray as well. Symbolics was having trouble finding the right sales and marketing mix. It was moving people from position to position—just as the hackers' screen saver had done—and had finally ended up with Howard Cannon as director of marketing. Howard, you will recall, was the youngster who had been given a Porsche for getting the company's first 3600s out the door. He may have had amazing technical skills, but he knew as much about marketing as Richard Greenblatt. Maybe less.

IBM looked at all this, and saw that it was good. This was a business that was now big enough for IBM to march into and conquer.

~

IBM's historical involvement in AI can best be described as "spotty." It has never had a reputation for innovation, relying more on the brute strength of its sales force than on the technical elegance of its products. It has some of the finest research centers in the world, notably the Watson Research Center in Yorktown Heights, New York, but it always seems to pass over the work of its own researchers in favor of outside technology (this is especially true in voice recognition).

The company's roots in AI go all the way back to the beginning of AI research. IBM was represented by three men at the original AI conference at Dartmouth in 1956: Nathaniel Rochester, Arthur Samuel, and Alex Bernstein. Interestingly, they were the only real "corporate" members of the conference, the others all being academics or consultants to RAND Corporation. Samuel and Bernstein were interested in AI from the perspective of getting computers to play simple games that required only basic intelligence. They worked on developing checkers and chess programs, respectively, in the late 1950s and early 1960s. To pursue their research, the two men were given access to IBM's internal computing systems, which at the time was the largest concentration of computer power to be found in any corporation anywhere.

Their game-playing programs caught the fancy of the popular press, namely *Life* magazine, which ran a story on how IBM's mechanical machines were being used to mimic the intelligence of people. The stories were slanted more to the game aspect of computing than to the AI aspect, however, which made it look as if IBM was using its resources for nothing better than playing checkers. At the first IBM board meeting following the publication of the articles, IBM chairman Thomas Watson, Jr. was accosted by stockholders who berated him for wasting the company's precious assets on such trivial pursuits. Embarrassed and chastened, Watson promptly shut down the AI pursuits of Samuel and Bernstein, who had to continue their work on the sly. For the next twenty years, AI was a no-no at Big Blue.

Even though basic AI research was carried out in IBM's labs, primarily in the fields of expert systems and voice recognition, the company refused to make any public acknowledgment of its involvement with the technology. Its customers were people who wanted traditional computer systems with dumb terminals, and there would be no use in getting them all riled up with talk of thinking machines. This relegating of AI to second-class status irritated many of IBM's expert system researchers, many of whom felt shackled by the warning to keep their AI work secret. Despairing of ever doing anything practical within IBM, four of the six AI scientists who were working in IBM's Palo Alto research facility quit in 1984 and started their own company. Called Aion (a takeoff on AI and eon), the goal was to create expert systems for personal computers and mainframes. The products would not, significantly, be written in LISP.

The defection of the Aion researchers severely hurt IBM's AI development work, but the company was determined to press on until it felt it could attack the AI market with a full contingent of products and services. The key was to make expert systems run on IBM machines, which traditionally couldn't handle the complexity of AI programs. IBM researchers, like those that had left for Aion, had to develop programming tricks to make AI work on IBM computers.

By the summer of 1986, IBM could wait no longer. The company was determined not to let AI pass it by, which would give critics another reason to claim that IBM had no talent for recognizing important new technologies. After some consideration, the powers that be at IBM decided to come out of the closet at the annual gathering of the AI believers, the AAAI Conference. The conference was slated for August 12th in Philadelphia, and IBM was determined to crash the party in a way that only a billion-dollar behemoth could.

The vendors in AI Alley got wind of IBM's plot to make its big formal AI announcement, and they planned accordingly. IBM's presence at AAAI was to be its way of saying "We're going to legitimize this business." Well, that intimated that AI was thus far some kind of illegitimate computer-child. The illegitimate children, the bastards, were more than ready for IBM.

Symbolics rented the Franklin Institute Science Museum for an evening, allowing thousands of guests to wander through the massive building with free drinks and hors d'oeuvres. Gold Hill, the upstart that was gaining credibility based on the success of its PC products, rented out the Philadephia Art Museum. Thousands more partied there until they were shut down by the proprietors.

And in all of this frenzy to dazzle and impress, IBM held a luncheon. A nice luncheon, but still nothing more than your basic hotel lunch. IBM apparently had not been ready for the glitzy counterattack unleashed by the AI companies, and the luncheon was almost solemn in comparison to what the AI companies were doing. IBM practically got lost in the shuffle of AI companies trying to impress each other as well as their prospective customers.

At the luncheon, IBM's group director of product and technologies, Herb Schorr, announced that IBM was going to support AI in earnest. Schorr is a tall man with the required IBM haircut, but he looks too easygoing to fit in with the pin-striped crowd at Big Blue. Schorr had been a research scientist at Yorktown Heights, and was given the mandate to make AI a reality for IBM, as well as to make it a viable business pursuit that would result in new sales for IBM. In his own words, "We are going into the commercial arena in full force with a lot of investment." Thus, IBM did not come unprepared. It had an expert system tool which ran on IBM computers, called ESE, the Expert System Environment. It had its own versions of LISP and PROLOG for sale. It was entering into agreements with a number of AI vendors, including Lucid and IntelliCorp. It had a working voice-recognition system that it was demonstrating in a series of national prime-time TV commercials.

The commercials showed a woman talking to a computer and saying, "Write to Mrs. Wright, right now." The words magically appeared on the woman's computer screen as she spoke, conveniently ignoring the fact that Mrs. Wright's name could have been spelled Reit, or Right, or Rite. While those in the computer industry knew that this demonstration was just so much hooey, it was a sure bet that plenty of people out there in TV land were dumping their Smith Corona typewriters into the garbage. Who needed a typewriter when IBM had a machine that took dictation as perfectly as any human?

Although it didn't take the time—or spend the money—to wine and dine the artificial intelligentsia, IBM dominated the rest of the conference. The company was all over the place. It bought enough booth space in the exhibit hall to house a third-world nation, and Schorr himself gave the keynote address at the conference, announcing that AI technology was ready for the mass market. All this validation of commercial AI was enough to make an old AI pioneer weep. "To see the world's major computer manufacturer take this position is a great victory," gushed Ed Feigenbaum.

IBM was the big story at the 1986 AAAI conference, but it wasn't the only one. LMI kept a low profile because it had just laid off sixty people—25 percent of its work force—in order to cut costs. Aion, the new expert system company made up of former IBM executives, introduced an expert system for mainframes that would compete directly with IBM's offering. Gold Hill introduced an expert system tool for PC users and took its company songfest to new heights by performing Gene Wang's version of "Mac The Knife" in front of a crowd of AI revelers. Sun Microsystems, DEC, and Hewlett Packard all showed up, most of them using Lucid's Common LISP to run AI programs almost as efficiently as Symbolics' machines could.

Of note to many attendees was the fact that Sperry had pulled out of the conference just days before the event began. There were claims that it was spending all its resources fending off the unwelcome advances of computer rival Burroughs Corporation, which in retrospect proved to be true.

One of the more uniquely annoying aspects of the conference was the presence of Microsoft programmers. Microsoft was not exhibiting, but it seemed like its programmers had been let loose on the exhibit floor like so many insects. The newly crowned "king of the nerds," Microsoft's Bill Gates, had joined the public fray with some quotes made during an interview with a computer magazine. His company, like Borland, was selling language packages to PC hackers, but it wasn't selling anything like LISP or PROLOG. Gates believed any computer application, including expert systems, could be written in any language, especially his company's main offering, BASIC. "I was doing AI stuff ten years ago," Gates bragged in the interview. "We (Microsoft) have a great awareness of the way in which AI techniques can be used in the types of products we do. But we don't see a market for AI per se."

If Gates' comment was to be believed, he was working on AI as a teenager. Since the computer power necessary to do even rudimentary AI projects was not readily available to the average teenager in the mid-1970s, it would be interesting to find out where Bill did all of his AI work.

Gates' disdain for AI-based products carried over to his minions. Microsoft programmers, who had been born too late to be part of the original hacking culture, stalked around the AAAI conference and exhibition, ostensibly to sneer at the LISP-based products. Microsoft's big emphasis was on its own BASIC language, one of the easiest and most primitive programming languages ever devised. Those Microsoft programmers who were especially enamored of Chairman Bill, which was essentially all of them, were fond of touting Bill's BASIC programming skills by saying things like, "What do you need LISP to do that for? Bill could do that in BASIC." Sure he could. Anybody could, if they didn't mind spending the rest of their lives writing millions of lines of BASIC code to match what LISP produced in a few hours.

The aftermath of the Philadelphia AI conference left the AI vendors exhilarated and exhausted. Many of them, including Symbolics and Gold Hill, had spent way too much money trying to set themselves up as big corporations when they were actually still living day-to-day on venture capital support and slowly increasing revenues. Many of the other AI companies had also seen the future as painted by IBM: it was time to make AI accessible to the mass market. That meant something very different from offering hacker tools and LISP consulting services. Corporate America needed something it could pick up and run with, and LISP didn't fit this description.

It was estimated that there were fewer than five hundred fully qualified and capable LISP hackers in the United States at the time of the AAAI 1986 Conference. Roughly two-thirds of them were already employed by AI companies, and most of the rest were at universities. This put the price for LISP hackers at a premium. If a corporation wanted to use the services of a LISP hacker, it either had to sign a consulting agreement with companies like IntelliCorp and Gold Hill, or it had to hire the hacker at a base salary that was quickly approaching the $80,000 level. Like plutonium, LISP hackers were too rare a commodity to be useful to a large segment of the population, and other alternatives had to be found in order to make AI a mainstream technology.

Inference, Carnegie Group, and Teknowledge all pledged to offer future versions of their products in C. This would allow owners of Sun workstations to run ART and S.1, as well as Carnegie's Knowledge Craft tool, on something other than a LISP machine. Teknowledge completely killed off its LISP development in favor of C. Only IntelliCorp refused to budge from its allegiance to LISP, claiming that a proper expert system required a proper expert system language. That language, obviously, was LISP.

The remainder of 1986, on into the end of 1987, was to be the most frenetic period in the short lifespan of the AI business, and IBM made sure that it was standing right in the middle of it. IBM opened an AI customer support center in Cambridge (where else?) in October 1986. In announcing the opening of the office, Big Blue's vice president for market development, Victor Goldberg, proudly proclaimed, "We are at the beginning of a new era. We can program expertise into a computer, set up rules by which it can be employed and then work with it. The marketplace is almost endless." IBM promised to set up an AI hotline and publish a newsletter for all of its customers who were ready to build their own expert systems—systems that would require IBM's help, of course. The company established three different AI facilities, one each in Palo Alto, Cambridge, and New York. Chairman John Akers even made an announcement from on high: "Emerging technologies such as image processing and artificial intelligence offer great promise for the future." Not exactly the boldest of statements, but what more could be expected from the guy whose name would eventually become synonymous with the decline of IBM?

For all intents and purposes, however, IBM's involvement in AI begins and ends right there. In its rush to capitalize on AI, IBM forgot to do one small thing. It neglected to tell its sales force that it was supposed to sell AI products. With all of its attention focused on flooding the media with its grand plans, the sales force—the backbone of IBM—was completely overlooked. They were, for the most part, completely in the dark about AI, or even the fact that IBM had AI products to sell. One simple story illustrates how absolutely clueless the IBM salespeople were. DM Data, an AI consulting firm, received a call from an IBM sales representative in early 1987. The rep, who had major accounts in southern California, was interested in AI, and so were some of his clients. Did DM Data know of any companies that sold expert system software that worked on IBM computers? The rep knew about the LISP machine-based software, but he had been unable to find anything that ran on IBM mainframes. "Where can I find expert system programs for IBM equipment?" he asked.

"Look in your own product catalog," was the reply. IBM itself sold AI products for IBM equipment. The sales rep was even given the page number of the listing for AI-related products in the appropriate catalog. The rep, either angry or embarrassed beyond belief, quickly hung up.

During the next several years, IBM moved its Knowledge Based Systems group around the country at least four times. It eventually wound up in San Jose, and for close to a year, the company directory in Armonk had no listing for the group. Herb Schorr, after becoming 1986's AI man of the year, disappeared off the executive radar. He quietly dropped out of sight, unable to raise AI to a full level of acceptance within IBM. (A Symbolics' manager snickered that Schorr "was the first corporate AI executive to be taken out and shot" by Big Blue.) For the next six years, the company's AI group became the "AI legitimizer's" very own bastard child. IBM introduced new expert system shells from time to time—including one called The Integrated Reasoning Shell—but customers didn't seem to care. This was probably due to the fact that IBM salespeople didn't care, either.

As of 1993, IBM had lost all interest in AI. Of course, it had other things to worry about, like the erosion of its core mainframe and PC businesses and its anemic financial health. Today, it still promotes voice recognition, but it is relying on outside vendors like Dragon Systems to provide it with workable products. IBM's record in AI, alas, is destined to always be "spotty."

The entrance of the world's largest computer maker into the AI market did put the fear of God into the AI vendors, who realized—a little too late—that all the fun and games of raising venture capital and trying to create intelligent machines ultimately meant nothing if customers weren't buying AI products. IBM infused a dose of reality into the AI business simply because IBM was market-driven, and none of the AI vendors ever had been. If customers weren't begging for something, then that something probably wasn't going to sell. IBM's salespeople were much more interested in selling products that the majority of their customers were clamoring for. AI wasn't all that high on the list.

As this reality settled in, IBM's brief attempt to take control of the future of AI served as a nasty wake-up call. But by that time, the AI vendors had already overslept.

28

The Edifice Complex and Donner Pass

New Offices and Gilded Towers

At the end of 1986, Symbolics reported record revenues of $114 million, while Lisp Machine, Inc. prepared to file for bankruptcy.

LMI had little life left. No amount of venture capital could save it from poor sales and poor product quality. Ward MacKenzie began looking for someone to buy the company, or at least take over its assets, since there were no longer any investors even remotely interested in throwing money down the drain. Unfortunately, one of LMI's primary assets had already left. The group that was developing the PICON expert system quit en masse during the summer of 1986, taking their combined expertise with them. They started a company called Gensym and wanted to build their own process control expert system—something along the lines of PICON. If that sounds like they took LMI's research and were planning to build a new company on it, that's what LMI thought, too. Until it solved its own problems, however, there wasn't much that LMI could do about Gensym.

Without any cash, LMI had no choice but to look for a "white knight" to keep it from bankruptcy. This time, no one rushed in. To save money, the entire company moved back to Cambridge into the cramped quarters that had been left behind for the hackers when everyone else had moved to Andover the year before.

Things looked better over at Symbolics, at least financially. After selling $114 million worth of LISP machines, the company built a new headquarters facility in rural Concord, Massachusetts, near the site of the Revolutionary War's first battle. The setting was idyllic and pastoral, worlds away from Cambridge or Boston, but only about a half-hour drive from AI Alley. Symbolics created a complete campuslike area in Concord that would provide a more "human friendly" environment than the increasingly congested area in and around Cambridge Center. Plus, the new site butted up against Hanscom Airfield, where Russell Noftsker kept his airplane.

Russell's new headquarters increased his board of directors' frustration with him. They wanted to keep costs down, even though Symbolics was selling more machines than ever. Yet Noftsker kept spending money on people and facilities. More than 900 people worked for Symbolics, and as of the fall of 1986, the company was spread all over the map with a manufacturing facility in Chatsworth, California, headquarters in Concord, and technical/hacker offices in Cambridge. (None of the AI companies that moved out of Cambridge ever suggested to the hackers that they might have to leave Cambridge. It just wasn't possible. If the hackers got too far away from the MIT campus, they might die from shock.)

This compulsion on the part of AI companies to build their own buildings and live in worlds of their own design has been called the "edifice complex." IntelliCorp had just done it, building a beautiful three-story building with a marble atrium and glass elevators in Mountain View, California. Even impertinent Gold Hill was considering moving out of its Armenian dance hall to a brand new building on the other side of AI Alley in Kendall Square.

The Symbolics board had put up with Noftsker long enough, and it was time to bring in the new president that they had been threatening him with for two years—since before the company's 1984 IPO. In November 1986, they hired Brian Sear, an executive who had been president of a semiconductor test company in California. Sear would serve as Symbolics' president, while Noftsker would remain as chairman and CEO. Russell had met Sear several years before and actually recommended Sear for the position. As far as Russell was concerned, Brian Sear reported to him. As far as the board was concerned, Sear was reporting to them.

This dichotomy was bound to be a source of trouble. However, something even more troubling became apparent in the light of the New Year 1987.

Everyone who wanted a LISP machine had one.

Symbolics had sold more than two thousand computers since its inception, and its customer list had grown to several hundred companies. They included such recognizable names as AT&T, GTE, Honeywell, American Express, Westinghouse, Hughes, Ford, RCA, McDonnell-Douglas, Alcoa, Merck, Sohio, Boeing, and General Electric, along with the usual roundup of government-sponsored labs and contractors. However, economies of scale had forced the price of LISP machines down month by month, and Symbolics had supplemented its product line with several "budget" models. This had taken its toll: the cost for a basic LISP machine had fallen from a high of $140,000 to about $40,000 in six years.

Increased competition from Sun Microsystems had also eaten into the company's market. Sun had become the darling of the high-end computer market, effectively bridging the gap between personal computers and mainframes with its multipurpose workstations. Sun's sales in 1986 were over $200 million and climbing sharply. Using Lucid's Common LISP, a Sun workstation could run KEE and ART and any other LISP program. These Sun workstations cost considerably less than Symbolics machines, ranging from $15,000 to $30,000. The Suns also ran general-purpose software such as databases and spreadsheets, and they could be linked together in groups which allowed users to easily share data. Symbolics' LISP machines still operated pretty much as stand-alone systems. Complicating matters further, Sun had aggressively pursued the AI development market, so much so that roughly 10 percent of its revenues came specifically from sales to organizations that were building AI applications.

Regardless of the type of computer that was the machine of choice for AI, the fact remained that the largest part of the computer market, which included data processing and information systems groups, still had not been given a compelling reason for buying LISP machines. DP managers were trying to figure out how to deal with the intrusion of PCs and workstations into mainframe environments and didn't want to be bothered with another type of computer—especially a LISP machine—that could not be readily integrated with their IBM mainframes.

The overwhelming bulk of Symbolics' customers still adhered to the 80/20 rule, with the vast majority of LISP machines installed at various government research centers. Some of these sites had dozens of machines, and there was simply no way that they could use any more. Saturation had been reached. Thus, everyone who wanted one, had one. Everybody else had to be convinced.

Many people associated with Symbolics saw the writing on the wall. LISP machines, per se, were not necessarily a guaranteed growth market. On the other hand, the ingenious software and the development tools that Symbolics had developed for LISP machines might be where its future lay. The company needed to focus on selling these powerful tools to other hardware vendors (the same argument has been applied to the Apple Macintosh since 1989). But the company's founders were reluctant to give up their beloved hardware. It had been the reason for starting the company and had been its lifeblood since the day of incorporation. Noftsker and the other executives refused to give up on the hardware side of the business, even though Noftsker claims he knew that the hardware business was headed for bad times when John Kulp fired the Portable LISP hackers in early 1983. Noftsker recalls tersely, "On the day that I found out John had cleared out the Portable LISP group, I knew that we were going to be in trouble. Richard Gabriel and Lucid ended up doing what we were going to do."

If Symbolics was indeed aware of the need to rethink its hardware and software priorities, it didn't act like it. Sun Microsystems executives at the time claimed to have been rebuffed by Symbolics when they approached the company about licensing Symbolics' software tools, known collectively as Genera. Sun offered to pay royalties to Symbolics for each version of the software it sold, which, given Sun's prowess at selling, would amount to a large number of licenses. Symbolics declined the offer.

Even though Symbolics had reported sales of $114 million in 1986, its earnings had dropped and its operational costs were climbing. The board wanted costs cut, people cut, and the new headquarters abandoned. It couldn't believe that Noftsker was still spending money on buildings and ever more people. In December, 1986 the board gave yet another ultimatum to Symbolics' management. This time there were no ifs, ands, or buts. If Noftsker and Sear, who oversaw the operations committee, didn't do something immediately, the board would kick them both out of the company. Reluctantly, the two men moved everybody back to the Cambridge offices in January 1987 and subleased the space in Concord. In addition, they laid off 160 people. It was not a pretty sight.

Three months later, on April 1, 1987—April Fool's Day—Lisp Machine, Inc. filed for Chapter 11 bankruptcy. Ward MacKenzie, knowing that the only survivors of a sinking ship are those that have a life preserver, immediately took a job with Data General to head up that company's OEM group.

Within a week of taking the job, rumors surfaced in the East Coast computer community that Data General was considering buying LMI and its assets. The hiring of MacKenzie, whose employment contract was considered an LMI asset (it ran until June), was seen as a way for Data General to get first dibs on LMI. Both Symbolics and Prime Computer had briefly considered the possibility of acquiring LMI; Symbolics to gain access to the customer base, and Prime to expand its workstation offerings. But both companies were put off by the $16 million worth of liabilities and the list of 526 creditors that were affixed to LMI like boat anchors.

Data General, too, ended up merely kicking the tires. After MacKenzie came on board full-time, the rumors about any possible acquisition ceased. MacKenzie had been LMI's best asset, and Data General already had him. It didn't need anything else. LMI slipped into the deepest depths of bankruptcy, where it remained for one month until a Canadian company called Gigamos purchased its remaining assets. Gigamos had been a distributor for LMI's Lambda machines in Canada and thought that there might be a possibility of using LMI to position Gigamos as a LISP machine vendor. Gigamos set up an office in Lowell, Massachusetts to try and rebuild LMI with the lone surviving member of LMI's executive staff: Richard Greenblatt.

The first thing that the Gigamos/LMI alliance did was sue Gensym for stealing PICON from LMI. The matter was eventually settled out of court, with neither side permitted to discuss the settlement. (Today, Gensym's process control expert system, G2, is one of the most popular AI software packages on the market, and Gensym is one of the most profitable of all expert system companies.)

Within a year of buying LMI's assets, Gigamos itself was broadsided by a lawsuit filed in Canada by one of its Japanese partners. Though unrelated to its LMI purchase, the lawsuit sunk Gigamos and drowned its assets, including those that had been related to LMI. Both Gigamos and Lisp Machine, Inc. then ceased to exist. Richard Greenblatt, the man who had helped to start an industry based on the notion that machines might be able to think, had nowhere to go. He was out of a job.

The only consolation for him this time was the fact that Russell Noftsker would soon be in exactly the same position.

❧

Scrambling like mad, many people in the AI industry didn't know which way was up. Like so many lab animals, they were all caught in the same cages and mazes, and they were unable to see their own problems in the failure of other companies. From the outside, it all seemed so simple, as it does to anyone who looks down on a maze or owns the key to the cage. The following few paragraphs are a description of the maze, so to speak, from a newsletter article written soon after LMI had gone bankrupt. It describes the way that AI companies were trying to navigate the maze, from start to finish. The article is representative of everything that was happening in the AI industry beginning in 1986 and continuing on up until today. The reason I insert it at this point is to compress all of the drive, determination, follies, and foibles of the AI companies into one simple morality play.

"The first thing you have to have when you start a new high-tech company is a bunch of people who used to work for a big company—like IBM, DEC, Wang, DG, HP, any of those. These are the kind of places where there is so much money floating around that people are encouraged to leave the lights on in the offices, or are asked to make four or five photocopies of every single document so that they get one that's just perfect.

"The people watching this kind of spending get disillusioned and say to themselves, 'You know, we could do this properly by eliminating all the waste that's floating around here. Look at this wastefulness! Let's start our own company and do it right!'

"So these people quit their corporate jobs, and with a business plan that shows their good intentions, round up some friends and venture capitalists to fund the new company. The first crucial months are devoted to figuring out what to name the company, and how to explain that name in press releases.

"This new company, usually four or five people, sets up shop either in a dilapidated building near the city hotspots, or in a new—but remotely located—industrial park on the outskirts of the city. The company gets going on product development, and then hires a few people to help the founders. These new people invariably are coworkers from the companies that the founders left. They get a piece of stock and a nice title for risking employment (and perhaps unemployment) at such an early stage of the start-up process.

"At just about the one year mark, the first product is released, surrounded by much fanfare and partying. This is followed by having exhibits and small press parties at trade shows. For some strange reason, the company sends one-half to three-quarters of its entire work force to these trade shows. This gives new meaning to the term 'overkill.' The new product introduction is also the first example of the start-up losing sight of its direction. There are about forty employees at this stage of the game, which is just about right for handling the work load. However, sending thirty-two of these people to a trade show to man a 10' x 12' booth is a little absurd.

"Next, the founders want to open numerous sales offices, usually in places they themselves would like to visit on occasion. Three offices are opened first (New York, San Francisco, and Washington D.C.), followed only a few months later by opening four more (Atlanta, Chicago, Dallas, and greater Los Angeles—preferably near the beach or at least the airport).

"The company is now a little over a year old, maybe two years old at the most. Yet forty becomes an inadequate amount of humans to staff such a fast-growing company. Although this number has been reached over many months, the company feels that it must double this figure in a four-to-six-month time span. This also coincides with a third round of venture financing, and the first suggestions from VCs that going public is not a sin. The company hires forty-seven new people to add to the existing forty and tells outsiders that it employs more than ninety. Not one of these new people is entitled to any stock, nor is any offered.

"Now the start-up is a growing big company. And its original headquarters are too small. However, there is nothing available in the vicinity that will do justice to the maintaining of the corporate culture. Never mind that most of the employees don't know each other now. Culture has to be preserved. The founders feel that the only way to do this is to build their own building. This building becomes a monument to their innovation and perseverance. Private offices are assigned. Lights are left on, and multiple copies are made for every single photocopied document.

"Someone, usually a board member, points out that spending is getting way out of hand, especially with free food and drink for employees, as well as from unregulated travel and entertainment expenses. The latter is due to the fact that executives no longer fly coach and stay in Holiday Inns. They now are booked first-class and stay in Ritz-Carlton's when they are available. If not, Westin resorts will do.

"The VCs are getting antsy. Sales aren't where they should be, and the company still isn't regularly profitable, if it is profitable at all. Someone must be made an example of. This is usually a founder who is in marketing or operations, but rarely the president or engineering VP. This designated founder is either replaced by an outsider and forced to take on 'unspecified duties' or 'special projects,' or is asked to leave quietly and watch from the sidelines.

"At this point, an interesting phenomenon occurs. The people who run the company start walking around with guns pointed at their heads, figuratively speaking. Only these people are holding their own guns. The guns have bullets which are individually stamped with such horrific phrases as 'Non-Existent Cost Control,' 'Too-Rapid Expansion,' 'Too Many Sales Offices,' and a variety of other poignant slogans. Yet when somebody from outside the company points out that there are guns pointed at everybody's heads, the reply is 'So what? We're not going to pull the triggers or anything!' This of course is not the point. The point is that the guns are there and that they are loaded. But the execs refuse to pull them away from their heads.

"So what happens? Guns start going off. Layoffs follow within eight months, usually involving a quarter to a third of the work force (that segment that never got to go to trade shows anyway). Advertising is killed. Another top executive is replaced, this time by another founder who must assume his duties. The first corporate defections occur, which the founders take personally. Trade show attendance is canceled for everyone, including the booth. Statements are issued labeling the events as a 'realignment.' NOW, says the press release, the company is really trimmed down, and ready to be the contender it always knew it was destined to be."

This was a sort of *Reader's Digest* abridged version of what was taking place in AI. Unfortunately, it ended up applying to more companies than anyone would have thought possible. That old saying about people who do not know history are condemned to repeat it is not applicable to the AI business. Everyone in AI knew of the mistakes that had been made by others, but they still went out and made them for themselves anyway.

&

At about the time that LMI was choking to death on its own red ink, Phil Cooper went out and bought space on a billboard in the center of Kendall Square. On the billboard, he put a photograph of himself and the employees of Palladian. The sign said "The Garden of Eden, Plymouth Rock, Kitty Hawk, Route 128, AI Alley. Great Beginnings." The Palladian logo was placed just below the picture.

The point was that AI Alley was the site of America's greatest new revelations and discoveries, and that Palladian was at the forefront of those new discoveries. The amazing thing about this particular billboard, besides being a huge manifestation of Phil's ego, was that it was completely frivolous. Even big companies like IBM—which had plenty of cash—never put up public love letters to themselves. It wasn't a prudent way to spend money. But for a company like Palladian, which thought nothing of buying arcade games or spending thousands of dollars a month to feed its hackers, the billboard was just another amusement to be indulged in.

Business for Palladian appeared to be good, with "appeared" being the operative word. Palladian's marketing machine reported robust sales of The Financial Advisor during 1986, its first full year of production. The software had been so successful, the company claimed, that Palladian was already beginning work on a follow-on product. But strangely, the same customer names kept showing up in the company's promotional material and in Cooper's interviews with the press: General Motors, Coopers & Lybrand, Texas Instruments, and Cigna. The list never seemed to grow or change, and Palladian, like most other AI companies, declined to name additional customers in public due to "client confidentiality."

In the summer of 1986, Cooper invested in a new AI start-up called Bachman Information Systems. He persuaded Russell Noftsker to help him raise funds for Bachman, and they were both put on the start-up's board of directors. Cooper was then named chairman of the company (Bachman employees were also featured on the AI Alley billboard). At the same time, Cooper was also named to the chairmanship of a multimedia company called New Media Graphics. As a self-promoter and on-the-go businessman, Cooper was suddenly everywhere—except Palladian. The expert system company was at a critical juncture in its growth and was moving out of start-up mode to become a fully operational large business. At this point, its investors would soon expect to start seeing some return on their investment. Yet, increasingly, Cooper's time and interests were wandering away from Palladian, which was now more than two years old. He'd sold Computer Pictures and made his first million in less time.

In 1987, Phil went out on the road to promote both The Financial Advisor expert system and a new software package for manufacturing called The Operations Advisor. The Operations Advisor was supposed to help manufacturing executives plan new manufacturing strategies. The software could create a model for manufacturing a new product and answer questions such as, "Can I achieve target and lead times with existing plant capacity?" and "What are the real costs associated with expanding production?" It would act as a manufacturing consultant to a company, albeit an expensive one. The cost for a single copy of the software was $136,000.

In talking about The Operations Advisor and its application to business, Cooper couldn't resist a dig at Teknowledge, which had investors that Palladian was trying to impress, like General Motors. "This expert system is nontrivial," he told the press. "It's something quite above choosing the right wine for dinner."

But on the technical side of Palladian's eleventh floor headquarters, a concern over product integrity was growing. The Financial Advisor had actually stalled in the marketplace by the end of 1986, contrary to reports, and Palladian programmers were getting worried. Initial customer feedback to The Financial Advisor was extremely negative. Many of the product's features simply didn't work, and the customers wanted to know why. The reason was simple, although it wasn't divulged to customers: In the rush to get the product to market, Cooper had instructed his developers just to get the damn thing out the door. Features and bugs could always be explained away or fixed later, he said. Meanwhile, Palladian hired more programmers to speed up work on The Operations Advisor, and Cooper went back to his investors for more money. The company now had over 100 employees and was burning through cash—fast. Maybe faster than LMI had.

There was a general feeling in AI Alley during the summer of 1987 that Palladian was in some kind of trouble and that Cooper's reputation was itself in danger. Palladian's hackers felt that their backs were up against the wall, and that Phil was making unreasonable demands on them. The word on the street was that some of the hackers were ready to quit rather than put their own careers at risk by continuing to work on Palladian's crippled software. Plus, many of them felt that Cooper was being dishonest by selling software that didn't work. That alone gave them all a bad feeling about continuing to work for Phil.

But Cooper's image problems weren't just related to Palladian. Cullinet Software, which had purchased his Computer Pictures Corporation, was having financial difficulty. The computer and investment communities were surprised, given Cullinet's strong growth over the years. Allegations leaked out that the company's poor performance was directly related to Computer Pictures, which had not been quite the moneymaker it had been portrayed as when Cooper sold it. Rumors abounded that Cullinet had been duped into buying Computer Pictures at a time when the company was already beginning to lose money. Though Cooper was not held personally accountable, Cullinet ended up shutting down Computer Pictures within 48 months of buying it, and wrote the acquisition off as a business loss. Not long after, Cullinet itself was acquired.

Several hackers at Palladian remember taking a three-day break from their nonstop hacking to go to Disneyworld during this period (one former Palladian executive claims that hackers regularly put in 110-hour work weeks). It was a spur of the moment thing, and the hackers grabbed an early morning flight out of Boston's Logan Airport bound for Orlando. While waiting to board the flight, the first edition of that day's *Boston Globe* was distributed at the airport. The newspaper featured an article on Computer Pictures, and how it had turned out to be a dismal failure despite all the appearances of success. Reading the article, the hackers came to a unanimous conclusion: The same thing was happening at Palladian.

Cooper ignored the insinuated attacks on his reputation and looked at the difficulties the company was having with The Financial Advisor. The problem was that it was a potentially desirable product that just didn't do what it was supposed to do. Its ease-of-use feature was hardly that, and users were confused by the way that the system arrived at its intelligent conclusions. Even Symbolics' CFO, Thomas Farb, privately admitted that he couldn't get the program to do what it was supposed to do, and he had nearly a dozen in-house programmers who were intimately familiar with The Financial Advisor to assist him. While it might appear that all this called for bold action, Cooper opted instead for a short-term fix based on what he knew best: marketing. He decided to change the name of The Financial Advisor, cut its price, and make it run on other computers. The new name was The Management Advisor, the new price was $35,000, and Palladian signed a deal with workstation vendor Apollo Computer to port the software to its machines. The agreement was an obvious break with Symbolics over software exclusivity, but it was a business decision that had to be made.

The Apollo deal involved a significant slight against Palladian's hackers. The same hackers that had seen the *Globe* article about Computer Pictures were approached by Cooper on a Monday morning to discuss the viability of porting The Management Advisor to the Apollo workstation. The hackers weren't sure that it could be done—the software took advantage of specific features on the Symbolics machine that weren't available on the Apollo— and told Phil that it might not be possible. Cooper was persuasive, and besides, he was the boss. He commanded the hackers to put all their efforts into making the software work on the Apollo machine. They had no alternative other than to give it their best shot.

Later that Monday morning, a member of Palladian's marketing staff approached one of the hackers and asked if he had prepared a schedule for the Apollo project. Bewildered, the hacker asked the marketing person how he knew about the plans, since the hackers had just finished talking with Phil about the Apollo project not more than an hour before. "Oh," replied the marketer, "Phil told us in a meeting last Friday that you were going to be doing it."

This set the hackers to seething. Such behind-the-scenes shenanigans caused a number of Palladian's technical staff to leave immediately. Some went to Gold Hill and Symbolics, while others went into consulting positions where they were hired to work on LISP projects for other AI Alley companies.

The Apollo agreement was used to help shore up Palladian's failing fortunes. Like LMI, Palladian was delivering a product that didn't work as promised, and customers weren't paying for it. On the other hand Apollo, like Sun Microsystems, was making a big name for itself in the workstation market, and Palladian hoped that a little of Apollo's cachet would rub off. From that perspective, the split with Symbolics had to be made in the best interest of Palladian. Besides, Symbolics itself was having some tough times, and Phil's buddy Russell Noftsker had been bumped out of day-to-day activities when Brian Sear was hired. Palladian couldn't afford to be loyal to one single hardware company anymore. It needed to expand its marketing options.

As far as Phil was concerned, cosmetic fixes would solve the sales problem for Palladian temporarily. Cosmetic fixes and vaporware—promising products which hadn't been finished yet—were part of the computer industry's modus operandi. Steve Jobs at Apple did it, Mike Manzi at Lotus did it, and Bill Gates at Microsoft was the acknowledged master of it. Unfortunately, the AI business was in a more precarious position than mainstream companies like Apple, Lotus, and Microsoft. Not delivering products as promised was more a matter of life and death for an AI company than it was for Microsoft.

No one outside of Palladian knew the troubles that the company's programmers were having trying to make the products work. Cooper continued to discuss Palladian's Fortune 500 customer base with industry analysts and editors, carefully neglecting to mention the fact that many Palladian users over the past year had been given free or discounted copies of the barely usable Management Advisor. Sales were literally nonexistent. When a published report of Palladian's problems surfaced in an industry newsletter, Phil fired off an angry letter claiming that nothing was wrong at Palladian and that everything was going according to plan. He omitted one salient fact, though: his investors had already pulled the plug on Palladian. The venture capitalists had discovered that his company was becoming a financial sinkhole, and they told him that he would receive no more cash; the well had finally run dry. In addition, they said, Palladian would have to take some drastic cost-cutting measures: it would have to get rid of half of its employees, including developers and programmers. No more dinners, no more toys. All of it had to go. So did Phil if he didn't shape up.

Cooper knew all of this, but he didn't say anything about it to the press or in his letter. To him, it wasn't that big a deal. He knew that investors always got spooked at some point during the first few years of a company's growth. But he'd been through this before, and he knew how to handle his investors.

The one thing that Phil Cooper didn't know as he obscured the truth about Palladian's success was that his investors had already found his replacement.

The man who promised to make artificial intelligence a real business was about to take a fall.

After Palladian's first layoff and first round of defections, there were more LISP machines within the company than there were hackers. This meant that Palladian was the only place on Earth where LISP hackers had as much LISP power as they could possibly use. Sure, some of the perks might have been yanked by the VCs, like the free food and games, but nothing was better than having two or three LISP machines all to yourself. Many of the hackers took to spending their free time just diddling around with the computers, like kids in an extra large sandbox.

On the last weekend of August 1987, the hackers were surprised to see Phil show up at work on a Sunday—Phil never came in on the weekends. Cooper was equally surprised to see them, perhaps because he figured no one would be there on a Sunday. Without saying much to anybody, Phil moved a few things out of his office, claiming that he needed them at home. The next day, at a company meeting, an announcement was made. Phil Cooper had resigned from the company he had founded "to pursue outside interests." This latter phrase is a euphemism for "getting fired."

Palladian's fortunes—or misfortunes—slid quickly from that point forward. The company was so far gone that nothing could help it. It had eaten up more than $18 million worth of venture capital, which was an extraordinary amount of money for a software firm. There was little left to show for it. The Operations Advisor was sold to Carnegie Group for $30,000, but even Carnegie couldn't make the product work. Palladian limped along for more than a year, laying off people and closing offices, and was finally shut down quietly in May 1989. Its last official location was the home of the company's chief financial officer, who spent several months tying up loose ends.

Phil Cooper briefly tried to start up his own venture fund, seeing as how he had shown such expertise at getting otherwise rational people to cough up large sums of money for risky ventures. He then went to work for Harvard's venture capital group, and finally left Cambridge to try his hand on Wall Street.

It is significant to note that Palladians' investors refused to discuss Palladian for this book. Randy Parker, the young programmer hired out of MIT to work at Palladian, looks back at the extraordinarily extravagant Palladian environment and laughs. "You know, it's hard to imagine that Palladian could have spent money faster than it actually did. I don't think there was a way that Palladian could have wasted more money. Unless, of course, it actually poured gas on it and burned it all."

༈

During that turgid summer of 1987, Symbolics and Teknowledge both announced losses, and IntelliCorp and Inference both had layoffs. Carnegie Group fired Larry Geisel and put one of its technical founders, Mark Fox, in his place as CEO. Carnegie wasn't making any headway against its competitors in the market, and Geisel didn't seem to know what to do about it—other than give more interviews to business trade publications. It seemed for all intents and purposes that the AI business was suddenly going to hell in a handbasket.

The essential problem was that new customers weren't being added in sufficient numbers, and the entire industry had hit a plateau. As a result, heads started to roll and people were let go. Media wags called the slowdown the "AI Winter." This concept was taken from the idea of nuclear winter, where all life ceases after a nuclear war and re-emerges only after the environment has cleansed itself and become hospitable once again. This term wasn't quite accurate, since it connoted a complete elimination of artificial intelligence from the business community, which wasn't the case. Perhaps more accurate was John Clippinger's assessment of the situation, "This isn't an AI winter. This is more like Donner Pass." Donner Pass, for those of you interested in American frontier history, was a particularly grizzly episode where Westward-bound pioneers, caught in a winter snowstorm in Nevada without any food, ended up eating each other in one of America's most celebrated acts of cannibalism. The AI business resembled Donner Pass in that only the strongest and most ferocious would survive the storm. In the process, the others would be devoured and never be heard from again.

The Donner Pass scenario is also relevant in that it occurred for one reason: a failure to adequately prepare for the future. AI companies fully expected that three to five years was an adequate amount of time for corporate America to fully embrace AI as a computer tool. The vendors were all moving at full speed by this five-year mark, but they had underestimated the time required for customers to learn about and understand AI. Mainstream corporations needed three years just to get comfortable with the concept of AI, and only after that time did the three-to five-year acceptance and buying cycle begin. AI vendors completely ignored the initial learning curve, lumping it in with the buying curve. If they had separated the two, the AI companies would have realized that they needed to work up to an eight-year buying cycle, not a five-year cycle. Of course, this wouldn't have gone over well with VCs, who would have demanded more results in a shorter period of time anyway. So maybe it's a moot point. But the AI companies were feeling intense pain in 1987. If only they hadn't been so eager and expended their resources so early, more of them might have been able to ride the storm out.

In essence, the AI companies were trying to sell sports cars to twelve-year-olds. A twelve-year-old can appreciate the beauty and power of a sports car, but he can't do anything with it. He doesn't have the requisite skills to be able to operate it. However, something like a mountain bike could be put to good use by a twelve-year-old without any learning curve or training. He can use it immediately. The AI companies treated their customers—the twelve year-old—as if they already had their driver's licenses, when in fact they should have given them something more suitable to their level of experience and competence.

As if this weren't a grim enough scenario, the stock market crash of October 19, 1987 was right around the corner. It drove all of the companies' stock prices down to rock bottom levels and also sent the VC community heading for cover. Any planned public offerings were scotched after Black Tuesday, because they would be too risky in a skittish market. The crash affected the spending habits of many of the mid-sized corporations that the AI vendors were wooing. The vendors wanted these companies to buy AI products in order to give them a foothold in the mainstream and thereby increase their revenues. With the market the way it was, though, those plans weren't going to materialize. That meant even tougher times awaited the AI companies over the next few months, maybe over the next few years.

For the AI pioneers, the party was almost over.

The Black Hole of AI

Symbolics Climbs In and Neural Nets Climb Out

Research into the basics of artificial intelligence had come to a screeching halt during the mass exodus of qualified personnel from the labs. Marvin Minsky's fear that no one would be left to work on the essential problems of how to make machines think had proven to be well-founded (although his company, Thinking Machines, did nothing to help matters). The academic labs looked like ghost towns for most of the 1980s.

Pure research did indeed suffer. Companies were more interested in selling products (for the most part) than in pushing the state of the art in machine intelligence. Businesses are rarely equipped to do pure research, simply because it rarely results in products—a concept with which Xerox was intimately familiar. Therefore, the labs have always been the best source of new ideas and technological breakthroughs. But without the necessary manpower, no one was left at the labs to do research. The best researchers were snapped up by industry as soon as they were old enough to vote.

The interest in AI from the general public, as superficial as it was, caused more and more university students to take AI courses. This new breed started graduating from the universities about the time that AI was entering its very own Donner Pass in late 1987. The result was that the hiring of new bodies slowed down significantly. Whereas their forebears had been universally scooped up by the AI companies, the new graduates had to go out and actually look for jobs. Some of them decided to stay in the labs rather than enter the real world, and as their numbers increased, the labs began to return to full capacity. It would be this generation of students who would ultimately return to investigating the hows and whys of human thought.

It was obvious that the first generation of AI vendors and researchers had not produced truly intelligent systems. Their systems were idiot savants, able to do only one thing well, and nothing else, like the Dipmeter Advisor or Cooker. Minsky, to his credit, was amongst the first to realize that they had all taken the wrong track, although he had been part of the misdirection through much of his career. It was now quite evident that no AI program could even do what a small child could do. To try and drive this point home, Minsky wrote a book called *Society of Mind*, a three-hundred-page book wherein every page was a chapter. It was a compilation of his musings about what actually comprised thought and intelligence. Although disjointed and occasionally tedious, *Society of Mind* nonetheless put forth concerns that had never been addressed by the AI community. Amongst the most intriguing of these was the idea that the brain thinks and creates images without ever having had direct contact with the outside world. It "sees" only because it is connected to eyes, which do the actual "seeing." It has no sense of touch, for it has no skin with which to "feel," yet it knows what things feel like because it is connected to skin. Perhaps the brain by itself wasn't enough to qualify as a "mind," or even a thinking organ.

Outside of the book, Minsky was in demand as a speaker and lecturer. Like his writing, his speeches tended to be rambling and not always obviously coherent to his listeners. But occasionally he would come up with a gem that gave those interested in AI reason to pause: Why, for instance, is it possible to do some things simultaneously, but not others? We can all walk and chew gum, but none of us can run two complete musical scores through our heads at the same time. How does the mind separate these types of tasks, allowing us to do some but preventing us from accomplishing others, no matter how hard we try? Questions like this caused almost everyone in AI to stop and re-evaluate the basic work that had been done in exploring the true nature of intelligence. As Russell Noftsker puts it, "Marvin can throw out one hundred ideas at any given time. Ninety-nine of them may be completely off the wall and not worth a thing, but that remaining one idea will be something so important that no one else could ever have come up with it."

Minsky was in the process of removing himself from his association with the AI Lab, believing that his ideas weren't being taken seriously. In addition, the new generation of AI researchers were more interested in practical AI; that's what had attracted them to the labs in the first place, especially since they thought they could get jobs relating to practical AI. As a result, Minsky's tutelage was not quite as in demand as it had once been. The theoretical aspect that he taught was less interesting to those who had first heard about AI from *Business Week* or "Doonesbury."

Another researcher who was working his way back into academia was Ed Feigenbaum. He, too, was a frequent speaker on the benefits of AI, and he had become a fixture at Texas Instruments' annual Satellite Symposium, a once-yearly program on AI produced by TI and then satellite broadcast to classrooms and conference rooms around the world. Ed also tended to spend more time at business-oriented conferences than Minsky did. At one of these forums, which was sponsored by EF Hutton, Feigenbaum managed to outdo his original "Japan will conquer us" rhetoric. In front of a congregation of some two hundred Wall Street executives, Ed said that the United States needed to speed up work in both voice recognition and natural language and do away with the computer keyboard, which was preventing many people from using computers. If the U.S. research community didn't eliminate the need for the keyboard by 1990, Feigenbaum claimed, then we should all start learning to speak Japanese, since by that time we'd all be using voice-activated systems designed and manufactured in Japan. A tad extreme, of course, but eminently quotable.

Actually, things weren't going so well for the Japanese and The Fifth Generation project. True to form, and counter to Feigenbaum's claims, the young researchers at ICOT were having difficulty developing new forms of software to address the problems of AI. They found themselves relying on American products—namely hardware from Symbolics and software from IntelliCorp and Carnegie Group—to accomplish basic research goals. Meanwhile, member organizations like Mitsubishi and Fujitsu were developing their own in-house expert system and machine translation products, and putting them to use in their various divisions and subsidiaries. All in all, The Fifth Generation Project remained very low-key during the latter half of the decade of greed.

There was one technology that ICOT stumbled upon for which it showed a particular propensity—neural networks. The lowly neural net had disappeared from the North American continent after Marvin Minsky and Seymour Papert had strangled it in their book, *Perceptrons*. The lone commercial exception had been the work done by Nestor, the Rhode Island company started at the outset of the AI revolution by the Brown University professors. There were also isolated pockets of study that remained at CalTech and Johns Hopkins University. On the whole, though, American researchers just weren't that impressed with the technology. They were too busy trying to improve expert systems.

The Japanese were thrilled with neural networks. More specifically, they were greatly impressed with an offshoot of neural nets called "fuzzy logic." Fuzzy logic was a computer technology developed at UC Berkeley by a researcher named Lofti Zadeh during the 1960s. The concept behind fuzzy logic was that the world was not made up of the "yes/no" and "on/off" binary conditions which existed in computers. Rather, there were multiple and even infinite stages which existed between "on" and "off." (Remember that computers respond to the on/off states of binary code, and, as such, their operations result in an exact answer, or no answer at all.) The real world, as Zadeh and most elementary schoolkids would attest, was not made up of such black-and-white answers to all questions and conditions. Instead, the world was mostly gray.

As an example, let's look at temperature. In a normal computer procedure, "hot" might be defined as 95 degrees F. "Cold" could be defined as 40 degrees F. Computers need to have this precisely defined in order to establish a value for hot and cold. But in many situations, hot and cold are relative values. In Arizona, an outside temperature of 95 degrees F is not hot; 110 degrees F is. By the same measure, cold in Arizona begins at approximately 55 degrees F and works its way down. However, in Sweden, 55 degrees F is warm to the point of being almost balmy.

According to Zadeh, such gray—or fuzzy—areas could only be addressed in computers by giving them the capability to make value judgments above and below certain defined points. Fat/thin, dark/light, far/near, big/small, major/minor and other similar values were relative to the environment in which they were found, and computers had to make allowances for that. He called his methodology for doing this fuzzy logic.

American and European researchers ignored Zadeh's technology, finding it to be too far outside the mainstream of computing interest to be worth pursuing. The Japanese, however, loved the technical elegance of fuzzy logic, and believed that it could be applied to all sorts of "intelligent" problems.

The first practical problem they applied it to was the braking system used on the bullet trains of the Sendai subway that scream out of Tokyo into the surrounding suburbs. Using traditional computers, and even expert systems, to control the brakes only allowed for variations in when the brakes were applied. And when the brakes were applied, they were either on or off—there was no in between.

Human train engineers who operated the brakes, however, knew just how much braking to apply to the train's wheels depending on how full the train was and the condition of the train tracks. If the train was full, there was more weight and more momentum on the train; thus, brakes needed to be applied more forcefully. If the train tracks were wet, however, a lighter touch over a longer distance was necessary. A human operator who slammed on the brakes every time they were needed was not a very capable operator. Variables always needed to be considered.

The Japanese installed electronic sensors on the train's undercarriage that measured the weight of individual cars (heavy, average, light) as well as the condition of the track (wet, oily, dry). It then fed that sensor data into a computer which used fuzzy logic to determine just how heavy, how light, how oily, or how dry the variables were. Based on a quick analysis of this information, the computer could then determine the appropriate amount of pressure to apply to the brakes, making for a comfortable stop at each station.

Although the system cost the Japanese government uncounted millions of dollars, it became a showcase for the benefits of fuzzy logic. The potential seemed to be enormous for use in other applications as well. Within just a few years, the Japanese would put the technology to use in simple consumer products such as cameras.

The Sendai subway notwithstanding, The Fifth Generation Project itself was not making the kinds of strides that it and Ed Feigenbaum had once predicted. Europe had attempted to join The Fifth Generation, but was rebuffed by the Japanese government even after the Japanese had said they would be willing to work with other nations in achieving machine intelligence. Donald Michie, for one, was particularly incensed by the Japanese method of wanting to take technology and ideas but not give anything in return. He called it "doing business with a vacuum cleaner."

Instead of working with Japan, the European Community banded together in 1984 to form ESPRIT, the European Strategic Programme for Research into Information Technology. ESPRIT was—and continues to be—an effort on the part of the European Community (EC) to coordinate and focus technology research in Europe so as to strengthen the capability of European companies to compete in world markets. This was done based on the perception that no single technology company could succeed on its own against The Fifth Generation, given the rising costs and risks of investment in new technologies and the increasing globalization of the market.

European companies participated in ESPRIT as members of either the European Community or the European Free Trade Association (EFTA), and they included EC members Belgium, Germany, Denmark, Spain, France, Greece, Italy, Ireland, Luxembourg, Netherlands, Portugal, and the United Kingdom, as well as EFTA members Austria, Switzerland, Liechtenstein, Iceland, Norway, Sweden, and Finland. Headquartered in Brussels, Belgium, the ESPRIT program was initially conceived as a ten-year project to address four major information technology domains: 1) microelectronics—the development of new hardware technologies, 2) information processing systems and software—the creation of new software technologies and applications, 3) computer-integrated manufacturing—application development for industrial use, and 4) business and home systems—moving advanced technology directly into the factory, office, and home.

This structure closely resembled that of America's private consortium, the MCC. Artificial intelligence played an important role in all of ESPRIT's domains, and most of Europe's commercial and academic AI organizations signed up for ESPRIT. Indeed, throughout most of the 1980s, ESPRIT produced the majority of AI work undertaken in Europe. Individual countries also had their own specific AI projects, sort of mini-Fifth Generation Projects, to complement ESPRIT. Notable among them were the Alvey Project in the United Kingdom and Nordforsk in Scandinavia. France had established a national AI consortium, Agence National du Logiciel, but it was intended strictly to promote the business aspects of AI by acting as a sort of international clearinghouse. The French had been interested in practical AI since the late 1970s through Schlumberger's Dipmeter Advisor and then the Elf Aquitaine and Framatone investments in Teknowledge. Several of IBM's early AI offerings, namely its PROLOG language, were developed in its Paris research center.

Europe didn't have quite the hacker rush to escape from the labs that the United States did, although a number of researchers did start their own companies. Michie started Intelligent Terminals, which built the RuleMaster expert system sold in the United States by Radian, and he also founded a research organization called The Turing Institute in Glasgow, Scotland. It was designed to be a meeting point between business and academia, something Marvin Minsky claimed to want to develop in the United States. Unlike Minsky, The Turing Institute actually achieved this goal, and throughout the 1980s it operated as a nonprofit center linking research and commerce.

Many in Europe saw the United States as the best place to commercialize their AI work. Two French nationals, Patrick Perez and Alain Rappaport, had developed an expert system which they called Nexpert. Perez, in particular, had been instrumental in launching the Apple Macintosh in Europe. The two moved to the United States in 1984 and set up a company in Palo Alto called Neuron Data. Although the market was seemingly glutted with plenty of expert system shells, Neuron Data offered the first one to work on the Macintosh. Most of the American AI community responded by laughing at such idiocy. The Mac was still considered a toy machine in the mid-1980s, and no one believed that it would be able to handle the processing demands of any AI application. The IBM PC barely could handle them, for that matter. To make matters even more ridiculous, Nexpert was written in C. How could these guys even think about doing real AI with a C-based Macintosh program? Who would even consider buying Nexpert?

Thousands of companies, as it would turn out. Neuron Data may have looked tiny and unthreatening in the turbulence that swirled around the major players in AI in the aftermath of the October 1987 stock crash. But that turbulence was causing more damage than any of the AI companies realized, and by the time it was over, Neuron Data would be one of the only AI vendors left standing.

This damage was especially evident amongst the AI pioneers. LMI was gone, which left Symbolics, Teknowledge, Carnegie Group, IntelliCorp, and Inference as the original torch bearers. Teknowledge's long-time difficulty in figuring out how to sell its products finally caught up with it in late 1987. Although the company had been issued the first ever patents for an expert system by the U.S. Patent office, this did not translate into more sales. M.1 had been forced out of the market by cheaper and more efficient PC tools, including a $99 program called VP Expert. This expert system shell, which cost $12,401 less than the original version of M.1, was sold by Paperback Software, a company started by Adam Osborne, who had also founded one of the world's first portable computer companies. His new company was in the business of selling cheap knockoffs of popular software, including spreadsheets and expert systems. Without even trying, Paperback Software sold ten thousand copies of VP Expert through magazine ads and a few retail outlets.

Executives at Teknowledge had reason to believe that VP Expert was built using code from M.1. They examined the inner workings of VP Expert—how it made decisions and how it stored knowledge—and saw enough similarity between the two products to file a lawsuit against Osborne and

Paperback Software. At the same time, Lotus filed a lawsuit against Paperback for infringing on the "look and feel" of Lotus's 1-2-3 spreadsheet program. Faced with both lawsuits, Paperback eventually was forced to shut down.

VP Expert had already adversely affected Teknowledge's sales. Even though M.1 was reduced in price to $1500, it still was less attractive than other offerings on the market, including Gold Hill's expert system, GoldWorks. Similarly, Teknowledge's S.1 was found to be wanting when compared to programs like ART, KEE, and Knowledge Craft, all of which were now available on regular workstations. It didn't have the power that sophisticated users currently expected from expert system shells.

Teknowledge went to work on creating a whole new set of expert system tools which it called Copernicus. Copernicus would incorporate all the features of M.1 and S.1, but this time they would be compatible with each other. The company had had success in selling lots of units of S.1 and M.1, but its customers wanted a more complete solution that wouldn't involve having to switch back and forth between M.1 and S.1, which were two very different products.

Teknowledge's revenues in fiscal 1987 were $20 million, an impressive amount of money for a software firm, but it had still lost $2 million for the year. Part of that loss was a $1.1 million equipment write-off—of LISP machines. Teknowledge no longer wanted to have anything to do with the LISP vendors or LISP technology. As Lee Hecht said in the company's 1987 annual report, "Teknowledge elected to distance itself from the 'Buck Rogers' aspects of artificial intelligence in favor of concentrating on practical applications of today's technology. We are not a 'me-too' company, and this was most evident during the year as we emerged as the only software products company with a real systems solution—integrated mainstream products, training and application support—for those customers wanting to acquire and apply expert systems technology."

Ummm, not quite. Those customers were primarily limited to Teknowledge's investors: Elf Aquitaine, FMC, Framatone, General Motors, Procter & Gamble, and NYNEX. These companies accounted for 39 percent of the company's total revenues.

What wasn't evident in the annual report was that Teknowledge was beginning to lose disenchanted employees. Jerrold Kaplan, the company's chief development officer and one of the founders, went to Lotus to become that company's principal technologist. Arthur Schwartz, the company salesman forced to demonstrate The Wine Advisor, went to Aion as VP of sales. Perhaps most disconcerting, as far as General Motors (Teknowledge's best customer) was concerned, was the departure of Barry Plotkin, the company's executive vice president and manager of knowledge engineering services. Plotkin had worked closely with GM on developing expert system strategies for the automaker, and he had suddenly left Teknowledge to start his own expert system company. GM was concerned that Plotkin might be trying to sell certain technologies that had been developed under contract to GM, and thus belonged to GM. It was also concerned that Plotkin's departure from Teknowledge would foul up some of the projects that were still in progress.

GM had grown somewhat tired of Teknowledge. The expert system company had for years tried to dictate the course of the relationship between the two companies, claiming that it knew best how to develop expert systems. GM knew what it wanted, but Teknowledge continually tried to push its own agenda. Teknowledge and its executives always acted like an exasperated mother trying to keep its child in line, only this child was the world's largest company and the mother was a tiny little software organization.

Over the course of their relationship, GM's Tech Center in Warren, Michigan, developed as much expertise in AI as that possessed by Teknowledge's employees. Presumably, it was GM that forced Teknowledge to start programming its expert systems in C so that they would be compatible with GM's huge installed base of computers. GM's knowledge engineers and AI managers also wearied of fighting with Teknowledge every time a project deadline was missed, or every time Teknowledge came back to GM and asked for more money to finish a project. GM was paying for the development of these systems, yet it appeared as if it was doing as much of the work as Teknowledge was. As far as GM was concerned, it had reached the point that it was giving more to Teknowledge than it was getting in return.

Instead of getting all worked up over Teknowledge and Plotkin and the attendant aggravation, GM simply decided to back off and cool its relationship with the company. It scaled back its plans for future contracts with Teknowledge and began to distance itself from the wayward AI company.

This happened none too soon. Teknowledge had only had one profitable year in its entire history, eking out just over $600,000 on sales of $14 million in 1986. But with M.1 and S.1 having outlived their usefulness and Copernicus still in development, the company had returned to its losing ways in 1987. As a stopgap measure, it brought in a former FMC executive, Peter Weber, to take over the president and CEO duties, limiting Hecht to the company chairmanship. In addition to getting rid of all of its LISP machines, Teknowledge also got rid of sixty employees. Then it hired an outside management firm to start looking for another corporate partner. Only this partner would not be a "strategic partner" like GM or Procter & Gamble. This partner would be someone interested in merging with Teknowledge.

Life was similarly unpleasant over at IntelliCorp. The company had been the only AI pioneer to remain committed to LISP, and no amount of coaxing would change its mind. With the slowdown in LISP machine sales, IntelliCorp found its own growth stunted. It, like Teknowledge, had broken the $20 million mark in sales during 1987, but had posted losses of $4 million. Tom Kehler, the former Texas Instruments engineer who had overseen the development of KEE, had risen through the ranks to become the company's chairman and CEO. Ongoing losses through 1986 and 1987 prompted the board to put Kehler back in touch with day-to-day operations in December 1987, making him president and CEO but removing him from the chairman's job. Then, in the single most bizarre executive change in the entire history of AI, the board brought Edward Feigenbaum back into IntelliCorp as chairman.

Feigenbaum's high profile had kept him in the news, but this hardly meant that he had gained any management experience in that time. The only possible reason for making him chairman was that the board couldn't find anybody else and that Ed was available. The other AI companies, including those that were in pretty sad shape themselves, laughed themselves silly over this appointment. IntelliCorp had confirmed that it was definitely a rudderless ship if it was going back to the labs for executives at a time when most of the lab founders were being replaced by real business people.

Russell Noftsker was one of those founders that was about to be replaced. Symbolics' sales in 1987 had shrunk from 1986's high of $114 million to $103 million, and it had gone from posting a profit of $10 million to posting a loss of $25 million. Operational costs were not only out of control, they were potentially lethal.

A substantial part of the new cost overruns was the purchase of a larger manufacturing facility in California, which Noftsker had approved. Even though the company was trying to figure out how to make viable use of its software products, the hardware division wanted more space and they got it. Thus, the East Coast administration, engineering, and sales staff continued to cram itself back into 11 Cambridge Center while the manufacturing group got bigger and better facilities.

Another reason for increasing space in California was that Symbolics had found an intriguing new market for its machines: Hollywood. The features of LISP machines were designed from the very beginning to provide the best development tools for high-level programming, which also included the creation of realistic graphics, animation, and 3-D simulation. While these were used primarily by scientists at places like NASA to perform lifelike renderings of satellite movements or planetary terrains, Hollywood special effects companies saw a potential use for LISP machines in creating unusual graphics effects for movies and television. The power and flexibility of LISP machines made creating such effects easier and less time-consuming than doing them on other computers.

As soon as it caught on to the entertainment industry's interest, Symbolics signed a deal with Pixar, a company already specializing in selling graphics systems to Hollywood. Pixar was the brainchild of George Lucas, the producer of the Star Wars and Indiana Jones movies. These films, and their sequels, made extensive use of graphic special effects, many of which Lucas's production company had developed especially for each movie. Sensing a market opportunity, Lucas started selling the software for these special effects through Pixar. Eventually, Pixar spun off from Lucas and his movie ventures to become an independent company. It was becoming a major player in Hollywood software circles by 1987, and it was only natural that Symbolics and Pixar should team up. By working together, the two companies could offer complete systems to both the movie business and the DOD's government labs.

Brian Sear liked the idea of expanding the California operation. His home was in California, and he pushed the board to move all of Symbolics out to Chatsworth to concentrate on hardware manufacturing. Noftsker was completely opposed to the idea. Symbolics had just finished the design of its own LISP chip, which would compete with the LISP MegaChip from Texas Instruments, and it was planning to put the chip in general-purpose workstations so that they could run Symbolics software. This would be done by making the chip part of an "add-in" board that would be inserted into computers such as the IBM PC and the Sun Microsystems' line of workstations. For Symbolics, the development and marketing of the chip would be the first step in creating a future customer base for Symbolics' software tools.

The company was also doing research into building its own RISC ship. RISC, which stands for "reduced instruction set computing" was a technology that IBM and Hewlett Packard had promoted throughout the early 1980s. RISC allowed computers to work faster by compressing many of the basic hardware and software components into one microprocessor. In that regard, it was like the LISP chip, but it had more widespread applications for traditional computing. Noftsker felt that having both the LISP chip, which the company called Ivory, and a RISC chip would give Symbolics leverage from which it could sell its software. If companies bought Symbolics' chips, the reasoning went, then they would be inclined to buy its software to run on those chips.

Sear thought this was nonsense. The company needed to take advantage of its existing products and stop playing around with new and untested areas such as building its own microprocessors. He and Noftsker could not come to an agreement over the matter, and the two men stopped talking to each other. In January 1988, they both took their cases to the board of directors. Sear wanted to shut down the East Coast operations, including the RISC chip R&D, and move everything to California. Russell wanted to continue funding the RISC chip, leave the existing facilities intact, and move more people out of manufacturing and into R&D.

At a board meeting that took on surrealistic qualities, the board couldn't decide which man it wanted to back. According to Noftsker, "We got all of the board members together, including one board member who had contracted brain cancer and was completely unable to speak. I asked the board to return control of the company to me and get rid of Brian. If they wouldn't do that, they should at least bring someone else in to take over the operations because Brian and I could not come to terms. Their brilliant reply was to tell Brian and I to go kiss and make up, and to work it all out. I told them that that wasn't going to work, but that I would do the best I could."

The company had another round of layoffs, and Noftsker could see no way to compromise with Sear. "After only a month, I went back to the board in February. I told them that it wasn't working, and that they should reconsider giving me control. Brian also made his case to them again, but they still couldn't make up their minds."

The board decided not to choose between Noftsker and Sear. Instead, it fired both men right then and there. No tears, no long goodbyes, no other positions within the company. Without warning, Russell Noftsker had just been kicked out of Symbolics.

Sear was the first to clear out, and the company announced his departure immediately. Shocked and sullen, Noftsker stayed as chairman for a couple of weeks, and then the board paid him $250,000 to go away and not come back. In his and Sear's place, a four-man "office of the president" was formed. The fact that the board called on four people to fill the president's position all at once was indicative of its inability to make a decision. The four who were selected included Ronald Derry, the VP of manufacturing; Donald Sundue, John Kulp and Thomas Farb. Kulp had left the company once already, but was brought back in by those board members who had been sympathetic with him during his attempt to overthrow Russell several years earlier. Farb, who at one time had served as the chief financial officer, had also left the company the year before. Farb and Symbolics' general counsel, Andrew Egendorf, had started a venture capital group called The AI Fund, which had intended to invest in AI start-ups using money from Symbolics' founders. With the slowdown in AI, though, there wasn't much interest in new AI start-ups. Farb came back to try and help Symbolics straighten out its financial and operational mess.

The four-man presidency was doomed even before it got started. The executives could not come to an agreement on what their respective duties were, and floundered helplessly about trying to find a common operational ground. Frustrated again, the board removed Farb, Kulp, and Sundue within a few weeks and kept Ronald Derry as the sole president. Derry was chosen almost by default; he was the only one with any real operations experience inside the company. As far as the board was concerned, he would be a good caretaker president until they found someone else.

A palpable malaise fell over Symbolics. The long months of executive infighting had not done much for the company's morale. Neither had the plans to move to the West Coast or the plans to kill the hardware group. With Russell gone, there was no focal point on which to base the company's identity. For all his managerial faults and run-ins with the board, he was still the man who had conceived of Symbolics and made it a reality. Noftsker's concept of a commercial LISP machine was one of the critical starting points of artificial intelligence, and he more than any other AI company founder deserved credit for bringing AI technology out of the dark recesses of the research lab. Richard Greenblatt may have invented the LISP machine, but Russell Noftsker was the one who packaged and promoted it.

Symbolics' problems were compounded even further during February when Texas Instruments announced a new product. Called the microExplorer, the computer was an Apple Macintosh II with a LISP MegaChip stuck into it. The Macintosh had become a powerful machine— with the release of the Mac II—in a relatively short period of time. Apple had been forced to create a better machine by CEO John Sculley's determination to compete with IBM-style personal computers. Thus, the Mac was no longer a joke in the computer industry, and it quickly started winning converts in the high-tech community who saw it as a low-end workstation. TI's decision to market the Apple computer with a LISP chip made the Macintosh II a mini-LISP machine. In a strange twist of technological fate, the Macintosh II was designed with a NuBus architecture—the same architecture that Texas Instruments, Western Digital, and LMI had all used for their computer workstations. Priced at $15,000, the microExplorer was the cheapest LISP machine offered by any AI company. It also had the added benefit of being able to run Macintosh software.

The announcement was quite a coup. Unfortunately, it was supposed to have been Symbolics' coup. The Ivory chip had long been slated to be put into general-purpose computers, but had encountered the usual delays in engineering and manufacturing. Symbolics was finally beaten to the punch by Texas Instruments. Coupled with the revolving door in the executive suite, this made things in Cambridge about as bad as they had ever been. They would, however, get much, much worse.

The board was desperate to bring in somebody who could turn around Symbolics' flagging fortunes. One of the board members recommended a young executive who had turned around a local software company called Management Decision Systems. MDS was a well-known vendor of high-end decision support tools, and it had gone through violent business shifts such as those Symbolics was now experiencing. The MDS executive responsible for salvaging it, Jay Wurts, was now a management consultant and was open to discussing the possibility of taking on another turnaround situation.

Hurriedly, the board made Wurts an offer and brought him into the company in May 1988 as chairman and CEO. The darkest days of Symbolics were now officially underway.

Wurts decided that operating out of Cambridge was too expensive. He leased space in nearby Burlington, Massachusetts and proceeded to move the company out there. He negotiated a deal to sell the 11 Cambridge Center building to another software group, and then Symbolics left AI Alley forever. Perhaps tellingly, the Palladian billboard that proclaimed great things in AI alley had already been torn down.

Next, Wurts cut the Symbolics work force by 30 percent, laying off a total of 225 people. Of the 400 that were left, Wurts instructed 100 of them to work full-time on the Ivory chip and get it out to market by August, which was the date of the next AAAI conference. Wurts also promised to focus the company's efforts on selling its Genera software tools, along with several other software packages that would help customers build expert systems and document management applications.

The board of directors was overjoyed. Wurts was saying and doing all the right things, something they could never get Russell to do. In his 1988 annual report statement, Wurts said, "When I accepted the Board's offer to direct Symbolics' turnaround, I took on a challenge that many people in the industry felt would be exceptionally difficult, if not impossible. I accepted this challenge because I knew that, despite its management and financial problems, Symbolics had extraordinary assets: significant cash reserves, proven technology, a large customer base, and unmatched technical expertise." He was, at this stage of the game, correct on all counts. Although revenues for the 1988 fiscal year would only be $81 million, and losses would be $46 million, Wurts was slashing costs like a piranha and was slowing down the bloody red ink that was marring Symbolics' income statement. It even looked like the company might soon return to profitability if Jay kept to the plan.

But Wurts didn't keep to the plan. Look back at his opening sentence from the annual report and note that Wurts uses the words "to direct." He wanted to direct, all right, in the most popular sense of the term.

Jay Wurts and Symbolics were about get out of artificial intelligence and go to Hollywood.

⤚

Former employees of LMI, Symbolics, Palladian, and other AI companies looked around for new ventures. It was hard to consider getting a job in a "regular" company after the excitement and wild abandon of being in an AI company. There were few alternatives other than to join AI groups at large companies, start businesses, or go back to the real world. Many of them did indeed go back to places like DEC and Data General, companies they had left in order to join the AI start-ups.

Only one area of the computer business held nearly as much potential for the ground floor thrills and challenges that had been part of the expert system and LISP machine companies: neural networks.

Like some kind of technological vampire, neural networks had arisen from the grave that was so conveniently dug for them by Marvin Minsky and Seymour Papert. Neural nets, as you might recall, were attempts to mimic the structure of the human brain by attaching processors together in a three-dimensional pattern that resembled the connections between neurons and synapses in the brain. The resurgence began in 1982, when a biophysicist named John Hopfield presented a paper to the National Academy of Sciences. Hopfield, a well-respected professor of biology and chemistry at CalTech who also worked under contract to AT&T's Bell Labs, wrote that neural networks could be made to resemble biological neurons by applying various energy states to them. The links and pathways between the individual neurons on a computer-based neural net could be governed by setting them to respond to specific energy states, ranging from low or nonexistent to high. In this way, the processors in a neural network could work on different pieces of a task simultaneously by assigning different energy values to each piece. (This is a simplistic, and by no means complete, description of Hopfield's paper. The original paper is technical beyond the comprehension of mortal man, this author included, and must be seen to be believed. Trust me on this. If, however, phrases such as "For N = 100, a pair of random memories should be separated by 50 +/- 5 Hamming units" or "This case is isomorphic with an Ising model" are of extreme interest to you, then I suggest you dig up a copy of Hopfield's "Neural Networks and Physical Systems with Emergent Collective Computational Capabilities" from the National Academy of Sciences.)

In essence, what Hopfield was describing was a computer chip—or more specifically, a neurocomputer—that could be made to work like a neuron; not exactly like a neuron from a biological perspective, but similar from a physical perspective. This was different from the original 1960s model of neural networks that were activated in an "all-or-nothing" fashion. Back then, a computer neuron reached a single point, and then it activated. Hopfield's model demonstrated that neural nets could be set to different levels before activating, thereby making them more adaptable. Using Hopfield's model, computers could be made to work on potentially large problems by dividing those problems up into small components that would be worked on simultaneously. The energy states would determine how the individual neurons behaved, which addressed Minsky's main complaint that neurons were unable to differentiate between similar types of data (based on the "all-or-nothing" argument). By adding multiple layers of neural networks, extremely complex problems could be tackled, which voided another Minsky criticism that said that neural nets were too simple to handle any large problems, and that they were no better than regular computers.

To demonstrate the fallacy of Minsky's argument, which Marvin continued to use even after Hopfield's paper was published, the neural net researchers cited the example of the traveling salesman. A salesman must travel to 10 different cities. What is the shortest route he can take to visit all 10 cities one after another? And, from which city should he start? For instance, should the salesman go from Boston to New York and down to Atlanta and then over to Chicago, or should he go straight to Chicago from Boston and then come back to New York before heading to Atlanta?

Most people would assume that this can be done simply by arranging all 10 cities in every possible combination, calculating the distances between each city in every combination, and then picking the answer with the least number of miles. What most people would not assume is that there are 181,400 possible routes involved in connecting ten cities. By adding twenty destinations to the problem, for a total of only thirty cities, the number of possible route combinations becomes 1,000,000,000,000,000,000,000,000,000,000. This number is fairly large by some standards, and downright incomprehensible by most others.

A traditional computer, which employs serial processing, would attack this problem one step and one possibility at a time. That's what serial processing does; works on one piece at a time, reaches a conclusion, and goes on to the next piece. With a personal computer, this process of calculating all the possible combinations could take the better part of a day or maybe a couple of days. People don't have that kind of time to wait for an answer.

But if a neural net with one hundred processors was put to the test, the problem could be solved in substantially less time. According to AT&T, it would take less than one second. This could be done by arranging the processors like a grid on a mileage finder on a road map. Mileage finders are those clever little grids and charts that you find at the back of a Rand McNally road atlas that list the distances between major cities. They're arranged in rows and columns, with all the cities listed down the left side and then across the bottom. By picking your starting point and then running your finger over to your destination, you arrive at the mileage between those two points. If you're going from Boston to New York, you find Boston on the left column, and then go across to where the Boston line intersects the New York line, which rises up from the bottom. The point where the two intersect gives you your mileage.

By creating a 10 x 10 grid of processor nodes that resembled the mileage finder, a neural net could be assigned to every intersecting space between the ten traveling-salesman cities. With each processor determining the mileage values simultaneously, and comparing their findings to the processor next to, above, and below them, the entire system would be able to select the best route in relatively no time at all. Many hands make light work, and all that.

With such a large number of possibilities, the neural network might come up with several selections which were all quite good, but it might not pick the single best route. This was due to the importance of time over exactness. Say you need to make a critical decision in the next five minutes, such as how much money to bet on a horse race. In that situation, you would take the best answer a computer had to offer rather than wait an hour for the perfect answer when the race was already over and the horses were back in the stable. Such is the logic of using neural nets; getting good answers fast and using them immediately instead of waiting until it's too late to get the right answer.

These time-critical situations exist throughout business, government, and the military. Making decisions about minute-to-minute changes in the stock market, correcting the trajectory of a rocket, or analyzing the signals from a radar are all processes that must be done as soon as possible with the best information possible. People in these situations can't wait until tomorrow afternoon to get a better answer.

When Hopfield's paper was distributed, all those neural net researchers who had been hiding in the closet began to emerge. Companies like IBM, TRW, and AT&T—Hopfield's employer—started building computer prototypes based on Hopfield's model. TRW had an exceptionally well-funded group that began building neurocomputers for DARPA. In 1986, it built a neurocomputer called the Mark III, which sold for $70,000—almost as much as an early LISP machine.

The man who led TRW's neural net research was Robert Hecht-Nielsen. Educated at Arizona State University, Hecht-Nielsen was one of the few people who had pursued neural net research during the death valley days of the 1970s. After completing the Mark III, he believed that neural nets could be sold to the mass market by adding them to PCs. A neural net add-in board would make a PC a neurocomputer in the same way that Texas Instruments had added its LISP MegaChip to the Macintosh II to make it a LISP machine.

Hecht-Nielsen is not your average nerd. Standing well over six feet, he is beefy like a construction worker or a redneck cowboy. His short-sleeved white shirts and ties give his identity away, however. He is a man who can, if necessary, outnerd the best of them from MIT or Stanford. But he is driven in the way that most technical people are not, which led him to create his own company, Hecht-Nielsen Neurocomputers, in October 1986. Known simply as HNC, the company started working on a plan to turn PCs into neurocomputers. It raised money quickly, and put some of the best and brightest from the traditional AI community to work on neural nets. Thomas Farb, the former CFO of Symbolics, was put on the company's board of directors. David Shlager, who had served as vice president of sales at Lucid after working at Symbolics, joined the HNC as a vice president. Hecht-Nielsen surrounded himself with people who knew the pitfalls of marketing a new technology because they had encountered them before.

Almost overnight, neural net companies started creeping out of the woodwork. Trade magazines ran brief articles on the technology, touting it as the next big thing. *Business Week*, in its usual overly optimistic way, ran a neural net article in June 1986 that described "Computers That Come Awfully Close to Thinking" and another one six months later that announced "They're Here: Computers That Think." Obviously, the magazine hadn't learned any lessons from the "Artificial Intelligence: It's Here" debacle of 1984—its editors even recycled the headline.

Expert system researchers largely ignored the resurgence of neural nets. The AI community dismissed neural networks, claiming that they were a means for creating thinking machines, but could not actually think themselves (thinking being a relative term). Sure, a neural net could solve large problems quickly, but it didn't reason or make decisions. Not true, countered the neural net researchers. Identifying patterns or recognizing trends and similarities or interpreting signals was just as much a sign of intelligence as performing logic functions.

Most people not intimately involved with the development or marketing of AI technologies tended to regard neural nets as an intelligent technology, and rightfully so. In its own way, it attempted to recreate human-based intelligence, albeit in a different way than expert systems did. People like Minsky tried to dissuade this association, claiming that neural nets did not work in the same way as the brain. As was often the case, Marvin missed the point in his eagerness to discount something he didn't agree with. The point was not that neural networks were an actual physical model of the brain. The point was rather that they handled complex problems in the way that the brain might be expected to. The debate raged on, primarily in the academic labs of MIT and Stanford, where expert systems and reasoning and logic were the key to AI, and at CalTech and Johns Hopkins, where neural nets were the next step towards creating thinking machines.

Either way, the marketplace didn't care. Potential customers of the technologies wanted something tangible to help them with their business problems, and for the most part, they weren't getting them yet. Successful expert system applications were few and far between, and expert system companies themselves were disappearing as fast as neural net companies were being formed. For every Palladian, there was a NeuralWare. For every LMI, there was a Synaptics.

Neural nets entered the technology spotlight just as expert system and LISP machine companies were falling out of favor with everybody from Wall Street to the press. The timing was perfect, but neural nets were as unproven in 1988 as expert systems had been in 1981. The question still remained: Would any of this stuff ever be used by a huge part of the marketplace?

The answer would end up being an unequivocal "yes," but a few more events had to transpire first, and they were improbably close at hand: Gold Hill Computers, run by the rowdies from the wrong side of the AI Alley track, would briefly be recognized as the most important company in AI. Roger Schank, the man who wanted to run an AI company and an AI lab, would be kicked out of both of them. And Teknowledge, the company with all the major corporate support, would bite the dust.

Chapter 30

Shakeout and Burnout

You Can Tell Who the Pioneers Are Because They're Laying Face Down in the Dirt with Arrows in Their Backs

The belief that the captain goes down with the ship does not apply to the high-technology industry. If at all possible, the captain will avail himself of a gilded lifeboat with just enough room for a few select friends and associates, and then watch his very own *Titanic* get sucked down into the blackness with most of the employees on board.

A few captains would probably be willing to go down with their ships, but they are usually tossed overboard before that happens. Russell Noftsker would have ridden it all the way down; Richard Greenblatt actually did; and the founders of Gold Hill were about to. They are the exceptions to the rule.

Lee Hecht was the rule. Teknowledge was a sinking ship with second-rate and outdated products and no immediate prospects on the horizon. Its customers had built some successful expert systems, like Charley, but the vast majority of those customers were currently looking elsewhere to have their AI needs met.

To lighten Teknowledge's load, Hecht started jettisoning cargo. The first entity to go was the company's Federal Systems Division, a group that had worked exclusively on government and DARPA contracts, including various aspects of the Strategic Computing Initiative like the Pilot's Associate. It was sold off for $1.5 million to a fledgling defense contractor, ISX Systems. This move only slowed the sinking; it didn't stop it. Something more drastic had to be done. Three senior executives were fired, including a founder. Then, for some strange reason, Hecht put the developer of M.1, Steve Hardy, in charge of mergers and acquisitions for Teknowledge. But Hardy was a software developer, not a mergers and acquisitions expert. Besides, who could Teknowledge possibly afford to buy? Hysteria had become the operative word at Teknowledge.

Teknowledge signed agreements with AICorp and Neuron Data to help those companies sell their products—since its own were no longer of any value—and to provide training and consulting to organizations that bought those products. In effect, Teknowledge was returning to its roots, selling basic services and assisting companies in developing expert systems. After all, it had started life five years earlier as "the largest knowledge engineering center in the world."

But living off of the handouts from other AI companies would not sustain a $20 million software company. During the summer of 1988, while trying to remember how to be a service provider, Teknowledge lost $2 million on service operations alone. By the end of fiscal 1988, sales had dropped to $14 million, and losses were nearly $10 million. Teknowledge was losing almost as much as it was making. Hmmmm. Maybe this service thing wasn't such a good idea after all.

One thing that Teknowledge did have was nearly $20 million in cash reserves, a phenomenal amount for a company that was in the process of losing money as fast as it possibly could. It also had one other attractive asset—it was a publicly traded company with a listing on the NASDAQ market. Both of these features could be attractive to another company that might want quick access to the public market as well as the use of some extra cash to service its own debt.

Teknowledge had already put out feelers into the AI market to see if any other vendors might be interested in some type of merger. A prospective marriage partner would have stable operations and an interest in Teknowledge's AI expertise, as well as a desire to put its own privately held stock on the public market. Carnegie Group seemed to be just such a company, and brief talks were held between the two companies about a possible union. Carnegie Group's business was targeted to building expert systems for industrial clients, which was similar to Teknowledge's business. The two companies had a great deal of experience in building custom applications-to-order for clients, and most of their clients were Fortune 500 corporations. They both had courted and won financial support from those same large corporations, so they each knew the advantages and disadvantages of dealing with rich, powerful, and oftentimes overly bureaucratic companies. Carnegie also had a new CEO, Dennis Yablonsky, who was determined that Carnegie not get sucked under by the rising anti-AI backlash. Having come from a successful mainstream software company, Cincom, Yablonsky was an A-Teamer who wanted Carnegie to define its market specifically and then pursue clients aggressively. He didn't want to run a generic AI company.

Rumors of the merger floated around the AI industry towards the end of 1988, and then the announcement was made: Teknowledge would merge with American Cimflex, a company that sold computer systems for manufacturing. Obviously, this caught everyone by surprise, including many Teknowledge employees. Not only was Carnegie left high and dry, but American Cimflex was one of the worst run companies in the United States. It was in even worse shape than Teknowledge.

❧

Amid all the turmoil, one company was having the time of its life. Gold Hill Computers had moved out of its Armenian dance hall and had taken over a new office building closer to Kendall Square. It was finally out of the projects and into the high-rent district.

Gold Hill's strategy of selling PC software had paid off handsomely for the company. The relatively low cost of its Golden Common LISP programming language and GoldWorks expert system had attracted a loyal following from universities and small companies that wanted to use AI but did not have Symbolics-size budgets. For a few hundred or a few thousand dollars, users could explore the pleasures of AI to their heart's content and not have to justify the cost to their bosses. However, like the vast majority of AI companies, Gold Hill derived most of its revenue from companies that were building applications for DARPA. In Gold Hill's case, this accounted for almost 40 percent of sales. As company founder Stan Curtis succinctly put it, "We were all addicted to DARPA cash."

Gold Hill was an unlikely success story. Two of its three founders, Curtis and Jerry Barber, had rotated in and out of the president's job in its first two years; its business plan was based on selling AI on personal computers, and it had absolutely no corporate structure in place. From day to day, the organization appeared to change depending on who appeared to be in charge of which project. Yet, it all worked. Gold Hill developed products that established the personal computer as a viable machine for building AI applications.

Unlike some of the culturally retarded nerds at other AI companies, the people at Gold Hill were creative individuals who took their fun seriously. All of the founders and many of the management staff were musicians who played together frequently, and interviews with prospective employees were often concluded with the question "Do you play any instruments?" Although not a condition of employment, adding a musician to the roster was always seen as a plus for the company.

Gold Hill gatherings were hardly formal affairs. With stocked refrigerators and free beer on the weekends, it would have been hard to impose rigid controls on any of the employees, whether they were hackers or salespeople. Most often, these diversions were led by the company's marketing vice president, Gene Wang, a Harvard business school student who had signed on as Gold Hill's first full-time employee. Wang had previously worked with Stan Curtis at one of New England's largest high-tech companies, Wang Computers, a hardware company started by An Wang. Despite the coincidence of the names, Gene was no relation to that company's founder. In fact, the outspoken Gene Wang, who insisted that his last name be pronounced in the traditional Chinese way—"wong"—had once confronted his former employer as to why the older man allowed his name to be Anglicized to "wang." An Wang explained that if he spent all his time trying to correct the mispronunciation of his name, he would never have time to attend to business. The entire episode was written up in a *Business Week* profile of An Wang, although it never identified Gene by name.

Most people, including his Gold Hill employees, got around the "wang" and "wong" confusion by simply referring to him as Geno, which was fine by him. Actually, anything out of the ordinary was fine by him. Geno reveled in his role as the upstart of the upstarts. He was not above jumping on tables during business meetings or throwing articles of clothing at people who enraged him. He would alternately cry or laugh hysterically at company functions. His enthusiasm for his job was such that when he hired ex-Symbolics sales VP Robert Lamkin to head up Gold Hill's sales force, he called analysts at home at three in the morning to tell them the good news. He then proceeded to entertain Lamkin on his first day at work with a musical revue, complete with Gold Hill salespeople dancing and lip-synching the words.

An accomplished flutist, Geno led the company in its various songfests, many of which he had no compunction about foisting on attendees at AI conferences. Lyrics such as Dire Straits' "I Want My MTV" became "I Want LISP on My PC" (it does fit); other popular songs received the same treatment. Geno had no pride; he would sing these songs at parties to which his competitors were invited, dancing around in a black suit or a costume and playing air guitar.

But there was also something of the fanatic in Geno. People who continually disagreed with him were blacklisted. Complete loyalty to him and the company was demanded. Bill Hoffman, who had left his job as Symbolics' marketing manager to run the ragtag marketing group at Gold Hill, remembers that Geno would scream and berate employees who quit, and then he would cry over their departure. Nonetheless, for all his overtly uncorporate behavior, Geno embodied the Gold Hill culture, more so than even the three founders.

After living life in this relatively carefree way for several years, Gold Hill's investors decided that the company was due for some real management. It needed somebody credible with previous business experience. Thus, the company's first, and perhaps only, attempt at corporate credibility was the hiring of Carl Wolf as CEO in 1985. Wolf was an extremely well-polished and knowledgeable executive who put people like Lee Hecht and Larry Geisel to shame. He was personable and well-spoken, and thought of himself as being somewhat debonaire, an image that he managed to convey to most people outside of Gold Hill. Wolf had been president of a small consulting firm, Interactive Data Corporation, but had earned his management stripes at Chase Manhattan Bank and at Xerox. His primary strength was his ability to understand, discuss, and market advanced technology. However, like the rest of Gold Hill, Wolf was oftentimes more interested in enjoying himself than in running a growing enterprise.

Bit by bit, the company established itself as a distinctive vendor of AI software. As 1988 was rolling around, Gold Hill was sitting in the AI catbird seat. It had sold more than 10,000 copies of its software, giving it the single largest penetration of any product in the AI business (with the exception of the $99 knockoff programs). Sales were approaching $10 million, and it had grown to more than one hundred employees. A number of other computer companies were so impressed with the upstarts that they started selling Gold Hill products, including Data General, Intel, Honeywell, Prime, and even Wang Computers.

Gold Hill was also the unabashed darling of the PC magazines, which were eager to write about something other than spreadsheets and databases. The company received regular write-ups in *PC Week* and *PC World*, and Carl Wolf was getting equal billing with other AI executives like Russell Noftsker and Phil Cooper. The three men were photographed together for *USA Today* as part of a story on the leaders of artificial intelligence. Interestingly, Gold Hill founder Jerry Barber shared Noftsker and Cooper's passion for flying, and the three of them were regularly flying around New England, either in their own small planes or in the B-25 that Cooper and Noftsker owned. The popular joke, or maybe it was a thinly veiled concern, was that if the B-25 ever went down, it would take all the leading developers in AI Alley with it.

Barber also was the source of a story that provided a small clue as to how sheltered people in the AI industry were regarding their lack of visibility in the outside world. As Barber tells the tale, a friend named Mark was travelling in Montana. Mark happened to strike up a conversation with a man he met while he was on the road. When Mark asked this man what line of business he was in, the man said that he was in AI, and was actually considered an authority in the field. Surprised, Mark said that he had a friend in AI named Jerry Barber. Did the man know him? No, was the reply. Yet, Mark and the man had found an area of common interest, and they began talking about AI: how close it was to the real thing, whether there were ethical considerations, how it could be made more natural through research, its limited success in the field, etc. They talked in this way for several minutes, when the man from Montana finally just shrugged and said, "Well, the cows don't seem to mind."

Cows? What did cows have to do with AI? Puzzled, Mark asked the man to repeat what he had just said.

"I said that the cows don't seem to mind," the man replied.

"Why would cows care at all?" Mark asked, completely mystified.

"Because they're the ones that we do it to," said the man from Montana.

"You do artificial intelligence to cows?"

"No, we don't do *that* to cows," the man snorted. "We artificially inseminate them. You know, AI—artificial insemination."

The two men had been discussing two entirely different subjects that happened to share the same AI acronym.

Back in that part of the world where everybody knew that AI meant artificial intelligence, Gold Hill reached the industry's zenith at the AAAI 1988 conference in Minneapolis. Symbolics had decided not to put on its traditional party; there wasn't any more money in the Symbolics' budget for that. Gold Hill had always had large parties of its own, starting with the 1986 Philadelphia show where it rented out the Philadelphia Museum of Art (site of the famed "Rocky" steps). The company bussed all its employees from Cambridge to Philadelphia just so they could party into the wee hours with the rest of the company. They were all sent home the next day after a night of revelry previously unknown in the AI community. The following year, at AAAI 1987 in Seattle, the company rented the entire Space Needle for a night, treating clients and competitors alike to an all-night bash at Seattle's most famous landmark, 600 feet above the city. Parties were definitely one of Gold Hill's fortes.

But AAAI 1988 was to be Gold Hill's biggest bash, as well as Gene Wang's swan song. The company took over Union Station, an elegantly renovated train station in Minneapolis, and invited every single attendee at the conference to come by for all the food and drink they could stand. Never mind that most of the guests ended up being competitors. (One can imagine the instructions issued at IntelliCorp or Neuron Data: "Drink all you can boys, it's on Gold Hill's tab. Maybe if you drink enough, it'll decrease their marketing budget for next year.") Gold Hill was going to make the world aware that it was the only serious pure-play contender left in the AI business.

Sun Microsystems had a party that year as well, renting out the Minneapolis Museum of Science and the Omnimax theater to show off its commitment to AI. But as soon as the Sun party was over, everybody, including Sun's employees, headed to the Gold Hill party. No one knew that it would be Geno's last AI party. No one knew that it would be Carl Wolf's last AI party. No one knew that it would be the last big AI party, period.

The annual meeting of the tribe had grown pale in just five short years. LMI was gone, Teknowledge was getting ready to go, Symbolics was a shadow of its former self, IntelliCorp was restructuring, and Carnegie Group and Inference were keeping low profiles. Palladian was on its deathbed, and Xerox had given up on selling AI products. Failing to market its way out of the proverbial paper bag, Xerox—the once and future AI powerhouse—had chosen instead to spin off a little start-up company in conjunction with Sun Microsystems. The new company, called en-vos, would be selling all the AI products formally marketed by Xerox, with the exception of LISP machines. No one wanted them, and there was no use beating a dead horse.

Xerox's fabled sale of $20 million in LISP machines to Applied Expert Systems was never consummated. Apex, which had gotten rave reviews from financial magazines like Forbes, had been unable to make a dent in its target market, the financial planning industry. The company's strategy initially seemed foolproof: It would sell its PlanPower expert system (running on Xerox LISP machines) to small and mid-sized financial institutions in order to help those organizations increase the number of plans that they generated, and thus allow them to compete with bigger institutions. That scheme backfired badly. As it turned out, smaller institutions did not have the basic economies of scale—the overall number of generated plans—to justify an initial investment of $50,000 in PlanPower. Larger organizations, however, could have used the expert system to achieve a greater level of consistency among the huge number of plans that they produced. They also could have afforded PlanPower easily.

Apex had a good idea, but it had terrible aim. That was its single biggest failing. That, and the fact that it chose to standardize on Xerox's brand of LISP machines.

Industry troubles notwithstanding, the 1988 Minneapolis conference still featured more than sixty exhibitors, including IBM, Hewlett Packard, Sun, and the pure-play companies. The exhibitors were all getting a little bit jaded, however. As one long-time AI marketing executive lamented, "It's weird enough that I know all the people who are staffing all of the other booths at the show this year, but it's even weirder that I recognize all of the attendees from past shows as well." Many of the AI salespeople were despairing of increasing their market share because they were all selling to the government and to each other or co-marketing with each other or jointly developing with each other. It was just becoming too incestuous. A salesman from Symbolics offered this comment: "We've been coming to these things for five years, and since there's never that much booth traffic or actual selling, you always wander over to your competitor's booth to see what those guys are doing. After five years of hanging out in each other's booths, we've all gotten to know each other pretty well. Finally, we figured we knew each other well enough that we decided maybe we ought to do some business together. It's probably the only thing we've gained out of sending people, booths, and resources to the AAAI conference all these years."

Well, not the only thing. Don't forget the parties.

On the last night of the conference, Gold Hill's party at Union Station went as long into the night as Minneapolis's liquor laws would allow. Gold Hill wined and dined the AI faithful like they'd never been wined and dined before. Or ever would be again.

Two weeks later, Gene Wang quit Gold Hill. Two months later, Carl Wolf was fired.

❧

Teknowledge had elected not to attend the 1988 AAAI conference. It would be bad form to show up at an artificial intelligence conference just as it was getting ready to kill off its artificial intelligence business.

Sometime during its brief and tentative overtures to Pittsburgh-based Carnegie Group, Teknowledge stumbled onto American Cimflex, which was also based in Pittsburgh. American Cimflex, a factory automation company, was founded in 1979 as American Robot Corporation. Originally, the company manufactured pedestal robots for use on assembly lines. These robots were the kind that most people are familiar with: mechanical arms that perform simple functions such as painting and welding. American Robot did not fare very well in this line of business, so it changed course in 1985 and became a systems integrator called American Cimflex, combining computers and manufacturing equipment to form a complete manufacturing system. This industrial merging of computers and factory processes is known as "computer integrated manufacturing," or CIM. The name Cimflex was designed to take advantage of the CIM acronym.

The company was created and overseen by Romesh Wadwhani and Sushil Trikha, neither of whom were accomplished managerial types. The two men raised $7.8 million from Ford Motor Company in 1985, and Ford became their single biggest customer, accounting for more than half of the company's revenues. American Cimflex used Ford's money to go on a buying spree and snapped up three small factory automation companies, each of which had developed products and equipment for different aspects of the automotive manufacturing process. This was how American Cimflex had become a player in the CIM world, by buying up existing companies.

As of late 1988, American Cimflex had had only one profitable quarter in its entire ten years of business, although Wadwhani and Trikha were paid salaries of nearly a quarter of a million dollars each—plus annual bonuses. There was no financial turnaround in sight, and there was no way that the founders were ever going to be able to take their hapless company public. With only one major customer and thirty-nine quarters of losses, American Cimflex was not likely to make a favorable impression on Wall Street. This must have been somewhat distressing for Wadwhani, who had more than a million shares of company stock, and Trikha, who had half a million shares. The only way that American Cimflex was ever going to be traded publicly was to take over—or merge with—a company that was already listed on the stock market. The ideal partner would also be involved in some business relating to computers and manufacturing in addition to being publicly held. Beyond that, the partner's business did not have to be specifically related to factory automation; being a public company was the key.

Whether it was kismet, fate, or greed, Teknowledge and American Cimflex found each other. They both had at least one quality that the other wanted. American Cimflex got access to the stock market, and Teknowledge found a company that was willing to take over its operations. The fact that Teknowledge really had no specific line of business left, other than consulting and knowledge engineering services, made the fit that much easier. It came to the party unencumbered by any real products.

The two companies agreed that their union would be a merger, although technically it was a takeover of Teknowledge by American Cimflex. The new company, to be called Cimflex-Teknowledge—the third name change in a decade for Wadwhani and Trikha—would be consolidated in Pittsburgh, and a small "knowledge systems division" would be left intact in Palo Alto. All management and non-technical employees of Teknowledge would be laid off, although there were several bonuses in store for top executives. Lee Hecht, whose salary had been $160,000 as chairman of Teknowledge, was given a $325,400 severance package, as well as $60,000 for two months of consulting. After that, he would be given $3,000 a month for unspecified consulting duties up until April 1991.

Teknowledge CEO Peter Weber did almost as well. His salary as chief executive officer had been $160,000, and he was given a $320,000 severance package. Weber was given $90,000 for two months of consulting during the transition stage, as well as the same $3,000 per month consulting deal that Hecht got.

Frederick Hayes-Roth, the chief technical officer and founder of Teknowledge, elected to stay with Cimflex-Teknowledge and preside over the remaining handful of AI employees in California. There was also a possibility that the new company might develop diagnostic expert systems for use in automotive manufacturing, and Hayes-Roth's expertise would come in handy should that plan ever come to fruition.

Everybody else in the deal pretty much got burned. General Motors, FMC, NYNEX, and Framatone—the corporate investors in Teknowledge—were now minority stockholders of the new corporation. Procter & Gamble and Elf Aquitaine had prudently reduced their holdings in Teknowledge prior to the merger. Not surprisingly, none of these original investors were inclined to continue their previous working relationships with the new company. The remaining one hundred employees of Teknowledge got zip—unless you count pink slips—and any other potential executive beneficiaries of the deal had already been fired earlier in the year by Hecht and Weber.

Arthur Schwartz summarizes Teknowledge's rise and fall with a single comment. "There was never anything at Teknowledge to build a company on. It wanted to be a software company, but you have to start with a product and build from there. Teknowledge never had real products or a real product strategy. Management just kept throwing stuff up in the air and against the wall, hoping that something would eventually stick. Nothing ever did."

The merger of American Cimflex and Teknowledge was finalized on February 27, 1989. The result of joining two severely mismanaged companies that couldn't make money was the creation of an even larger mismanaged company that couldn't make money. Over the next five years, Cimflex-Teknowledge accumulated bigger losses and validated its reputation as an also-ran in the factory automation market. In 1993, it started selling off and closing the various business divisions it had purchased or developed over the past decade.

The only part of Cimflex-Teknowledge that remains today, remarkably, is the small group of original Teknowledge employees that remained to do knowledge engineering work in Palo Alto. Everything else, including Wadwhani and Trikha, has been disposed of. Frederick Hayes-Roth, the founder of Teknowledge, is Cimflex-Teknowledge's chairman. He is attempting to rebuild the company's fortunes by selling a new version of the old M.1 expert system, a package called M.4. In its last financial statement, though, Cimflex-Teknowledge admitted quite candidly that it may not have enough money to keep alive.

The company was dropped from the stock market in November 1993 for lack of trading activity. At the time, its stock was worth half a dollar.

❧

The LISP market had stalled dead in its tracks by the end of 1988. A number of factors were to blame. The shutdown of LMI and Symbolics' recent financial troubles had a domino affect on the other LISP-based companies, primarily IntelliCorp. Customers saw the problems at Symbolics and believed that those problems must be directly related to a lull in LISP interest. This was partly true, especially since the initial buyers of LISP products were glutted with hardware and software, but it was equally a case of Symbolics growing and expanding faster than it should have.

Other mitigating factors seeped finto the equation. In 1988, the basic personal computer was much more powerful than it had ever been, especially with the introduction of Intel's 386 microprocessor. The increased power allowed users to create more advanced software for the PC using low-level programming languages such as BASIC. Sun Microsystems was also dominating the workstation market by selling an operating system called UNIX. The UNIX system was developed by Bell Labs in the late 1960s specifically for the purpose of allowing computers to communicate and share data with other computers. An adjunct of UNIX was a programming language called C, which was optimized for use with UNIX. Applications developed in C that ran on UNIX had no problem running on general-purpose workstations like the Sun (which alleviated the types of problems typically encountered on PCs, such as sharing files between, say, the DOS and Macintosh operating systems). As the Sun workstations became more popular, so did UNIX and C.

The most important trend in computing, however, was a growing interest in object-oriented programming. This was a departure from the standard method of programming, where a hacker would normally write hundreds and thousands of lines of code to make the computer perform a specific operation. With object-oriented programming, however, certain functions were already represented as a specific object, and the programmer simply had to insert that object into his or her code instead of writing that function out line by line.

Think of it this way. If you wanted to automate the control of your stereo all on your own, you could buy a frequency transmitter, a number of small electronic parts, a frequency receiver, some wire, and some plastic casing. You could assemble all of these together by hand in order to create a customized system that turned your stereo on and off and adjusted the volume. This meticulous process would be like coding a normal software program. If, on the other hand, you went out and bought a universal remote control that already had all the gadgets inside it, that would be like using an object. With object-oriented programming, much of the routine or repetitive work was already done.

One version of the C language, called C++, was an object-oriented form of C. Programmers found it extremely versatile and it allowed them to create applications in less time than before. Coincidentally, many of the best features of LISP were found in various object-oriented programming languages, and there were a number of LISP derivations that resembled languages like C++. The advantage that C++ had over LISP was that it didn't use as much memory as LISP did and could run quite efficiently on both workstations and PCs.

By 1988, the interest in object-oriented programming had grown to such a level that companies like Microsoft and Borland were offering object-oriented versions of their programming languages. The LISP community argued that LISP was better than these object-oriented languages, and that LISP should still be considered for complex programs. LISP may have been better, but it was still difficult for many programmers to learn, and it was unnaturally slow on PCs. It was so slow, in fact, that Gold Hill sold add-in accelerator boards for PCs to compensate for LISP's slowness.

Suddenly, even inexperienced programmers had access to programming tools that were able to do much of what LISP could do. Hacking with objects and symbols was no longer the exclusive domain of well-funded hackers and computer researchers. For a few hundred bucks, any programmer could create an object-oriented program. In most cases, there was no longer any need to use high-level programming languages like LISP in order to create elaborate applications.

An added benefit of this was that the object-oriented languages, which were usually derivations or mutations of traditional languages, could easily integrate with other applications. If a programmer wanted to create, say, a report generator for an existing scheduling program, it was a relatively simple matter to integrate the new application (the report generator) with the existing application (the scheduling program). This was very difficult to do in LISP, because LISP didn't recognize many of the operations of programs written in traditional languages. This was the same reason that many of the expert system companies had begun rewriting their LISP-based tools in C the previous year; it made it easier for users to add intelligence to existing computer programs.

Of the AI pioneers, IntelliCorp was the first to recognize the potential for leveraging its LISP experience in the growing object-oriented programming market. It had been working with its own object-oriented tools, called Units, when it developed the KEE expert system. There was a market there that it could capitalize on, but IntelliCorp had to get its musical chairs style of management together before it could venture into new market areas. Tom Kehler and Ed Feigenbaum were still running the company, which didn't necessarily lend itself to moving forward and away from LISP-based expert systems.

Just after the 1988 AAAI conference, IntelliCorp hired Aion's senior vice president, Katherine Branscomb, to become its new chief operating officer. Branscomb, who preferred to be called KC, had directed the marketing operations at Aion, and was considered quite accomplished in the art of selling AI technology. Prior to her stint at Aion, she had been partners in a consulting firm with Richard Karash, one of the founders of Apex. (See how incestuous this all is?) Even before that, she was the daughter of Lewis Branscomb, the chief technologist at IBM, and perhaps one of the best known computer researchers in the United States.

Branscomb was brought into IntelliCorp to straighten out the company's operations and try to rectify its sagging LISP fortunes. Tom Kehler was put back into the chairman's spot, and Ed Feigenbaum went back to Stanford to work on yet another book. This one would be called *The Rise of the Expert Company,* and would describe how expert systems were changing the face of corporations throughout the world. Needless to say, it was substantially thinner that any of his previous works.

There were lots of things to clean up at IntelliCorp. The company had recently finished working on IBM versions of KEE that would run on mainframes and PCs, work that had actually been done as part of a contract with IBM. Once IBM KEE was delivered, though, IBM had no clue as to what to do with it. Despite all the work that IntelliCorp had done—almost a full calendar year's worth—IBM let the product die a lingering death, buried alive on some back page of an obscure IBM software product catalog. IntelliCorp had touted this work in a slew of announcements, and now it found out that it was just another IBM partner that had gotten lost in the shuffle of doing business with Big Blue.

Other products had been preannounced and never completed, either because they were impossible to create or because customers had responded with minimal enthusiasm. The most notable was the well-named IntelliScope, which was supposed to allow KEE to connect to computer databases. It, like Teknowledge's Copernicus, never saw the light of day.

Fiscal 1988 revenues for IntelliCorp were $20 million for the second year in a row, and it had reduced its losses from $4 million to $1.5 million. KC Branscomb had her work cut out for her, though. She had to get the company moving quickly towards object-oriented programming so as to avoid getting sucked into the LISP vortex.

Either that or she could pull a Teknowledge and sell everything to the highest bidder.

❧

Although Gene Wang was technically the first employee of Gold Hill and not a founder, he was granted founder status in 1985 by the board of directors for all his hard work and loyalty. This accorded him rights to certain types of stock options and also recognized his contribution to the company's success.

That success was coming unraveled by mid-1988. Though some of Gold Hill's executives saw it coming, they were not adequately prepared for the sudden appeal of object-oriented languages on the PC. This left their

LISP-based PC products competing with a whole new class of software products, products that were easier to use and more efficient than their LISP products.

It tried to extricate itself from this potential conflict by investing time and money in the development of GoldWorks, a PC expert system written in LISP. Initial reaction to the product was positive, but then it died. GoldWorks didn't work as it was supposed to—a theme that by now was so common throughout the AI business that it was almost a cliché. LISP hackers were sent out to fix the problem, but customers were billed for the hackers' consulting time. This, perhaps, was not the best way to win customers' hearts.

The initial version of GoldWorks was also overpriced beyond comprehension. Gold Hill charged $7,500 for the expert system, apparently believing that if Teknowledge had gotten away with charging more than $10,000 for the original version of M.1, lightning might actually strike twice. It did not. The company added salespeople to sell the product, but advance word on its flaws killed much of the potential enthusiasm among the existing customer base. The salespeople were reduced to selling copies of the Golden Common LISP programming language, which was primarily a direct order product.

Even as it was throwing its 1988 AAAI bash, Gold Hill knew it was in trouble. The past six months had shown a dramatic drop-off in sales from the previous year, despite the fact that there were more employees trying to sell Gold Hill products. Sales had literally hit a wall; nobody was buying LISP tools like they used to. Seemingly, it had happened almost overnight. LISP was losing its nobility and cachet among the programming community, and it was dragging Gold Hill down with it. Cheaper and more conventional programming tools were the brand new name of the game.

Outside of Microsoft, the biggest name in PC programming tools was Borland International. Borland was considered an upstart amongst mainstream PC vendors in the same way that Gold Hill was among AI vendors. Borland's founder, Philippe Kahn, was a French national who had started an American software company in order to stay in the United States when the government refused to renew his green card. He was a rotund and abrasive executive who played saxophone at company functions. Kahn also encouraged his employees to form a company band. Sound like anybody we've already met in this story?

Borland approached Gene Wang about heading up its programming languages group. Geno would be a perfect fit, they would pay him handsomely, and he would get to move to California, where his family lived. Plus, he would get to play in the company band.

Geno had seen the handwriting on the wall. LISP was dying. Borland was selling the kind of tools that programmers wanted now. Torn by his allegiance to Gold Hill, Wang agonized over the decision. Ultimately, he had to go with the best bet for the future, and that was Borland. After he returned to Cambridge from the AAAI conference in Minneapolis, he told Carl Wolf about his plans. Wolf didn't try to stop him, and Geno announced to his employees that he was leaving Gold Hill to go work for Philippe Kahn.

It was a painful event, and many in Gold Hill, including some of the founders, felt that the company was losing its best asset. Geno was told that he would be welcomed back if at any time he wanted to return. In his farewell address to the troops—as it were—Geno cried and told everybody how hard it was to say goodbye. Then he left, nonchalantly taking several Gold Hill employees with him.

The exact same scene was to be played out precisely four years later, tears and all, when Geno quit Borland to go to work for rival software firm Symantec. That particular departure, however, would result in a 21-count indictment against Geno for conspiracy and attempted theft of trade secrets. His case would become the most notorious computer scandal in the history of Silicon Valley. Gene Wang would no longer be just a fanatical guy singing weird songs in a peculiar little AI company. He would be an accused felon waiting to be tried in a criminal court by the State of California.

Carl Wolf was a different story. Geno's departure had served to divert Gold Hill's attention from its precarious state of affairs only temporarily. The problem of steadily mounting losses remained. The board of directors, which included two investors who also served on Symbolics' board, was shocked by the company's sudden reversal of fortune. Looking for a quick fix, in the way that investors will often do, they decided to get rid of Carl Wolf. It was Wolf who should have been paying better attention to things, they reasoned, and thus he should be handed the blame. Wolf was given his walking papers, and Jerry Barber was installed as president. Barber had already served as president in the early days of Gold Hill, and the investors figured he would take a greater interest in the company than Wolf did. After all, Barber was a founder and wouldn't want to see his company go down the tubes.

❧

Teknowledge, Gold Hill, Symbolics, Palladian, and the other AI pioneers had established a high-flying corporate culture that attracted a lot of media attention in both the good times and bad. The companies went from receiving favorable reviews in *Business Week*, *Fortune*, *Forbes*, and *USA Today* during their heyday to scathing denunciations in those same magazines during the Donner Pass days at the end of the decade. The press had helped to build them up, and the press was helpful when it came time to tear them down.

One company that had never garnered any significant amount of press for itself was Cognitive Systems. Although founder Roger Schank was more than happy to glare into the camera for yet another personal profile in national magazines such as *Psychology Today* or *Insight* or *Computerworld*, Cognitive rarely got equal billing. The story was Roger, and Roger alone.

As both chairman and part-time employee of Cognitive, Schank received a salary of $90,000. Despite this part-time status, he demanded that the company give him a car, which had to be a luxury model BMW 735i. Roger insisted that the reason for choosing this particular BMW model was simply because of its safety record. When the board suggested that a Volvo might be just as safe and perhaps a bit more economical, Roger was unmoved. He wanted a BMW, damn it, and that was the only car that would be acceptable. The board leased him his expensive—but safe—luxury car.

In the process of building his company, Schank had obtained $2.8 million in financing, much of it from Reliance Group Holdings, the investment company headed by Saul Steinberg. Steinberg was one of the 1980s' most famous greenmailers, along with people like T. Boone Pickens and Carl Icahn. (Greenmail was the money paid to hostile takeover artists to remove themselves from specific corporate mergers and/or acquisitions deals.) Among his noted greenmail escapades were attempts to take over Chemical Bank and the Disney company. Reliance used its greenmail for somewhat more legitimate purposes, such as corporate investments. Interestingly, two of these corporate investments went to AI companies: Cognitive and Nestor. Since Schank was only a part-time employee (a fact which was even stated in the company's prospectus), Reliance put one of its own hired guns, David Fox, into Cognitive as a full-time president. Fox had served as director or president of several companies funded by Reliance, and his job was to oversee the daily operations of Cognitive. Somebody had to, since much of Schank's time was spent commuting back and forth to Yale in his BMW.

Cognitive remained a small company. Unlike Teknowledge or IntelliCorp, companies against which it competed, Cognitive grew to only about thirty employees. It had a tiny but elite client list, consisting almost solely of Citibank, MCI, General Foods, and Belgium's Generale Bank. There was also some government contract work for both DARPA and the Coast Guard. The bulk of this work was built on an advisory system—a combination natural language/expert system—called ATRANS, which stood for Automatic TRANSfer. ATRANS automatically scanned an organization's incoming electronic data messages and sorted out time-critical information—

specifically money transfer orders—for immediate action. This allowed companies like MCI and Citibank to minimize the amount of time involved in obtaining and processing monetary transactions. And since time is money (a fact of life in the finance business similar in importance to $E=mc^2$), extracting these transactions from the hundreds or thousands of other daily data messages was critical to taking advantage of transfers in the shortest time possible. ATRANS became Cognitive's claim to fame.

Cognitive went public in May 1986. Its IPO had the distinction of being one of the most low-key public offerings in the entire AI business. It sold a million shares at $6.50 a share, but almost no one in the high-tech business noticed. Much of this had to do with Cognitive's out-of-the-way location in Connecticut, off the beaten high-technology paths of Route 128 or Silicon Valley. Nearly as much of it had to do with the fact that the AI companies (and some of the press) just didn't feel like acknowledging Schank or any of his endeavors. Cognitive got lost in Roger's shadow.

So did the AI Lab at Yale. Roger split his time between Yale and Cognitive, refusing to give into either organization's request that he pick one or the other and stay there full time. His determination to run an academic AI entity as well as a commercial AI entity did not endear him to the people who were actually committed to each organization. Those at Yale believed Schank's real allegiance lay with Cognitive, while Cognitive employees were convinced that Roger was more enamored of the Yale AI Lab. Neither the Cognitive board of directors nor the Yale administration was happy with the arrangement, and Schank's penchant for antagonism did nothing to resolve the conflict.

Schank had also worn down and outlasted his verbal sparring partner, Yale president Bart Giamatti. Giamatti resigned from Yale in 1986 to pursue a lifelong love of baseball and became the head of the National League. This did not end Roger's public feuds with the powers-that-be at Yale, however. The university still had not warmed up to the idea of professors and lab directors making money from work that was originally developed as part of their tenure at Yale. If they were receiving a Yale paycheck, they should be devoting all their time to Yale.

By the summer of 1988, Roger had become insufferable. Cognitive Systems went through various chief executives after David Fox moved on (he was being sent by Reliance to take over Nestor), and Roger himself had moved back into and out of the president and CEO positions. Being the head guy at both Cognitive and the Yale AI Lab was okay with Roger, but not with anybody else. Cognitive's board of directors hired a marketing vice president from MCI, Steve Mott, to take over as company CEO. Mott had first encountered Cognitive during his years at MCI, a company that was one of Cognitive's primary customers. Mott had also had extensive marketing experience at McGraw-Hill and McKinsey & Company, and wasn't about to let an academic like Roger run riot over his plans for managing the company.

In June 1988, the near-universal animosity towards Schank and his AI fence-straddling caught up with him. The Cognitive board of directors decided that Roger was contributing far too little to the company, and was actually more trouble than he was worth. It demanded that he resign as chairman. At the same time, things were getting ugly over at Yale. Yale's administration decided that Roger's personal business endeavors didn't serve the best interests of the university, and that his interests were not the same as those of Yale. Though the exact details are shrouded in rumor and innuendo, Roger and Yale came to "an agreement" whereby he would give up control of the AI Lab and leave the university.

Grudgingly, Schank resigned from both positions. Regardless of what the specifics were, Roger had gone from running two AI organizations to running none. This indicates that maybe things hadn't gone quite the way that Roger had foreseen. He packed up his bags and his reputation and moved away from Yale and Cognitive. Actually, he moved out of the entire state of Connecticut.

Steve Mott makes no bones about the condition of the company that Schank left behind. "I came to Cognitive after being a customer, and found out that the company was made up mostly of prototypes and unfinished product releases. It was amazing because Cognitive had already gone public. Things had gotten to the point where the board had no choice but to ask for Roger's resignation.

"In dealing with Roger and other AI researchers, I think that they felt that they had some divine right to profit from their own work. Other researchers had done it in other fields of technology, but it was different in artificial intelligence. The people in AI wanted to profit disproportionately from their work. They may have been smarter than other researchers, but they were also greedier."

Mott would plug away at Cognitive's problems for the next five years, finally turning it into a profitable company in 1993. Schank went into hiding for a year after leaving Connecticut, and then re-emerged in Chicago. In June 1989, he started an AI Lab at Northwestern University, funded in large part by management consulting firm Arthur Andersen. Schank was given three tenured professorships by Northwestern: one for Electrical Engineering and

Computer Science, another for Psychology, and a third for Education and Social Policy. Most professors are lucky to get one tenured position, and two is considered the maximum. Three is virtually unheard of in American universities, but Roger managed to pull it off. Plus, his AI Lab was given an initial grant of $2.5 million by Andersen.

If nothing else, Roger Schank had found the ultimate playpen.

ᔦ

Considering the tribulations that the original AI companies had gone through during 1988, most of them were extremely glad to have the year over and done with. They believed 1989 had to be a better year (it certainly would be for Roger). The stock market crash would be that much further behind them, the computer market would settle down, and life would resume some semblance of normalcy. It was bound to be better after the New Year.

Maybe.

Chapter | **31**

Success Stories Make the Rounds in Corporate America

Coming Out of the Closet

While everyone in AI was hoping to lay low during 1989, including Symbolics, Russell Noftsker was not so inclined. He was incensed at what he saw as a "slash and burn" mentality on the part of Jay Wurts and the Symbolics' board of directors. These people were yanking the life out of the company one vital organ at a time.

Noftsker decided to make one last stand. Even though he had been out of the company for a year, he still believed very much in its potential, and it was still very important to him. Symbolics had been his baby. It had been taken away from him against his will, and he wanted to get it back.

At the annual stockholder's meeting in January 1989, Noftsker caused quite a stir by confronting the Symbolics' board with accusations of irresponsibility and neglect. He demanded that he be voted back into the company to effect a proper turnaround.

The board, and the majority stockholders, gave this proposal the thumbs-down. Everybody appeared to be happy with Wurts' performance, and Jay was going to be allowed to keep plugging away. There was no room for Russell in the new Symbolics. He was out for good.

❧

Keeping out of sight was a way for most AI companies to take a deep breath and figure out just what the hell they were going to do with themselves. Many of them reorganized. Many of them rethought their product strategies. Many of them just wanted to crawl off into a corner and die in peace. No publicity, no obituaries, no stockholder's lawsuits. They just wanted to be left alone to fade away in whimpering silence.

The timing of all of this was somewhat inopportune. As the AI vendors were giving up the ghost, their customers were coming out of the closet. The expert systems that had been such a big secret for years in large corporations were now proving their usefulness. Some of them had been so successful that users were ready to brag about them—in public and in print.

The first of these success stories came out of American Express. Even though it had suffered through the K:Base fiasco involving Symbolics, Gold Hill, Brattle Research, and Bruce Gras, senior executives at American Express were convinced that AI had potential for helping it to improve some of its operations. One of these executives was Lou Gerstner, who would eventually go on to replace John Akers as head of IBM. He and several other managers believed that AI could be applied to help out the company's largest business, its credit card division. Specifically, they felt that the authorization of credit card purchases, a very time- and people-intensive process, could be handled by some form of artificial intelligence. The existing system was somewhat cumbersome and needed to be streamlined.

American Express provided each of its retailers (stores, hotels, restaurants, bars) with one of its automated validation, or authorization, systems. (They are almost ubiquitous in stores; you know them as the little cash register gadgets that the card gets slid through.) These devices allowed merchants to check the status of the card and the customer's ability to pay at the time of purchase. Thousands of these transactions were telecommunicated to a central American Express authorization office in Phoenix, Arizona, every minute, every hour, every day, for twenty-four hours a day.

The logistics of such an operation were mind-boggling. For years, American Express had used IBM mainframes to handle the basic authorization procedures involved in each card check. These computers stored all the data on individual cardholders, amounting to millions of data files. These files were accessed by more than a hundred operators at individual terminals, who would look up an individual cardholder's past spending history, and then make an authorization for each purchase. Authorizations were based on a number of variables, ranging from spending patterns to recent purchases. Unusual or very large transactions often required that supervisors or experts handle some of the authorizations.

American Express wanted one vendor that could provide it with the tools and the consulting services necessary to build an expert system from start to finish in order to avoid the problems it had encountered with K:Base. The goal was to build an "authorizer's assistant" that would work in real-time and could be connected to the existing mainframe database. Amex did not want just a prototype, or a semi-useful, occasionally employed expert system. It wanted something truly useful on a twenty-four hour basis.

The criteria for the authorizer's assistant were fairly straightforward. It had to minimize fraud and credit losses from improper or incorrect authorizations. It had to assist authorizers in making more accurate authorizations more frequently and more quickly. It had to reduce necessary training time and associated costs for authorizers. Finally, it had to stabilize authorization staffing levels by transferring certain responsibilities to the computer system. Other less obvious requirements included the necessity that the Authorizer's Assistant be able to show its chain of reasoning at given points in the operation— a fairly common capability in most current expert system tools and shells. The system also had to be easy to maintain, with the ability to incorporate new corporate card policies in a minimal amount of time.

American Express went hunting for the appropriate products and services, eventually settling on Inference Corporation to help out with its large-scale development plan. (Teknowledge's S.1 had been dismissed as too simple to handle the gargantuan task, and IntelliCorp did not have a noteworthy consulting group.) Inference agreed to immerse itself in the development of the formally titled Authorizer's Assistant so that it would conform to all of American Express' guidelines. With this agreement, Inference couldn't just sell American Express the most recent version of ART and say "have at it." The system had to be fully deployable for American Express' internal use, and Inference' reputation would be staked to that goal.

Begun in early 1986, the system began with several prototypes. The companies used a Symbolics LISP machine for development purposes, given that

Inference's ART had not yet been fully reconfigured in C. The main theme to be addressed in terms of knowledge engineering was the reasons for approving or denying a purchase. This was not as straightforward as it may sound because American Express is different from other credit card companies in that it has no pre-defined credit limit. The company imposes spending ceilings for individual cardholders based on their ability to pay their monthly statements, which are always due in full. So oftentimes, users of the card may not know how much they are allowed to spend in a given time period until the company determines that maybe the cardholder is in over his or her head. An authorization dilemma arises if an individual who customarily runs up a maximum of $300 per month on the account all of a sudden decides to make a purchase for $15,000. This is something that would require human authorization because a number of mitigating factors are involved.

In this instance, primary concerns might be "Is the card being used by someone other than the original cardholder? Could it be stolen? Could it be a fake? Or could the cardholder just be on an expensive shopping spree?" Coupled with these problems, other factors come into play. If Monday's authorization for this card came in from Sacramento, and Tuesday's authorization for the same card came from Manila, and Wednesday's came from Stockholm, Thursday's from the Bahamas, and then Friday's from Anchorage, there is probably something strange going on with that particular card number. The system would have to be able to track unusual travel patterns given the location of previous authorization sites.

The system also had to address the real-world problem of how to handle situations where the discrepancies occurred. For example, how would the customer be queried? The Authorizer's Assistant couldn't just give the instruction to have the cardholder detained or arrested. It was decided that the program would help by supplying a set of "courteous" questions to the merchant on the other end in case a problem arose.

The first prototype took almost six months to complete and consisted of 520 rules (over the years, it has grown to more than a thousand rules). The Authorizer's Assistant was transparent to Amex's users, who still utilized the same IBM terminals and system software that were in place before the expert system project began. For them, it appeared as if the regular system had just taken on a new level of intelligence. The regular system, however, was linked into a network of Symbolics machines that were responsible for running Inference's ART software. There, authorization decisions were made and sent back to the mainframe, which then returned the approval or disapproval over the phone lines to the original merchant and cardholder.

American Express claimed that it saved tens of millions of dollars per year using the Authorizer's Assistant. It did the work of seven hundred authorization employees, many of whom were transferred to other, less routine job functions. AI had proven itself a success in one of America's most famous corporations.

The accolades didn't stop there. Expert system tales began to pour out of companies that were pleased with themselves for making the technology work in ways that could be measured against the bottom line: cost savings, time savings, improvement in response time, and personnel reduction. This latter didn't endear expert systems to many employees, but companies were realizing that they had to start making better use of their work force, as well as cut bloated employee ranks. If an expert system could help with reduction, then so be it.

Coopers & Lybrand, one of the country's major accounting firms, was next in line to sing the praises of expert systems. The company was once one of the Big Eight accounting firms, but turmoil in the corporate accounting business had reduced the Big Eight to the Big Six, and it was certain that the Big designation would include fewer firms in the coming years. Coopers had always had an interest in technology development, an expertise that it liked to pass on to its customers. (This same mentality resulted in the founding of Roger Schank's Northwestern AI Lab by accounting firm Arthur Andersen.) In particular, though, Coopers wanted to apply AI technology to the difficulties that it encountered in keeping up with the escalating changes in the corporate tax code. The majority of auditors were not able to embrace all these changes because they worked out in the field. Thus, they relied on specific experts within the company to assist them in working through thorny issues relating to the mutations in the tax structure.

Take a look at a typical audit. In order to examine a client's financial records, Coopers would send junior accountants to the client's offices. This often involved having Coopers' accountants spend several days and even weeks at the client's facilities examining records, documents, and other related financial material. One of the tools employed during this audit was a set of questionnaires. These questionnaires covered a wide variety of information, often in varying degrees of detail. They served to standardize auditing procedures as a whole, but due to their generic nature they could not cover the fine points of each individual client. To complicate this lack of standardization, Coopers' junior auditors (and those from every other accounting firm) were not overly well-versed in the innuendoes and intricacies of tax law. These people tended to be lower-level personnel sent on fact-finding missions who would return to their offices and review the paperwork they had generated with their managers. Once presented with this basic data, Coopers' senior accountants had to decide on a strategy for addressing the needs of the specific client.

As soon as this strategy was defined, accountants were again deployed to the client to gather even more data. Depending on how well the client had organized its records, this phase of the task could either be a very tedious affair or a budding accountant's journey through hell. Either way, the process got more complex as Coopers tried to pin down the client's tax strategy, not only for the year of the audit, but also for the next fiscal year.

When all the paperwork relating to this strategy was rounded up, Coopers utilized higher-level managers to analyze the data in preparation for the filing of the tax statement. Even with these individuals working on the client's taxes, there was still a lot of running back and forth to the client's office to ensure accurate account reporting. It would not look good for Coopers & Lybrand to put its name on an audit and overlook the fact that the shipping clerk's assistant had received weekly bonuses of $15,000 for the past two years. Hence, attention to detail was very, very critical.

Like American Express' authorization procedures, Coopers was faced with spending more and more time on routine operations: time spent obtaining data, subsequent time analyzing data by more experienced accountants, more time spent obtaining data, reevaluation of all previous data in light of new data, various levels of experience being brought to bear on the same data, and on and on. While this was necessary for devising a good tax strategy for the client, it was less than efficient.

In an attempt to streamline these procedures, and improve overall audit efficiency, Coopers decided to develop a computerized method of assisting with the corporate audits. The company's Auditing Directorate, which was entrusted with research and implementation of new auditing techniques, joined forces with the company's Decision Support Group. The mandate of the Decision Support Group was to assist the financial services divisions with the deployment and integration of computer technology. This included areas such as decision support tools, MIS services, and artificial intelligence.

This particular project had to achieve several important goals: reduce the time spent between the start and finish of a complete audit, achieve that goal by reducing the time needed for each individual audit step, reduce the time required for using high-level managers and audit experts, and ensure that the quality was consistent with that achieved by Coopers' own internal experts. From an implementation perspective, the program had to be highly interactive, taking into account the novice level of the potential end-users, who were the junior accountants. Thus, screen design and familiarity with what was to be displayed were important. This proved very important in the decision not to use a standard software application or even a typical expert system shell for development.

Coopers decided to create the system as an interactive, intelligent questionnaire based on the forms that the company had been using. One of the limitations of the paper questionnaires was that they were too generalized in the early stages of the audit, which necessitated repeat trips to the client's facilities for additional—and more specialized—information as the audit progressed. By incorporating intelligent capabilities into the computerized questionnaire, the system could achieve some of the goals outlined above; namely, reducing overall audit time by reducing the time spent in going back for more information at each audit step. Plus, the intelligent analysis capabilities would come from a knowledge base created using the expertise of high-level personnel, thereby minimizing the time that those experts had to devote to each audit.

Hardware considerations also played a critical role. The program had to be delivered on a machine that was easily accessible to the scores of staff accountants throughout the country. Based on the proliferation of IBM PCs throughout Coopers & Lybrand's more than ninety individual branch offices, it was determined that the final package would have to be delivered on PCs and fit comfortably on a 10-megabyte hard drive. The Decision Support Group reviewed several expert system shells for the PC, but decided to develop its own shell in LISP, primarily because this would give them control over construction of several crucial features such as screen design. It chose Gold Hill's Golden Common LISP, since Coopers had been using Golden Common LISP internally since 1985. Work on the system, known as ExperTAX, began in the spring of 1986.

Coopers developed an expert system shell called Q-Shell, or Questionnaire Shell. Q-Shell was basically an inference engine in much the same way larger tools like IntelliCorp's KEE and Inference's ART were. It was a rule-based system that utilized a technique called forward-chaining, meaning it began by assembling the facts of an audit, and then worked towards a specific goal. (Backward-chaining, on the other hand, was a condition in which you already had a problem, such as ill heath, and had to work backwards to find the cause.)

As soon as Coopers had settled on a basic design for ExperTAX, it then had to build a knowledge base. The Decision Support Group determined that four sets of tax specialists, representing varied levels of expertise and specialty, would be necessary to create a comprehensive system. But once the knowledge engineering process began, it was obvious that the experts had difficulty coming up with tax strategies off the tops of their heads. They needed actual scenarios in order to offer detailed advice. In order to extract this knowledge from the experts, Coopers' AI group decided to simulate an actual audit process, using the questionnaires and a junior staff accountant.

In an inventive use of knowledge acquisition tactics, perhaps inspired by the fabled Turing Test, the staff accountant with the questionnaire was seated at one end of a table, separated from the other end by a curtain. Behind the curtain sat the specific expert whose knowledge would normally be used for that phase of the audit. As the staff member verbally proceeded through each question on the form, he would receive verbal help from the hidden expert. The catch was that the expert was not allowed to view the forms or the information about the client. Thus, all communication between the staff accountant and his hidden expert had to be oral.

By creating a highly communicative verbal environment, the expert had to both explain his or her reasoning and prompt the staff member to investigate other aspects of the audit. In this way, the expert (and the knowledge engineers) could create pockets of expertise throughout the questionnaire, without having to wait until all the general questions were completed to go back over them again. This simulation helped to shape a structure for the actual knowledge acquisition, and the knowledge engineers could then convert this information into computer code. Over the course of 1986, roughly two dozen experts contributed over one thousand man hours of time to the creation of ExperTAX. The end result was that Coopers & Lybrand spent almost $1 million on the development of ExperTAX, based in a large part on the number of hours needed from high-level experts at the management level. Total man hours to develop ExperTAX weighed in at seven thousand, including the one thousand hours of time provided by the individual experts. All ninety-six of Coopers' U.S. offices were then set up with the system. Thus, Coopers had ninety-six computer clones of its experts installed in each office, all of which could now produce consistent and sophisticated tax strategies. ExperTAX was so successful that Coopers & Lybrand began offering it as a separate product to its individual clients, who could then use it for their own internal accounting operations.

Both Coopers & Lybrand and American Express were financial institutions that used AI for streamlining and improving personnel-intensive tasks that were part of their core businesses. Other industries were finding that this same methodology could be applied to their businesses, as dissimilar as they might be to the financial services world. The most unlikely company to exploit this benefit of AI was Mrs. Field's Cookies, one of the most popular and successful retailers of chocolate chip cookies and brownies.

Retailing is a very difficult business to put parameters on. Unlike the financial services business, where certain methods work better than others in certain situations, retailing is oftentimes a catch-as-catch-can business. It is a matter of certain processes working better for some companies than for others. If all things were equal in retailing, Burger King would sell as many burgers as McDonald's, Lee would sell as many jeans as Levis, Keds would sell as many high-tops as Reebok, and Pontiac Firebirds and Chevrolet Camaros would sell in equal amounts. After all, each of these is a commodity product that is essentially the same in quality, and not much different in appearance. One could argue that there are specific details that differentiate these products, such as the way that Lee stitches its jeans versus the Levi's method, but by and large these differences are based more on perceptions created by sales and marketing professionals.

Marketing is a highly objective endeavor, and is therefore very difficult to pinpoint and predict. There are rarely any specific and universal "right answers" in marketing. For example, will a display of sweaters sell better in the front of the store during the winter than it does on the center aisle during spring? Why or why not? Do Egg McMuffins with ham sell better in Cleveland at 8 A.M. than they do in Columbus? If so, why? In addition, a lot of marketing and sales techniques are based on psychology and demographics, hardly the two most concrete sciences known to man.

However, other aspects of retailing, such as efficiency, service, and control measures, can be gauged, and their impact on retailing can be observed and defined. It was these areas that Mrs. Fields' opted to concentrate on. The best strategy appeared to be expert systems. Interestingly, Mrs. Fields' corporate literature on the use of technology in retailing read like an expert system primer: "Competitive advantage comes by making the inevitable happen sooner. Companies that accurately anticipate tomorrow's retail environment and effectively exploit it before their competitors do, create more than an edge in the industry, they establish market dominance. Anticipation is driven by information...An organization which gathers data monthly, is always a month behind...If the chief executive could run each store, virtually no location would fall short of its maximum potential. In multistore management, individuality seems impractical...This succeeds only in pulling the best stores down while failing to significantly improve less productive locations...Management is singularly focused. It is either adept at controlling costs, or driving sales. Rarely both...Expertise is pivotal. Experts are a limited resource. Leveraging their knowledge is crucial. Transferring proven expertise enables every manager to perform beyond his ability...Paperwork is the antithesis of productivity...Complex computer systems sit idle. For a system to be successful, it must be easy to use."

Mrs. Fields' Cookies was started by Debbi Fields and her husband Randy, a former IBM systems programmer, in 1977 in Palo Alto. This location would eventually be smack dab in the middle of the expert system companies that would emerge from Stanford and SRI International. The Fieldses decided from the outset to make their company virtually paper-free, and to make full use of computers to handle the mundane task of data management. Upon opening their second store a year later, the Fieldses, under Randy's administration, were on their way to computerizing everything that could possibly be computerized within the company.

As the company grew through the 1980s, Randy Fields and his data processing department embarked upon the task of spreading headquarters expertise to each of the company's locations. After a decade, these locations had come to include more than one hundred La Petite Boulangeries, numerous Fox Photo stores, nearly eight hundred cookie shops, and dozens of combination stores. Fields wanted all of these locations to do as well as the original stores that he and his wife had run in the early years. It was evident that the first few stores succeeded in large part due to Debbi Fields' marketing techniques; she set hourly sales quotas for herself, baked up the day's inventory based on daily experience, and even went out on the sidewalk to hawk her cookies with free samples on slow days. This was all in addition to the fact that the cookies were of high quality and passed the basic consumer requirement—they tasted good.

Unfortunately, the growth of any retail organization means that the original entrepreneur's ideas get assimilated into the bureaucracy of corporate culture, and some of the early methodologies and practices get lost—for better or worse. The company did not want Debbi Fields' ideologies and beliefs to get lost, but it also did not want individual stores to lose sight of the potential for selling millions of chocolate chip cookies. Since cookies were not exactly a high-ticket item, revenues were dependent upon high unit sales. Debbi Fields had already proven she had some of the right ideas to move chiploads of cookies. With this in mind, headquarters wanted every store to have access to her expertise in selling cookies.

Using IBM mid-level and personal computers, the company created an integrated series of expert systems using IBM's original expert system shell, ESE. Fields called the system ROI, or Retail Operations Intelligence. The components that were contained in the overall ROI included the Daily Sales Capture, Sales Reporting & Analysis, Labor Scheduler, Interviewing, Skill Testing, Daily Production Planner, Lease Management, and several others.

These system components ran on each store's personal computer, which were all linked into the thirty-eight IBM minicomputers that collected nationwide data at Mrs. Fields' Utah headquarters.

Though designed to work together, each component had its own specific area of retailing expertise. For instance, the Labor Scheduler took full advantage of the expertise of Mrs. Fields' senior executives. These people had years of employee management experience, especially in employing minimum-wage personnel, which was the predominant variety used to staff the counters at the cookie stores. The LS scheduled employees based on knowledge of labor and work force-related conditions such as the labor laws of a particular state, employee work preferences, and store characteristics. Using the knowledge of the company's senior execs, it drew up a work schedule, including breaks, for optimizing hourly employee time. Thus, a store manager could optimize the use of his or her staff by minimizing overtime and providing workers with a potentially more flexible schedule.

Because retail employees tended not to stay with any particular job much longer than a summer or perhaps a year—there aren't many fast food lifers—interviewing prospective employees was an ongoing task at every store. The Interviewing module of ROI was designed to help store managers assess the potential of prospective store personnel. It also provided a means of making sure that each employee throughout the company was asked the same set of questions, ensuring a certain level of employee quality. The system analyzed applicants by weighing responses to basic questions and could generate probe questions to cover key areas or flag contradictory responses to assist a manager in making a hiring decision. ("You say you worked as a sales rep for IBM from ages 17 to 22?" "Uh, yeah." "But in a previous answer you stated that you were at Johns Hopkins Medical School from ages 17 to 22." "Uh, yeah, well, school wasn't that hard so I had a lot of free time.") The company believed that this took the guesswork out of the interviewing process by identifying undesirable applicants, reducing the amount of time spent in interviews, and enforcing a standard interview in every company location.

For the day-to-day retail operation, there was the Daily Production Planner, an expert system that served as an intelligent and interactive Day-Timer, Appointment Book, Diary, Hourly Schedule, and To-Do List all bundled into one application. Every store manager logged into this application about thirty minutes before the store opened and entered that day's date and date-specific information, such as whether the day was a weekend day, or perhaps a holiday. In the case of a potentially high-traffic cookie day—say Valentine's Day—the system would check the previous year's store traffic for that date, and would also factor in such things as weather conditions. If there happened to be a hurricane on the verge of slamming into Manhattan, the system would recommend a reduced level of cookie production. If, on the other hand, it happened to be a sunny Beverly Hills day, it might recommend making a substantial number of additional cookies, especially those with white chocolate chips, because they sold well in Beverly Hills on Valentine's Day.

The Planner created a full day projection for the amount of dough that had to be prepared, the ratio of macadamia nut cookies to toll house cookies, etc. It also performed this process on an hourly basis to chart actual store traffic and progress and would make decisions on cutting back production or even whether to offer free samples to passing customers to increase sales. All of this was designed to place the emphasis where it counted the most in a retail baking operation—maximizing profit potential but minimizing leftovers and loss. At the end of a full day, the store manager could measure performance against projection, and then use all of that data again the following year to help boost sales.

According to Randy Fields, "The system has leveraged Debbi's ability to project her influence into more stores than she ever could without it." The company was so pleased with the results that it created its own software company, Park City Group, to market ROI to other companies in the retail industry. Early customers included Burger King and The Disney Store.

On the other side of the coin, the airline industry is an ostensibly retail-based business that involves more than just offering a product to a customer. For every seat sold, there are hundreds of logistical operations that need to be accomplished in order to move a passenger from Point A to Point B. The airlines began to invest heavily in AI to make these operations, such as maintenance, scheduling, and gate assignments, more efficient. The first attempt at exploring airline AI, Northwest Airlines' Seat Advisor, had fallen victim to Northwest's merger with Republic Airlines and Sperry's merger with Burroughs. Other airlines, however, were not in this same state of flux and needed to improve operations in the continued frenzy of deregulation. Some of the world's largest carriers, including American, SAS, Air Canada, Iberia, British Airways, Delta, and United, all began spending a great deal of money with AI companies, primarily Symbolics, Texas Instruments, Inference Corporation, and a small company formed by MIT's Patrick Winston called Ascent Technology (which, coincidentally, had set up operations in Gold Hill's old Armenian dance hall location).

The issue for the airlines was how to make schedule-based operations a more cohesive procedure. This included the scheduling of maintenance, which involved taking planes out of service and re-routing them to a service location; scheduling of routes, which involved assigning planes to those interconnecting routes that would give them the optimum number of passengers per flight; and scheduling of ground crew operations for each flight as it arrived and departed from an airport gate. In the case of this last operation, gate assignment, the airlines' methods were so antiquated as to be almost prehistoric. For example, United Airlines' gate controllers made gate assignments every hour. These gate controllers, especially those at Chicago O'Hare's "Terminal of Tomorrow," had to assign more than four hundred flights daily to one of fifty gates in that terminal. But the assignments had to take into consideration that planes like DC-10s and 747s didn't fit into every available gate slot, such as those designed for 727s, and that runway backups and weather affect how quickly individual flights could get in and out of gate areas. Unbelievably, controllers relied on a large, room-sized magnetic board to keep track of gate positions and moved little airplane magnets manually around the board according to flight plans and existing airport conditions.

Realizing this was a half-baked way to perform gate operations, United contracted with Texas Instruments to create an intelligent gate assignment system. TI then knowledge-engineered a half dozen experts from United's gate operations team to create the knowledge base for Gate Assignment Decision System (GADS). The system was built on a TI Explorer and used a graphic representation of the magnetic wall board to allow controllers to input and manipulate more graphic information than they could with their cute little magnets. It also freed these personnel from making routine assignments so that they could focus on more critical assignments such as runway and tarmac backup, loading delays, etc. United and TI claimed that the system took just ten months to develop, and after two test-phases, it was installed in both O'Hare and Denver's Stapleton airport in July 1987. Although GADS was originally a stand-alone system, it was eventually linked into United's main computer system, Unimatic, which maintained all information on flights, schedules, fares, and customers. Unimatic fed flight information directly into GADS, which could then update its decision-making process based on the flight status of incoming and outgoing planes. It was able to show this information, as well as an aerial view of gates, to the controllers on the Explorer's screen.

In addition to the cases listed above, the expert system success stories just kept on coming. They were followed by descriptions of hundreds of others, literally.

The IRS announced that it had more than a dozen expert systems underway. Prodded by the General Accounting Office to provide better service to taxpayers, the agency created an application called the Correspondex Expert System to automatically generate those nasty audit letters that the IRS sends to fifteen million people annually. Prior to Correspondex, each letter had to be created manually by clerical personnel who literally "cut and pasted" individual letters together with paragraphs from a library of three hundred master letters. All told, this correspondence process utilized three thousand full-time employees at ten national IRS centers. The Correspondex Expert System was created to handle taxpayer correspondence by evaluating the specific situation and retrieving the proper standardized paragraphs from its knowledge base. The IRS hoped to reduce its error rate in sending these letters out from 30 percent to less than 10 percent.

The Seattle Police Department bought a natural language system to help it track down the Green River serial killer. The system, developed by Information Access Systems, was able to understand that words like knifed, cut, stabbed, sliced, and slashed all referred to the cutting of human skin with a sharp object. In Virginia, the FBI developed an expert system for profiling the character traits of serial killers.

The Baltimore Police Department cloned the expertise of its burglary investigators to create an expert system for analyzing routine household break-ins and burglaries. Funded by the National Institute of Justice, and using Gold Hill's LISP products, the program improved the city's arrest rate for burglaries by 15 percent.

The New York Stock Exchange created an expert system called the Surveillance Expert that monitored stock trading in order to catch unusual or illegal trading activity. The Chicago Board of Trade created a microExplorer-based system that allowed it to accept international transactions after U.S. business hours.

Johnson Wax used Aion's expert system shell to develop an application that helped the entire company wade through the product regulation maze. As the maker of Raid and other insecticides, Johnson was required to follow very stringent local and federal laws governing toxicity and environmental concerns. Not only did the company have to adhere to EPA guidelines and submit product applications as part of a nightmarish paper chase, but it also had to conform to a variety of state laws, which, not surprisingly, made it legal to sell certain products in one state but not another. Using the Aion Development System software on an IBM mainframe, Johnson developed a registration system called REGI (short for Registration). The system, developed in roughly six months, contained knowledge about all of the different federal and local insecticide regulations and helped outline product requirements in order to meet these mandates. A significant number of product application rejections were routinely based on clerical failings in filling out the applications, and Johnson believed that REGI kept this out-of-hand rejection percentage down to less than 10 percent.

Siemens AG, one of the world's largest and most well-known electronics firms, developed a "context understanding" machine translation system to deduce meaning from words and phrases. Called METAL (Machine Evaluation and Translation of natural Language), the product could translate up to two hundred pages of documentation a day.

Raytheon developed a neural network for anti-submarine warfare, with the specific goal of hunting down enemy subs. By way of metaphor, hunting submarines was a lot more difficult than finding a needle in a haystack. For one, the needle kept moving. For another, the haystack tended to be a few miles deep and hundreds of miles wide. And lastly, the needle oftentimes knew that it was being looked for, and chose to hide in various nooks and crannies scattered throughout the haystack. Thus, part of sub-seeking was based on the gathering and analyzing of data from sonar and other signal capturing equipment. It involved the tracking of a specific object believed to be a submarine, but since that object couldn't be seen, determinations had to be made from this signal processing and subsequent data analysis. Even with the amount of data that was collected by these computerized systems, it was still quite an imposing task to try to figure out just where a sub was, what kind of sub it was, how fast it was moving, and ultimately, whether it was actually a sub at all, and not just a slow moving school of fish. To address these problems, Raytheon set up a system with neural net vendor NeuralWare to perform feature analysis on the signal data once it had been collected. The system evaluated all the information and attempted to recognize patterns or specific features in the signals. Over a continuous period of time, the network would analyze enough information to provide specific details about the object being monitored: whether it was indeed a submarine, what its location was, and even what type or class of submarine it was—which was a crucial factor in identifying whether the craft was friend, foe, or neutral.

Even voice recognition got into the act. Both Renault and Audi announced automobiles that would use limited voice recognition to control minor functions, such as radios, thermostats, and the dialing of cellular phones. Many of the Bell Companies began employing voice recognition to replace human operators in the management of collect calls. In all of these cases the recognition was limited to about a dozen utterances, such as the numbers zero through nine, yes and no, on and off. The world still hadn't gotten the voice-activated typewriter that Ray Kurzweil had promised, but it was getting a small taste of things to come.

❧

These are only a handful of the applications that were contributing to the success of AI throughout government organizations and large corporations. By 1990, there were several thousand of these applications in all different shapes and sizes. These AI programs didn't just occur overnight; many of them had been in development since early 1984. But, like celebrity substance abuse and unusual sexual predilections, all of a sudden it became fashionable to talk about them in public.

In many cases, it was too late. Like the cavalry, the stories arrived after some of the AI vendors had gone under, and others were so malnourished that there was no hope for them. A few hung on long enough to reap the glory of their success, but they didn't hang on for long. Their condition was already fatal.

32

The Final Irony
AI Companies Don't Live Long Enough to See the Fruits of Their Labors

The macabre chill of AI's Donner Pass appeared to thaw during 1989 and 1990. The AI vendors let the press cover the stories of their customers' emerging success, but had to content themselves with remaining in the background lest their own internal faults be revealed.

Most AI companies worked at improving their products so that they would actually work as promised. Others concentrated on getting their operations in shape. Cognitive posted its first quarterly profit ever. Symbolics posted its first annual profit in three years, closing fiscal 1989 with $67 million in sales with a profit of $1.8 million. IntelliCorp rang up sales of $22 million, with a profit of almost a million dollars. For Symbolics and IntelliCorp, however, these profitable years would be the last they would ever see.

Symbolics had shipped its Ivory chip as an add-in board for the Macintosh and called it MacIvory. It was an effort to make the Macintosh a little LISP machine in the vein of the Texas Instruments' microExplorer. But LISP machines were routinely being shoved off to the side by major corporations and replaced with Sun workstations, so the marketplace greeted the MacIvory with a huge yawn.

Jay Wurts saw no future in AI for his company. He had slashed Symbolics to the bare bones and made it profitable in the process. It was lean, not quite mean, and ready to go in any direction that he desired. That direction was towards the entertainment industry.

Wurts felt no affinity for AI, and saw it as the root of many of the company's problems. This view was shared by almost no one within Symbolics, especially the bulk of its employees, many of whom still worked with customers like Alcoa and Delta Airlines in building expert systems. Wurts ignored this fact and treated Symbolics' AI endeavors as unwanted children. This treatment also extended to the people involved in those AI endeavors.

Symbolics' PR people were instructed to talk about the company only from the perspective of its involvement in the graphics and animation business. Creating flashy commercials and movie title sequences was what the company was all about now. The only endeavors that Symbolics and Wurts would discuss publicly related specifically to these new business areas. Information about AI was eliminated from the company's marketing documents and press releases. As far as the outside world was to know, Symbolics was working exclusively on developing entertainment industry toys such as "videographic workstations" and high-definition TV.

This infatuation with the graphics industry alienated many long-time Symbolics employees. Regardless of what Wurts and his puppet PR people claimed, AI was still responsible for more than half of the company's revenues. Hiding references to AI because Jay Wurts didn't want to have anything to do with the company's prior business could not negate that reality.

Wurts was not well-liked within Symbolics. Many new executives are disliked simply because they effect painful changes within companies, no matter what their personality may be like. Wurts, on the other hand, was simply not a likable guy. He took personal credit for almost all the accomplishments of the company during his first two years as CEO. He brought in old friends and former employees as vice presidents, people with little knowledge of Symbolics' business. He ignored some of the impressive advancements the company had made in helping to get expert systems developed, notably the American Express Authorizer's Assistant.

Wurts was also disliked by the analyst community, which wasn't sure of his actual agenda. He talked magnanimously of his financial turnaround of Symbolics, but he wasn't precise about the company's future direction. Graphics and animation were all well and good, but Symbolics was a second-tier player relative to companies like Silicon Graphics and even Apple. Wurts seemed not to care; his mission had been to pull Symbolics out of the hole, and he had done that. What happened in the future was of little consequence.

His slashing and burning had been successful in cutting costs, but it had left Symbolics with little idea of what to do from there. Wurts created five business units and then shuffled them around with absolutely no apparent rhyme or reason. This juggling left the remaining employees, and even some of the board, completely bewildered. Wurts' primary skill had been in slashing operational expenses, and from there he seemed lost. This became evident in 1990's annual report. With no defined product or corporate strategy, Symbolics' sales dropped to $53 million and its losses were $6 million. Jay had contributed all that he could to the company. When there was nothing left for him to cut, he had nothing left to offer.

~

The one significant event during this two-year "blackout" period was AICorp's IPO in June 1990. The little company founded by Larry Harris as a natural language provider had grown into a large IBM software house specializing in creating expert systems for IBM computers. In the process, it had changed its name from Artificial Intelligence Corporation to the less obvious AICorp. With the backing of a group of companies including Liberty Mutual, Transamerica, and Southern California Edison, AICorp had transformed itself into an expert system vendor with a tool called KBMS, the Knowledge Based Management System. This corporate transformation had been overseen by an A-Team executive named Robert Goldman, who had once been the heir apparent to the presidency at Cullinet, the company that was brought down by its purchase of Computer Pictures.

Goldman and AICorp were extremely aggressive by AI industry standards, working their way into numerous IBM mainframe sites at insurance companies and state and federal government agencies. Their only competition was Aion, which had actually been the first company to target the IBM market with AI applications. Aion had faltered along with the rest of the AI industry, but was regaining its footing. The two companies shared a common identity problem, however: it was hard to tell them apart. Their products did essentially the same things and ran on the same computers—IBM mainframes and personal computers. There were technical differences—the Aion expert system tool was more flexible—but customers were almost reduced to a coin toss in choosing between them.

Nonetheless, AICorp went public, marking the first AI IPO in almost four years. The company had been profitable for several years, and its sales were

$15 million in 1990. AICorp was one of the only companies on the upswing, and it was one of the only ones to make any noise about its activities in artificial intelligence.

The "stay down and shut up" mentality of the rest of the AI vendors during 1989 and 1990 caused the press to miss the one and only story of an AI company and its founders cashing out of the business with their pride intact. A tiny LISP company called Coral Software had labored away on the outskirts of AI Alley, operating in the slums near Gold Hill. If anything, it was even more dangerous over in Coral's neighborhood than in Gold Hill's. The little company had developed a LISP that ran on the Macintosh and ran very fast. It had become popular in the fanatical Mac community, yet Coral had never grown to more than a handful of employees. Apple itself took notice of this interest and decided it wanted to offer LISP capability to its legions of Mac adherents. In January 1989, the founders of Coral quietly sold their little organization to Apple Computer for a little over a million dollars. They took their money and disappeared from the AI world, happy at having realized the dream that eluded almost everyone else in AI Alley: get rich and get out.

If Coral's founders had waited even two or three months longer, they might not have made out as well as they did. Rather, they could have ended up in the same predicament as Gold Hill Computers. That company's sales stall had turned into a sales fall, and employees had bailed out in increasing numbers since the end of 1988. LISP was no longer a salable commodity and Gold Hill had no other commodities to sell. The three founders tried to sell their business to a number of other companies, including Symbolics, but in the end, there was no way out. They had opened for official business on February 29, 1984—leap day—and closed that business on March 1, 1990. It was as close to being six years to the day as they could get. Stan Curtis, Jerry Barber, and John Teeter settled all the accounts with their investors and creditors, and then performed one final act.

They sold the assets of the company for a dollar.

One dollar. It was largely a symbolic gesture, but significant nonetheless. The company's administrative director, Celia Wolf (no relation to ex-CEO Carl), wanted to continue to serve the installed customer base and was willing to upgrade the LISP products on a regular basis. It would be a small operation, only three or four people, but it would have an existing client list of more than ten thousand licenses to work with. The three company founders gave Celia the assets to Gold Hill for a buck, along with the rights to the name and the customer base. Then Curtis, Barber, and Teeter returned to the Pacific Northwest region from which they had originally emerged, each to pursue other careers. Curtis went to work for Arthur Andersen in

Portland, Barber went to desktop publisher Aldus in Seattle, and Teeter set up a research center sponsored by Fujitsu just outside his original Gold Hill ranch in Idaho. Celia Wolf continues to run Gold Hill from a small suite of offices in the building that was Gold Hill's second and final home.

The AI shakeout took its toll on organizations other than the vendors who inhabited AI Alley and Silicon Valley. The businesses that had supported AI imploded. Several conferences that had focused on the commercial aspects of AI folded, notably an annual conference held in Long Beach each year by Tower Conference Management. An annual expert systems conference sponsored by the Engineering Society of Detroit, an organization funded by General Motors, Ford, and Chrysler, was allowed to fade away into nothingness.

The AAAI Conference of 1989 was held in Detroit, a location that was considered to be representative of America's industrial decline. This was, as they say, a "bad choice." The 1990 AAAI Conference was held in Boston, the heart of the "Massachusetts Massacre," and barely managed to drum up an attendance of two thousand. There were no parties to speak of at either of these shows. They resembled wakes.

AI newsletters disappeared without so much as a whimper. From a high of nearly twenty publications dedicated to AI in 1987, only three newsletters and two magazines remained. One coincidence almost went unnoticed: The woman who had been the single most influential recruiter of AI talent died in 1990.

AI Alley began to look like the remains of a neutron bomb explosion. The people were all gone, but the buildings were left standing. Restaurants closed, including the Daily Catch. The Catch had become an AI investor and executive favorite, and had advertised on the Palladian billboard after that bit of egotism was torn down. The restaurant's other Boston-area locations were hallmarks of city dining, but it could not sustain life in AI Alley once the AI companies were gone.

The fire station in Kendall Square had once placed a bumper sticker in its top window that read "Welcome To AI Alley." The sticker had been scraped away by the end of 1990.

In 1987, one could have stood on the corner of Vassar and Broadway streets in Cambridge's Kendall Square and had access to over one thousand AI company employees within shouting distance. Now, there were barely one hundred of these people left. Symbolics, Palladian, Apex, Gold Hill, Coral, Lisp Machine, Inc., and a handful of others were all gone. The only company that remained was Thinking Machines, and it had taken over larger quarters closer to the Charles River. You could almost hear the wind whistle through the streets in anticipation of some Clint Eastwood spaghetti western theme music. The only thing missing was the tumbleweeds.

Around the country, corporate AI groups were faring no better. Hewlett Packard, which had acquired rival Apollo Computers in order to mount a joint workstation effort against the seemingly unstoppable Sun Microsystems, had never been able to get its AI effort off the launching pad. Its AI group had dissolved in one sad episode of political infighting. At a meeting in Palo Alto, the company had brought all of its various AI researchers and group leaders together, along with a number of consultants, to discuss the future of AI. Chairman John Young even prepared a "State of AI" address to be shown on videotape for the occasion. Barely two hours into the meeting, the company's East Coast AI group—which was standardizing on LISP and working with Carnegie Group—found out that its West Coast counterparts were trying to standardize on PROLOG. The gathering deteriorated into a shouting match between the two factions, each accusing the other of keeping its AI agenda secret from the other. Hewlett Packard's AI efforts never recovered from the pettiness of that meeting, and the company gave up on AI shortly thereafter.

Digital Equipment had tried to introduce a modified version of its low-end VAX computer as the "AI VAXstation." It started selling Neuron Data's Nexpert tool and created a group of nearly four hundred people to address the development and marketing of AI to its customers. But its biggest customer was itself. The only thing customers wanted from DEC was AI training, since DEC had proven to be so successful at building its own expert systems, such as XCON. DEC had never been known as a capable marketing company, always relying on its technical and engineering expertise, and it wasn't any better at marketing AI. The AI group was continually reorganized, and the company's marketing misfits always seemed to end up trying to manage the AI group. The company's primary business units were suffering as well, and AI never got the attention it needed to sustain itself.

Data General moved its AI group three times in three years, from Massachusetts to Colorado and back to Massachusetts. IBM did the same thing with its AI group, to the point that customers decided it was simpler to go do business with Aion and AICorp—something that IBM's internal divisions ended up doing as well. Bolt Beranek & Newman opened and then closed two separate groups built around AI, eventually spreading its AI expertise to smaller groups within existing divisions. Unisys tried to keep the three AI groups it had inherited from the merger of Sperry and Burroughs together, but the new company had a hard enough time just keeping its core customers satisfied. It decided to get its AI expertise from the outside, primarily from small expert system vendors who were hired under contract.

The biggest, and quietest, AI group shutdown was at Texas Instruments. An exodus of the company's senior executives, including George Heilmeier, left the Advanced Systems Group without any direction. The gradual shutdown of the LISP machine business accentuated this problem, and all of a sudden, TI wasn't selling AI products anymore. It was that uncomplicated and painless, kind of like dying in your sleep.

Of the AI pioneers, only Inference and Carnegie Group had managed to sustain their businesses at the levels equal to those that existed before the market slowdown in 1988. They didn't necessarily grow, but they didn't nosedive, either. Each began to focus on specific market niches and brought in A-Team executives to help it weather the bad times. Part of their ability to do this may have been the fact that they weren't public companies and thus avoided some of the scrutiny that befell the others. Yet, Carnegie continued to build solid custom applications for its customers, while Inference made its ART product available on every computer architecture available.

IntelliCorp was not so fortunate. In the spring of 1990, it acquired MegaKnowledge, a small developer of an object-oriented tool called KAPPA. The plan was to build awareness of IntelliCorp as an object-oriented company by focusing on KAPPA and de-emphasizing the company's bread-and-butter expert system, KEE. This went over like a lead balloon among the company's LISP contingent, which had been the only LISP expert system holdout when all the other AI companies had switched to C. Now, chairman Tom Kehler and chief operating officer KC Branscomb were telling them that LISP was out and this newly acquired KAPPA product was in. Ten years of expert system work in LISP was being flushed down the drain in an effort to refocus the company. Internal development was replaced by an outside product.

Tom Kehler believed that the new strategy had a great deal of promise. He told one analyst that there was no reason that IntelliCorp couldn't capitalize on its long association with objects to become the leader in object-oriented programming. If things went well, he said, IntelliCorp could become a $100 million dollar company, far surpassing any of the accomplishments of its former expert systems competitors.

That was if things went well. But they weren't going well. The transition from KEE to KAPPA confused IntelliCorp's customers, and they stopped doing business with the company, choosing to wait until they knew exactly what was going on with IntelliCorp's product line. And even though 1990 had been the year of IntelliCorp's greatest revenues with $22.8 million in sales, the company had slipped back into the loss category. Like Gold Hill the year before, IntelliCorp suddenly found itself hitting a wall: customers stopped buying altogether.

Objects were hot, but IntelliCorp was not. Kehler and Branscomb found themselves in the same position that Teknowledge had been in two years earlier: an old and outdated product line was being supplanted by a new product that was not quite ready for the market. Like Teknowledge, IntelliCorp found itself reduced to one choice. It had to be sold, or it had to be shut down.

IntelliCorp's executives started shopping the company around, playing up its object-oriented programming expertise. Time was running out, though. Fiscal 1991 revenues were $13.9 million and losses were $14.8 million. The company was losing more money than it was making.

It attracted the interest of KnowledgeWare, a publicly held company that—despite its name—had no interest in AI. It was a software engineering company headed by Fran Tarkenton, the former New York Giants quarterback and infomercial pitchman. Tarkenton had actually been quite successful with KnowledgeWare, building it into the leading vendor in the computer-aided software engineering (CASE) business. KnowledgeWare was interested in adding object expertise to its product line, and in August 1991 agreed to buy IntelliCorp in a deal that involved a stock swap worth $34 million.

IntelliCorp executives and board members were ecstatic. They would cash out of the company having done their duty and filled their pockets. Kehler, the man who orchestrated the buyout, would be given a senior vice president title at KnowledgeWare. KC Branscomb, however, was not going to the new company. In what appeared to be a split with Kehler, she was not given a golden parachute.

One condition of the sale was that IntelliCorp had to get rid of all of its LISP machines. Eighty of them. They were of no use to KnowledgeWare, which didn't want eighty boat anchors cluttering up its halls.

IntelliCorp tried to sell them to anyone and everyone, even to the point of asking Carnegie Group to take them off its hands. No one wanted them; they were like exposed nuclear waste. Eventually, IntelliCorp sold the machines for $500 each to a Silicon Valley computer parts dealer. He bought all eighty machines, stripped their disk drives out of them, and sold the drives for $1,000 apiece. He was the only one who profited from the deal. The once great LISP machines, originally costing upwards of $100,000 each, had been sold for parts.

Then the unthinkable happened. In November, KnowledgeWare announced a huge quarterly loss in the midst of completing the deal to acquire IntelliCorp. Reeling from the unexpected red ink, KnowledgeWare management decided that it couldn't afford the costly takeover. With just days to go until the final papers were signed, KnowledgeWare backed out.

Ecstasy at IntelliCorp turned to rage. The board, which had already started counting its blessings—and its dollars—was left holding a bag that it thought it had gotten rid of. Looking for a human sacrifice to ease the hurt, the board tossed Kehler unceremoniously out on his ear, the final reward for a decade of service to the company. He had been the man responsible for making the buy out happen, and he was now going to be the scapegoat in its failed aftermath. To rub salt on the wounds, control of the company was given to the executive who had been something of an afterthought, KC Branscomb.

Three thousand miles away, Symbolics was sinking even deeper into its own financial losses. On sales of little more than $40 million in fiscal 1991, it had lost nearly $10 million. Clearly, Jay Wurts was found wanting when it came to long-term corporate management that entailed something more than closing offices and laying off workers. The board hired Kenneth Tarpey, a former Prime Computers executive, to take over Symbolics' day-to-day operations.

Tarpey, a practical and affable New Englander with a keen sense of corporate culture, realized that Symbolics had one business and one business only: high-end software tools like Genera. Not graphics hardware and not LISP workstations. Flying in the face of the corporate despair that Wurts had spawned, Tarpey sold the Symbolics' graphics division to a group of former employees and a Japanese hardware distributor. He moved the company's headquarters out of the offices in Burlington and back to the original Concord site that Russell Noftsker had built near Hanscom airfield. This reduced the lease strain on the company, which still had a financial interest in the Concord facility. He even sold one of Symbolics' software tools, called Macsyma, to Russell Noftsker. Macsyma was a programming tool created at MIT to perform complex mathematical functions in scientific applications. Symbolics had marketed the tool for a time during the 1980s, but it no longer fit into the company's product strategy. Noftsker believed that he could build a small business around selling Macsyma to universities and research labs. Tarpey sold Macsyma to Russell for $115,000.

❧

The relative quiet of the AI business continued into 1992. The media continued to harp on the fact that AI was helping corporate America solve some of its most difficult computer-based problems. "Smart Programs Go To Work" announced *Business Week* on March 2, 1992. It followed this up with "Smart Computers Are Starting to Help Executives Plot Strategy" in November 1992. *The Wall Street Journal* named Kurzweil AI, Nestor, and Thinking Machines as advanced technology companies to watch in the future. Note that the term "artificial intelligence" was not used. It had become an anti-quated buzzword, one that promised more hype than reality.

But using simple intelligent systems that helped to make traditional sys-tems smarter was a good thing. People stopped thinking of these AI programs as stand-alone brains that would take over all aspects of business. From the 1980s heydays when one Symbolics executive had confided, "I can see a world where AI grows in tandem with the regular computer world, and then re-places it," a much more acute sense of what the corporate world really needed emerged. "The problem in AI was that we tried to replace the human expe-rience," says Ken Tarpey, Symbolics' chairman. "What we should have been focusing on was enhancing the human experience."

Companies started to add intelligence to their databases and their job schedulers and their inventory control systems, all of which had reached the point in their evolution where they weren't going to get any more efficient. These applications were, however, pervasive throughout the world's busi-nesses. By making them smarter through the process of embedding intelli-gence deep into them, these mainstream applications now reached a new level of efficiency—the next stage in their computer evolution, as it were.

These smarter systems manifested themselves in a variety of ways. Speigel, the merchandise giant, applied neural networks to the task of selecting the customers on its mailing list that would be most inclined to buy from spe-cific catalogs. Wendy's, the hamburger chain, installed a corporate expert system that let store employees call up a help desk to assist in the repair of various ovens and fryers. The U.S. military claimed that expert systems had helped it to manage the massive movement of men and materials to Saudi Arabia in record time during the Gulf War. It had also used expert systems, primarily from Carnegie Group, to help diagnose and repair equipment prob-lems in the harsh desert environment of the Middle East. NYNEX, the former partner of Teknowledge, relied on Inference to create a maintenance expert called MAX that helped to solve customer problems over the phone, elimi-nating the need to send repair personnel out to a problem site for every call.

One result of all of this publicity was a new concern about the ethics of artificial intelligence. This came to the fore as the medical community started using AI as part of its need to cut costs while offering more comprehensive care. The possibility that computers were making medical decisions scared many people, who felt that the world had truly turned control over its hu-manity to the machines.

Medical expert systems had long been part and parcel of the research community's interest in AI. MYCIN and DENDRAL had medical founda-tions, as did IntelliCorp's first product offerings when it was called

IntelliGenetics. These, however, did not address the issues of human health. Only one system did that in the early days of AI, a program called CADUCEUS. This medical expert system was started in the early 1970s at the University of Pittsburgh. CADUCEUS, which was named for the twisted snake and staff symbol of the medical profession, was the brainchild of the university's chairman of medicine, Jack Myers. He was interested in the possibility of developing a computerized diagnosis system to provide a ready source of information to medical internists. Myers originally envisioned an interactive textbook format, as the idea of expert systems was not very widespread at the time. Myers joined forces with Harry Pople, a computer scientist also with the University of Pittsburgh. Although both felt that the application could be developed over time, they were faced with a single awesome obstacle: Myer's specialty was internal medicine. Unlike subspecialties that deal with the quirks and foibles of specific organs, appendages, and systems, internal medicine covered one of the widest sets of medical application. Yet Myers' forty years as an internal specialist gave the project an appropriate expert, so work commenced.

The original version of the program was actually called INTERNIST and covered 500 different diseases classified as part of internal medicine. In addition, 350 disease variations and some 100,000 symptoms were included in the program. It was developed on a DEC-10 using InterLISP (remember, this was the 1970s). Interestingly, there was not a computer in Pittsburgh powerful enough to run the program at the time, so the developers used one of the National Institute of Health's computers. This computer was actually part of John McCarthy's multiple access system that had been installed at Stanford University.

INTERNIST initially suffered from an inability to deal with complex medical situations that involved a number of different diseases. Myers and Pople went back into the knowledge base and created a revised version of the program in the late 1970s that became CADUCEUS. The new program did not contain any more significant information about specific diseases, but it did make up for the information exchange deficiency in INTERNIST. The aim of CADUCEUS was to do high-powered diagnosis at a very active level—in effect, the system drove the diagnosis process, leaving little control in the hands of the physician.

The possibility of actually deploying CADUCEUS was discussed in 1982, but met with resistance from the medical community. Plus, Myers was reluctant to release the product until it contained all the information he could possibly stuff into it. At the time, Harry Pople figured there were probably fifty man-years in the creation of CADUCEUS, and if all the computer time and resources could be calculated along with the value of human resources, the system might actually have cost somewhere around $7 million.

Myers and Pople renamed the application one last time, calling it QMR, for Quick Medical Reference. QMR was designed to be more interactive with physicians than its predecessors. It ran on a Symbolics machine and contained information on some 650 different diseases related to internal medicine. This was short of the roughly 800 diseases known in the field, but Myers believed the addition of another 50 would make the system workable, and more importantly, practical. But medical knowledge changed monthly, as evidenced by the numerous papers and journals published regularly throughout the field. Such a rapid rate of change meant that the system would have to be maintained on a routine basis, and Myers didn't think that was wise until the knowledge base as a whole was more complete. There was a benefit in getting QMR into the hands of physicians as a reference system, though, since QMR could be updated to be more timely than textbooks. Myers claimed that textbooks were often outdated by the time they got off the printing press, and he actually liked to think of QMR as more of an electronic textbook than an actual expert.

As LISP machines faded away, Myers and Pople rebuilt QMR for use on personal computers, using Borland International's Turbo PASCAL to fit it all onto a single PC hard drive. The University of Pittsburgh then tested QMR at its VA Hospital for two months in 1987. The decision to use the system on specific cases was determined at the time of a patient's admission to the hospital. The doctors who were evaluating QMR would decide which admissions were appropriate to test with the system, and then used QMR as an integral part of the diagnosis process. One-third of all admissions over this period were eventually diagnosed with QMR. Of those admissions, 75 percent were diagnosed correctly by the computer. Myers maintained that the remaining 25 percent of the diagnoses were incorrect because of lack of information in the knowledge base.

In practice, an internist examining a patient could input ninety-five positive and negative answers to the machine's questions about the patient. Each of these questions used "evoking strengths" and "frequency strengths" in determining an analysis. These "strengths" are more commonly known as confidence or certainty factors. At the end of its analysis, QMR presented up to fifteen possible diagnoses for the situation at hand. These were ordered in degrees of most likely to least likely, and all were considered possible within the scope of the diagnosis. QMR also allowed for interaction on behalf of the user, who could ask the system to evaluate other considerations and consider different conclusions.

The program was introduced commercially in 1989 by a company called Camdat. By that time, other researchers had developed similar medical expert systems. The University of Utah and the LDS Hospital in Salt Lake City developed a program called HELP with the assistance of Control Data Corporation. HELP, which eventually became the core of 3M's Health Information Systems division, was designed to prevent adverse drug events, such as reactions, as well as to monitor hospital-acquired infections.

Even the Russian government was interested in the possibilities of such systems. Byelorussian State University in Minsk began developing a series of PC-based expert systems in the late 1980s for use by the medical community in the (then) Soviet Union. Like U.S. expert systems, they were developed to help advise existing practitioners, but the Russians also viewed the programs as being essential to training medical students. Even more importantly, they could be used to supplement the lack of medical expertise in rural and impoverished areas or in practices where medical knowledge was at a low level. The systems developed by the University's Specialized Medical Complex were fairly vast in their scope, and included DILTOAD, an expert system that diagnosed illnesses in children over the age of four years, such as severe stomach aches and appendicitis; DONEVZ, which was used to diagnose diseases of the central nervous system ranging from encephalomyelitis to meningitis; DOLNAR, a system for the treatment of heart conditions; DIOHIP, which was intended for diagnosis of diseases of the abdominal cavity organs such as the pancreas and liver; and CHELIT, a system designed to assist in the treatment of maxillo-facial injuries, primarily those involving the lower jaw. According to the Russian developers, these programs addressed a minimum of 80 percent of all the diseases or problem conditions found in Russian patients.

None of these programs made much initial impact on the commercial world or even in the press. Then, in 1992, *Newsweek* and *Business Week* ran stories about a system called APACHE, an expert system which was perhaps more terrifying to the average person than either CADUCEUS or the Russian systems. APACHE made life and death decisions.

APACHE was an acronym for Acute Physiology, Age, and Chronic Health Evaluation. It was developed in 1989 by an intensive care physician at George Washington University in Washington, D.C., named William Knaus. The goal of APACHE was to determine the odds that a patient in the intensive care ward would live or die, and to prescribe treatment accordingly.

The procedure for using APACHE was stark and straightforward. When a patient was admitted to the hospital, doctors would input twenty-seven pieces of data into the APACHE workstation. This information detailed patient specifics such as vital signs, level of consciousness, initial diagnosis, lab results if any, and presence of chronic diseases. This information was used by APACHE to create a patient profile record, which was then compared against the records of 17,448 other patients in its knowledge base. These patient treatment records had been compiled over three years from forty different hospitals throughout the United States. Each record was actually a case history against which the new patient's case could be compared. This form of AI was known as case-based reasoning. Case-based reasoning systems made decisions by comparing existing problems with a library of similar "cases." Instead of using rules to make "if-then" judgments, a case-based system could examine historical precedents to a problem, utilizing its expertise in the context of past experience. ("This problem is similar to that one, and the solution in that case was....") Based on the similarity of the new patient's condition to previous cases, APACHE would make a determination of the new patient's chances for survival.

Once this determination was made, APACHE assigned a number from 0 to 100 to the patient. These numbers were color-coded, ranging from green for a good chance of survival, such as 0 to 10 percent, on down through the color spectrum to red and 100 percent, where death appeared to be the inevitable result. Using this scale, APACHE would also predict the costs and resources that would be utilized in caring for the patient. The doctor could then make his or her own determination about how to care for the patient and whether or not the amount of treatment was justified by the possibility of impending death. To assist the physician during the course of the patient's treatment, APACHE updated its diagnosis and prognosis twice daily, continually adapting and adjusting its data based on changes in the patient's condition over time.

As cold and clinical as this may sound, APACHE was a valuable tool in aiding physicians who were involved in life and death situations. It was not their only tool, however, and it was not intended to replace a doctor's own expertise. APACHE was an advisory tool, as most expert systems were, used primarily to assist the user. Interestingly, APACHE also proved useful in an unexpectedly humane way: It helped doctors present information to friends or relatives of the patient. Instead of relying on the standard medical terms like critical, stable, or grim, the doctors could use the computer's graphics to show where the patient lay on the recovery or mortality scale.

Knaus formed APACHE Medical Systems to market the program, which sold for $350,000. By the end of 1992, more than two dozen hospitals had purchased the APACHE expert system. Many claimed that the daily updates helped them respond to patients' conditions more quickly than normal, and that they were better able to allocate resources to each patient as needed. With resources getting more costly and expertise becoming less available, APACHE provided an objective analysis of which patients would most benefit from available resources.

An immediate concern in the medical and religious communities was the possible use of APACHE as a way to cut off patient treatment once certain spending limits were reached. The fear was that insurance companies might refuse to pay for patients who were admitted to a hospital with a certain mortality rating as supplied by APACHE.

◌◌

All the while, the commercial forms of AI mutated and grew into new products. Carnegie Group started combining expert systems with neural networks to create applications that took advantage of the strengths of both technologies. Inference and Cognitive introduced case-based reasoning systems. Neural nets and fuzzy logic were combined with statistical analysis at financial institutions to spot fraud and to extract trends from data sources that were too huge to be analyzed by humans. Companies like Canon and Ricoh started putting tiny fuzzy logic programs into cameras, copiers, and even washing machines. These programs allowed the appliances to make decisions about light levels and shutter speed, or to determine the temperature of water needed for specific levels of dirt in clothing.

This renewed focus on the importance of AI, or smart computing as it came to be called in the press, did not save many of the remaining AI companies. Syntelligence, the SRI spin off, went belly up. Voice recognition vendor Votan was acquired, as was expert system company Cogensys. The Xerox and Sun group, en-vos, was even worse at marketing than Xerox was and shut down.

Much of this paled in comparison to the final days of The Fifth Generation Project. As the end of the project approached, the Japanese were about to lose face in front of the whole world.

Ending It All

On June 1, 1992, The Fifth Generation Project ended—not with a successful roar, but with a whimper. Like some elderly and infirmed animal, it was left behind to be picked apart by scavengers.

Ten years after it had begun, the project had failed to develop anything remotely resembling a thinking machine. The Japanese had developed several expert systems and neural network applications, but primarily had nothing concrete to show for a decade of work. Instead of unveiling a world-dominating technology, Japan offered the meager results of its Fifth Generation work to any company that could make use of it. For free.

The Japanese tried to play down the failure of The Fifth Generation. "Ten years ago we faced criticism of being too reckless," said Kazuhiro Fuchi in his address to the final Fifth Generation conference. "Now we see criticism from inside and outside the country because we have failed to achieve such grand work."

The years had taken their toll on Fuchi, who looked strained from a decade of trying to keep his project on track. Even though he was entrusted with its success, he could not be held personally accountable for the failure of The Fifth Generation. Indeed, there were a myriad of reasons for ICOT's failure. The single most important reason had to do with an unforeseen flaw in the basic premise of The Fifth Generation. The Japanese had wanted to develop an actual machine, a single hardware device, that would be able to perform logic functions and learn from experience. The project's emphasis had been directed toward hardware, and not the development of software.

But the world of computer hardware had changed dramatically in ten years. Computers in the early 1980s were the province of the well-funded few, limited to those organizations and individual researchers lucky enough to afford and have access to mainframes, supercomputers, and LISP machines. In the 1990s, personal computers and general-purpose workstations made computing a commodity. A $2,000 PC in 1992 had more processing power and memory than a $100,000 LISP machine from a decade before. Thus, economies of scale and advances in hardware technology had passed The Fifth Generation by. Japan, Inc.'s legendary tenacity and its determination to stick with its original goal prevented it from dealing with this reality.

The cultural traditions of Japan also impacted ICOT's ability to create a free-thinking climate of renegade technology development. As many had predicted, the natural Japanese tendency to conform and fit in, coupled with a cultural belief in management by consensus, had hampered The Fifth Generation from the outset. It took several years worth of precious research time just to convince researchers that it was okay to think for themselves. Ed Feigenbaum's warnings notwithstanding, the Japanese had been unable to rise above centuries of social conditioning.

So, too, the consortium fell prey to the primary interests of its corporate participants—themselves. Fujitsu and Mitsubishi and Toshiba and NEC all were more concerned with their own corporate financial advancement than they were in turning over their best and brightest researchers for two- and three-year stints at The Fifth Generation. Indeed, some of these companies pursued their own AI agendas. Fujitsu created the Facom pseudo-LISP machine, Mitsubishi had contracted with American AI companies to develop neural network hardware, and Toshiba had set up an endowment at MIT to study new technologies. The person who was selected as chairman of the Toshiba endowment was none other than Marvin Minsky.

Japan did get one tangible benefit from all of its efforts to create true artificial intelligence: scores of researchers who were intimately familiar with the potential of intelligent technology. Estimates were that more than a thousand researchers had passed through ICOT's labs during its ten-year run, all of whom had worked together to achieve a common goal. They had all been well-trained in one of the world's most difficult computer disciplines, and more importantly for the Japanese, they had undertaken to produce advanced forms of software. The Japanese had always ranked behind the United States and Europe in software development, and now there were hundreds of capable software programmers in companies throughout Japan. Despite its obvious failures, The Fifth Generation had proven to be a breeding ground for the country's first generation of software creators.

The ashes of The Fifth Generation had hardly been swept under the rug when the Japanese government began constructing a sequel to the project. The Ministry of International Trade and Industry announced the formation of the Real World Computing Project (RWC), a national research and development program that would pick up where The Fifth Generation Project left off. Like its predecessor, RWC was to be a ten-year project, with government funding approved at $500 million. The total financial commitment might end up being even higher, since MITI was going to encourage foreign partners to participate in as much as 15 percent of the total program. Thus, overall funding could be as high as $800 million, significantly more than the funds given to The Fifth Generation. The RWC would include many of the Japanese conglomerates that had signed on for The Fifth Generation, including Toshiba, Fujitsu, Oki, Mitsubishi, Hitachi, and NEC.

RWC research would concentrate on three core areas of development and two areas of fundamentals or theory. The core technologies were defined as parallel processing, neural networks, and optical computing. The first of the fundamental exploration areas would create methodologies for problem-solving through the use of statistical analysis and inferencing or self-learning systems. This was called Soft Logic. The second would develop the types of applications that could actually be created with these problem-solving methodologies, such as self-adapting and self-organizing systems.

While all of the five groups had overlapping functions and goals, the neural computing component was one of the most pervasive of the themes. In optical computing, the Japanese hoped to develop an optical neural net technology for use in software, hardware, and storage devices. The Soft Logic project also hoped to establish a structure for the use of neural nets in all aspects of intelligent computing.

Interestingly, Japan, Inc. began soliciting participation from around the globe and claimed to have a number of "Western" organizations interested in research partnerships. These partnerships would take the form of either direct membership in the RWC—which would allegedly give an international organization the same privileges as Japanese members—or the Western organizations would be subcontractors to RWC members. Either way, the Japanese government tried to convince overseas participants that the RWC was designed to benefit all interested organizations. It did this by laying out the plans for an open-door technology program that would welcome any and all interest. This was a concept that had never been tested in any of Japan, Inc.'s research endeavors, past or present.

The Fifth Generation Project had been an amazing impetus to the growth of the artificial intelligence industry worldwide, yet it had also been overly ambitious and culturally inappropriate for Japan's computer industry during the 1980s. RWC was a more practical, less ambitious project, and its goals were much better defined than the "world domination" agenda set for The Fifth Generation. The Japanese had failed in a big way once and were not interested in having that happen again.

Rocked in the early 1990s by governmental corruption and scandal, a slowing economy, and a concerted effort by the United States and Europe to prevent it from overtaking their lead in computing, Japan was ready to regroup and take on the world one more time. After the failure of The Fifth Generation, it had nothing to lose and everything to gain. In the minds of the Japanese, computer domination was a matter of time. And this time, it seemed that the country would stop at nothing to succeed.

While The Fifth Generation may have been a lot of saber-rattling, the RWC did not appear to be just another example of saber-rattling; rather, it appeared to be a concise outline of Japan, Inc.'s technology development plans for the remainder of the decade and on into the early years of the next century. To dismiss the RWC would be folly, for it was in the decision to keep RWC from being too grandiose that Japan may finally have found a vehicle for its advanced technology development. Failing to realize the potential of the RWC could end up being fatal to those countries who dismissed the new technology efforts of Japan, Inc. with the passing of The Fifth Generation.

❧

In the United States, the pioneering AI vendors were fighting their last corporate battles. Aion and AICorp decided to stop playing the indistinguishable roles of Tweedledee and Tweedledum, and merged on October 1, 1992 to form a single company called Trinzic. The new entity continued to sell IBM-based AI applications, but decided to embed most of its AI capabilities in a suite of products designed for use with more traditional software such as databases.

That same month, KC Branscomb quit her job as CEO at IntelliCorp to join Lotus Development Corporation as a senior vice president. IntelliCorp's 1992 sales had fallen to $9 million, the lowest level in seven years. This figure was eerily matched by $9 million in losses, the second largest loss in the company's history. IntelliCorp was in a tailspin, and Branscomb strapped herself into the ejector seat and bailed out. The company was taken over by its chief financial officer, but its expert system days were over. If IntelliCorp survived at all, it would be on the strength of the object-oriented technology in KAPPA; a technology that IntelliCorp had not created itself, but purchased from someone else.

Surprisingly, the one place where things were going well in the post-Fifth Generation months was at MCC. The consortium, which had been created specifically in response to The Fifth Generation, had had its share of rocky moments over the past decade. Most of these were related to member defections, which in turn were prompted by the consolidation of the high-tech industry in the 1980s. Sperry pulled out when it merged with Burroughs, and several semiconductor companies gave their notice when they were purchased by foreign organizations or could no longer afford the cost of pure research. Bobby Ray Inman left the consortium in 1986, convinced that the group was on the right track. One can picture him standing at the entrance to MCC's Austin headquarters, hands on hips and feet spread apart, gazing over the Silicon Prairie and claiming "My work here is finished."

He would disappear into obscurity until January 1994, when he was chosen by President Bill Clinton to become the secretary of defense. But in a bizarre episode reminiscent of Ross Perot's campaign for president, Bobby Ray withdrew from the nomination, claiming that there was a media conspiracy that was designed to smear his good name. The ultimate spook had finally had enough of government and politics and vanished back into the shadows.

Despite all the odds against it, MCC actually managed to produce usable technology for its members. MCC's biggest claim to fame, though, was not any of its products; it was its pure, unadulterated AI research. Over the years, the AI aspects of MCC had gravitated toward one specific program, known as Cyc. The name was short for "encyclopedia" and was indicative of the program's goals. Cyc sought to create a computer system that contained all of the world's knowledge, or more appropriately, all of the world's common sense. Begun in 1984, Cyc was overseen by Douglas Lenat, a former student of Feigenbaum's who had also taught at both Carnegie-Mellon and Stanford. Lenat was widely regarded to be the brightest of the second generation AI researchers, and thus he was recruited to head up MCC's AI effort by Inman.

The scope of the Cyc project was enormous, and was to become quite possibly the largest computer programming effort ever undertaken anywhere on the face of the Earth. Yet the underlying concept was one that even a child could grasp. In order for people to understand information and use it intelligently, they must have common sense as a preexisting condition. This common sense includes an understanding of the basic truths of the world: "A dog is not a cat." "Food in a restaurant must be purchased with money." "In fast food restaurants, the food is paid for before it is eaten." "A physical object cannot be in two places at once." "An unsupported physical object will fall downwards." "Horizontal is side to side, vertical is up and down." "A person cannot be older than his or her biological parents."

It was the view of the Cyc team that this understanding of the world was necessary in order to understand specific information relating to expertise or domain knowledge. One could not be a doctor or a lawyer or a plumber if one did not understand the way the world worked. From this perspective, Cyc was seen not as an encyclopedia of knowledge, but as the compilation of the common sense that allowed people to use encyclopedias. Lenat referred to this common sense as consensus reality: facts and concepts that people know and which they assume all other people know.

The task, then, was to build a common sense infrastructure upon which all future knowledge bases could be built. Task, though, hardly describes the size of the project. Lenat and his knowledge engineers figured that Cyc would take at least ten years to program, and maybe as many as fifteen. It would include several million rules, or common sense facts, and require several hundred man-years worth of programming. At the outset, Lenat and Inman gave the program less than a 10 percent chance of achieving its goals.

Others in the AI community couldn't believe that Lenat was actually going to attempt such an outrageous feat. In order for Cyc to succeed, the project would have to entail the arduous task of manually putting the minutiae of common sense into a computer, piece by piece. But Lenat countered that until a computer knew the things that every human took for granted, it would never be able to learn. If that meant inputting data into Cyc one painstaking bit of data at a time, then that's what they would do.

The cynics notwithstanding, a lot of companies were interested in finding out if Cyc could really work. Apple Computers, Microsoft, Eastman Kodak, Digital Equipment, AT&T, Motorola, and a number of the regional Bell Companies put up an astounding $25 million to give Lenat a crack at accomplishing his goal. Working with twenty-eight knowledge engineers— who were referred to as knowledge *enterers*—the Cyc group began putting two hundred rules a day into their program, using a custom LISP-based language called CycL.

By the summer of 1993, Cyc was considered the premier AI research effort in the world. The university labs had not quite fully recovered from the exodus of the 1980s and The Fifth Generation Project was becoming a fleeting memory, but the knowledge enterers at MCC had made surprising progress. The Cyc program contained more than two million rules, and Lenat and others at MCC told the press that the probability of Cyc's success had gone from less than 10 percent to better than 90 percent. By the end of the decade, they claimed, Cyc would be 100 percent complete.

The AI community, what was left of it, was impressed with the Cyc group's achievements. Even if people were not convinced of its ultimate success, they were awed by the amount of work that MCC had done. Richard Greenblatt even called it "the only place where anybody cares about pure AI research."

The companies that were funding Cyc hoped to put the monstrous Cyc knowledge base to work in their own organizations. For instance, the system might act as a kind of fact-checker that would weed out inconsistencies in their database, or those of their customers. An insurance company could use Cyc to determine that it was impossible for twenty-nine-year old John Doe of Scottsdale, Arizona to be the same twenty-nine-year old John Doe who lives in Scottsboro, Alabama. Though common sense would dictate this to be true, a computer could easily confuse the two. And unfortunately, confusion of this type occurs regularly in criminal records and credit reports, as well as in government files. Cyc could also be used to provide the basic intelligence for future expert systems in every field, since many of the facts pertaining to a general understanding of the physical world would already be included in Cyc.

Cyc was the last remaining link to the research environment that had spawned the artificial intelligence business. It had found common ground between the theoretical and the practical, something that had never been a concern of AI companies. Nor should it have been. The AI companies were founded to sell the commercial products that had been built on AI theory and research. They were not in the business of selling theory.

In the long run, the AI companies and their products had actually been built on too much theory, as well as too much hype, too many promises, and too many expectations. The promises of AI had been handed out like Halloween candy; promises fueled with funny money from a none-too-diligent investment community and by the egos of researchers who thought that they could get rich from playing God. This was too weak a foundation to build a business on. For all the advanced technologies that the AI companies had brought to computing, there were a similar number of technological disasters.

Not every AI company that failed had been founded on charlatanism, but in light of the overwhelming number of failures, it was hard to think otherwise. In truth, many founders, including those at Symbolics and Gold Hill, as well as most of the industry's first employees, had believed they were about to change the world with their technology. What they never realized was that the world wasn't ready for them or for their brand of artificial intelligence.

The largest single year of AI corporate revenues, 1988, reached a level of approximately $1 billion. This included all the combined sales of LISP machines, expert system tools, natural language products, neural networks, voice recognition systems, consulting and development services, programming languages, and peripheral business areas such as additional hardware needed to support individual systems. In contrast, the amount of money spent on cat food in the United States that same year was in excess of $2 billion—more than twice the amount spent on AI. The business that was planning on changing the world had never put its own importance into perspective relative to the other concerns of the world. Looking at these numbers might have helped.

There was one final act to be played out. The AI business had started with Symbolics. It was now ready to end with Symbolics.

Chapter 34

The Future of Artificial Intelligence

Controlling the Human Brain with a Computer

On January 28, 1993, Symbolics filed for protection under Chapter 11 of the Federal Bankruptcy Code of the United States. Its legacy of bloated operations and reckless spending had dragged Symbolics down to the point where it could no longer operate without the fear of going out of business entirely. Reorganizing while in Chapter 11 gave the company some breathing room to try to fend off creditors while it looked for additional investment to fund its software product development.

Sales had continued to drop, and Ken Tarpey cut the employee ranks to a mere seventy people. The company was still burdened with problems that had their roots in the mid-1980s, especially the California manufacturing facility that the hardware group had demanded and received from

Noftsker. Not being in the hardware business anymore, and faced with a downturn in California's economy, Symbolics was stuck with tens of thousands of square feet of factory space that it could not use or unload.

Tarpey was optimistic that Symbolics could be run as a mid-sized software company. It would specialize in the development of software tools for the same class of high-end customers that had originally bought Symbolics' LISP Machines. These products wouldn't necessarily be called artificial intelligence software tools, but if customers wanted to develop intelligent systems with them, so be it.

~

Only three of the earliest expert system companies managed to emerge from the wreckage of the AI business—Inference, Carnegie Group, and Neuron Data. Each of these companies redirected their AI businesses to new target markets. They no longer called themselves AI companies, nor did they refer to their products as AI products. Instead, they sold their goods and services using less threatening terms such as "knowledge management tools" and "re-engineering software" and "intelligent development environments."

Their low profiles in the Donner Pass days gave these companies enough of a running start in this new direction that they were able to effectively change their corporate strategies without seeming to blunder about as IntelliCorp or Symbolics did. Inference, in particular, found that many of its clients were using its tools to create help desk systems. Every major company has a help desk. They are the support centers at the corporate end of toll-free numbers that allow customers to call a company for technical assistance, whether it's installing a garage door opener or trying to set up a personal computer. Help desks are often staffed by personnel who have to wade through huge instruction and repair manuals in order to find a potential solution to the customer's problem. These manuals often occupy many feet of shelf space, forcing the customer service representative to rummage about until the appropriate piece of data is found. The time spent doing this ties up the company's phone lines and also irritates the customer, who has probably spent several minutes either on hold or just trying to get through.

Intelligent help desks, which were basically expert systems, allowed the customer service representative to input the customer's questions or problems right into a computer system, which would then search its knowledge base to find the correct solution. This saved time and the system was usually more efficient than the humans who couldn't possibly remember all the different types of problems that occurred within huge product lines. Having these smart assistants at the fingertips of the customer service personnel reduced phone time and improved customer satisfaction. This latter concern had already become the watchword of all corporations in the 1990s, and intelligent help desks helped to make it a reality.

Companies ranging in diversity from Nintendo to Compaq Computers to Color Tile all installed intelligent help desks and were more than happy to talk about them. After all, these expert systems were tangible manifestations of their desire to better serve the customer, and they wanted customers to know just how much effort they were putting into customer service in the high-tech 1990s.

Carnegie Group continued to develop specific applications for its strategic investors, especially Ford and US West, through a program it called IMKA, the Initiative for Managing Knowledge Assets. In Ford's case, Carnegie created the Service Bay Diagnostic System, or SBDS. This system addressed the problems involved with dealer servicing of cars still under warranty. Due to the increasing complexity of newer model car components, many auto technicians or mechanics were finding it easier to swap out entire auto subassemblies rather than find a specific component that needed to be repaired. Thus, a subassembly consisting of numerous components, instead of an individual component, was thrown away even when much of the subassembly was in working order. This increased the cost of warranty repair to Ford Motor, since the cost of all the parts was passed back to the automaker by the dealer.

Ford wanted to have more detailed repairs carried out with less part returns, thereby holding warranty expenditures down. The idea behind the SBDS was to put a PC with a 20,000 rule diagnostic expert system in every dealership service bay, and to have it guide mechanics through the diagnosis and repair procedure. This way, a more precise repair could be made, which eliminated the wholesale swapping out of parts. It also minimized the time it took for the repairman to find the problem, which meant that the customer got the car back sooner, which in turn meant that Ford looked better when it came time to publish the latest J.D. Power satisfaction ratings. And since the engines on new cars were beginning to look more and more like the inner workings of a supercollider, the SBDS assisted mechanics in staying current with the changes in automotive design.

An interesting aside to this project was that Carnegie developers discovered an unusual fact about auto mechanics: a significant proportion of them were dyslexic. This prevented these mechanics from getting more skilled engineering jobs such as product engineers or hardware engineers. In order to address this concern, Carnegie created an intricate natural language front-end to SBDS to make the system more accessible to all Ford's mechanics.

Neuron Data, for its part, designed its software tools so that they could be invisibly embedded in other applications. A programmer using Neuron Data products could create a new program, such as a job scheduler, and easily insert rules or objects into that program without having to connect it to an outside expert system. Plus, Neuron Data offered these tools on almost every computer known to man—from Macs to mainframes. The ease with which Neuron Data's products could be integrated into the programming process made it extremely popular with developers, and Neuron Data became the biggest seller of AI-based tools, boasting more than ten thousand licenses for its product line. The company that had entered the AI world amid laughter over its Macintosh expert system ultimately had the last laugh.

Companies like Microsoft and the major database vendors started offering AI facilities in their products, although they didn't dare call them AI facilities. Microsoft embedded Inference's case-based reasoning technology into its Windows NT development environment to provide intelligent user assistance to developers. Other companies started offering facilities which, like those from Neuron Data, enabled programmers to build mini-expert systems right into their basic code. There was no need to go out and buy an expert system when one could be built right into the very soul of the program.

Eventually, all computer programs will have this intelligent capability. None of us will think anything of it because machine intelligence will become pervasive and even expected. Thus, the ashes of the AI industry's burnout are not destined to rise like the Phoenix. Instead, they have already seeped down into the ground water, where they have permeated the mainstream of computing and have now started filtering into everyday applications. The AI industry's full frontal assault on traditional computing has given way to a more clandestine operation, one which promises greater success than the original AI pioneers ever could have hoped for. The result will be that computers will be capable of the things that people always thought they were capable of, until the reality of strange commands and difficult operations set in.

Other AI technologies finally found their niche as well. Voice recognition took off in 1992 after years of disappointing results. Apple Computer demonstrated a voice-recognition system early in the year called Casper (as in "the friendly ghost") that promised a new step forward in the ability to control computers with human speech. Analysts and developers alike suddenly believed that voice recognition would facilitate the use of the next generation of small hand-held computers like the Apple Newton. The need for a keyboard would be eliminated, and a simple microphone could be built right into these little devices. Apple had taken a hapless technology and made it "cool."

Ray Kurzweil backed off the idea of populating the world with his talkwriters, but his company became extremely successful in creating a suite of voice-recognition products for the medical community. Collectively known as VoiceMED, these systems allowed doctors in various specialties—radiology, pathology, etc.—to dictate their analyses directly into the computer. VoiceMED created an interactive environment that followed the doctor's normal reporting routine, and then fed the doctor's spoken words directly into a formal report. This freed doctors from the task of having to handwrite the information or dictate it for later transcription. Given the universal illegibility of the medical profession's handwriting, VoiceMED was soon adopted at hundreds of hospitals and clinics around the country. The success of the technology gave Kurzweil AI the credibility to go public in August 1993.

⌁

Neural networks are the heirs to, or survivors of, the AI industry as it once existed. Companies like HNC have targeted the financial services industry with their neural net products to help financial institutions analyze huge amounts of data and make sense of it all. One example is an HNC product called AREAS, an automated property evaluation system. AREAS performs appraisal operations on specific properties by searching for recent comparable sales in the neighborhood and in surrounding areas. Once comparable sales have been identified, the product uses the characteristics of both the subject property and the comparable properties as inputs to neural network models. These models are trained to reflect the recent patterns of price behavior in a particular real estate market. Applying these neural network models to the subject property—and the data about comparable properties—yields both a market price estimate and a range of confidence around the best estimate. The entire evaluation, according to HNC, can be done in less than a minute.

Big corporations love neural networks. Even Nestor, which is now publicly traded and still hasn't turned a decent profit in almost twenty years, continues to attract attention just because it is a neural network company. Many of these big corporations, however, are actually learning that neural nets work best when combined with expert systems. The neural net can find patterns or trends or relevance in massive amounts of data, and then the expert system can make decisions about that data.

While this might be the best of all possible AI worlds, the point is that no single AI technology has ever proven to be a panacea for the shortcomings of traditional computers. Certain AI technologies work better in some situations than others, while the use of several at the same time may be much more beneficial. The expert system companies can be excused for sneering at the neural net companies, and vice versa, but in the end, neither technology has all the answers to what constitutes intelligence. Applying a little bit of this here and a little bit of that there ultimately seems to work best for customers. Maybe it takes all of these different forms of technology—and more—to create something that even remotely resembles human intelligence in a machine.

The immediate future of artificial intelligence—in its commercial form—seems to rest in part on the continued success of neural networks and other "biologically based" technologies such as cellular automata, chaos theory, and genetic algorithms. This latter group take their inspiration not so much from the logical functions of the brain, but rather, they attempt to model computer data as if it were a living organism.

The concept of cellular automata treats pieces of data like biological cells. In living entities, individual cells are affected by what happens to cells around them. Sometimes, the death or malfunction of one cell will adversely affect those cells closest to it, while leaving others unscathed. To put this more graphically, the cells around a knife wound in the hand are more likely to die or be thrown into disorder than are cells located half a body away in the leg. Applying this metaphor to the stock market, particular stocks are more likely to react to economic changes than other stocks, given their proximity to an economic upheaval, such as falling interest rates. By modeling all stocks as a biological entity, and then applying outside forces to it, financial analysts can see how that specific stock, or cell, reacts.

Genetic algorithms take a similar concept and apply it to the theory of evolution. Within the context of evolution, organisms survived or disappeared due to their ability to respond to changes in their environment. The strong survived, the weak disappeared. Genetics determined which organisms would go where, based on those biological traits that adapted best to changing conditions. Using the financial market again—which, not coincidentally, is a big believer in genetic algorithms—data can be modeled as a primordial or genetic soup. As that data evolves, financial analysts can watch how it deals with environmental factors. In the models, these environmental factors are represented as market conditions, which are then thrown into the path of the various organisms' evolution. Those organisms, or stocks, with strong and adaptive genes survive the changes in the market; those without the prerequisite flexibility wither away and die. Analysts can then determine which stocks seem to have the best potential for "evolving" over time.

Chaos theory is less a matter of looking at how an organism has survived and more a matter of where it will end up. By trying to explain random events as predictable and mathematically definable events—something all of science wishes it could do—the growth of an organism can be predicted out into the future. Thus, a stock's growth or stagnation can be charted based on the line of chaos that it has already followed to get to the current point in time. Determining how it will behave in the future, then, is a question of ascertaining the path that it is already on and following it to its conclusion.

While all of these technologies are extremely experimental and just as extremely controversial, they have their adherents, many of whom are in the same position of influence as the early AI researchers were in the mid-1960s.

☙

Or maybe machines are best utilized as adjuncts to the human mind. A number of science fiction stories, most notably William Gibson's Neuromancer, have dealt with the possibility of enhancing human intelligence by connecting computer hardware directly to the brain. As an element of fiction, this form of intelligence involves the ability to insert microchips into the brain, where they serve as temporary and removable encyclopedias and experts. Given the proper connection, perhaps an input plug behind the ear, a person could be outfitted with a pop-in microprocessor that contained, say, all the available knowledge on cardiovascular surgery. The user's brain would then access the chip just as if it were a medical encyclopedia or cardiovascular textbook. The wearer would be able to discuss the intricacies of cardiovascular surgery for as long as the chip was implanted. Once it was removed, though, the knowledge would be removed as well.

Don't laugh. This method of providing humans with their own personal artificial intelligence is not as far-fetched as it sounds. Implanting chips in biological entities is an intriguing area of research. Although at the early exploratory stage, small advances have been made. Researchers at Stanford performed an experiment where they were able to control the leg movements of a cat by inserting a microprocessor into the nervous system of the animal. The chip was inserted into the space between two ends of a severed nerve, which were then reattached to each other using the chip as a junction. By sending the appropriate commands to the chip, which was hardwired to a workstation controller, the researchers were able to simulate those brain commands that directed the movements of the cat's leg. A similar principal is being used by Motorola to develop neuroprostheses, artificial limbs which are hardwired into an amputee's nervous system and then controlled by specific reflexes. There are already prostheses that allow a wearer to flex certain muscles and activate certain nerves; the limb then reacts in a specific way to that nerve stimulus. People outfitted with such limbs learn to flex these muscles in a manner that aids them in controlling the movement of the arm and its attached hand, say, to open and close a fist. Adding a microprocessor with programmed logic to these devices is an obvious evolutionary step.

And, finally, what about controlling computers with the human brain? Or more appropriately, eliminating the physical contacts between man and machine and operating computers as if they were another human limb or organ? There are a number of disparate and unrelated research programs around the world that are attempting to use the electronic signals generated by the brain to manipulate computer data. The primary researchers in this area are Fujitsu and Nippon Telephone & Telegraph, the New York State Department of Health's Wadsworth Center for Laboratories and Research in Albany, the University of Illinois, and Graz University of Technology in Austria. The efforts undertaken in these institutions deal mostly with the potential of aiding the handicapped in moving a computer cursor around a computer screen or identifying a particular image when it is flashed in front of a user. The research does not yet deal with any problems more substantial than this; nonetheless, with advances over the past few years in reading brain waves—through the use of positron emission tomography (PET)—researchers have found that certain areas of the brain show increased electrical activity when performing certain functions. When a subject hears a certain word, for instance, or an expected sound, the brain shows a measurable response. The same is true when a subject is exposed to certain flashes or colors of light. Researchers are now using this response activity to guide cursors in a particular direction around a computer screen in a somewhat binary manner: high activity, the cursor goes up; low activity, the cursor goes down. Not how far up or down, as yet; just up or down. Subjects have found that they can control the cursor movement by thinking intensely or thinking about strenuous activities (cursor up, for instance), or by relaxing and thinking about mild activity (which might relate to cursor down). Other research uses a slowly presented alphabet to activate brain activity: when the subject sees the letter he or she is waiting or expecting to see, the recognition triggers a slight brain response.

Thus far, these brain responses are so minute in their level of electrical voltage output that it takes a very controlled environment to even detect them; an environment that requires millions of dollars worth of computer and medical equipment and many hours worth of preparation and study time. The alphabet method alone only produces a single character about every thirty seconds. A large part of the difficulty comes from just trying to separate these little blasts of specific energy from those normal brain bursts that relate to breathing, blinking, and other autonomous activities.

Obviously, though, there is an underlying attractiveness in the possibility of getting computers to work with humans on a truly "hard-wired" level. The idea of using a direct link to the brain that would allow computers to siphon off facts, experiential knowledge, expertise, and even emotions would certainly make for a much more advanced and more intelligent machine. The act of programming intelligence would be a thing of the past; direct knowledge input would be the most efficient way to create smart computers. The opposite could also be true: humans might be able to extract information from machines by a reverse process that would let the brain understand the information processing operations of a computer. Artificial intelligence and natural intelligence could ultimately be one and the same.

Yet this will create moral, philosophical, and theological dilemmas on a scale never previously encountered or imagined by the human race. Machines that possess true intelligence will have a value never before accorded to man-made entities. In a world where machines will do what humans do, and technology will threaten to replace God, who will decide how much power and privilege to entrust to these machines? Conversely, will machines that learn be able to learn about themselves and understand their relationship to mankind? Will they also learn to make demands on their human creators? And, finally, will people be ready to deal with the ramifications of such a scenario should it ever come to pass?

Such questions for now will be left to our descendants, who most assuredly will have to come to terms with the concept of dealing with machines that may be smarter than they are. For us, it is only a matter of curiosity and science fiction, but it is something that has nevertheless been a subliminal social fear since the earliest days of computing. Nowhere has this fear been more eloquently stated than in a short piece of fiction called "Answer," written in 1954 by Frederic Brown. In the story, a scientist creates a link between all of the computers in the world, producing a single machine that can draw on all the computer power in existence. At the ceremony that is held to honor the moment when all the computers are joined together, the scientist throws a single switch that activates the giant machine. When the computers are linked, he asks the machine the one question that has intrigued mankind forever: "Is there a God?"

A sudden flash of electricity fused the switch to the "on" position as a terrified world watches, and the computer replies menacingly, "Yes, *now* there is a God."

᪐

The future of AI belongs primarily to our imagination. Just as today's use of artificial intelligence was fostered nearly fifty years ago in the mind of Alan Turing, the development of tomorrow's thinking machines will require both technological daydreams and forethought. All the while, it will mutate and be manipulated by its human masters, none of whom know how it will all turn out.

The past has already had its chance to create a machine that thinks like a human. Advancements were made, but not in the way that the early researchers and vendors expected. Today, very few of the people who populated the original artificial intelligence community are left to savor AI's growing acceptance in the traditional world of computing. In some cases, this is rather sad. In others, it is only fitting.

Alex Jacobson of Inference still remains with Inference, the only founder who didn't lose his AI company to bankruptcy, merger, or investor disgust.

Russell Noftsker now runs day-to-day operations at Macsyma, an Arlington, Massachusetts company that is named for the product it sells. Macsyma has a dozen employees, all of whom have access to their own LISP machines. One of his employees is Howard Cannon, who doesn't drive his Porsche as much as he used to.

Richard Greenblatt operates a software consulting business in Cambridge, in an office next door to the old Lisp Machine, Inc. headquarters. Much of his work, which is funded by the Small Business Innovation Research program, involves trying to get complex data transmitted over phone lines for medical outpatient purposes. He says he has two CADRs and a Lambda LISP machine in his garage, and a microExplorer in his house. AI is primarily a hobby these days, but he is thinking about getting an Apple PowerBook so he can do some LISP hacking when he travels.

Tom Kehler, Lee Hecht, the founders of Gold Hill, and many others have gone back to work for more established companies, or are involved in small software companies in industries subject to less turmoil than AI.

Gene Wang, the Gold Hill marketing VP with a flair for the dramatic, sits in the limbo of the California justice system. He was indicted in March 1993 on charges that he stole trade secrets from his post-Gold Hill employer, Borland International, and forwarded them via e-mail to his new employer, Symantec. The case has taken on national proportions due to the complexity of the laws involving computer trade secrets and the confidentiality of e-mail. He continues to serve as the company's vice president while awaiting trial, and is fully supported by the company's CEO, who was also indicted.

Hubert Dreyfus continues to teach at UC Berkeley and says that he is still amazed that people take AI seriously. He has very few people left to argue with.

Peter Hart, the founder of FLAIR and Syntelligence who purchased the first Symbolics machines, is now a neural net researcher at Ricoh. Randy Davis, who founded Applied Expert Systems, worked with MIT to install an intelligent e-mail system in the Clinton White House. He is the MIT Lab's associate director. Patrick Winston is still the director of the lab, a position that he has now held for more than twenty years, ever since Marvin Minsky was asked to resign.

Marvin doesn't go back to the AI Lab much anymore. "Why should I spend time there?" he asks. "They don't pay attention to my ideas, so I might as well be somewhere else." Somewhere else is MIT's Media Lab, where Marvin gets to do whatever he damn well pleases as Toshiba Professor of Media Arts and Sciences. His company, Thinking Machines, continues to push the boundaries of computer power, but it has suffered from bad management and tremendous financial losses.

Ed Feigenbaum is still at Stanford, although he is keeping away from start-ups. In 1991, he was elected to the American Academy of Arts and Sciences. He was also the first recipient of the Feigenbaum Medal—surprise, surprise—an award established in his honor by the World Congress of Expert Systems. He still speaks at various AI-related events, mostly about something he calls "the tiger in the cage." AI is the tiger, according to Feigenbaum, and it is caged by lack of support from government and industry. He believes that government should use knowledge-based systems to improve its efficiency and better serve its people. More than that, he still believes that government should "organize the development of a second generation of knowledge systems science and technology, including the underlying basic AI research, as part of a national information infrastructure." This infrastructure is better known as the information superhighway. In Ed's own words, "Government support nurtured the tiger; now help remove the bars of its cage!" Obviously, things have changed little in Feigenbaum's mind since the first days of The Fifth Generation Project, and even less has changed in the wake of its failure.

Ed and I sat together on a technology panel several years back, and I decided to question him about something that had always intrigued me. What, I asked, was the best thing that had happened to him professionally as a result of writing *The Fifth Generation*, the book that was singularly responsible for jump-starting the worldwide commercialization of artificial intelligence?

Without missing a beat, he replied, "It got me on the Merv Griffin show."

I think he was joking. But I'm not sure.

Endnotes

Much of the information in the preceding chapters comes from my own work covering AI since the early 1980s. I had countless interviews with the key players in *The Brain Makers* over that same period of time, ranging from formal sessions to late-night discussions held in bars all over the United States. I also received innumerable company documents ranging from press releases to confidential materials over the last decade. Much of *The Brain Makers* is culled from these sources.

Since I cannot admit to being omnipresent or omniscient, however, I have relied on a fair number of books and articles to fill in the gaps in my own personal knowledge. Whenever I have taken information specifically from a source other than my own, I have cited it below. Mistakes should be attributed to me, and not to any of these sources. I may not be omniscient, but I am willing to take the blame.

Chapter 1

Party description based on author's attendance.

02   *Symbolics was… working closely with agencies such as The Pentagon, etc.*
      Information culled from Symbolics' IPO prospectus (September 19, 1984) and marketing documents from 1984 to 1989. Additional information provided to author by current and former Symbolics' emloyees.

02   *only a matter of a few years before every computer in the U.S.…*
      Author discussion with Symbolics' executive.

05   *Outraged and fearful...*
      This story is legend in the AI industry, and was actually verified in an
      interview with Russell Noftsker. Author interview 1993.

Chapter 2

13   *IBM announced publicly that it was going to legitimize the artificial intelli-*
      gence market...
      "IBM Finally Jumps into AI with Both Feet," *Electronics Magazine,*
      August 21, 1986:30.
13   *Hewlett Packard saw a big chance to make money in AI...*
      Based on author's notes from attendance at Hewlett-Packard meeting.
14   *6000 cubic feet of...*
      The first computers, such as the ENIAC and Mark I, routinely covered
      spaces of approximately 10'H x 40'W x 15'D (including power and
      peripherals) when they were completely installed.

Chapter 3

20   *best known of them was Hephaestus...*
      Greek myths mentioned here and later in the chapter were verified in the
      Grolier New Electronic Encylopedia (San Francisco: Grolier, 1991).
22   *The first of the religious talking heads belonged to Pope Sylvester II...*
      The Oxford Dictionary of Popes (Oxford: Oxford University Press, 1986),
      136-138.
23   *The next Catholic dignitary to dabble in the mechanical arts was Albertus*
      Magnus...
      Albertus Magnus and Roger Bacon are both extensively profiled in Lewis
      Spence, *An Encyclopedia of Occultism* (New Hyde Park, New York:
      University Books, 1960).
24   *Only a dozen years after automaton made its way into the vernacular...*
      Grolier New Electronic Encyclopedia.
24   *Descartes was obsessed with putting forth a philosophical determination...*
      For René Descartes' philosophy on thinking and existence, see *Meditations*
      of First Philosophy, Meditations I and II (1641); on humans and animals,
      see *Discourse on Method,* (1637).
25   *the golem, a manlike creature made out of clay through magical means...*
      The Golem tradition is taken from Marshall Cavendish, ed., *Man, Myth &*
      Magic, Volume 4 (New York: Marshall Cavendish, 1985), 1135-1136.
      Psalm 139 has been variously interpreted as comparing man's basic nature
      to that of the golem, as well as being a reference to beings without souls
      such as the golem.
27   *There were a few attempts at continuing to create lifelike machines...*
      Vaucanson's duck, Jacquet-Droz's writer, Descartes' metallic girlfriend, and
      other mechanical oddities are described in Isaac Asimov and Karen Frenkel,
      Robots (New York: Harmony Books, 1985), 1-7. Vaucanson's duck is also
      described in "Maelzel's Chess Playing Machine, An Essay" by Edgar Allan

29   *The unusual grimness of the summer weather… led Lord Byron to suggest a particular literary diversion for the group…*
Tale of creation of *Frankenstein*: from Mary Wollstonecraft Shelley's own introduction to *Frankenstein*, (1818).

31   *Charles Babbage was a man who, by all accounts, could be accurately described as both…*
My portrait of Babbage is a composite of many encyclopedic and biographical sources, as well as *Robots* (mentioned above). Some people argue that Babbage was not overly mean, but was simply misunderstood, and there is no doubt that there are conflicting accounts of his personality. I have chosen the personality that seems to pervade his own writings. A novel by science fiction writers William Gibson and Bruce Sterling, *The Difference Engine* (New York: Bantam, 1991), presents a bizarre nineteenth-century world transformed by the successful completion of Babbage's machine.

33   *Lord Byron, who was actually the first person in literary circles to be described as "mad, bad, and dangerous to know,"…*
This was a quote from an 1812 journal entry of Lady Caroline Lamb, cited in William Heath, *Major British Poets of the Romantic Period* (New York: Macmillan Publishing, 1973), 526.

33   *it's not inconceivable to suppose that Ada and Mary Wollstonecraft Shelley were related…*
Specific details of Mary Shelley's life also come from Heath's volume, pages 777-780.

Chapter 4

41   *Turing's sexuality was not out of the norm at King's College, where he was just an "ordinary English homosexual atheist mathematician."…*
From Andrew Hodges, *Alan Turing: The Enigma* (New York: Touchstone, 1983), 78. A majority of this chapter's specifics were taken from this book as well as from the paper "Computing Machinery and Intelligence," by Alan Turing (1950). (Turing's paper has been published in Edward Feigenbaum and Julian Feldman's *Computers and Thought* (New York: McGraw-Hill, 1963). *Alan Turing: The Enigma* is an incredibly thorough biography of Turing and is highly recommended for both mathematicians and those interested in more details of Turing's life.

Chapter 5

46   *Norbert Weiner… A child prodigy who had received his Ph.D. from Harvard at the age of 18…*
Background of Norbert Weiner's life supplied by the MIT Museum, from the Insititute Archives and Special Collections.

47   *Shannon felt that a machine could not and should not try to…*
Claude Shannon's interest in thinking machines, from Claude Shannon, "A Chess Playing Machine," *Scientific American Magazine*, February 1950:182.

48   *As far back as 1835, Edgar Allan Poe wrote an essay called "Maelzel's Chess Player,"…*
Edgar Allan Poe, "Maelzel's Chess Playing Machine, An Essay" (1835).

49   *In 1956, two years after the death of Alan Turing, McCarthy and Minsky*
      approached their old summer job mentor Claude Shannon with the idea of
      bringing together a group of people...
      Specifics of the 1956 Dartmouth Conference were obtained from a number
      of different sources. These include:
          Oliver Selfridge, "An Interview With Marvin Minsky," *Access Magazine,*
      Spring 1992, Volume 2, Issue 1:10-12. (Published by GTE Laboratories.)
          Linda Witt, "A Mind of Their Own," *Chicago Tribune Magazine,*
      September 21, 1986:8.
          Henry Mishkoff, *Understanding Artificial Intelligence* (Dallas: Texas
      Instruments Learning Center Series, 1985), 31-36.

54   *Artificial Intelligence, as a phrase, "keeps our eye on the goal,"...*
      This quote and McCarthy's involvement and remembrances, as well as his
      decision to leave MIT were taken from "A Mind of Their Own," by Linda
      Witt, *Chicago Tribune Magazine,* September 21, 1986, page 8.

58   *Marvin Minsky, on the other hand, was prematurely bald, had a biting if not*
      somewhat condescending manner...
      My opinions of Minsky in this chapter, as well as the next, are based on
      several conversations I had with him when I first met him in 1986.

59   *MIT would act as if Stanford never existed...*
      I interviewed a number of former MIT researchers and students who
      confirmed that this was the prevailing attitude of the school.

Chapter 6

62   *He claims that no one paid any attention to a robot arm that he built...*
      This and other Minsky stories are from Minsky's speech to AZAI on July
      29, 1985.

64   *The first big ARPA project that affected the AI group at MIT was a 1963 grant*
      worth more than $2 million...
      The origins of Project MAC are catalogued extensively in the *MIT 25th*
      Anniversary of Project MAC Brochure, printed 1988.

71   *Marvin built an artificial neuron during his days at Harvard...*
      This and other details of Minsky's work at MIT are from Marvin Minsky,
      Society of Mind (New York: Touchstone, 1988), 322-325, and also Oliver
      Selfridge, "An Interview With Marvin Minsky," *Access Magazine,* Spring
      1992, Volume 2, Issue 1:10-12. (Published by GTE Laboratories.)

73   *Minsky and Papert side-stepped this issue by stating, "We have not found any*
      other really interesting class of multi-layered machine."...
      This and other Minsky ideas about neural networks from Marvin Minsky
      and Seymour Papert, *Perceptrons* (Cambridge, Mass.: MIT Press, 1968).

75   *"Did Minsky and I try to kill connectionism?"*
      This and other Papert quotes, as well as Papert's admission of hostility
      towards connectionists, are found in the essay by Seymour Papert, "One AI
      or Many?" *Daedalus,* Winter 1988:1-14.

Chapter 7

78   *John McCarthy came to Stanford in 1962...*
Descriptions of John McCarthy are from Philip Hilts, "The Dean of
Artificial Intelligence," *Psychology Today*, January 1983:28-33, and Linda
Witt, "A Mind of Their Own," *Chicago Tribune*, September 21, 1986:8.

81   *Alan Newell and Herbert Simon had gone back to work... after the Dartmouth
Conference with the feeling that they were really quite a bit further along...*
Much of Simon's AI work is recounted in his autobiography, *Models of My
Life* (New York: Basic Books, 1991).

82   *The result was a program called EPAM (Elementary Perceiver And Memorizer)
which ultimately had much more to do with psychology than business...*
Edward Feigenbaum and Julian Feldman, *Computers and Thought* (New
York: McGraw-Hill, 1963), 295-307.

84   *A user, acting as the patient, would type a statement...*
Descriptions of ELIZA sessions are from my own use of the program.

85   *Daniel Bobrow, tackled natural language and logic together in a program he
called STUDENT in 1964...*
Details from Avron Barr and Edward Feigenbaum, *The Handbook of
Artificial Intelligence, Volume 1* (Los Altos, California: William Kaufmann,
Inc. 1982), 284-285.

86   *Lederberg... approached Feigenbaum in 1965...*
Information from Edward Feigenbaum and Pamela McCorduck, *The Fifth
Generation* (Reading, Mass.: Addison-Wesley, 1983), 61-63.

Chapter 9

105   *Besides that, he whined, he was nothing more than a "rank amateur"...*
Hubert Dreyfus, *What Computers Can't Do* (New York: Harper Colophon,
1972, revised 1979), 84. Most of Dreyfus' beliefs can be found in this
book.

106   *The victory over Hubert was not enough to sate the wounded pride of the
denizens...*
From "The Artificial Intelligence of Hubert L. Dreyfus: A Budget of
Fallacies," Project MAC Memorandum Number 154, January 1968. See
Preface, Chapter 1.5 "Computers Can't Play Chess," and 1.5.1 "Nor Can
Dreyfus."

106   *One fact that Dreyfus finally did accept was that he was unwelcome at MIT...*
This and other details about Dreyfus from author interview with Dreyfus,
January 1994.

Chapter 10

111   *Clarke states in his novel that HAL stands for Heuristically programmed
ALgorithmic logician...*
Arthur C. Clarke, *2001: A Space Odyssey* (New York: Signet, 1968), 95.
References to Minsky and Turing are made on pages 96 and 97, respectively.

117 *Though the government discontinued funding for academic research into machine translation in 1966...*
Specifics of ALPAC and machine translation from *Critical Technology Trends,* (Scottsdale, Arizona: The Relayer Group, 1993.)

Chapter 12

In this chapter, Ed Feigenbuam's *Handbook of AI* was invaluable in providing details on methodology and accomplishments of individual research projects. I highly recommend it for anyone interested in the technical aspects of AI development.

139 *Shakey was a mobile robot created by the Stanford Research Institute...*
Isaac Asimov and Karen Frenk, *Robots* (New York: Harmony Books, 1985), 22-24.

141 *The first program it funded using this more stringent policy was called SUR, or Speech Understanding Research...*
The technical descriptions of various SUR Projects, including HEARSAY, HARPY, and HWIM, are from *The Handbook of Artificial Intelligence, Volume 1*, pages 325-361.

145 *The last major publicized breakthrough at the AI Lab had been a natural language program called SHRDLU...*
Description of SHRDLU from Barr and Feigenbaum, *The Handbook of Artificial Intelligence, Volume 1*, pages 295-299.

Chapter 13

148 *PROLOG... was originally developed in 1970 at the University of Marseilles...*
The history of PROLOG was derived from many sources, chief among them being Susan Scown, *Digital Equipment: An Introduction To The Artificial Intelligence Experience* (Maynard, Mass.: Digital Equipment, 1985), 77.

150 *Japan wanted artificial intelligence—badly...*
The Japanese concern for their future was taken directly from the writings that were published for the announcement of The Fifth Generation. In particular, see *Fifth Generation Computer Systems, Proceedings of the International Conference on Fifth Generation Computer Systems* (Amsterdam: North-Holland Publishing Company, 1982), 1-120, which contains the introduction by T. Moto-Oka and the presented paper by Kazuhiro Fuchi.

151 *Lighthill was not impressed...*
Report description from Brian Oakley and Kenneth Owen, *Alvey: Britain's Strategic Computing Initiative* (Cambridge, Mass.: MIT Press, 1989), 115. Donald Michie and the United Kingdom AI programs, interview by the author.

152 *On April 19, 1979, Fuchi organized the first meeting of a national committee...*
Fuchi's initial committee meetings were documented in Shohei Kurita, "Japan: The Policy of the Fifth Generation," *Electronic Business* magazine, June 15, 1985:84.

Chapter 14

156 *While these areas attracted all the publicity, two small blips appeared...*
Details of Nestor and Artificial Intelligence Corporation are from AICorp's IPO prospectus, Nestor's annual reports, and both companies' marketing documents.

159 *"hated his guts"*
Winston's saying that he hated Noftsker's guts was recalled word for word by Noftsker in an author interview in Fall 1993. Noftsker claims to have been shocked by the intensity of Winston's loathing for him (author interview, 1993). Winston remembers it differently, according to author interview, 1994.

164 *this scale consisted of "Blatts," short for Greenblatt.*
The "Blatt" stories are an itegral part of MIT's AI Lab lore, and they were verified by a number of former MIT employees, including Russell Noftsker, who stated that "we had a ritual in the lab where we would drag Richard outside from time to time and hose him off." Author interview, 1993.

167 *"We begged and pleaded and haggled and placated..."*
Noftsker interview, Fall 1993.

167 *"We will give you a year..."*
Ibid.

168 *"whether Russell could be trusted"*
Quote from Richard Greenblatt during Fall 1993 interview. Comments and observations about the business meetings with the hackers are from author interviews with both Noftsker and Greenblatt. Obviously, both men have different recollections of what exactly transpired, so I have included their quotes verbatim as given to me during interviews.

168 *"Every one of us, to a man..."*
Op. cit. Russell told me, "If there is one thing I want you to know, it's that we all wanted Richard working with us."

169- *"We were using a DEC-10...", "So the next thing I did..." and "I told him*
170 *that we had money"...*
Quotes from author interview with Alex Jacobson, Fall 1993.
LMI specifics from internal company documents, including financial documents, and author interviews with Richard Greenblatt and Alex Jacobson in 1993.

173 *Minsky as "exile"*
David Freedman, "Artificial Intelligence's Angry Exile," *The Boston Globe Magazine*, January 19, 1992:16.

Chapter 15

178   *Feigenbaum's second, and perhaps most famous, AI project, called MYCIN...*
Description of MYCIN from Avron Barr and Edward Feigenbaum, *The Handbook of Artificial Intelligence, Volume 2* (Los Altos, California: William Kaufmann, Inc., 1982), 177-192. In the MYCIN session described here, I have simplified the actual interview reported by Shortliffe and Buchanan in order to keep the technical and medical terms to a minimum. A complete and exact description can be found in Bruce Buchanan and Edward Shortliffe, *Rule-Based Expert Systems* (Reading, Mass: Addison-Wesley, 1984).

185   *In 1980, three primary participants on the medical side of MOLGEN decided to make use of the AI methodologies that they had learned...*
IntelliGenetics description from corporate public documents, including the company's IPO prospectus and marketing literature.

Chapter 16

192   *Despite all of the potential, not one investment company offered to put any money into Symbolics...*
Details of Symbolics start-up pains are from the author interview with Noftsker, 1993, and IPO documents.

195   *Stallman had come to the AI Lab in the early 1970s...*
Jay Fraser, "Keeper of the Faith," *EDN*, October 1, 1990:174-177.

196   *I will wrap myself in dynamite and walk into Symbolics' offices, and I will blow the whole the company up.*
Noftsker's recollection of the contents of the message, author interview, Fall 1993.

196   *I fought Symbolics with all my might...*
These comments were sent to the author via e-mail in February 1994.

198   *Apparently, one Saturday morning when none of the hackers were around...*
The exchange between Bobrow, the VP, and ELIZA is excerpted from ACM SIGART Newsletter, June 1968 and December 1968.

202   *In 1978, SRI developed an expert system with a decidedly unmilitary bent called PROSPECTOR...*
PROSPECTOR specifics are from *The Handbook of Artificial Intelligence, Volume 2*, page 155; also *Business Week*, July 9, 1984:54-55.

204   *Dipmeter Advisor became the first expert system developed specifically...*
Dipmeter Advisor specifics are from an article by James Baker, "Dipmeter Advisor," in Patrick Winston & Karen Prendergas, eds., *The AI Business: Commercial Uses of Artificial Intelligence* (Cambridge, Mass.: MIT Press, 1984), 51.

205   *It was this "infinite variety" concept that plunged DEC into the AI world...*
XCON specifics: see Susan Scown, *The Artificial Intelligence Experience: An Introduction* (Maynard, Mass: Digital Equipment, 1985), 112.

Chapter 17

210 *"In making our way through this new age, informationization and information industries that center around computers are expected to play a big role."*
Quote from T. Moto-Oka's opening address: *Fifth Generation Computer Systems, Proceedings of the International Conference on Fifth Generation Computer Systems* (Amsterdam: North-Holland Publishing Company, 1982), 14-15.

211 *"The various researches described (at this conference) must be aggressively carried forward."*
Quote from Kazuhiro Fuchi, Ibid., page 120.

Chapter 18

223 *Yet, TI had bigger plans in mind than merely buying some start-up's AI product...*
Comments on Texas Instruments, Lamont Wood, "TI Turns to AI for the Long Run," *Computer Decisions,* Summer 1986:50.

226 *"I think my mission in life—if I have a mission—is to put AI in perspective."*
Schank quoted in Mary Emrich, "Expert Systems in Manufacturing," *Manufacturing Systems* (insert to the magazine, page 25).

227 *"One task in AI, strangely enough, is to get the computer to forget about the words."*
Quote from Roger Schank, *The Cognitive Computer: On Language, Learning, and Artificial Intelligence* (Reading, Mass.: Addison-Wesley, 1984), especially page 96. Descriptions of Conceptual Dependency and Yale AI programs are also in this book.

230 *Schank, in particular, would incur the wrath of his boss, Bart Giamatti...*
Commentary on Bart Giamatti and Schank: see Frank Kendig, "Getting Computers To Understand English," *Psychology Today,* April 1983:28-36.

Chapter 19

233 *"None of the artificial intelligence groups in industry is doing really basic research...*
Quote by Minsky on industry vs. universities from "The Problems and the Promise," *The AI Business* (Cambridge, Mass.: MIT Press, 1984), page 247-248.

234 *"Within a generation, the problem of creating artificial intelligence will be substantially solved."*
Marvin Minsky, *Computation: Finite and Infinite Machines,* (New York: Prentice Hall, 1967), 2.

234 *As AI progressed into the 1980s, he was no longer sure of that...*
Minsky and the future of AI, along with Thinking Machines information, from Bob Davis, "Superfast Computers Mimic the Structure of the Human Brain," *The Wall Street Journal,* February 19, 1986:1.

234 *"In the laboratory we regard the term expert system with a certain amount of scorn"*
Ibid.

234   *"I think that Cognitive Systems will succeed because our people were all trained by me."*
Schank's quote on industry vs. universities from "Intelligent Advisory Systems," *The AI Business*, 146-147.

238   *"Those who disagree with McCorduck invariably begin by quoting Santayana"*
The Fifth Generation, page 155.

238   *"We are writing this book because we are worried."*
Ibid., page 3.

239   *"We can form industrial consortiums to meet the Japanese challenge and as citizens insist that the Justice Department take a reasonable stance..."*
Ibid., page 225.

Chapter 20

244   *"We finally fell for the Symbolics' hype, and we chickened out."*
Quote from author's 1993 interview with Richard Greenblatt. Other Greenblatt comments are from this same interview. Specific LMI data is from LMI financial documents.

246   *Heilmeier returned to the commercial world when he joined Texas Instruments in 1977...*
Heilmeier's career: see "White House Honors Bellcore President," *EDGE Magazine: On & About AT&T,* Sept 23, 1991:19. Includes Heilmeier's résumé.

248   *"If someone is going to get rich out of the technology developed here, it ought to be the people who developed it."*
Reddy's comment on getting rich from "The Academics Cashing In At The Carnegie Group," *Business Week,* July 9, 1984:60.

249   *This was the formal incorporation of America's technology consortium, the MCC...*
MCC specifics: see Robert Lineback, "MCC: The Research Co-Op's Surprising Fast Start," *Electronics,* December 16, 1985:49.

251   *"We need some new American heroes."*
The Fifth Generation, page 224.

Chapter 22

260   *"I would buy him the Porsche of his choice."*
Quote from author interview with Russell Noftsker, 1993.

264   *IntelliGenetics created its own version of the EMYCIN shell and called it KEE...*
IntelliGenetics specifics: see "AI Trends Annual Report 1984" (Scottsdale, Arizona: The Relayer Group). Also, corporate documents, including IPO prospectus.

267   *Like Symbolics, it had found itself badly wedged between an old and a new product line...*
LMI specifics are from author's 1993 interview with Richard Greenblatt and corporate financial documents from 1984 and 1985.

269 *"I remember very distinctly, ever since I was five, knowing that I'd be a scientist"*
Quote from Paul Attanasio, "What The Inventor Saw," *Esquire*, December 1984:120. Also see: Herb Brody,"Kurzweil's Keyboard" *High Technology*, February 1985:27, and Leslie Helm, "This Whiz Kid Isn't Such a Whiz At Business," *Business Week*, January 18, 1988:66.

Chapter 23

272 *"I had to go along with what the board wanted, since you're supposed to do what your board of directors says to do"*
Quote from author interview with Noftsker, 1993.

276 *"It's like being at Kitty Hawk."*
Citations from "Artificial Intelligence: It's Here!" *Business Week*, July 9, 1984:54-62.

283 *Accolades for K:Base came fast and furious… Gold Hill joined the ranks of media darlings in the nascent AI business…*
William Marbach, "Big Things On The Way," *Newsweek Access*, Fall 1984:54. Additional Gold Hill information from author interviews with Stan Curtis and Jerry Barber, Fall 1993.

284 *suddenly K:Base was an orphan…*
K:Base specifics: see Wendy Rauch-Hindin, "Bankers and AI Experts Team Up for Greater Revenues," *Systems & Software*, October 1984:105-108, Other K:Base details from author's 1993 interviews with John Clippinger and Russell Noftsker.

Chapter 24

295 *"One of our biggest liabilities in the beginning"*
Author interview with Noftsker, Fall 1993.

296 *"They had no idea what a salesman really did"*
Author interview with Arthur Schwartz, 1993. Details of The Wine Advisor are also from this interview. Additional facts were obtained from Teknowledge promotional documents.

299 *"All the sales and marketing people entered the room…"*
Author interview with Bill Hoffman, Fall 1993.

299 *"There was a real passion that I haven't seen in any other business."*
Ibid.

Chapter 25

Investor specifics for Teknowledge are from company documents and IPO prospectus.

303 *"That hurt us, and it hurt us bad."*
Quote from Noftsker during author interview, 1993. Specifics of the TI and MIT deal were obtained from Russell Noftsker, as well as confidential sources. Additional material came from *The Wall Street Journal*, October 19, 1984:33.

309 *Sperry was anxious to get involved with AI...*
Sperry specifics are from the company's AI marketing documents, and its company newsletter "Newsbriefs, Volume 1." See also *Automation News*, August 12, 1985:22.

310 *"the most advanced artificial intelligence package available today."*
Sperry quote from marketing brochure.

Chapter 26

315 *"You can't just go out and buy AI any more than you can go out and buy art,"*
Cooper's quote from William Bryant Logan, "Don't Follow the Leaders," *Venture*, October 1986:38.

316 *"In a public speech during my road show for the IPO in 1984..."*
Noftsker quote from author interview, 1993.

318 *"Other companies in Cambridge were offering normal salaries to software engineers..."*
This, and other descriptions of Palladian hacker life, from author interview with Randy Parker, Fall 1993.

319 *"Phil would bring clients or investors up to his office..."*
Ibid.

320 *"You would always come in early on Tuesdays, because Ralph went shopping..."*
This quote, and comments on the quality of Gold Hill's kitchen, ibid.

321 *"I think our transportation bill for buses and limousines that night alone was about $20,000"*
Bill Hoffman quote from author interview, 1993.

Chapter 27

328 *Neither Campbell Soup nor General Motors had anyone within their monstrously huge organizations...*
Charley specifics are from a General Motors press release, whereas Cooker specifics are from "AI TRENDS," January 1986:15. ("AI TRENDS" is a newsletter published by The Relayer Group in Scottsdale, Arizona.)

338 *"We are going into the commercial arena in full force with a lot of investment."*
Schorr's quote from "IBM Finally Jumps into AI with Both Feet," *Electronics Magazine*, August 21, 1986:30.

339 *"To see the world's major computer manufacturer take this position is a great victory"*
Ed Feigenbaum's quote from *Electronics Magazine*, ibid.

339 *"I was doing AI stuff ten years ago"*
Mitch Irsfeld, "An Interview with Bill Gates," *Computer Systems News*, October 7, 1986:13.

341 *"We are at the beginning of a new era."*
Goldberg's quote from *PC Week*, October 7, 1986:175.

341 *"Emerging technologies such as image processing and artificial intelligence offer great promise for the future."*
Akers's comment from an IBM marketing document.

341   *"Where can I find expert system programs for IBM equipment?"*
       IBM sales rep conversation with the author.
       Charley specifics are from a General Motors' press release, where as Cooker
       specifics are from "AI TRENDS," January 1986:15.

Chapter 28

346   *"On the day that I found out..."*
       Noftsker quote from author interview, 1993.

347   *Gigamos had been a distributor for LMI's Lambda machines in Canada...*
       LMI and Gigamos specifics are from author's interview with Richard
       Greenblatt, 1993. Additional bankruptcy specifics are from *The Boston
       Globe,* April 4, 1987:30.

348   *"The first thing you have to have when you start a new high-tech company..."*
       HP Newquist, Editorial, "AI TRENDS," March 1988:2-5.

351   *"This expert system is non-trivial...It's something quite above choosing the right
       wine for dinner."*
       Michael Ball, "AI-Based Software for Factory Control Debuts from
       Palladian," *Automation News,* November 10, 1986:14.

355   *Palladian's fortunes—or misfortunes—slid quickly from that point forward.*
       Palladian financial specifics in this section are from bankruptcy documents.

355   *"You know, it's hard to imagine that Palladian could have spent money faster
       than it actually did."*
       Author interview with Randy Parker, Fall 1993.

356   *"This isn't an AI winter. This is more like Donner Pass."*
       Quote by John Clippinger, "AI TRENDS," December 1986:3.

Chapter 29

361   *"Marvin can throw out one hundred ideas at any given time..."*
       Noftsker quote from author interview, 1993.

361   *...we should all start learning to speak Japanese...*
       Feigenbaum quote from EF Hutton Conference on AI, as reported in "AI
       TRENDS," June 1985:7.

366   *"Teknowledge elected to distance itself from the 'Buck Rogers' aspects of artificial
       intelligence..."*
       Lee Hecht's comments in the Teknowledge 1987 Annual Report.

370   *"We got all of the board members together, including one board member who
       had contracted brain cancer..."*
       Quote from Noftsker, author interview, 1993.

372   *"When I accepted the Board's offer to direct Symbolics' turnaround..."*
       Wurts's comment from Symbolics' 1988 Annual Report.

373   *The resurgence began in 1982, when a biophysicist named John Hopfield
       presented a paper...*
       Hopfield's paper is from *The Proceedings of the National Academy of Sciences
       '79,* pages 2554-2558.

374 AT&T's traveling salesman problem
Otis Port, "Computers That Come Awfully Close to Thinking," *Business Week*, June 2, 1986:94. See also *Otis Port*, "They're Here: Computers That 'Think'," *Business Week*, January 26, 1987:94.

Chapter 30

381 "We were all addicted to DARPA cash."
Author interview with Stan Curtis, 1993.

384 "Well, the cows don't seem to mind."
Story related during author interview with Jerry Barber, 1993.

386 "It's weird enough that I know all the people who are staffing all of the other booths...
Quotes from the AAAI show: see "AI TRENDS," September 1988:10.

388 "There was never anything at Teknowledge to build a company on..."
Quote by Arthur Schwartz from author interview, 1993. Additional specifics of Teknowledge merger from annual reports and merger documents.

396 ATRANS became Cognitive's claim to fame.
Cognitive and ATRANS specifics are from Cognitive company documents and IPO prospectus, as well as *AIEXPERT*, May 1991:65-66.

397 "I came to Cognitive after being a customer, and found out that the company was made up mostly of prototypes..."
Author interview with Steve Mott, 1993. Other quotes are from this same interview.

397 In June 1989, he started an AI Lab at Northwestern University...
Schank at Northwestern: see "AI TRENDS," July 1989:6.

Chapter 31

401 American Express went hunting for the appropriate products and services...
Details about Authorizer's Assistant: see "In Practice" column, *AIEXPERT*, April 1987:63.

403 Coopers & Lybrand...was next in line to sing the praises of expert systems.
ExperTAX specifics: see "In Practice" column, *AIEXPERT*, March 1987:57.

407 "Competitive advantage comes by making the inevitable happen sooner..."
Mrs. Fields specifics are from company marketing documents and promotional literature.

410 "The system has leveraged Debbi's ability to project her influence..."
Randy Fields quote, ibid.

411 Realizing this was a half-baked way to perform gate operations...
GADS system outlined in *AIEXPERT*, May 1990:67.

Chapter 32

424 "The problem in AI was that we tried to replace the human experience"
Ken Tarpey quote from author interview, Fall 1993.

425   *CADUCEUS, which was named for the twisted snake and staff symbol of the medical profession...*
Specifics of this program are from the "In Practice" column, *AIEXPERT*, May 1987:69-71.

427   *APACHE made life and death decisions.*
APACHE system specifics: See Jean Seligmann "Software for Hard Issues," *Newsweek*, April 27, 1992:55.

Chapter 33

431   *"Ten years ago we faced criticism of being too reckless,"*
Fuchi quote from Andrew Pollack, "'Fifth Generation' Became Japan's Lost Generation," *The New York Times*, June 5, 1992:D3.

433   *Like its predecessor, RWC was to be a ten-year project...*
RWC specifics from "AI TRENDS," January 1993:2-12.

434   *IntelliCorp's 1992 sales had fallen to $9 million, the lowest level in seven years.*
For information on IntelliCorp's failed merger with KnowledgeWare, as well as the Aion and AICorp merger, see "AI TRENDS," November 1993: 1-10.

435   *Cyc sought to create a computer system that contained all of the world's knowledge...*
MCC specifics: see Doug Lenat, et al, "Cyc: Towards Programming with Common Sense," *Communications of the ACM*, August 1990:30-49. Also see Glenn Rifkin, "Cyc-ed Up," *Computerworld*, May 10, 1993:104-105.

Chapter 34

449   *"Why should I spend time there?"*
Quote by Minsky regarding his frustration with the AI Lab: see *The Boston Globe Magazine*, January 19, 1992:26.

449   *"Government support nurtured the tiger; now help remove the bars of its cage!"*
Feigenbaum's quote from a copy of his presentation to the AAAI 1993 Conference.

Index

T